LIFE CHANGING
CONVERSATIONS

LIFE CHANGING CONVERSATIONS

A single conversation can be a life changing event.

Jon Connelly, LCSW

www.RapidResolutionTherapy.com

Second Edition

Printed in the United States of America

Dedicated to Kimberly Austin

Her Light is Strong, Yet Gentle

"If the doors of perception were cleansed, everything would appear to man as it is, infinite."

~ William Blake

Foreword

By Courtney Armstrong, LPC, NBCFCH

Magic. That is what it looked like when I attended my first Jon Connelly workshop on his Rapid Resolution Therapy (RRT) method in the year 2006. Through videos and live demonstrations that weekend, I witnessed him turn experiences of trauma into triumph for dozens of people who emerged feeling liberated and downright gleeful after a single session with him! I had never seen someone with such an amazing ability to uplift clients and create compelling, felt experiences that caused them to see themselves in a new light. I was astounded by his talent, but slightly skeptical. How was it possible to transform traumatic events for survivors of horrific events like incest, brutal gang rape, combat trauma, the 9-11 World Trade Center bombing, and the murder of a loved one in less than an hour? It seemed too good to be true. Then, on the last day of the training, Jon transformed my own traumatic grief experience in less than 20 minutes! After that, I was a believer.

Even though I experienced transformation within myself, I doubted I could reproduce the same results with my clients. But I began to apply what I learned from Jon little by little and was astonished by how quickly my clients experienced change. More important, my clients loved this new approach and enjoyed its use of humor and multi-level communication to empower them. As clients shared their successes with others, referrals began to pour into my practice, nearly doubling it in a year's time. My RRT colleagues reported having similar experiences.

Jon is masterful at creating new meaning experiences using novelty, warmth, humor, playfulness, imagery, metaphor and movement. That is how he engages the emotional brain and causes the change. Jon is also a wizard with words. But it is not the words themselves that evoke change. It is the delivery, idea, and intention behind the words that prompts change.

In this book, with its twenty-one life-changing scripts, Jon shares his ideas and intentions that lead to each client's emotional transformation. In every chapter, he explains why he selected particular interventions, how to craft language to lead your client towards what is desired, and how to deepen change experiences with enjoyable and powerful transformational tools.

If you have trained with Jon, this book will further inspire you and improve your therapeutic skills. If you have not trained with Jon, read this book and attend one of his trainings. It will not only transform your professional life; it will change you personally. My life and my work with clients are so much more joyful, optimistic, and satisfying since training with him and I know yours will be too.

Courtney Armstrong, LPC, NBCFCH
Author of Rethinking Trauma Treatment,
The Therapeutic "Aha!" and Transforming Traumatic Grief

Introduction

It is possible to change someone's life with a single conversation.

How often do we hear someone say that they wish they could stop doing something, feeling something or thinking something? People say they wish they could get themselves motivated in order to get themselves started and then they could try to keep themselves going. No other life form ever has thought like that. If a crow is on one branch and wants to be on another branch, he is not thinking about how to get himself motivated so that he could get himself started so that he could try to keep himself going. If he wants to be on another branch, he is already on his way. If crow wants to stop doing something, he has not hired another crow to meet with him once a week to talk about it. If he wants to stop, he already has.

People are the way they are due to genetic and environmental factors. People do not select their DNA. They do not select the thoughts that occur to them, their emotions or the sensations they experience. Much of the turmoil people are going through is because of things that are happening, have happened, or they believe might happen.

Therapists attempt to make people feel responsible for their feelings and their thoughts. People who have been over-therapized take the blame for things that they never did. They say things like, "I allow myself to feel jealous" or "I allow myself to be resentful" when actually they have simply reacted in the only way they could have. Traditionally, therapists believe that if someone takes responsibility for something, they can then change and improve it. Therapists bring people through processes that cause them to feel bad in order to get them to feel better. If their clients do not cooperate with this process, they are accused of being "resistant" or "not ready to change."

Universities that prepare students to be licensed mental health professionals conduct the entirety of their training without ever showing the student how to do what they are being trained to do. I have asked many mental health professionals how many hours they spent during their graduate training observing their professors doing what they were teaching them to do. The average number of hours is zero. Not only are the professors not demonstrating how to do psychotherapy, they are not observing their students as they begin doing it. Instead of seeing what is being done, the student describes it to the supervisor in weekly supervision sessions. Their supervisors, who have never met the students' clients, are attempting to improve the students' work without ever having observed it. No other profession would consider teaching people how to do something without ever showing them how to do it or observing them doing it. The concern for confidentiality has created an educational process in mental health fields where no one gets to see anyone doing what people are there to learn to do.

Psychotherapists are mandated to attend "ethics" courses in order to maintain their professional licenses. These classes are geared to protect psychotherapists and their malpractice insurance companies from their clients.

The first "ethics" class I took was held at a private for-profit psychiatric hospital that was sponsored by a malpractice company where the instructors were attorneys. The belief that one should "do no harm" was coupled with the even stronger belief that one should avoid being sued. This concern causes therapists to approach the process of facilitating positive change to be diluted with fear and timidity. This can affect whom the therapist is willing to work with so that the most "difficult clients" (therefore, the ones who are most in need) are avoided. It also affects the way therapists work and promotes working with an obsessive need to document what is being done in order to protect against clients who could sue and insurance companies who might refuse to pay.

People are plagued with shame and even feel ashamed for seeking psychotherapy. Therapists respond by stating that it is extremely important to not only keep people's secrets, but to keep secret the fact that they are being seen at all. The ethics classes stress that the therapist should make sure not to greet people they have worked with in public in order to protect the secret that they have been seen. In doing this, the therapist is buying into the belief that it is shameful to seek assistance with psychological issues.

Therapists, substance abuse treatment centers, and private psychiatric hospitals are economically motivated to come up with the worst possible view of their clients in order to justify the most treatment possible. Almost all substance abuse treatment centers and private psychiatric facilities have staff members whose jobs are to convince insurance company representatives that the individual is as sick as possible in order to get the insurance company to provide the maximum amount of funds. Psychotherapists are frequently speaking to insurance companies themselves trying to convince them to continue paying for visits by describing how troubled and needy their clients are.

Treatment facilities, psychiatric hospitals and private practice psychotherapists are financially motivated to see their clients as troubled and disturbed as possible. This, then, affects the way that clients are viewed and treated. Therapists who are motivated by their own economic well-being, feel a sense of dependency on their clients. This reliance causes the therapist to encourage the client to become dependent as well. Clients who have financial resources or good insurance may be encouraged to engage in endless visits while those with limited resources are likely to be subject to a forced and abrupt ending, regardless of their needs.

Once a long-term schedule has been facilitated (for the economically sound client), familiarly between the therapist and the client then develops. This can breed contempt and any power the therapist has had initially to facilitate change becomes increasingly diminished. I have spoken to numerous individuals who wanted assistance in "breaking up with" a therapist they had been seeing for years and I have met with therapists who wanted help in "breaking up with" a client, when the aggravation had exceeded the economic benefit of continuing.

I went to graduate school to become a psychotherapist. In my very first year, I was sent to a county mental health clinic that offered counseling to people who did not have the financial means to pay for it. My very first client was a man who was in his early forties. He told me that it was very difficult for him to come in for help and that he would hate it if anyone found out he had done so. He explained that there was a problem he was having with his oldest son and that he was confused about how to handle it and needed some advice. I listened to what he told me and told him what I thought he should do.

He returned for his second visit. He had done what I recommended, and the situation was resolved. He said he only came back because he wanted to thank me. This visit only took a few minutes. We shook hands and that was that.

I was excited to share this good news with my clinical supervisor. She was horrified. She said I had missed the opportunity to provide him with deep, on-going treatment and that I was not supposed to have given him advice at all. She said that I had committed a grave therapeutic error and labeled it as "premature termination." I am afraid that she would not be a fan of what I am doing in this book.

In contrast, the method I present is fast, effective, and painless, regardless of the economic status of the individual. The process is built upon gain (rather than deficit), openness (rather than secrecy), and happiness (rather than pain). What I am suggesting is a way for therapists to improve their abilities and their practice.

I never try to engage anyone in an ongoing process involving multiple sessions. Instead, each meeting is approached with the thought that this will be my only opportunity to be of value to this individual. My intention is to influence individuals in ways that will improve the quality of their life and, hence, improve the world.

I begin the meeting by conceiving of the person as I intend them to be. I see them with their mind only entertaining what has value. By that, I mean things that would be possible to do and good to have done, good for the person and good for the world. I see their mind attaching interest and appeal to these things. Because they are possible, interesting and appealing, the person will be drawn to engage in the doing of them and the person's mind will attach pleasure and satisfaction to the completion.

I conceive of the person with the process of maintenance and repair turned up to full. Healing is going on with full power within their body and supported by those behaviors that create health and well-being. I conceive of this individual with all of their powers and resources fully available. This would include their intelligence, logic, reason, creativity, sense of humor, playfulness, compassion, passion, and wisdom. I conceive of the individual as flexible and adaptive. The things I do and the words I say during our meeting will flow from the intention I have for the person I am with. I continue getting new and more complete information during our meeting and the intention continues to become more detailed and powerful in compelling what I say and do.

I intend, and I expect, a significant and lasting improvement for the individual I am meeting with. I do not tell them that getting better is their responsibility and I certainly do not believe that it is. If a positive change does not take place, it indicates that I lacked the skill and it will, therefore, be my intention to become more skillful. I never think or suggest that a meeting was not successful because the individual I met with was resistant, lacked motivation or did not really want to change. If someone is "not motivated," then it is my job to motivate them. If that person did not want to change, perhaps that indicates that there was something conflictual that I should pinpoint and resolve.

Although I take full responsibility for the meeting being successful, I give the participant all of the credit for the success that is achieved. I intend the individual to recognize and experience that what is good for the world is best for them and that what is best for them is, therefore, best for the world. The most selfish thing they can do is, be loving and the most loving thing is to be selfish.

I utilize reason, logic, imagination, persuasion, connection, credibility, touch, humor, action, drama and altered states of consciousness. I delight in this individual's presence and passionately intend that the quality of their life improve. I take full responsibility for causing changes in how the person's mind processes information and celebrate how successfully they have already navigated a very difficult environment.

I do not encourage the individuals who see me to forgive their self or to forgive others. I do not ask them to examine their thinking or to try to control their thoughts. I never tell people that they deserve to be happy or that they deserve to be treated well. I do not encourage self-analysis, insight, or introspection. I never tell people they need to adjust their attitude or think more positively. I do not tell people that they need to build their self-esteem. I never tell people that they need to love themselves. No other life form does any of these things and they are doing significantly less harm to themselves, to each other, and to the planet than we are.

Human beings are the only life forms that are pre-occupied. By pre-occupation, I am referring to anything that takes someone out of the present and decreases their power. Pre-occupations include guilt, shame, resentment, grief, anxiety, heartbreak, chronic pain, self-consciousness or worry. Conscious pre-occupation is a distraction and it drains energy from what there is to do in the present. Even if preoccupation is not conscious, it can still drain energy, slow down the healing process and negatively affect mood and behavior. I intend to eliminate any pre-occupation that has been blocking joyful living, emotional freedom and success.

People are often looking through the lenses of their own perceptions as if they are seeing what is actually there. Just as beauty is in the eye of the beholder, meaning is in the mind of the perceiver. It is as if the individual looking through a blue lens is thinking that things that are being looked at are blue. My intention is for people to be experiencing things as close to how they actually are as possible. The more accurate the map is, the easier the journey will be. I would like people to realize aesthetic evaluations (such as ugly or beautiful) or meanings (such as good and bad) are happening within the individual who is experiencing something rather than within what is being experienced.

I want people to realize that our senses are far from perfect so that what they bring in is not ever complete or accurate. What is brought in is being filtered through judgment and meaning and is, therefore, always distorted. Our senses are limited so that the information they bring in is never accurate. For instance, the earth appears flat and the sun seems to circle the earth. You look at a large boulder and it seems to be solid and still, and yet, it is made of tiny particles that are always moving.

In the following pages, I provide transcripts of meetings I had with twenty-one individuals whose lives were changed after only one visit. Some had lives that seemed very normal while others experienced events so horrible that they were hard to listen to. They were dealing with painful emotions, troubling thoughts, and problematic behavioral patterns. They experienced grief, anxiety, depression, relationship issues and a variety of other problems. I learned a great deal from each one of them.

For many years, I have been conducting training programs for mental health and health professionals in what I call Rapid Resolution Therapy®. It has been wonderful to teach others and to hear about their successes in working with people this way. They report amazing results with a very wide variety of people dealing with many different issues. This book is intended to show you a different way of thinking and practicing. My passion is to fearlessly and creatively pursue what is in the client's best interest and to make it possible for people to live happy and productive lives.

How to Benefit from These Transcripts

Each transcript includes commentary in order to better understand the reasons behind what I said and did. Some of the print is in bold. This is the meat of what I wanted to bring into that person's mind in order to create the shift. These are the things I want the individual to understand, experience and feel. I also recommend you read the conversations first, then my commentaries.

If you read only the bold print, you may agree that if the individual completely bought in to what is said and fully experienced, and accepted it on all levels, they would no longer be stuck, and the turmoil would disappear. The challenge is two-fold. The first part is determining what there is for the individual to feel, think and experience. That is what is in bold. The next challenge, though, is getting that individual to buy in and to have that experience.

Often, people try to learn something new by trying to understand how it might be similar to something they already know. I would strongly discourage you from attempting to learn these methods in this way. You are better off not comparing at all, but, if you do, focus on what is different rather than trying to find out what is similar.

Put a piece of paper over the page you are reading and then uncover it line by line. Read what the participant said and then decide what you would say. Then read what I said and notice how they are different.

Read one transcript and put the book down. Pick it up again at another time. This will make these tools and concepts much more available to you than if you were to read one transcript after another.

If you are reading this book to benefit yourself personally, I would suggest that you create a character in your own mind that is similar to you, but different. Consider how what happened in the transcript would apply to them and your mind will apply it to yourself automatically. By keeping your own issues at a distance in this way, you will benefit even more than if you applied it to yourself directly.

My intention is that reading these transcripts will not only increase your ability to assist others but will also be personally beneficial.

Kristin

I met Kristin when she was 22 years old. She had been having seizures and needed to walk with a three-pronged cane and wear a helmet for protection. Her father called me and told me a friend of his suggested that he bring his daughter to see me. He told me she had been receiving expert medical and psychological treatment for seizures, nightmares, anxiety and depression at the world-renowned Mayo Clinic for the past 11 months with no positive results. He said she was extremely despondent and had attempted suicide. He started to cry and told me he would do whatever it took, even carry her on his back to me if he had to, but he needed me to see her. After an 11-hour trip, they arrived at my office.

Jon: I am glad to meet you. **What should we get done?**

OUR MEETING BEGINS WITH THE EXPECTATION AND PLAN THAT THIS WILL BE GETTING SOMETHING DONE THAT HAS VALUE. IT IS A DIFFERENT SET UP THAN "WORKING" ON SOMETHING, WHICH SEEMS TO IMPLY NOT GETTING IT DONE.

Kristin: I want to learn how to deal with strong emotions because I realize that the physical symptoms I have are from repressed stress. When the Mayo Clinic diagnosed me with conversion disorder, they put me on Klonopin. I have seen some reduction in my symptoms, but they still happen, particularly if I get stressed. I start having tics or twitching or I start having seizures. The doctors at Mayo call them pseudo-seizures. My whole body jerks uncontrollably and it's really awful. I don't know what to do. I get really angry and extremely afraid. I had to drop out of school, and I can't work. I can't go out to a store. I can't watch a television show. I can never take a step backwards. All of these things trigger the seizures. I don't want to live like this.

Jon: **I'm familiar with the stuff that you're talking about and I'm familiar with the diagnosis of pseudo-seizure. I'm excited to collaborate with you** on these issues and **get things working in a better way.** I understand there have been very disturbing physical symptoms as well as strong and painful emotions.

I LET HER KNOW I AM FAMILIAR WITH WHAT SHE HAS BEEN EXPERIENCING AND EXCITED ABOUT COLLABORATING WITH HER, WHICH INCREASES HER SENSE OF SECURITY AND ADDS TO MY CREDIBILITY. I AM EMOTIONALLY RESPONDING TO WHAT IS GOING ON IN THIS PROJECT RATHER THAN RESPONDING TO THE MATERIAL SHE IS DESCRIBING. I AM EMOTIONALLY RESPONDING TO WHAT WE ARE DOING RATHER THAN WHAT SHE IS THINKING ABOUT. WHAT SHE IS TALKING ABOUT IS HORRIBLE. WHAT WE ARE DOING IS FINE. I STAY EMOTIONALLY PRESENT AND KEEP HER WITH ME, AND THEN SHE WILL BE EMOTIONALLY PRESENT AS WELL. OUR CONNECTION ACTS AS A MAGNET SO THAT SHE RESPONDS MORE AND MORE TO THE PRESENT ALONG WITH ME.

Kristin: I still have strong emotions about things from my past. So, things that happen remind me of them and I feel those same things and I still don't know how to deal with them. I just try to stay away from it rather than deal with it. I try to listen to music or distract myself because I'm afraid. If I try to deal with these things, I have nightmares, or I lash out. I feel out of control and I get really, really depressed.

Jon: **That's exactly what I deal with**. I'd be more than happy to **get that done for you**. You told me, though, that you want to learn to deal with strong emotions. I would prefer to **clear them away** so that **you don't have to deal with them**. You've seen counselors or therapists, right?

BY TELLING HER THAT THIS IS EXACTLY WHAT I DEAL WITH, I CAUSE HER TO EXPERIENCE REASSURANCE AND TO SEE ME AS CREDIBLE. SHE IS IN THE RIGHT PLACE AND WITH THE RIGHT PERSON TO GET THE ASSISTANCE SHE DESIRES. I TAKE RESPONSIBILITY FOR CREATING THE CHANGE BY SAYING I INTEND TO GET IT DONE FOR HER. MOST OFTEN, COUNSELORS BURDEN THE CLIENT WITH THE RESPONSIBILITY OF GETTING BETTER. MY INTENTION IS THAT SHE IS LIGHT AND AT EASE RATHER THAN HEAVY AND BURDENED SO THAT I TAKE ON THE BURDEN MYSELF. SHE HAS BEEN THINKING, AND PROBABLY BEEN TOLD, THAT SHE HAS TO DEAL WITH THESE PAINFUL EMOTIONS IN ORDER TO GET BETTER. I DISAGREE. PEOPLE DON'T GET BETTER BY EXPERIENCING EMOTIONS ABOUT SOMETHING THAT IS NOT HAPPENING. SHE HAS BEEN EXPERIENCING AN EMOTIONAL RESPONSE TO SOMETHING THAT IS NOT HAPPENING. SHE HAS BEEN EXPERIENCING AN EMOTIONAL RESPONSE TO SOMETHING THAT IS NOT GOING ON OR THE EMOTION WOULD NOT BE TROUBLING. IF ZEBRA IS RUNNING FROM LION, SHE IS AFRAID, BUT NOT TROUBLED. IF SHE WAS CONTINUING TO BE AFRAID WHEN NO LION WAS AROUND, THAT WOULD BE TROUBLING. RIGHT FROM THE BEGINNING, THE GOAL IS DIFFERENT FROM OTHER THERAPISTS SHE HAS SEEN.

Kristin: I believe four now.

Jon: And they had you talk a lot about yourself and they asked you many questions.

TELLING HER WHAT HAPPENED TO HER WHEN SHE WENT TO OTHER THERAPISTS IS AMUSING TO HER AND IT CONTINUES TO BUILD MY CREDIBILITY. IT ALSO DISTINGUISHES WHAT WILL BE HAPPENING IN OUR MEETING FROM PREVIOUS THINGS THAT WERE DISADVANTAGEOUS.

Kristin: Yes. That is exactly what happened.

Jon: Let's **break with that tradition**. I'll talk about how I view things so you and I can be looking through the same lens before we get to anything else that has been going on for you. **This will be interesting for you to learn about**. **Don't try applying these things to yourself**. Instead, **make sure you approve** before deciding whether or not we should apply this way of thinking to you. Make sense?

Kristin: Yes, it does.

BY SAYING OUR MEETING WILL BREAK WITH TRADITION, KRISTIN REALIZES OUR MEETING WILL BE DIFFERENT THAN THE OTHERS. WE WILL BE DOING THINGS DIFFERENTLY AND GETTING DIFFERENT THINGS DONE. I DON'T WANT HER TO THINK OF MEETING WITH ME AS MORE OF THE SAME AND I DON'T WANT HER LIFE TO BE MORE OF THE SAME. I TELL HER THE WAY I VIEW THINGS WILL BE INTERESTING TO HER. I WANT HER INTERESTED IN THINGS OUTSIDE OF HERSELF AND I CERTAINLY WANT HER INTERESTED IN WHAT I'M DESCRIBING TO HER. BY ASKING HER TO NOT APPLY THESE THINGS TO HERSELF, THINGS WILL MOVE MORE QUICKLY. SHE IS RELIEVED OF ANY RESPONSIBILITY TO RELATE TO WHAT I AM SAYING; HENCE, SHE WILL BE MORE PRESENT. SHE WILL BE MORE OBJECTIVE, WHICH ELIMINATES DISTORTION THAT IS CAUSED THE CLOSER ONE IS TO

SOMETHING. IN ADDITION, OBJECTIVITY RELIEVES THE EMOTIONAL PAIN SHE HAS BEEN EXPERIENCING WHEN SHE WAS LOOKING AT HERSELF. SHE WILL FEEL GOOD WHILE SHE IS WITH ME AND WHEN SHE LEAVES.

Jon: I'm not suggesting that what I'm telling you is the truth. Instead, I'll just be suggesting a view I think will be useful for here and now as we meet.

Kristin: Okay.

WHEN HEARING A NEW WAY OF THINKING, ONE MAY GET BOGGED DOWN TRYING TO DETERMINE WHICH IS TRUE, THE OLD WAY OR THE NEW WAY. I TOOK TRUTH OFF THE TABLE, SO IT WON'T SLOW US DOWN.

Jon: Perfect. Most people think that things that happen cause feelings. A guy is standing in a lunch line. Another guy comes over, gives him a shove and says, "You can wait. I'm important." The guy that just got shoved is madder than a hatter, right?

I TELL HER A STORY THAT AMUSES HER. I DESCRIBE A SPECIFIC SITUATION INSTEAD OF JUST A GENERAL CONCEPT, ENABLING HER TO VISUALIZE IT MORE EASILY. BY GETTING A SENSORY RESPONSE AS SHE SEES AND HEARS WHAT I AM DESCRIBING, I AM REACHING HER SUBCONSCIOUS MORE EFFECTIVELY THAN I WOULD WITH THEORIES AND GENERALITIES. THE STORY IS INTENDED TO TEACH WHILE BEING FUNNY AND INTERESTING.

Kristin: (*Laughing*) I am sure he is.

Jon: People who see this think about his anger as coming from what just happened to him. That is the normal way to think.

Kristin: Right.

Jon: Instead of thinking about it in the ordinary way, let's think that the guy is angry because of how his mind processed information.

Kristin: Okay.

I WILL BE OFFERING A NEW WAY OF UNDERSTANDING THINGS. SO, I WANT HER TO KNOW THAT THE WAY SHE HAS BEEN THINKING OF THEM UP UNTIL NOW IS NORMAL. SHE HAS BEEN DEALING WITH PEOPLE WHO HAVE NOT BEEN VIEWING HER AS NORMAL AND SHE HAS NOT BEEN VIEWING HERSELF AS NORMAL. BY REFERRING TO IT AS "ORDINARY," SHE IS INCLINED TO REJECT "NORMAL". SHE LONGED TO BE NORMAL BUT IS READY TO BREAK AWAY FROM ORDINARY.

Jon: This guy isn't going to tell you that. He's not going to say, "Yeah, I'm angry because of what my mind is doing." He's going to say, "I'm angry because that jerk shoved me." But if we think of it resulting from how mind is processing information, **it gives you and I more power** so that **I can adjust how your mind processes information** and the **painful emotions will disappear**.

BY SAYING, "IT GIVES YOU AND I MORE POWER," I PUT SHE AND I TOGETHER AS A TEAM – AND A POWERFUL TEAM TO BOOT. THIS MOVES HER TOWARD MY INTENTION FOR HER. I TELL HER PAINFUL EMOTIONS WILL DISAPPEAR BECAUSE THIS IS EXACTLY

WHAT I WANT HER TO BELIEVE AND EXPERIENCE. I SUGGEST THE PROBLEM RESULTED FROM HOW HER MIND PROCESSES INFORMATION. THIS IS DIFFERENT THAN THAT THE PROBLEM IS HER; HENCE, PROTECTING HER IDENTITY.

Kristin: I understand.

Jon: Since you've seen four therapists, you've probably been told that people are negatively affected by past events because emotions were strong and weren't expressed and, therefore, haven't been released. You have been told that the feelings need to be dealt with for you to get better. By "dealt with," it was implied that you needed to feel them and process them and get them out.

BY TELLING HER WHAT SHE HAS EXPERIENCED WITH OTHER THERAPISTS, I BUILD CREDIBILITY AND I SEPARATE WHAT WE WILL BE DOING FROM THINGS THAT HAVE NOT WORKED.

Kristin: Yes. (*Laughter*) That is exactly what they have told me, but the feelings are so painful I do my best to stay away from them. They tell me I am resistant.

Jon: Staying away from painful emotions indicates that **you are intelligent, not resistant.** If you were resistant, you wouldn't have shown up. You do not have to deal with painful emotions to get better. No other life form ever tries to deal with its emotions. A hawk is not trying to deal with her emotions or to release her feelings and hawks are doing fine. When something happens that is very disturbing, terrifying, weird, ugly, painful, whatever, it slams into awareness and can leave an impression. I am going to use a visual aid. (*I grab a pillow and slam my hand into it, leaving an impression.*)

TELLING HER THAT SHE IS RESISTANT CAUSES HER TO RESIST. TELLING HER THAT SHE IS NOT RESISTANT CAUSES HER TO COOPERATE. IT ISN'T USEFUL TO TELL SOMEONE THAT HE IS RESISTANT UNLESS YOU WANT HIM TO RESIST YOU.

Jon: And there we have an impression. You see the difference between the hand slamming and the handprint.

Kristin: Right.

Jon: The deeper part of the mind is likely to confuse handprint with hand slamming. It doesn't know hand isn't slamming until we do this. (*I move my hand over the pillow and smooth away the impression.*) I will do this for you. Okay?

THE PILLOW IS A POWERFUL METAPHOR. IT CLARIFIES THE DIFFERENCE BETWEEN THE THING THAT HAPPENED AND THE IMPRESSION THAT IT LEFT, AND THAT THE MIND HAS NOT DISTINGUISHED BETWEEN THE TWO. SHE SEES THE IMPRESSION DISAPPEAR RIGHT IN FRONT OF HER. THEN, I TELL HER THAT I WILL GET THAT DONE FOR HER. NO ONE ELSE HAS TOLD HER THAT THEY WOULD GET IT DONE FOR HER AND THIS LIFTS THE BURDEN FROM HER.

Kristin: Yes. (*Nodding her head*)

Jon: The part of your mind that just caused your head to nod when you said "yes" is a different part of your mind than is following along with the things that I'm saying. It was your inner mind that nodded your head, not your intellect. Did you know you were nodding your head?

Kristin: When you pointed it out, I realized it, but I didn't know I was doing it.

Jon: Even if you were aware of doing it, you weren't doing it on purpose. You were not doing it with the part of your mind that you call "I." It wasn't done consciously. There are different facets of your mind. It's advanced and it's complicated. If you take a hammer and throw it down the stairs and you go pick it up, it will work fine, but don't try this with your computer. Right?

DESCRIBING THROWING THESE THINGS DOWN THE STAIRS CREATES VISUAL IMAGES IN HER MIND. THESE IMAGES ARE FUNNY, AND THEY MAKE WHAT I'M SAYING INTERESTING. I AM CAUSING HER TO BE ENGAGED AND FOCUSED OUTSIDE OF HERSELF. SINCE THIS IS HOW I WANT HER WHEN SHE LEAVES, I CAUSE HER TO EXPERIENCE IT WHILE SHE IS WITH ME.

Kristin: (*Laughter*) Right.

Jon: Your computer is much more likely to be damaged because your computer is much more complex. Our minds are much more complicated than our computers. You need to take a new Toyota in for tune-ups more than you would need to take the hammer in for tune-ups. The Toyota is much more advanced than an old-fashioned Model-T Ford. It's not only advanced, it's integrated so that all components work together. But, you know, the Toyota is all thought out before anybody starts building it. In other words, they don't build it and then, when they're done, decide to install an air conditioner. They thought of it before they started. If, on the other hand, you took a Model-T Ford and then you started putting in new-fangled devices like cruise control and a power moon roof, you're going to screw that thing up because it isn't built to support those things. Unfortunately, our minds are not built like a Toyota. It's more like an old-fashioned, black-and-white television set with a phonograph and then someone attached a Blu Ray player to it.

Kristin: Okay. I follow you. This is interesting.

Jon: Do you know what a planned community is? Before they started building it, they designed it. So, for instance, on the drawing board, they are saying, "Let's make sure the community center is here, where everybody in all the surrounding places has access to it. And we want everybody to be about the same distance from the swimming pool and the park." They draw it out and plan it before they build it. On the other hand, let's say you're in the city and there's a huge residential area in one place and a workplace in another location. Every morning, people commute from the residential area to the work area and, every evening, they travel back. There is a small bridge over the water they have to cross, and someone asks you what kind of idiots stuck a little tiny bridge in between these two big places? You might say, "Well, when they put that little bridge in there, those places didn't exist."

Kristin: Yes, that's right.

Jon: So, that was an unplanned…

Kristin: …community.

Jon: Exactly, and that, unfortunately, is how our minds work. They were not built like a planned community. So, there are disruptive things that just naturally go on. People are sometimes amazed when their minds aren't working in a way that's ideal, but they're not amazed when their computers aren't. We're not amazed when our car isn't. We just figure, well, of course it would screw up. It screws up when you use it.

I called my computer guy the other day and I said to him, "This thing doesn't work again, and you just came in and charged me a whole lot of money to fix it and I haven't used it! So, how did it break?" And you know what he says to me? He asked me, "Has it been exposed to air?" I told him I was pretty sure it had been, and he said, "Well, that explains it." That's what happens to our minds. Things can go wrong on their own just because mind is doing what it does. However, things are even more likely to go wrong when someone is exposed to certain stuff.

Kristin: That makes sense. This is why people's minds go off track so frequently.

PSYCHOTHERAPY BEGINS WITH LOOKING FOR AN UNDERSTANDING OF WHY THINGS ARE NOT WORKING IN THE BEST WAY. PEOPLE BEGIN THE PROCESS OF LOOKING WITHIN TO TRY TO FIGURE OUT WHY THINGS ARE GOING WRONG. FEELING LIKE SOMETHING WITHIN THEM IS BROKEN OR DAMAGED, THEY TRY TO UNDERSTAND SO THEY CAN EITHER FIX IT OR MORE SUCCESSFULLY COPE WITH IT. INSTEAD, I START FROM THE UNDERSTANDING THAT THE BUILD OF THE HUMAN MIND MAKES DYSFUNCTION INEVITABLE.

WE MIGHT BEGIN BEING CURIOUS ABOUT HOW SOMEONE IS SURVIVING AND FUNCTIONING AT ALL INSTEAD OF BEING PUZZLED THAT THERE HAS BEEN A PROBLEM. PSYCHOTHERAPISTS USUALLY BEGIN BY RIGHT AWAY EXTRACTING LARGE AMOUNTS OF VERY PERSONAL INFORMATION FROM THE CLIENT. THE INFORMATION THAT IS OF INTEREST TO THE THERAPIST IS LIKELY TO CONCERN WHAT HAS BEEN TROUBLING INSTEAD OF WHERE THERE HAVE BEEN SUCCESSES AND TRIUMPHS. KRISTIN IS RELIEVED THAT OUR VISIT DOESN'T START BY PROBING HER WITH PERSONAL QUESTIONS. THIS RESULTS IN HER FEELING LESS EXPOSED AND BROKEN THAN SHE HAS IN OTHER THERAPEUTIC EXPERIENCES.

Jon: Yes. Good job. If something happens that is disturbing, the mind will attach a meaning to it. I'll give you an example. This gal was attacked on her way out to her car, which was parked in the parking lot right outside of her office, which she was walking to about a half hour after the workday was over. She stayed a little late to finish up a couple of things. A guy jumped out of a car, hit her in the head with a rock, abducted her, and did awful things. She told me she has never forgiven herself for putting herself in danger, but she didn't put herself in danger. She simply walked to her car and then that maniac hurt her. That is what actually happened and then her mind attached meaning to it. Our minds attach meanings which are always distorted. The more disturbing something is, the more distorted the meaning is likely to be. If I'm walking out to the car and somebody hits me with a brick, you don't say, "Look at that silly guy putting himself in danger." You say, "Somebody just hit that poor fellow with a brick."

Why would she be blaming herself? Because, when she was a little girl, she learned something that is absolutely untrue. She learned it from children's television and children's stories and all kinds of places. She learned that things are good if you are good. All the children's stuff implies that. Later in life, she learned things that contradict that. She learned that things can go badly even if someone is "good," but the later learning didn't eliminate the earlier learning. When something happened that wasn't good, it meant…

Kristin: …she did something wrong.

Jon: Yes. It was her fault. She was bad. The meanings get embedded in the impression and enlarge and distort it even more. The deeper part of the mind can be experiencing this thing as ongoing and can be experiencing it as meaning something that makes it even worse than it was. What happened to her was bad enough, but the meaning her mind attached to it made it even worse. "I'll never be clean. It was all my fault." All that stuff. When that impression is still active, the mind scans around for anything that has structural similarity and is likely to confuse that similar thing with this thing that it doesn't know isn't happening. A combat veteran is hiding under the couch in his suburban living room because someone lit a firecracker. Doesn't he know the difference between a firecracker and a rifle? Sure. But, the part of his mind that doesn't know that the gunfire isn't happening is searching, finding this and confusing it with that.

SPECIFIC EXAMPLES ABOUT THINGS THAT CAN HAPPEN TO OTHER PEOPLE ARE EDUCATIONAL AND CAN EVEN BE ENTERTAINING DEPENDING ON HOW THE STORY IS TOLD. THIS ENGAGES KRISTIN AND PUTS HER AT EASE. SHE ISN'T REQUIRED TO BEGIN ANSWERING PERSONAL QUESTIONS FROM A TOTAL STRANGER, BUT, INSTEAD, GETS TO BE EDUCATED AND EVEN ENTERTAINED.

Kristin: I understand.

Jon: That can also happen in a subtler way. You introduce this guy to your friend, who is really sweet. He says to you afterwards, "She just gave me the creeps." You say, "But why?" And he says he doesn't know. The structure of her voice tone was similar to a gal that was mean to him a long time ago. He doesn't even remember her, but it still affects him. **I have the solution** and it has nothing to do with dealing with painful feelings.

Kristin: Like smoothing the pillow?

Jon: Yes.

Kristin: I got it.

Jon: I never encourage people to re-live painful events and experience painful feelings in order to get them out. Therapists encourage people to feel and express painful feelings about things that aren't happening. They tell people they need to do that to become okay. But that doesn't make sense to me because people who are okay are not doing that. Nobody ever does that if they're okay.

This 37-year-old man is holding his face and screaming. When you ask what's wrong, he explains that when he was 12 years old a guy punched him in the face, and he lost a tooth. You quickly realize that this dude is far from okay. If someone is feeling pain from something that is already finished, this is a problem. Therapists often think it is the solution. I never ask people to try to figure themselves out. Therapists encourage people who are having a hard time to try to figure themselves out. Intelligent people are naturally introspective when they are feeling troubled and the therapist is likely to encourage this and join in a collaborative analysis. People are encouraged to try to figure out what might have happened in their past and how it might relate to what is currently troubling. Nobody ever does that if they're okay. Introspection is a symptom of emotional disturbance and, therefore, it is not the cure.

Kristin: (*Laughter*) Right.

Jon: You <u>have</u> experienced troubling feelings and one of those feelings <u>was</u> anger.

Kristin: Yes. Anger, fear, guilt and shame.

KRISTIN HAS BEEN WITH ME FOR A WHILE AND, INSTEAD OF BEING ASKED PERSONAL QUESTIONS, I GAVE HER INFORMATION ABOUT A WAY THAT THINGS CAN BE UNDERSTOOD. SHE HAS HAD A TIME TO BE WITH ME AND BE OKAY WITH IT AND NOW I AM GOING TO ADDRESS ISSUES THAT HAVE BEEN AFFECTING HER.

Jon: Let's start with guilt. Purposely feel a little of that for less than five seconds. Nod for me when you have accomplished that. (*She nods*) Perfect. Now, here's what just happened, Kristin. You cooperated with me. I asked you to do something, and you did it. I asked you to feel a feeling, and you felt it. You did something with your mind that caused a feeling to happen. The problem was your mind has been doing this on its own. That's what's on the table for us to clear up. So, let's first find a way to represent this problematic thing that your mind has been doing. Not the feeling, but the mechanism that processes information outside of conscious awareness that has been causing the guilt. Represent it as a design. Create a design that will represent not the solution, but the problematic way the mind has been processing information. Would it be dark or bright?

I BEGIN BY ESTABLISHING THE BASELINES THAT REPRESENT OUR STARTING POINT. THE FIRST ONE IS CREATED BY ASKING HER TO PURPOSELY EXPERIENCE THE FEELING OF GUILT FOR LESS THAN 5 SECONDS. THE SECOND BASELINE IS A DESIGN I CALL THE BASELINE VISUAL METAPHOR. IT DOES NOT REPRESENT WHAT HAPPENED NOR WHAT SHE HAS BEEN FEELING. INSTEAD, IT REPRESENTS THE WAY HER MIND HAS BEEN PROCESSING INFORMATION SINCE THAT IS WHAT WE ARE LOOKING TO CHANGE. LATER, WHEN DIRECTED TO TRY TO EXPERIENCE THE FEELING OF GUILT OR TO AGAIN LOOK AT THE DESIGN AND SHE IS NO LONGER ABLE TO, SHE REALIZES THAT SHE IS SUCCESSFUL IN CREATING A VERIFIABLE SHIFT WITHIN HER MIND.

BEFORE DEALING WITH ANY DISTURBING FEELING OR EVENTS, I WANT TO GET HER PRESENT, FEELING A CONNECTION WITH ME AND EXPERIENCING ACCEPTANCE, ENGAGEMENT AND CLARITY. FROM THAT PLATFORM, WE CAN LOOK AT THE DATA ABOUT EARLIER EXPERIENCES WHILE REMAINING EMOTIONALLY PRESENT. I DON'T SAY LET'S "WORK ON" THE GUILT FIRST. INSTEAD, I SAY THAT WE WILL "CLEAR IT".

Kristin: I would say dark.

Jon: Good job. Is it more jagged or smooth? Is it big or small?

Kristin: I would say big and jagged.

Jon: Good. Got it?

Kristin: Yes.

I AM NOT ASKING THOSE QUESTIONS FOR ANY DIAGNOSTIC PURPOSE, BUT TO CREATE A BASELINE THAT WILL LATER SHOW THE PROGRESS WE HAVE MADE.

Jon: **I am looking toward what I am intending for you. I see you like this.** You are experiencing the present each and every moment that you're alive. You are sourced from within with energy, power, clarity, strength, flexibility, joyfulness, grace, and balance. Your mind attends only to what is beneficial and possible. You are aware of what you can do. **I see you** as your body is working to your best advantage with healing going on in a deep and powerful way that keeps you energized and healthy. You are naturally inclined to do things that you will be glad you did. You experience deep satisfaction from your accomplishments, and this fuels energy and interest in other accomplishments. You can also enjoy intense pleasure and beautiful and revitalizing rest.

Kristin: That would be great.

I BEGAN SEEING KRISTIN THIS WAY THE MOMENT I MET HER. BY CHOOSING ATTRIBUTES I AM LOOKING TO INCREASE, I AM NOW CREATING THE PICTURE OF THIS SO THAT IT CAN BECOME OUR SHARED INTENTION. WITH IT "OUT IN FRONT" AS THE PLAN, BOTH OF OUR MINDS BEGIN TO ORGANIZE IN A WAY THAT SETS UP FOR IT. THINGS OCCUR TO BOTH OF US TO SAY OR DO. HENCE, WHAT IS PLANNED IS REALIZED.

Jon: A ship at sea is being affected by the current and even by the wind. It can't stay on course. It is up to the captain to continue to bring it back on course again and again. I see you doing that. You **bring yourself back on course over and over.**

Kristin: Wow! That's perfect. It is just what I want.

Jon: Inner mind is responsive to symbols. That's why every country has a flag. Let's create a way to symbolically represent what you are heading toward. What wild bird or animal would be inspirational?

Kristin: A butterfly.

Jon: Butterfly is the perfect symbol. It is what your mind has chosen and, therefore, what your mind will respond to. Is the butterfly moving or still?

Kristin: Flying.

Jon: What color?

Kristin: Pink.

I ASK FOR DETAILS CAUSING HER MIND TO FORM A PICTURE. A PICTURE WILL BE MORE POWERFUL THAN A CONCEPT. IF YOU ASK PEOPLE TO VISUALIZE SOMETHING, THEY MAY FEEL THEY LACK THE ABILITY. THIS WAY, THAT PROBLEM IS AVOIDED. INSTEAD OF ASKING HER TO VISUALIZE, I CAUSE HER TO VISUALIZE.

Jon: Whenever butterfly comes to your mind, your mind is drawn toward what we intend for you. Can you do two things at exactly the same time?

Kristin: I believe so.

Jon: Okay, because this is going to require you to both breathe and think. *(She giggles)* Picture butterfly and inhale nice and deep. *(She does)* Your mind is taking that in and responding.

So, Kristin, the way we're viewing things is that people are feeling what they're feeling because of something their mind is doing, rather than something that's happening or that did happen. I am suggesting that you think this way with me, not because the other way is wrong, but because this will **give us power to accomplish good things for you.**

Kristin: Yes. I can definitely do that.

Jon: Your emotions and thoughts are due to the way the information processor within your unconscious mind has been managing information. Your mind has been making you feel bad a lot. Do you think your mind wants you to feel bad?

MENTAL HEALTH PROFESSIONALS FREQUENTLY SUGGEST THAT THE INDIVIDUAL IS DOING THESE BAD THINGS TO THEMSELVES. THEY USE WORDS LIKE "SELF-DESTRUCTIVE". THEY CREATE A DIAGNOSIS AND THEN TELL THE INDIVIDUAL THAT IT IS WHO SHE IS BY REFERRING TO HER, SAYING THINGS LIKE, "SHE IS A BORDERLINE." ONCOLOGISTS DON'T REFER TO THEIR PATIENTS AS CANCERS. TWELVE STEP PROGRAMS AND SUBSTANCE ABUSE TREATMENT PROGRAMS ENCOURAGE PEOPLE TO INTRODUCE THEMSELVES AS IF THEY ARE THE ADDICTION. "HELLO, MY NAME IS BEN AND I'M AN ADDICT. MY DRUG OF CHOICE IS CRACK." I WANT TO ALWAYS PROTECT HER IDENTITY. IT'S NOT THAT SHE HAS BEEN DOING IT, AND IT ISN'T EVEN ABOUT HER, AND IT CERTAINLY ISN'T WHO SHE IS. IT IS, INSTEAD, JUST SOMETHING THAT HER MIND HAS BEEN DOING, SOMETHING THAN CAN CHANGE AND SOMETHING THAT I CAN CHANGE.

Kristin: No.

Jon: You're right, it doesn't. It's been making you feel bad, but it doesn't want you to feel bad. Do you think it wants you to feel good?

Kristin: Yes.

Jon: You know what I've discovered, Kristin? Your mind doesn't give a rat's ass how you feel. It truly doesn't care. Why does the mind get people to feel stuff? To understand the whole thing, you need to understand something about rabbits. Now, Rabbit's mind makes Rabbit feel bad when the wolf gets near. Rabbit's mind makes Rabbit feel bad when his stomach is empty. Rabbit's mind makes Rabbit feel good when Rabbit is eating carrots. Rabbit's mind makes Rabbit feel good when Rabbit's having sex. So, what do rabbits do? Stay away from the wolf, eat carrots and have sex. The mind of the rabbit isn't interested in the emotions of the rabbit for their own sake. In other words, the rabbit's mind isn't saying, "I really want the rabbit in a good mood," or "I really want the rabbit in a bad mood." Instead, it's saying, "I want the rabbit eating carrots, staying away from the wolf and having sex." Rabbit can't think about anything it can't do. Unlike other animals, people can think about things they can't do. People can think about things that don't even exist, but the animal can't. Imagine there's a little hill right here with a flag on it. Good, you did it. Let's say you said the same thing to a moose. He can't do it. Right?

Kristin: (*Laughter*) Right.

Jon: If a moose can't do it, a moose can't think it. Make sense?

Kristin: Yes.

Jon: Wolf was hunting. She steps in a hole and she hurt her paw. It's going to get better, but it's sore. So, now she's walking more carefully. Do you think she's thinking she should have been much more careful?

Kristin: (*Laughter*) No.

Jon: A guy with a long red beard approaches the wolf and says, "Miss Wolf, you should have been more careful when you were walking. If you had been more careful, you wouldn't have slipped into that hole." Wolf is confused and asks, "I should have been more careful when?" "In the past, on the way to the hole," he answers. And she says, "Where is 'on the way to the hole'?" And he says, "You know, in the past!" Wolf says, "What are you talking about? Where is this thing you are calling the past? I don't see it." Then she kills him because he doesn't make any sense and has no value. She can't think it because it actually doesn't exist. Make sense?

Kristin: (*Laughter*) Uh huh.

Jon: One day I brought some bread to the duck pond. Do you like to feed ducks, sometimes?

Kristin: Yes, it can be fun and relaxing.

Jon: Oh, it's great. I had this piece of bread. I lob it out and Mr. Duck grabs it in his mouth. He's so happy for about a second until this other duck, Duck #2, pulls up alongside him, yanks that piece of bread out of his mouth and quickly swallows it. You know what Duck #1 did? He sailed away peacefully. I found that so interesting because I don't know anybody who would do that. I wanted to discover what it was about, so I swam out to Duck #1 and said, "Mr. Duck! What about the bread?!" Mr. Duck said, "What bread?"

Mr. Monkey sees another monkey trying to monkey around with his monkey girlfriend and he gets really mad. Mr. Monkey makes loud angry monkey sounds and then he bites the other monkey. The other monkey runs away. It's finished. Mr. Monkey is relaxing, and his monkey girlfriend is sitting next to him and scratching between his shoulder blades. He loves when she scratches that spot. Do you think that, as he's sitting there and feeling his girlfriend digging in and making his itch disappear, that he is thinking about how pissed he is at that other monkey? No, because, for the monkey, if it's not happening, it's…

Kristin: Over.

Jon: Not exactly. For a monkey, it's not over. If you say to the duck, "What about that other duck taking the bread?" He doesn't say, "It's over." He says, "What bread?" And, if you ask Mr. Monkey about that other monkey who was trying to mess with his girlfriend, he doesn't say, "Well, it's over." He doesn't say, "It's in the past." He just asks, "What monkey?"

Kristin: (*Laughter*) Okay, yeah.

Jon: Got it? Because for a monkey, if it's not happening, it doesn't exist. On the way to the duck pond that day, I saw Harry sitting on the bench. He looked like he was in a bad mood, so I said, "Harry, how are you doing"? And, he said, "I'm pissed!" I told him that I hope things work out better. Afterward, I went and fed the ducks and, a few hours later, I was on my way home and guess who was on the bench?

Kristin: Harry?

Jon: Yeah. I said, "Harry, how are you?" He says, "Are you stupid?! I told you how I was just a few hours ago!" It was about a month before I took a walk to that duck pond again. Guess who was on the bench?

Kristin: Harry.

Jon: I said, "Harry, how are you doing?" He says, "Man, you're totally stupid! I've already told you twice." Harry's mind is not functioning as well as the mind of the duck.

Kristin: (*Laughter*) That's funny.

Jon: All right. So, remember that most of my mind is functioning on about the level of the mind of a donkey. The emotions are never coming from the top part. They're coming from the mind that is outside of consciousness. When somebody has an emotional response, it's not because he has decided to. It's not in his appointment book: "At 7:30 PM, I have to remember to feel surprised. At 8:00 PM, I have to remember to get back into feeling resentful." So, the feelings have happened, and you have not been deciding on them. Let's check back in with the wolf. You'll be relieved to know her paw is doing quite a bit better. She didn't see any nice, fat rabbits, but she did see a nice fat bird that was on the ground. She began running toward the bird, but, before she got to it, the bird takes off into the air and flies away. Do you think Miss Wolf is saying, "This is just wrong! If that stupid thing can fly, I should be able to fly, too"?

Kristin: No. She just accepts that things are the way they are. I would like to be a wolf.

Jon: This guy who speaks "wolf" comes over and says, "Miss Wolf, there don't seem to be any rabbits around here today, but there is an abundance of rabbits in Australia." Does she wish she could be in Australia? Nope! You might sometimes wish you were a wolf, but she never wishes she could be a Kristin. For a wolf, if she can't do it, she can't think it.

When you call the dog, you say, "Come!" Does he ask, "When?" You say, "Sit!" Does he ever say, "Give me a few moments."? For Wolf, it is always "now". Wolf isn't thinking, "You know, right now I'm sleepy, but later I think I'll kill that rabbit." or, "I'll kill the rabbit now, but later I'm taking a nap." It's not considered if it's not present. The wolf can't consider the past, and if we try to explain to the wolf where it is, she can't see it. What I want to suggest to you is the reason she can't see it is because it isn't there. There is no past.

Kristin: Wow!

Jon: When these two really bright psychologists are discussing the past as if it's there, the duck is actually functioning on a higher level. What they're talking about, as if it exists, actually doesn't exist. When I do trainings for mental health professionals, I give them this question. I say, "I'd like you to picture a little, wavy line in the moist sand near the ocean. A wave comes and leaves the sand smooth and clear. Where is the line?" Here are the answers: "It's under the sand. It's been swept into the ocean. It's in the past." Somebody said, "the line is actually in our minds." Lots of people agree with that. I say, "Please imagine, for a moment, that you are an electrician instead of a psychologist. I'm going to ask you the same question. There was a line. A wave eliminated the line. Where is the line?" And, as electricians, they said, "There is no line."

Kristin: (*Laughter*)

Jon:	So, do you know these crazy trucks that you need a ladder to get into? Super big gaudy trucks that some guys like. The wheels of it are taller than you. There was this big yellow one that was making me very nervous the other day because my little car was backed next to a wall, so I couldn't back up, and this huge thing was backing up toward my car. Now, somebody thoughtfully installed these warning beepers during the backup thing, so, as it's backing up, the lights on the back are flashing. It flashes and beeps, which is really handy because it makes you aware that you're about to get run over, but there was zero I could do about it. And this thing is backing up, and I'm thinking, "If this guy, this stupid ass guy, checks his rearview mirror, all he's going to see is a cloud or something because I'm on the ground and he is up in the air. I'm a goner here."
Kristin:	Did he hit you?
Jon:	Just in the nick of time, he stopped and went in the other direction. I was really relieved. So, the question I have for you is, where is the truck backing up into me? Somebody might say it's in the past, but is there a thing called the past where we can find a truck backing up toward my car? No. My mind took in information about something that does not now exist. See, if we say, "The beer is in the fridge," it means what? It means, there's a fridge, there's beer, and the beer is safe within the fridge. When someone says, "It's in the past," the mind perceives that there is a past, and something is in it. So, if your friend gets raped, don't tell her it's in the past.
Kristin:	I understand that, yeah.
Jon:	Well, then, is it in my mind? I want you to look at me very carefully and determine whether or not there is a truck in my head.
Kristin:	(*Laughter*) No.
Jon:	Good, good. So, it's not in my mind and it's not in the past, and it's not under the sand, and it's not in the ocean. So, the answer to "where is this?" is that "it doesn't exist." Make sense?
Kristin:	Yeah.
Jon:	My primitive mind, like a donkey, figures that, if I can think it, it is in existence. If you ask the donkey to imagine a castle, he might say, "I can't imagine a castle because there is no castle." If you show him a castle, there is a castle. If there isn't a castle, there isn't. Primitive part of the mind functions like a donkey. It figures, if you're thinking it, it is. You can tell me to think of a palm tree, and I think of a palm tree. If you ask me to think of a palm tree flying around the room, I can think of that, but it doesn't mean it is. The wolf can't think it. Primitive mind figures that if I'm thinking it, then it must be. That is why someone can be scared watching a horror movie. The primitive mind figures that if it is being thought about, then it must exist.

In addition to that, mind figures that it won't come to mind unless there is a chance that it can get done. If I'm thinking of it, possibly I can do it, because the only thing that a wolf could think is something that a wolf might be able to do. "I might be able to outrun that rabbit," not, "I might be able to fly like a bird." When the primitive part of the mind wants to cause the animal to do something, it causes a thought, a sensation, an emotion or some kind of impulse to cause an action. These are feelings we might think of as bad feelings, like fear to get the animal to run, anger to get her to attack or hunger to get her to eat. They are not bad if they are doing what they are intended to do which is to cause immediate action. The purpose of the feeling, however, is not to cause the animal to feel bad. I don't think the animal is feeling badly if he is engaging in the action that is intended. The zebra running from the lion is experiencing fear. Because fear turns into action, Zebra is not feeling emotional pain. When mind wants Zebra to keep doing something, it causes a feeling we might think of as pleasure. If Zebra begins eating and her mind wants her to continue eating, it will cause pleasure as she eats. If it no longer wants her to keep eating because it has determined that she has eaten enough, it stops causing pleasure and she stops eating. This is the primitive part of the mind and, if it wants you to do something, it makes you feel uncomfortable.

Now, this guy said to me, "Well, that's terrible! I don't like it making me feel uncomfortable every time it wants me to do something. Why doesn't it do it in a better way than that?" And I said, "Well, it doesn't know how to text you. It can't send a fax or e-mail. It's functioning like a donkey. So, all it can do is make you feel uncomfortable or make you feel good, and it isn't going to make you feel comfortable if it wants you to do something else, because if you feel good, you'll just keep doing what you're doing." If she wants him to get off the couch, she doesn't walk over and start rubbing his shoulders.

Remember I asked you if your mind wants you to feel bad, and you said no? Does it want you to feel good? It doesn't care about that either. What it does care about is you doing something. That's it. It just wants you to do something. This has not been obvious to the intellect because the things your mind has been asking you to do frequently are not things that are possible and, because they are not possible, your intellect didn't understand what was going on. So, rather than just address that as either doing it or saying, "I can't do that," this part of the mind (*pointing to the top of my head)* didn't think it was being asked to do something. It thought it was being asked to consider something, to feel something, come to grips with something, have a perspective on something. Of course, donkeys don't ask you to do that.

Kristin: (*Laughter*)

Jon: So, I'll give you an idea, sort of how it's been operating. We go into this restaurant together. The food server comes over and I say to this guy, "You know, I'd like you to bring me some hot soup." He says, "I know that I should have realized that. I apologize." I say, "Well, okay, but bring me some soup." He says, "I think it's a pattern. I find that often people want soup and I haven't brought the soup, and I should have gotten the soup, but I didn't think of the soup and I don't know why it repeats." And I say, "Uh huh," because it doesn't make a damn bit of sense to me. So, all I say is, "Ah, well, you know what? Bring me some soup here." Now, at some point, the guy says, "Oh, we don't have soup. I can't bring soup. I'm sorry. We don't have soup." Do you think then I say to him, "Well, then, bring me some soup?" No. Then I say, "Okay, never mind." So, if this guy wants me to stop asking him for soup, there are two things that could happen. One is, he brings soup. Two is, he says, "I can't bring any soup." Either way, I stop asking for soup right away. Does it make sense?

Kristin: Yes.

Jon: But, if I say, "Bring me soup," and he goes into some crazy thing about "I know it's something I have to realize…I should have done it," and he sounds like a blithering idiot, and I just repeat it, "Yeah, but bring me some soup." "But I don't know how to adjust the air conditioning," and I say, "All right, but bring the soup." "You know? I can't bring soup." Oh, never mind. It's over. Got it?

Kristin: Uh huh.

Jon: So, your mind has been making you feel bad. It keeps asking you to do stuff you can't do, and you haven't realized what it was asking, so you couldn't answer it. The answer is to say, "No, I can't," or to say, "Nothing needs to be done," because then it will stop asking. It's a donkey. It's got no other issue. Do this thing. Why does it think you can do it? Because you can think it. "If you can think it, do it." I could say, "What do you mean if I can think it, do it? I can think things I can't do." The donkey says, "What are you talking about? If you think it, do it."

Kristin: (*Laughter*) Uh huh.

Jon: "Well, I can imagine things that aren't there." "What are you talking about, imagine things that aren't there? If it's there, do something with it. If you're thinking it, it must be there. How can you be thinking it if it isn't there?" Kangaroo doesn't get this whole "imaginary castle in the corner of the room" thing. It just gets that, if you're thinking it, do it, until you say, "I can't" and then it's done. If you just respond to your mind in a way it understands, it will stop requesting that you do things that don't need to be done in ways that cause you problems. When you respond, your mind will finally just shut up.

Kristin: That sounds great. How can I make that happen?

Jon: I'm going to give you some practice saying, "I can't." You've been taught that "I can't" isn't a good thing, but "I can't" is really a good thing. So, we're going to get practice with "I can't." Here we go. I'd like you to please get here 10 minutes earlier than you got here today.

Kristin: I can't do that. (*laughter*)

Jon: Then, if you would please just have a big glass of water before you walk in the door.

Kristin: I can't do that.

Jon: Um, I'd like you to wear a different top this morning, please.

Kristin: I can't.

Jon: Good. **You're getting it**. So, you see, "I can't" can be a good answer.

Kristin: (*Laughter*) Okay, yeah.

Jon: Right? It's not a bad answer. It's a good answer. It's an accurate answer. Now, I'll show you what I mean by that. Watch. Put your feet flat on the floor. Now, can you push your feet through the floor?

Kristin: No, I can't.

Jon: No, you can't. And you know that?

Kristin: Yes. I know I can't do that.

Musle Test w/imagination

Jon: Okay. I want you to put your arms out like this. (*I indicate that she should hold her arms out straight in front of her*) Think of your arms like bars of steel so there's no way I could push them anywhere, okay? I try to push, and they're not going to go anywhere. (*I push on her arms, but they don't move*) See? And now, I'd like you to imagine something. I'd like you to imagine that you should be able to push your feet through the floor. You know you can't, actually, but think about it. Get into that mindset and think, "Well, I should be able to do that." And, as you're thinking you should, remember when you were strong. I'm going to push your arms down and you try to resist. Think you should be able to do it. Okay? Here we go, one, two, three. (*Her arms have become weak and I easily pushed them down.*)

Jon: Interesting, huh? Should you have been able to push your feet through the floor, actually?

Kristin: No.

Jon: No. So, you know that. Right?

Kristin: Yeah.

Jon: Ok, push your feet through the floor in the past. Hurry up. You say, "I can't."

Kristin: I can't.

Jon: *(I push her arms that are once again strong)* Good and notice I can't get anywhere. There's strength. Feel it?

Kristin: Yes.

Jon: Now, I want you to think for a moment that you should have. So, say, "I should have done that" and believe it. Act it. Be an actress. Say, "I should have done it."

Kristin: I should have been able to put my feet through the floor. *(Laughter)*

Jon: Good. Say it, and really try to resist. Say, "I should have been able to put my feet through the floor."

Kristin: I should have been able to put my feet through the floor. *(I push, and her arms are again weak.)*

KRISTIN FINDS THE STUFF I AM DOING WITH HER ARMS AND HOW HER STRENGTH VARIES IN THE WAY I PREDICT TO BE FASCINATING. SHE IS OUT AND FOCUSED, INVOLVED WITH THE WORLD RATHER THAN INVOLVED WITH HERSELF. SHE UNDERSTANDS THE THOUGHT THAT SHE SHOULD HAVE DONE MORE IS ONE THAT WEAKENS HER, NOT JUST MENTALLY, BUT EVEN PHYSICALLY. SHE CAN NOW ELIMINATE ITS POWER BY SIMPLY SAYING, "I CAN'T".

Jon: I'm going to say to do something and you answer by saying, "I can't. I'm strong." I will be trying to push your arms down, but you will see that you become very strong when you say, "I can't." Wear a different blouse this morning.

Kristin: I can't. I'm strong. *(I push her arms, but they are strong and don't move.)*

Jon: There we go. Got it? So, the "I can't" is accurate. Let's think about putting that blouse on this morning. Where is that? Where is you putting on that blouse?

Kristin: In the past.

Jon: Well, we used to think so, didn't we? But where is it actually?

Kristin: It's not there anymore.

Jon: It's not, is it?

Kristin: No, it's not there.

Jon: Okay, so, it's not in the past. Is it in your mind? You can recall it, but does that mean there's a closet in your head? Or a dresser? Clothes? So, where is it? And the answer is: it doesn't exist. Do you get that?

Kristin: I do.

Jon: Put on different shoes this morning.

Kristin: Right now? *(Laughter)*

Jon: Well, everything's right now, isn't it? So, put different shoes on this morning.

Kristin: I can't.

Jon: Right. And, why not? And the answer is, "it doesn't exist." Do you get it? If it doesn't exist, can you change it? No.

Kristin: No.

Jon: Okay, well, here. This dresser here, this one, will you paint it blue for me? No? (*I am pointing to the air where there is no dresser.*)

Kristin: No.

Jon: Why?

Kristin: Because it doesn't exist.

Jon: And then, could you put a few knickknacks on it?

Kristin: No.

Jon: Why not? Because it doesn't exist. Can you just wake up a little earlier this morning, please?

Kristin: No.

Jon: Why not? It doesn't exist. So, "No, I can't. It doesn't exist" are accurate answers. Accuracy gets your mind enlightened so you're thinking clearly like a monkey. Got it? Because the monkey is seeing what is. And you say, "Boy, I bet you're really pissed about that other monkey." "No!" "Well, why not?" There's no other monkey. There's banana, girlfriend, no other monkey. Monkey is clear and enlightened, like the duck. You get that, right?

WITH LOTS OF SILLY EXAMPLES, KRISTIN IS REALIZING WHAT THE PROBLEM HAS BEEN. HER MIND HAS BEEN TRYING TO GET HER TO DO THINGS THAT SHE CAN'T DO AND DOESN'T NEED TO DO. I TEACH HER TO RESPOND TO THESE REQUESTS BY SIMPLY THINKING, "NO, I CAN'T." HENCE, HER MIND WILL STOP ASKING. WITH MIND QUIET AND FREE OF TURMOIL, I BELIEVE THERE WILL BE SIGNIFICANT IMPROVEMENTS. THE EXAMPLES AND THE EXPERIENTIAL PROCESSES KEEP HER ENGAGED AS THE COMMUNICATION REACHES VARIOUS FACETS OF HER MIND.

Kristin: Yes.

Jon: Your mind has been causing you to feel pain, but it doesn't want you to be in pain. It doesn't care how you feel. It's all been trying to get you to do something because you thought you should have done it. Since you didn't know that, you didn't just say, "It doesn't exist. I can't." You said stuff like, "Well, I'll have to take a look at that. Bring me some soup! Well, I'll have to take a look at that. Yeah, I see what you mean, but bring me some soup." Over and over, endlessly until we say, "It doesn't exist. I can't." So, that feeling, was it more like shame or more like guilt?

Kristin: I think, guilt.

Jon: Okay. We're going to now take that apart. Ready to do that?

Kristin: Yes, I want that very much.

Jon: The guilt that you experienced, get just a smidgen of it now. Got it?

Kristin: Yes.

Jon: It's about something that you did or didn't do? Which?

Kristin: Did.

Jon: Did. When?

Kristin: Recently. Like a month ago.

Jon: A month ago. Okay. So, what did you do a month ago?

Kristin: I have a good friend and I love her, but sometimes she's really needy. She called and left a message saying she was upset and needed to talk. I lied and texted her that I was sick and couldn't talk. I turned my back on my friend when she was hurt and asking for help.

Jon: Okay. Think about it for a second. Feel the guilt?

Kristin: Yes, I do.

Jon: Now, the guilt is saying, "Don't do it. Don't do that thing a month ago." When?

Kristin: Now.

Jon: Now. Exactly, because if the monkey is telling me to do it, it's when?

Kristin: Now.

Jon: So, here we go. I'm going to speak for the part of your mind that's like a monkey. Don't lie to your friend last month.

Kristin: It doesn't exist?

Jon: Right. It doesn't exist. You are not even doing it, so you cannot do something you are not even doing. As you simply say, "I can't. It doesn't exist, and nothing needs to be done," it clears.

Kristin: Really? Just like that?

Jon: Yes. Let's stay with it. Don't lie to your friend last month. Hurry up.

Kristin: I can't. It doesn't exist, and nothing needs to be done.

Jon: That's the first time there's been a reasonable answer to that question. You follow?

Kristin: Uh huh.

Jon: Say, "Bring me some soup" Say it to me. Say, "Bring me some soup."

Kristin: Bring me some soup.

Jon: "You're right, I should have." That's not a reasonable answer.

Kristin: (*Laughter*) No.

Jon: The donkey wants you to feed him and he goes, "UHHH." You say, "You're right, I should have done it." So, don't lie to your friend last month. Hurry up.

Kristin: I can't.

Jon: Good, now check with the guilt.

Kristin: I don't feel it. Oh, my goodness! It's gone!

I TAUGHT KRISTIN A WAY OF THINKING AND A PROCESS TO APPLY IT TO ON AN ISSUE THAT SHE HAD SOME CONCERN ABOUT, BUT IT WAS NOT THE ISSUE THAT WAS MOST SIGNIFICANT. I THINK IT MAKES SENSE TO TEST IT BEFORE IT IS APPLIED TO THINGS THAT ARE EXTREMELY SIGNIFICANT.

Jon: Yeah, there you go. I bet you're thinking, "This could not be this simple. There's no way this could be this simple." But think about what you've been doing to solve this problem. You've been seeing people who have suggested two things. One is, you need to figure out why you've done things. Tell me anybody who is figuring out why they did things who is not screwed up.

2   Two is, you need to get in touch with and release those feelings. You tell me anybody who is releasing feelings about anything that isn't in existence who isn't completely crazy. So, the reason you were having trouble is because the people you were going to were telling you to do things that would cause somebody to have problems even if they weren't having problems. Right?

Kristin: That seems really clear. The medication reduced the symptoms, but certainly hasn't eliminated them. The talk therapy doesn't seem to have done a thing.

Jon: Monkey is having a really great day until someone convinces him that he needs to figure himself out and start experiencing emotional responses to things that are not taking place. If he gets right on that, he's one screwed up monkey. That's what was happening with you. Got it?

Kristin: Yes. This makes so much sense. Nothing they were telling me was making sense to me and it made me feel like I was even more crazy. I felt like I was too disturbed to benefit from therapy for people who were disturbed.

Jon: Everybody has been doing their best or, more accurately, people have been doing the only thing they could have done at the time. Your mind is fine. It just needed a tune up. Let's do another one about guilt because what will happen is, we're not going to get to everything, but we're going to get to a bunch of things, and **then your mind is going to take what you learn and generalize it to everything we don't get to**. Like, if you teach a little boy how to tie a pair of shoes, then you teach him on another pair of shoes, then you bring out the third pair of shoes. You know what he says? "Hey, lady, I think I'm getting the concept here. You don't have to bring out every pair of shoes in the world." Your mind is going to apply what you learn to everything. Tell me about something else, guilt or shame. Tell me the biggest one.

Kristin: My sister, before she died. My parents were really hard on her because she came out of the closet as being a lesbian. My dad was a pastor and he was really religious. Both of my parents were really religious, and my sister didn't want to be anymore, and there was a lot of turmoil in our house. So, I feel guilty for not being able to stand up for her. I followed my parents instead.

Jon: Good. Here we go. Try to defend her from your parents in the past.

Kristin: I can't.

Jon: Good. Where is dad making her feel guilty about being gay?

Kristin: Nowhere. It doesn't exist.

Jon: There we go. Paint this bookshelf. (*I point to the air where there is no bookshelf.*)

Kristin: I can't. It doesn't exist. (*Laughter*)

22

Jon: Get Dad to stop making...what's your sister's first name?

Kristin: Bethany.

Jon: Okay. Make Dad stop making Bethany feel guilty about being a lesbian.

Kristin: I can't.

Jon: Why not?

Kristin: Because it doesn't exist anymore.

Jon: No, not "anymore". It doesn't exist. Make your father treat Bethany differently, how long ago?

Kristin: Five years.

Jon: Make your dad act differently to Bethany five years ago.

Kristin: I can't. It doesn't exist.

Jon: There it is. And now, feel that "I can't." Feel the "I can't." Your mind has been doing all this stuff that's been making you feel crappy, not because it's interested in you having insight, Kristin. It just wants you to do it. You get it? It's a monkey. It's not trying to get you to be self-aware. It's like, "Do it." So, I'm going to be the monkey, and I want you to answer me head to head, straight on and clear. Do it.

Kristin: I can't.

Jon: Good. Here we go again, just like that. (*Slapping sound*) Jam it into me. Do it.

Kristin: I can't.

Jon: Yeah. Perfect. Once more. Do it!

Kristin: I can't.

Jon: Good. Now, check for the feeling.

Kristin: I don't feel it. Wow! It's gone. The guilt is gone.

Jon: Perfect. Ready for anger?

Kristin: Yeah.

Jon: The guilt was to get you to do something differently in the past. Of course, there is no past and there is no you in the past who could do anything differently. So, your answer was perfect. It doesn't exist. Bingo. Done. We don't have soup.

Kristin: (*Laughter*) Okay.

Jon: Bring me soup. We don't have soup. Okay, never mind. And that took care of it. When there's anger, it's designed to get somebody else to do something differently in the past. Where is Dad five years ago, now?

Kristin: He's not there.

Jon: Right. So, the answer is, simply, it doesn't exist. Got that one?

Kristin: Yes.

Jon: Okay. Where is Dad five years ago?

Kristin: It doesn't exist.

Jon: Good. I want you to keep answering me back the same way and it will get clearer and clearer each time because, as obvious as this is, it's brand new. It's totally obvious, but it's brand new. So, where is Dad five years ago?

Kristin: It doesn't exist.

Jon: Where is Dad four years ago?

Kristin: It doesn't exist.

Jon: Where is Dad a year-and-a-half ago?

Kristin: It doesn't exist.

Jon: Twenty-four years ago?

Kristin: It doesn't exist.

Jon: Good. Get Dad to act differently 27 years ago.

Kristin: It doesn't exist.

Jon: Get Dad to act differently 17 years ago.

Kristin: It doesn't exist.

Jon: Get Dad to act differently seven years ago.

Kristin: It doesn't exist.

Jon: Get Dad to understand things he didn't understand two years ago.

Kristin: It doesn't exist.

Jon: Get him to know something he didn't know six years ago and get him to know it six years ago.

Kristin: (*Laughter*) It doesn't exist.

Jon: Okay. Get Dad to treat Bethany differently five years ago.

Kristin: It doesn't exist.

Jon: Good job. Get Dad to treat Bethany differently five years ago.

Kristin: It doesn't exist.

Jon: Good. You have to stop Dad from criticizing Bethany five years ago. Hurry!

Kristin: I can't. It doesn't exist.

Jon: Again. Get him not to do that five years ago. Hurry up. (*Slapping sound*)

Kristin: I can't. It doesn't exist.

Jon: Good job. Now, check for the anger.

Kristin: (*Laughter*) I am not angry at all. Oh, my goodness. I am not angry.

Jon: Beautiful. And so, let's say there was somebody, a surgeon who was about to operate on somebody you loved. How guilty do you want her to be?

Kristin: Guilty?

Jon: Yeah. She's about to start her surgery. How guilty would you want her?

Kristin: None.

Jon: Zero guilty. Okay. How resentful do we want her?

Kristin: None.

Jon: You didn't even say, "Why? What did she do?" Did you? You didn't care, did you?

Kristin: No. (*Laughter*)

Jon: "Well, did she have an affair? Lie to her friend? Did she kill two hundred kittens?" Well, if she had an affair, lied to her friend or killed two hundred kittens, how guilty do you want her to be? She's about to do surgery.

Kristin: None.

Jon: Right. What if her father used to make fun of her? What if her father tried to have sex with her? How angry do you want her to be while doing surgery?

Kristin: Not a bit. (*Laughter*)

Jon: And she'll do it better, won't she?

Kristin: Yes.

Jon: So, now that your mind is clear, you can't not do better. You can't not do better. Everybody around you will benefit, and your body and mind will heal. It has to. Got it?

Kristin: Yes. I really do. Finally, I understand. (*She is both laughing and crying.*)

Jon: Those are good, clean tears. They are tears of relief.

Kristin: Yeah.

Jon: Good job. Okay. You know, it's so fun to work with you because **you are really smart**. You're so smart, and it makes you so easy to work with.

Kristin: I'm studying psychology.

Jon: That made it harder, but we still got it done.

Kristin: (*Laughter*) I am really interested in helping people.

Jon: You'll be good at it.

Kristin: I hope to get a master's or open up a practice, but the thing is, I don't want to learn to do it the way people have tried to help me.

Jon: You don't want to do it the way it's been done to you.

Kristin: (*Laughter*) No. Definitely not.

Jon: Well, you won't. What **you'll learn is to enlighten** so that **there's light** and **things are light.** Much of what you've experienced was heavy and in shadows. Didn't people say things like, "You really need to take responsibility for this," and "It's time now for you to let it go."

Kristin: That is what all of the therapists have been telling me.

Jon: "It's really necessary for you to do this and you have to understand the importance of this, and you have to come to grips with this, and you need to forgive yourself first and love yourself, and if you love yourself, you can start to love other people, but you have to first be compassionate to you, and give yourself permission to feel horrible." (*Laughter*) Does that sound familiar?

Kristin: (*Laughter*) Yes. That was what they were all telling me. Not in just those words, but that is what it was.

Jon: That's why it didn't work. It was well meaning, but it couldn't have gotten you anywhere. But here you are, and **things are getting clear now**. I want to give you another way of looking at things that will be useful to you. I want to give you a way of understanding the way people think about things. There are four major views of explaining why people do what they do or don't do.

The first and most popular by far is moralistic. Moralistic is the view held by most people who are four years old. It goes like this: Why didn't she do that? Because she was a bad girl. Why did he do it? Oh, because he was a good boy. Of course, that's the way four-year-old children have been taught to think. It's also the way most of the grown-ups you know think. People have been taught to understand themselves and others by applying praise or blame, pride or shame. That is what I mean by moralistic thought. It's the way most people you know think. It sounds like it is the way your parents thought.

Kristin: Right.

Jon: And he should have been good because he was bad, and bad people should be good, and good people should be good, and all of that.

The second way of thinking is higher purpose. You've definitely heard this one. Higher purpose means that things seem bad, but they're not bad if we take a broader view and see things we haven't been able to see, then we'd see that the things we thought were bad were good. Sweet old guy gets stabbed to death. Somebody says, "Oh, it seems awful, but actually he drew that energy into him in order to ascend to a higher level or God had a good reason to take him." You've heard this, right?

Kristin: Yes.

Jon: A little girl has a disease and dies, and somebody says to her mother, "God took her because he needed a special little angel." So, did you hear a couple of those when you went through some stuff?

Kristin: Yeah.

Jon: I'm going to give you a third, okay? This is the one you've never heard. This is the one nobody talks about. This is the one that, after you're with me and you want to talk to people about it, don't bother. They won't get it. This is one that's completely out of the box. It's called science.

It goes like this. If you see a branch has fallen off the tree, you might say, "I wonder what made it fall." You won't say, "I wonder if anything made it fall." Do you get that? You'll say, "I wonder WHAT made it fall," but you won't say, "I wonder IF anything made it fall."

Kristin: Something made it fall.

Jon: Something made it fall. How do you know?

Kristin: Because it's fallen.

Jon: Yes. So, the event proves there was a cause, doesn't it? It doesn't answer what caused it, but it answers that it was caused.

Kristin: Yes.

Jon: We can make up a cause. Let's say it fell because it was hit by lightning. It fell right in that spot. How the lightening hit the tree caused it to fall exactly where it fell. Could it have fallen a little further to the right?

Kristin: No.

Jon: To the left? No. Earlier?

Kristin: No *(Laughter)*.

Jon: It happened so you know it was caused. Because it was caused, it had to happen. Now, watch this. There's a bridge and pedestrians cross this bridge, only pedestrians. It's over white-water rapids with sharp, jutting rocks. You definitely don't jump off this bridge. These four gals are crossing the bridge and they hear a child scream. There's a little girl. She is somehow in the white water. She's going to go under the bridge and down the falls, and definitely die. People are horrified. They are frozen, except Judy, who instantly has thrown herself off the bridge. Her ankle shattered against one of the sharp rocks, but her arm reaches out as she grabs this kid's collar, and she hobbles out of that water, and she's being interviewed that night, and people say,

"My God! I mean, you're amazing. You're such a hero. I mean, there were good people on that bridge, really good women on that bridge. Everyone else froze. You jumped. You sacrificed your ankle. You'll never walk again the way you had, but this child is alive because of you. Why did you jump when nobody else jumped?" You know what she says? "I don't know." Got it? She doesn't know. She says, "All I know is I heard that kid and then my ankle hurt like hell." Why did she do it? We don't know exactly all the things that preceded it, but we know that if it happened, it was caused, and the cause had something to do with genetics. It had something to do with environmental influences. Those two things caused that tree and that branch to be exactly where they were and Judy to be exactly as she was. There was lightening. There was the child. Branch fell. Gal dropped. Could she have not?

Kristin: No.

Jon: No, got it? Now, Jean, sweetheart of a gal who would give her life for a child, didn't jump. She just stood there. Could she have jumped?

Kristin: No.

Jon: Bingo. Now, here's the other part. You're not going to like Joey. You know why?

Kristin: Why?

Jon: It was Joey who took this little girl to the river. He picked her up, and she looked at him with loving, trusting eyes, and he says, "Ha!" and he threw her in the river, and she screamed in horror, and he clapped his hands (*slapping sound*) and said, "Goody!" I don't like him. Do you? Could he have not done that? Should he have not done that?

Kristin: Now, I'm not sure. I would have said, "Of course, he shouldn't have done that," but now, I just don't know.

Jon: Does he have a higher level of consciousness than our hero?

Kristin: No.

Jon: Is he functioning on a higher level than her?

Kristin: No.

Jon: We wouldn't say he has more awareness, more choice, or more ability, would we?

Kristin: No.

Jon: So, could he have not done what he did?

Kristin: No.

Jon: So, we're glad we didn't have that role in this movie. I mean, I wouldn't want to have to play him. Sit here and tell you about it, "Yeah, I walked the kid to the river, threw her in." As we look through View Three, if there's something you did that you don't like, you may still not like it, but you no longer are thinking that you could have not done it.

Kristin: I understand that, yes.

Jon: Yeah. Now, if you could have not done it, should you have not done it?

Kristin: No.

Jon: Don't try to explain it, because nobody is going to get it, but you're getting it.

Kristin: Okay.

Jon: If it was something I didn't do, you don't even need to know what it is, I didn't do it. Should I have done it?

Kristin: No.

Jon: Right. I did do it. Should I have not done it?

Kristin: No.

Jon: You don't care whether it was horrible or wonderful. It doesn't have anything to do with it. There can't be a "should" without a "could." And, there wasn't a "could" so there couldn't have been a "should." Got it?

Kristin: (*Laughter*) Yes.

Jon: So, let's take something that's really been a big one for you. Dad was critical of your sister's sexual…I don't even think the word "preference" is accurate. Do you? Let's say, instead of preference, it was her inclination, because it wasn't something she sat around one day and picked off the menu. Right?

Kristin: (*Laughter*) Right.

Jon: It was how it worked. Why? I can tell you exactly why. Something to do with environment, something to do with genetics. Probably more to do with genetics than environment. But, whatever, it certainly was not picked off the menu. So, anyway, he was critical of that, right? Could he have not been?

Kristin: No.

Jon:	Should he have not been?
Kristin:	No.
Jon:	Bingo. (*Laughter*)
Kristin:	Thank you! I don't even know how long it took for me to realize that!
Jon:	You got it? The person that was driving the other car when Bethany was killed had been drinking, How has that been making you feel? You must have been angry.
Kristin:	I have been so angry at him. I have tried to let it go, but it's just not possible.
Jon:	Is it okay if we look at this one as well?
Kristin:	I already get it. It couldn't have happened any other way. Thinking things shouldn't have happened the way they did has been making me sick. No one ever pointed these things out to me like you have. None of it could have been different and it doesn't make sense to think that it should have.

THE CONVERSION DISORDER WAS ROOTED IN HER BELIEF THAT THINGS SHOULD HAVE BEEN DIFFERENT THAN THEY WERE. HER PARENTS SHOULD NOT HAVE BEEN CONDEMNING TOWARD HER SISTER. SHE SHOULD HAVE STOOD UP FOR HER SISTER. HER SISTER SHOULDN'T HAVE BEEN KILLED IN THE ACCIDENT. THE DRIVER OF THE CAR THAT CAUSED THE ACCIDENT SHOULD NOT HAVE BEEN DRINKING. THE PROCESS I TOOK HER THROUGH ATTACKED AND DESTROYED THE BELIEF THAT THINGS SHOULD HAVE BEEN DIFFERENT BY ELIMINATING THE BELIEF THAT THEY COULD HAVE BEEN DIFFERENT. I BEGAN WITH THINGS FREE OF EMOTIONAL ATTACHMENT, LIKE THE BRANCH FALLING FROM THE TREE, AND THEN APPLIED THE SAME PRINCIPLES TO THINGS THAT SHE HAD STRONG EMOTIONAL RESPONSES TO.

Kristin:	There's other stuff, too. I recently got married in January of 2008 and there's just tons of ways my husband has talked to me that remind me of my dad….
Jon:	It's the number three thing, remember?
Kristin:	Yeah, and, so…
Jon:	Is he a little moralistic?
Kristin:	Yes.
Jon:	Hello!
Kristin:	(*Laughter*) He's almost exactly like my dad, and I didn't even realize it when we got married, but now, I understand so much more. I've been unhappy but feel badly that I don't want to be intimate with him. Now, I'm making the decision of, should I call it quits now or do counseling…
Jon:	Kids yet?

Kristin: No. But there's never been a divorce on either side of my family. They are all in the ministry…

Jon: Well, we've got to make sure that you're no different than everybody else. (*Laughter*)

Kristin: (*Laughter*) I know that's not the biggest thing. I don't have…because of my severe conversion disorder I had, I have no money and I have no…

Jon: Right, it doesn't need to be completely figured out today or tomorrow but hang with this new way of experiencing life for a little while and then let's see how it bubbles up. There's no way to have gone through what you went through today without significant positive physiological and psychological benefit. Does it make sense? I mean, how could you? So, it has to do that. The anger that was there for a long time based on thinking that Dad should have been different isn't there any longer. The anger at yourself isn't there anymore. There is no longer shame or guilt. All that **energy is now released and there for healing.**

KRISTIN'S MARRIAGE AND HER TURMOIL ABOUT IT IS A SITUATION THAT IS ONGOING. HER MIND CLEARED FROM THE PAST TRAUMA WILL FREE UP RESOURCES SO THAT SHE CAN DEAL WITH THIS MUCH MORE EFFECTIVELY AND IN A WAY THAT IS BEST FOR EVERYONE.

Kristin: Yeah.

Jon: Sometimes that old golden rule thing is a very useful tool for dealing with this kind of situation. Let me make up a situation for you. You've met a guy and you fell in love with him, and you built your life around him, and he's getting that he just doesn't feel it for you. You're just not a turn on for him. He's thinking the gal he is waking up with is not somebody he is attracted to, not somebody he has fun with, not somebody that he really wants. So, imagine that situation. You are that gal.

Kristin: Okay.

Jon: What would you want the guy to do? Would you want the guy to just decide to stay with you, go home at night saying, "I'd really rather have fun, but I'm going to do the right thing? I'm going to be with Kristin again"?

Kristin: Not really, no.

Jon: And then the next night, would you want him to say, "I'm going to do it again. I'm going to do the right thing. In fact, I'm even going to touch her sexually tonight. I don't want to, but I know it's what I promised." How would you like that?

Kristin: No. That would be awful.

Jon: So, now, you're going to do me a favor and do the right thing and get into bed with him and do what you should. Right? So, I mean, if this fella is dying from a terrible disease, then I think we need to take that into consideration.

Kristin: No, he's fine.

Jon: Does he have arms? Legs?

Kristin: (*Laughter*) Yes.

Jon: Okay. If you dropped him in the shopping mall, do you think he'd be okay?

Kristin: (*Laughter*) He'd be fine.

Jon: Does he know how to use a cell phone?

Kristin: (*Laughter*) Yeah.

Jon: Okay. Those are good things to know. Eliminate your sense of obligation and **NEVER have sex because of obligation.** The little flame of romance and sexual interest up against the ocean of obligation doesn't have much of a chance. Now that we've done something about the ocean, let's see whether the flame sparks up. Give it a little while.

SO MUCH HAS BEEN ACCOMPLISHED THAT I DON'T THINK KRISTIN SHOULD BE TRYING TO MAKE DECISIONS ABOUT HER MARRIAGE WHILE SHE IS WITH ME. TELLING HER TO NO LONGER FEEL OBLIGATED TO BE SEXUAL OR EVEN TO STAY WITH HER HUSBAND CAUSES A SHIFT IN HOW SHE VIEWS HER MARRIAGE. THIS SHIFT WILL EITHER IMPROVE THE MARRIAGE OR GIVE HER MORE CLARITY ON HOW TO PROCEED.

Kristin: Okay.

Jon: Let's see if there's a little bit of flame without the ocean, because the ocean was all about you have to, you need to, you should, you've got to, it would be wrong, all that. Let's get rid of the ocean and then let's see what it will be like without that. It may be that, without that, you may realize he could do better than you because he could find a gal who would be happy about wanting to be close to him, and, if so, the best thing you can do for him is to get the freak out of the way.

I AM SHIFTING KRISTIN'S VIEW OF WHAT HAS BEEN GOING ON IN HER MARRIAGE. SHE HAS BEEN FEELING STUCK AND GUILTY ABOUT NOT WANTING TO STAY WITH HER HUSBAND. I HAVE TURNED THAT AROUND USING THE GOLDEN RULE. I RELIEVE HER GUILT OF THINKING SHE COULD DO BETTER THAN HIM BY SUGGESTING HE COULD DO BETTER THAN HER.

Kristin: (*Laughter*) Right.

Jon: Right? And, if that's the way it shows up, that's the way it shows up. But, sometimes, people go out for a drink to celebrate their divorce and go home together. You know why? I mean, that's weird, but I've met people who are happily living together, and the way they got into happily living together is they went out, said, "You know what? We've been through it, we're finally divorced. I'll tell you what, let me buy you a drink and at least we should smile at each other once." And she says, "You know, that's so crazy that I'll actually do it, Harry." And, after two drinks, she went home and to bed with him, and decided, "You know what? You really are cute." And you know what happened? The ocean was gone. Got it?

Kristin: Okay. Yeah.

Jon: There was no obligation to live with this guy after she divorced him, so the ocean was gone, and the flame came back. So, let's give it at least a little while, do you think?

Kristin: (*Laughter*) That's good.

Jon: Is there anything that comes up that you want to ask me about that we didn't get to? We've gotten to a lot of stuff.

Kristin: I have a lot of reoccurring nightmares. I don't know if this will help prevent them.

Jon: Let's take care of them. Tell me about one of them.

Kristin: One is me being violent with my mom, like us getting into an argument that escalates into violence. That started happening after an incident where she wouldn't stop talking to me. I asked her to give me some space, and she physically started touching me. I was getting really angry and I pushed her, and she accidentally fell over a baby gate, because I had a puppy in the room, and I felt horrible about that. She can hurt me with her words a lot. If we start to get in an argument, I just immediately walk away or change the subject. I'm almost scared to talk with her because of how much she can hurt me. In my dreams, she'll say something that hurts me. I yell at her and end up actually getting physical with her and hurting her.

Jon: I understand how the dream works. Our minds sometimes bring to our attention things that we are threatened by. You have been threatened by mom's words being hurtful and you have been even more threatened by hurting her. Fear and anger are emotional and physiological responses to perceive threat. Dream Mom poses no real threat. Let's think of a dream tiger. He isn't a real tiger, so he can't actually hurt anyone. If it were an actual tiger, you'd want to run from it. If it was a dream tiger, you could just lay down.

The only thing Dream Tiger can do is make somebody scared and run. But, if you stopped running, there isn't anything he could do if he caught you. With that principle, we can defeat dream things just by surrendering to them. So, first, let's just clear away the response you've had to the kinds of things Mom has said. So, tell me the kind of thing that Mom would say that you would have found really hurtful. Go for it, right to the biggest punch.

34

Kristin: The biggest one was while we were eating dinner one time. I was talking about how I was going to miss my sister because she wouldn't be there this summer for us to hang out. We had, since I was born, gone to camp and everything like that. Real casually, Mom said, "Kristin, you wouldn't have hung out with your sister. You guys got further away from each other since you went to college, and now she's dead."

Jon: Let's take that and blow it up and make it worse. So, let's put worse words than that. What would they be?

Kristin: "You didn't love Bethany."

Jon: "You didn't love Bethany. You only care about yourself." That's a big one. If Mom were to say that, where would that be coming from? Mom learned, as a kid, if you're good, things will be good. If things aren't good, it's because somebody was bad. That little-kid part of Mom's mind is coming up with those words. That's not any kind of an adult conversation. You get that? Adults wouldn't think that.

BY REFERRING TO IT AS THE LITTLE-KID PART, I REMOVE MOM'S CREDIBILITY SO THAT KRISTIN IS NOT HURT BY THESE WORDS. I ALSO REMOVE ANGER BY REMOVING THREAT.

Kristin: (*Laughter*) Right.

Jon: So, it's coming from that kind of distorted, wounded-kid thing. You know what a Rorschach test is? Ink blots?

Kristin: Yes.

Jon: So, the psychologist shows this guy an ink blot, and the guy looks at it and he says, "It's a flower garden." And, she shows it to the next guy, and he says, "That guy's torturing a zebra!" Now, did the psychologist learn anything about the ink blot?

Kristin: No.

Jon: No. She learned about the person she showed the ink blot to. So, when Mom is talking about stuff like this, is it about you?

Kristin: No.

Jon: No. You're an ink blot. So, what is it actually? Is it somebody torturing a zebra?

Kristin: (*Laughter*) No.

Jon: Is it a flower garden?

Kristin: No.

Jon:	It's ink dropped on the thing, folded in half, and unfolded. And all that other stuff is projection and has to do only with what is going on inside of the person who is seeing it, not the thing they're seeing. Now, just fully know that and get that. Today, your awareness has been moving in toward where **at your center you are light. There is wisdom and total clarity. At your center, you see things exactly as they are.** So, from your center, hear Mom saying that. I want you to close your eyes and see her face. Hear her say that, but **you are soft and clear and light.** Come from and be in touch with where **you have access to amazing wisdom and clarity.** You're seeing Mom who is hurt, distorted, childlike saying, "You didn't love her. It's all your fault." Good. Now, open your eyes. What happened?
Kristin:	I felt like she didn't know what she was talking about.
Jon:	And was there hurt within you?
Kristin:	No.
Jon:	Was there anger within you?
Kristin:	No.
Jon:	Good. Let's expand it. "You didn't defend Bethany and that's why she is dead. You didn't love her. That's why she's dead. You are a terrible person. You were a horrible sister." What about that one?

I PROVE THE WORK I DID WITH HER WAS EFFECTIVE BY SAYING THINGS IN AN EVEN WORSE WAY AND CHECKING HER RESPONSE. AS SHE REALIZES THERE IS NO NEGATIVE RESPONSE, SHE KNOWS THAT THINGS HAVE DRAMATICALLY CHANGED AND IMPROVED.

Kristin:	I didn't feel it.
Jon:	Okay. Because it doesn't make any sense, does it?
Kristin:	(*Laughter*) Right.
Jon:	There aren't any buttons to push on you, are there?
Kristin:	No.
Jon:	So, there's no anger coming up from it. I want you to be <u>Mom</u>. I'm going to be **you, clear and enlightened.** So, say the most awful thing you could say.
Kristin:	"You should have spent more time with your sister and loved her before she died."
Jon:	"Mom, I know how much you love her and love me and how much this has hurt you." Got it? You don't even have to say it, because you so totally got it. What you know

is, "You're in trouble. You're hurt. You're distorted." You don't have to say all that. You can just say, "I know, Mom." So, now you close your eyes and hear her angry. Just respond soft, "I know, Mom. I'm sorry. I love you."

Kristin: I know, Mom. I'm sorry. I love you.

Jon: Bingo. Got it?

Kristin: Yeah.

Jon: Perfect. You just took care of it. Got it?

Kristin: Yeah. I believe I do. I believe that I won't feel the same way, even in my dreams.

Jon: No, you won't, because…here we go in your dreams. Close your eyes. Mom is coming at you saying, "I wish it was you who was dead. You killed her. You're the one who made her a lesbian. It's your fault." You say, "I know, Mom. I love you."

Kristin: I know, Mom. I love you.

Jon: There we go. Bingo. Got it?

Kristin: (*Laughter*) Yes.

I HAVE GIVEN KRISTIN WAYS TO THINK AND WORDS TO SAY WHEN MOM IS CRITICAL, WORDS THAT COULDN'T BE SAID IF MOM WAS A THREAT. SAYING THEM INDICATES THAT MOM IS NOT A THREAT.

Jon: I was saying the worse stuff I could come up with. It wasn't doing a thing to you. Your shoulders stayed soft. You were just so open. So, perfect.

Kristin: It's amazing because I've had so much tension in my body for so many years…

Jon: Yes. What about Dad? Is there something Dad could say that would bother you?

Kristin: I've been afraid of him commenting on anything I do because of the way he'd scold Bethany in front of me and my younger brother, like finding out stuff about her being with girls.

Jon: I want you to picture Dad saying, "You are evil. You want to leave your husband because you have no integrity. You are a disgusting slut. All you think about is your own gratification, and you've put the nails into Jesus' hands."

Kristin: I just don't believe it. None of it can affect me now.

Jon: There you go. Isn't that nice?

Kristin: Yeah, because I did believe all those horrible things about myself.

Jon: "Your husband is suffering. Jesus is suffering. Your mother is suffering. All because of you." You don't have to defend. Just say "Okay, Dad. I understand,"

Kristin: Okay, Dad. I understand.

Jon: Bethany is totally loving you, and she's so excited about what you're doing today. She's right there loving you, feeling your love. She's right there, loving you, and she feels how much you love her.

THERE WAS GRIEF FROM THE EXPERIENCE OF THE "LOSS" OF BETHANY. RATHER THAN ASKING FOR KRISTIN TO ACCEPT AND COME TO GRIPS WITH HER "LOSS," I SUGGEST THAT THERE IS AN ONGOING CONNECTION. THERE IS NO LOSS AND, THEREFORE, NO GRIEF.

Kristin: (*Crying*)

Jon: And she is clear, and she's got it, and she is just jumping all over the place that you're getting it. She's, like, so good that there's light and wisdom and clarity. Can you feel her? I can see her right here with us. Can you feel her right there with you? Loving you?

Kristin: (*Crying*) Yes.

Jon: **Excited for you, hugging you. She is so sparkly, and she's so excited. And you are so beautiful and so smart, and she's fine.** She says, "There were a few scary moments there, but I'm doing fine, Kid."

Kristin: Thank you.

Jon: Yeah. You feel good with that, with her?

Kristin: I've always been wondering if she thought I should have done more, stood up for her more, that I was being the hypocrite. I just wonder about how she would think about my life.

Jon: So, let's think about it. How do you think she's thinking about you and your life?

Kristin: I think that she just loves me and has a better perspective than even I have now. I think she realizes what's important and what's not. And she realizes why people do things the way they do. Like you said, that she's in the light and in that clarity…

KRISTIN EXPERIENCES HER SISTER AS PRESENT RATHER THAN AS FINISHED AND IT CAUSES A CONNECTION. SHE NOW HAS A DIFFERENT WAY OF UNDERSTANDING HUMAN BEHAVIOR WHICH IS FREE OF MORALISTIC THOUGHT. THIS NEW WAY OF VIEWING HERSELF AND OTHERS ELIMINATES THE ANGER SHE HAD TOWARD HER PARENTS AND EVEN THE DRUNK DRIVER WHO

KILLED HER SISTER. SEEING HER SISTER WITH MORE CLARITY THAN SHE HAS HERSELF ASSURES HER THAT BETHANY HAS NO ANGER OR RESENTMENT TOWARD HER. ANY GUILT IS NOW GONE.

Kristin: …and she sees even probably why Mom and Dad did things.

Jon: Exactly. She's like a duck.

THE SUBCONSCIOUS IS RESPONSIVE TO ASSOCIATIONS. PAVLOV TAUGHT ME MORE THAN FREUD. I REFERENCED "DUCK" EARLIER AS BEING PRESENT AND CLEAR. NOW, I CAN BRING THE EXPERIENCE OF PRESENT AND CLEAR TO HOW SHE THINKS ABOUT BETHANY BY ASSOCIATING HER SISTER WITH A DUCK.

Kristin: (*Laughter*) A happy duck.

Jon: She's saying, "What thing do you think you're supposed to be doing or didn't do or should have done or shouldn't have done? What are you talking about?" Or, "What bread?" **She's right with you, and it's totally all about now and it's all about love.**

Kristin: This feels so good. It is so good. It's like I am waking up from an ugly dream. (*Deep sigh, then laughter*) I feel like I have her back.

Jon: You never lost her. She is with you. She always had you and you have always had her, but your awareness was blocked by distortion. Kind of like when the guy goes out and looks at the sky, and it's dark and cloudy, and he says to his girlfriend, "Oh, no sun." And his girlfriend says, "You know what, fella? It's still there." The sun doesn't go away at nighttime and it doesn't go away on a cloudy day. Our human senses are limited. They only bring in a portion of what is there and what they bring in is not accurate. It looks like the earth is flat and still, but we know that it is round and that it is always moving. Something looks solid and still, but everything is moving. Nothing is solid. All of it is energy. She's always going to be right here. You've always had her, but you weren't always sensing it. Now, you sense her.

Kristin: Yes, I do, and it feels so good.

Jon: So, I want to do another little process with you that's going to be vibrating energy up and getting the healing going even more rapidly and completely for you. So, here's what you do. Take this hand and put it like that. (*I extend her arm, so it is out in the handshake position.*) Good. Then, look here. I'm going to put my hand near yours without touching. (*I put my hand out like to shake hands, but my hand is about four inches from hers. With my other hand, I touch a spot on her hand.*) Look at that spot. You'll begin to feel my hand even without it touching. You can feel it there.

BY FOCUSING KRISTIN'S AWARENESS IN A PARTICULAR WAY, I CAN PRODUCE AN ALTERED STATE OF CONSCIOUSNESS. THIS DEEPENS AND ACCELERATES THE INTEGRATION OF THE EXPERIENCES SHE HAS HAD WITH ME AND THE PERSPECTIVE SHE HAS ACQUIRED.

Kristin: Yes. I feel it.

Jon: Yes, you feel the energy within and between our hands. Very slightly and with just tiny movements, begin to pat the energy and you can feel it still more. Each time you pat, you feel it, and then you feel it even more with each pat. Stronger, stronger, and stronger. You don't have to move your hand on purpose anymore, you just feel that energy. Your awareness is heightened. As I pull my hand back, you continue to feel it, *(I move my hand still further from hers.)* even this far away. Don't do anything consciously to move your hand. I'll move your hand from way over here. You start noticing little twitches, jumps, jerks, fits and starts, and then, as the fingers begin to ever-so-slowly separate, you'll notice that the vibrations become even clearer, and you'll feel and see your fingers vibrating. The pinky is already vibrating and moving in ways that nobody can purposely cause. *(Her hand is vibrating more and more.)* Look at your fingers starting to vibrate and moving in ways that nobody can consciously cause. *(People can consciously move the hand, but not consciously vibrate it.)* Each movement is the outward sign that your inner mind is responding.

Kristin: This is amazing!

Jon: And it's responding to pink butterfly. It's responding to our combined intention that **you are peaceful, powerful, excited and well.** Every movement means **your mind is organizing toward what is in your best interest.** As it continues, you'll notice that sometimes your eyes blink. You'll realize that your eyes close when they blink. And since every time they blink, they close, *(her eyes blink more and more rapidly and then just close),* and since your eyes close, your eyes rest, and since your eyes rest, you rest, and your eyes continue resting closed. Your hand continues moving even more definitely, even more dramatically as your awareness is drawn into the light of wisdom. *(Hand moves more and more.)* Next time, as you see your hand, you'll see it moving. You'll see it moving even much more. You'll see it moving in closer to your face, so when it touches your face, you will drop down like a rock being dropped into a lake. Open your eyes and look at that spot. *(Her eyes open and she focuses on the spot on her hand that I have indicated.)* Watch as your hand begins to move in closer to your face. *(Her hand is moving with twitches and jerks toward her face. It is clear to her that she is not consciously causing the movement because the movement is different than any movement she could consciously cause.)* And each time you see a tiny movement, silently say the word, "yes." Continue to say "yes" over and over as your mind integrates all that you have learned and felt.

There is so much that you know, and I know that you know even more, even so much more than you know that you know. Even now, as you know so much more and clear, so very **clear, light, butterfly, health, strength, flexibility**, as the light shines, you are guided to shine as the healing power that you become for others.

Mind is responding to the butterfly, to that you who's leaving here today that we aimed at, that **you are going to leave with all that stuff intact, clear, light.** As soon as it touches, *(her hand continues toward her face)* you just drop like that rock into the light that you are. Everything is loose and limp and it's liquid. Now, think about even three times, still deeper, as you feel the chair move *(I move her chair)* everything releases. And **the healing process becomes** even ten times, 110 times 1,000 and 10 times stronger. You remember the energy you felt between our hands. As I put my hand near your forehead, you feel it so much more. Now, it's pouring in like light pouring into the plant, absorbed in and down to the roots, **clearing, cleansing, freeing, light, energy.** Perfect. And then **feeling better than you have felt in such a long, long, long, long, long time.** There you are. Eyes open.

Kristin: Wow!

Jon: And that beautiful gal who we both imagined soon after we met who is **clear, present, sourced from within,** whose mind is showing her things that are beneficial, appealing and possible… She is **light, joyful, energized, healthy, excited** and **having fun.** She is learning to utilize her own power to heal and clear others.

Kristin: (*Laughter*) Yes.

Jon: Remember her? Who is that?

Kristin: It's me! (*Laughter*)

Jon: There we go! And you'll remember there was a picture, and it was dark and jagged. Tell me what it looks like now.

Kristin: I don't see it.

Jon: That's like a thermometer that was giving a reading on the internal environment within your mind regarding the issue you put on the table. It represented the problematic way mind was reading information that was causing the distortion that caused symptoms and issues and turmoil. When you look at a thermometer and there's a different reading, it means what? There's a change in the environment. So, **there's been a dramatic change in the environment within your mind.**

Kristin: Yeah. I don't see it anymore. It's not even there!

Jon: That's as big a difference as you can get in a reading. **The healing is just going and going,** so picture butterfly. Inhale (*breathing*). Exhale and melt. Do that over and over during the day, and **you'll just melt into your center, to that place of peace, wisdom, and power.**

Kristin: This is so good.

Jon: Perfect.

Kristin: I feel good now. I feel like the principles you taught me, I feel like I can apply them, like you said, into different situations daily or whatever I need. I've even heard that you have an institute or a learning program or something like that?

Jon: How would it be with you if the recording that you and I made was made available to people who are learning to do this with others?

Kristin: Oh, that's fine.

Jon: You are putting this out into the universe where it can be saving lives and helping people.

Kristin: Of course, yeah. I mean, I was having pseudo-seizures that were grand mal in nature many times each day, and was taken to the hospital, and they would give me three shots of Ativan and they couldn't stop the seizing. I mean, I didn't even know why it was happening, so they ran all the tests they could for months at the Mayo Clinic, so anyway…

Jon: So, I'll be really glad to hear how things progress for you.

Kristin: Right, I mean I was using a cane and wearing a helmet because I never knew if I was going to crack my head some time because of the seizures. Anyway, I even used to sometimes twitch and jerk even thinking about them, or if I remembered them, but now I don't.

Jon: **No anger, no shame, no guilt and no grief.**

Kristin: And I feel like there's not anything to be afraid of.

Jon: **You don't need to be afraid anymore**.

Kristin: No. Not any more….

Grief Almost Killed Me, But I Survived:
My Story of Hope and Healing

BY <u>KRISTIN RIVAS</u> · PUBLISHED MAY 15, 2016 · UPDATED FEBRUARY 28, 2017

When I was 18—a freshman in college visiting home one weekend—my dad woke me from sleep to break the news to me. My older sister, Bethany, had been in a car accident. The driver had been drinking. The four words my dad spoke to me that morning shattered me.

"Bethany didn't make it..."

That life-changing sentence as well as the impact of the crash and those words on my life, on my psyche, was immediate and ongoing. I didn't realize it then, but the idea that began to overtake my mind upon hearing of my sister's death was what happened to my sister was not okay. Nothing would ever make it okay and, therefore, I could never be okay.

The night after her funeral, my parents had to hold me down as I writhed and screamed, begging them to let me go sleep on her freshly covered grave, so she wouldn't be alone in the dark with the thunderstorm raging outside. I remember waking up the next day realizing it wasn't all a bad dream. This was the new reality I was going to have to face as life moved on without her.

I thought that, now, I had to take my place as the older sister. I had to be strong. I handled my grief mostly by keeping as busy as possible. I was in college, majoring in psychology and missions, a member of Army ROTC, and many clubs on campus, taking a full load of classes while also working part time as a nanny. Later that same year I got engaged to my first love while serving on a missions' trip to help orphans suffering from AIDS.

Outwardly, I seemed okay, but I was afraid to process my feelings; they were all so strong, yet so muddled. It seemed like they were a dark edged abyss in the back of my mind. I was afraid that if I let myself explore them, I could lose myself, like I might drown in a deep dark sea, boiling with anger and pain, that I wouldn't be able to escape.

I didn't tell anyone I was having trouble falling asleep, keeping disturbing thoughts at bay, only to then have nightmares of my sister dying in some new way, night after night, without me ever being able to save her.

My fiancé suddenly broke up with me in 2006, months before our wedding date. For three days, I literally did not eat or sleep. I cried as I poured over my sister's photo albums. The floodgates had opened up on my grief. I flipped back and forth between thoughts of my sister and my ex-fiancé. My hormonal 19-year-old brain now had a crazy person at the wheel.

I felt that my pain would always be there. It would always hurt this badly, or worse. The only way for me to end the pain was to end my life.

I grabbed a knife from the kitchen drawer, and a bottle of my dad's pain pills from the bathroom cabinet. As I felt myself beginning to fade, I remember thinking about what a horrible thing it would be for all my friends and family to have to go to my funeral less than a year after my sister's. I remember feeling scared that I couldn't take it back, but thinking, *"I just want to be free of the pain and be with Bethany, wherever she is."* When my eyes opened, I was in an ER trauma room with bandages on my wrists.

Fast-forward a few years. It's my senior year of college. I'm folding laundry when suddenly, everything looks blurry and I start having double vision. A mental fog comes over me. My tongue feels swollen and numb. I notice ringing in my ears. My ability to speak, see, and think disappears. I lose consciousness.

Later that night, I find myself in the emergency room. The doctors give me a series of tests, but my results are all normal. They chalk it up to stress and send me home with anti-anxiety meds and tell me to take it easy.

The same thing happens again the next day, and then two more times that week. My memory and ability to concentrate rapidly declines as mental fog, slurred speech, and fainting spells become a daily occurrence. Attacks of vertigo, panic, and seizures happen without warning. A complete a loss of muscle tone, tingling, and numbness invades my limbs so strongly that I experience sudden falls that leave me in a heap on the floor.

Repeated trips to different doctors, emergency rooms, and neurologists yield no explanations or help. I'm referred to the Mayo Clinic and wait for my case to be considered. My husband and I have no clue what to do in the meantime. We end up going to a Walgreens to buy a seizure helmet and four-pronged cane. I quickly realize there's no way I can pull this look off. Especially after my husband adds the final touch—an envelope with my emergency contact information pinned to my chest.

I take one look in the mirror and burst into tears. I say, "I can't take it. I'm dropping out of my classes."

I now spend my time "taking it easy" as per the doctors' advice. My symptoms become even worse. Long days of isolation, boredom, and worry take their toll. Seizures begin striking at any moment—day or night—violent fits that come while I'm wide awake or fast asleep. They are triggered by feelings of vertigo that happen when I see things zoom in or out, or even take a few steps backwards. They are resistant to, or become worse with, medication. Scans and tests say nothing's wrong. With up to 9 attacks per day, I start using a wheelchair to get around for my own safety.

By the summer of 2008, I'm finally taken on as a patient at the Mayo Clinic. Tedious diagnostic testing goes on month after month with no answers or successful treatment. My symptoms escalate while my spirit fades.

In May of 2009, the Mayo Clinic officially diagnoses me with Post Traumatic Stress Syndrome, Major Depressive Disorder, and Conversion Disorder; my primary symptoms are pseudo seizures. They believe I'm suffering from traumatic grief—my body converting stress into physical symptoms. Due to the frequency, length, and severity of my symptoms, and the fact that I've seen six different mental health professionals with no improvement, I'm given a 20% chance of recovery.

There's one alternative left. The Mayo Clinic recommends that therapy with a qualified, experienced professional has been shown to be particularly helpful for this kind of thing. My dad finds and calls Dr. Jon Connelly, the founder of Rapid Resolution Therapy. On June 20, 2009, I have one session lasting about two hours. It's the most life-changing conversation I've ever had.

As Dr. Connelly speaks to me, I feel peace occurring for the part of me that's had nightmares reliving my sister's death every night, trying to prevent it from happening. My anger, my shock, and the overwhelming pain of traumatic grief seem to wash away.

As I open my eyes, I feel lighter, and notice that I can see and think more clearly. I know I'm okay. As Dr. Connelly opens the door to the waiting room, I lock eyes with my dad and we both start crying. I run backwards around Dr. Connelly's office and I'm seizure free—to this day!

Life hasn't been perfect. I've had my moments, but I haven't had a seizure, anxiety attack, or depressive episode since that session. I went on to train with Dr. Connelly and other healers and was even invited to give a Ted Talk that has now reached more than 500,000 people.

If there is anything I've learned from my experience with traumatic grief it would be that it's important to find a way to healthily process emotions instead of trying to avoid them and that it's equally important to commit to finding an effective form of treatment. Rapid Resolution Therapy is fast, painless and complete. I can only wish the same for everyone else dealing with tragedy or challenge in their life.

Misty was 42 years old when we had this conversation. She was happily married and quite successful in her career. But, in spite of these things, she felt insecure and often worried about how other people felt about her. She had been in therapy for many years so could pinpoint what had contributed to her insecurity but had never been able to shake loose of it.

Jon: I hear that there has been something that has been troubling you. I want to understand.

Misty: So, it's been an issue that I've been feeling for many years. I am married to a man that I love, and he loves me. I have a successful business as a photographer, and I teach courses in photography. I am much more successful than I expected I would be. My life is good, and I appreciate what I have. But I have this issue of the need to be liked and I think I know where it comes from. I go out of my way when I feel someone doesn't like me. I over-compensate to make sure that they do like me. It affects me in a lot of ways where I have a lot of anxiety around it. Like, even when I teach some of my photography classes, if someone walks out in the middle of class, I feel like I've done something wrong and I can't stop beating myself up. I have this kind of burning issue that I can't clear. I just can't clear it. I have friends, but then I feel like when I leave the room and they talk about me. I just feel that all the time and it drives me crazy.

Jon: I get it. You said you think you know where it comes from.

Misty: Yeah. I think. I'm not sure. I don't know. It sounds silly to me sometimes, but I felt not good enough as a teenager growing up. I was the black sheep, the rebel. I was the youngest of three and my older brothers didn't want much to do with me. I suffered through that, but I was popular in elementary school. I was really popular until sixth grade and then it was like every kid started to hate me. Every single desk, something was written bad about me in my private school. I hated that. I started getting bullied and made fun of. I can't have anyone hate me ever again because that was the worst feeling in the world. I try to make sure everyone is happy with me all the time.

Jon: I get it. **Your mind works very well** but it is a complicated instrument. Advanced and complex instruments run into glitches and benefit from tune up and repair. Your mind understands that connection is more useful than isolation. Your mind has been causing these thoughts and feelings to get you to maintain connection with others. Does that sound wrong?

I AVOID ASKING SPECIFIC QUESTIONS. INSTEAD, I SIMPLY SAY, "I WANT TO UNDERSTAND." THIS ALLOWS HER TO DECIDE WHAT IS BENEFICIAL FOR ME TO KNOW. MANY PEOPLE BELIEVE THAT THEIR MINDS ARE THEIR OWN WORST ENEMY. I DEBUNK THIS BY TELLING HER THAT HER MIND IS WORKING WELL. SINCE SHE FINDS CONNECTION WORTHWHILE, HER MIND UNDERSTANDS THE VALUE OF IT AS WELL. BECAUSE OF THIS, HER MIND HAS BEEN CAUSING UNPLEASANT THOUGHTS AND FEELINGS FOR THE PURPOSE OF PROMOTING CONNECTION. RATHER THAN ASK HER IF SHE AGREES, I ASK HER IF IT SOUNDS WRONG BECAUSE, IF THERE IS DISAGREEMENT, THIS INVITES HER TO STATE IT. IF I, INSTEAD, SAID, "DON'T YOU AGREE?" THIS WOULD ENCOURAGE HER TO REPORT AGREEMENT EVEN IF IT WAS NOT FULLY THERE. THAT WOULD NEGATE CONNECTION AND CREDIBILITY AND MAKE HER LESS LIKELY TO BELIEVE THAT WHAT WE WILL BE DOING TOGETHER WILL HAVE VALUE.

Misty: No, that's right.

Jon: There <u>has been</u> fearfulness. I get that this <u>has been</u> painful and exhausting. Even though you objectively realize the **fear has not been serving you,** it hasn't gone away. Am I close?

I AGAIN GIVE HER ENCOURAGEMENT TO CORRECT ME BY ASKING, "AM I CLOSE?" RATHER THAN SAYING, "DON'T YOU AGREE?"

Misty: Yeah.

Jon: The way mind has been processing information is what has caused the issue. This is something that is going on outside of consciousness so there is no way you could have just decided to make it stop, no matter what the heck is going on. So, the way mind has been processing information has been causing this thing. Let's create a baseline so we can keep track of where we are starting, purposely cause the feeling for about four seconds. *(She does and there is a shift in facial expression.)* Good job. Next, create a design that will represent how your mind has been processing what has caused these feelings. Just make one up.

I EXPLAIN HOW HER MIND HAS BEEN PROCESSING INFORMATION HAS CAUSED THE ISSUE. THIS SEPARATES HOW SHE IDENTIFIES HERSELF FROM THE PROBLEM, ELIMINATING ANY SHAME ASSOCIATED WITH INABILITY TO CONTROL HER OWN THOUGHTS AND EMOTIONS. IT IS A LOGICAL AND EASILY UNDERSTOOD EXPLANATION OF WHAT HAS BEEN GOING ON.

Misty: It's dark with diamonds and zigzags.

Jon: Hold out your arm and resist when I push down. I will say different things and check your muscle response, and it will give me useful information. Some people don't like goats. *(I push her arm and her arm stays strong.)* People might decide they no longer like you. *(Her arm got weak.)* We have three baselines: the feeling, the muscle test and the design. Good job. Now I have a good sense of how to proceed. I see what's intended for you and I know what to do. I see you with **this thing out of your way and gone.** I don't need you to **see it too,** at this point, but I want you to **see that I see it.**

THE MUSCLE TEST IS ANOTHER BASELINE THAT CAN BE UTILIZED TO INDICATE ACCOMPLISHMENTS. BY SAYING, "I NOW HAVE A SENSE OF HOW TO PROCEED," MY CREDIBILITY IS INCREASED. IT ALSO DEMONSTRATES THAT WE ARE DOING SOMETHING,

TAKING AN ACTION, RATHER THAN JUST TALKING ABOUT IT, WHICH STRENGTHENS HER BELIEF THAT THIS PROCESS WILL BE USEFUL. I TELL HER SHE DOESN'T HAVE TO SEE IT, WHICH REMOVES ANY BURDEN FROM HER. AT THE SAME TIME THAT I'M TELLING HER SHE DOESN'T HAVE TO SEE IT, I'M TELLING HER TO SEE IT.

Misty: Ok.

Jon: Let me know if it would be all right.

Misty: Yeah.

Jon: What else should I know to really get it?

THIS QUESTION AGAIN PUTS HER IN THE POSITION OF POWER. WHAT SHE WILL CONVEY TO ME ARE THE VERY THINGS I NEED TO KNOW IN ORDER TO EFFECTIVELY ASSIST HER.

Misty: You've got it.

Jon: Perfect. So, I've got that, but do **you get what I'm telling you about**? Because you're telling me how it's been and I'm telling you about the intention. The intention isn't history. Do **you get what I'm saying** in terms of intention?

PEOPLE WHO HAVE BEEN STUCK ARE OFTEN THINKING THAT THE PAST AND THE FUTURE ARE THE SAME. THIS MAKES IT DIFFICULT TO MOVE FORWARD BECAUSE FORWARD IS NOT EVEN CONCEIVED OF.

Misty: Yes.

Jon: As I'm looking at what's intended, I'm seeing you where **the thing that has been troubling you has disappeared.**

TELLING HER MY INTENTION ELIMINATES ANY STRESS THAT SHE IS REQUIRED TO CONCEIVE OR BELIEVE IN HER OWN SUCCESS. I SEE IT, BUT SHE DOESN'T HAVE TO.

Misty: Ok.

Jon: If something is being held down under water because it is tangled up, untangling it eliminates what has been holding it down. Then **it just naturally floats.** With that untangled, **you just float up.** As we **untangle your mind** from this glitch that has affected information processing, your mood and **joyfulness just floats up.** As **mind clears, there is resolution** and **the shifts are powerful and automatic.**

Misty: Yes.

Jon: Tell me a about a recent time you noticed the fear?

Misty: A woman walked out in the middle of a class I was teaching. People pay quite a bit to take my course and she just stood up and walked out. This was about three weeks ago, and she never came back. I started to worry that I was not interesting as a teacher. I worried that she didn't like me. What If I'm not good enough? What if she hates me?'

Jon: If someone is training to be a Navy Seal and they think it's just too hard, they can ring a bell and then leave. The bell means that it was just too hard. She rang the bell.

Misty: Right. That is how I would like to feel. Instead, it just eats me up inside.

Jon: I'm hearing how it has been, but I also see what I am intending for you. I am seeing future you. A woman stands up as you are teaching. She shakes her head in disgust and says, "I am not going to waste any more of my time." You are thinking, "Whoa, I guess she just rang the bell."

Misty: Yeah, she's done. I can see that. It's about her.

Jon: **We have the same intention; our energy comes together**. I'll ask your mind to scan back to a particular experience so that as we look at it together, energy will be freed. **This energy will power the shift that untangles** the way information has been stuck so that **you are clear** toward the intention we have for you. Something will come to mind. You found it. How old were you?

Misty: In my early twenties.

Jon: Let's put it on a shelf for later. And another one?

Misty: Seventeen.

Jon: Good job. Now younger.

Misty: Twelve.

Jon: Ok. Good. And now something earlier than that. Don't try to find it. Let that just come.

Misty: Ok, I got it.

Jon: Yes, and how old were you?

Misty: Five.

Jon: There was a thing that you accomplished that there was a sense of real satisfaction when you accomplished it. What was that?

Misty: I was given an excellent evaluation on my photography class. It filled up and there was a waiting list. That happens regularly now, but I am remembering the first time. It was really neat.

Jon: Ok, remember that? (snap)

Misty: Yes.

Jon: And anything you did academically you felt good about? *(She nods and smiles.)* Sports, athletics, vacations, a special time... *(She smiles again.)* A moment where there was a special connection with someone. *(Big smile)* The five-year-old girl is on her way to some wonderful stuff. When you were five, you had that troubling experience.

Misty: It happened a lot. My older brothers acted like I was disgusting. I just wanted them to like me. Sometimes my mother tried to get them to take me with them when they went out, but they acted like they hated me.

Jon: So, here's what we do. Think of a photograph you were delighted that you took. *(She smiles and nods.)* Think of a moment that felt good when teaching. *(She smiles and nods again.)* A time you really enjoyed with your husband. *(She smiles a big smile.)* Look through those wonderful moments to see the little girl who we know is on her way to some wonderful stuff. She begins to realize that she's on her way to something really cool.

Misty: Yeah.

Jon: **She drives past it. She's on her way past it.** Look at her breathing, open up. **She is on her way to something really cool** and **it's absolutely going to happen, and it's guaranteed.** Make some sense?

Misty: Yes.

Jon: Now, how is she doing?

Misty: She's cool. She gets it. Yes. I feel more peaceful.

Jon: What are your brother's names?

Misty: Roger and Eddie.

Jon: They are both older, yes?

Misty: Three years and five years.

Jon: She is a five-year-old little girl and he's an eight-year-old boy and he's acting disgusted by his little sister.

Misty: Unwanted, like doesn't like me. He wants nothing to do with me.

Jon: Right, he's an eight-year-old boy who wants nothing to do with his five-year-old sister.

Misty: Right.

Jon: What does that mean about her?

Misty: He just doesn't like me.

Jon: Yeah, but what does that mean about her? Be here with me as a grown up and look out at the little girl. Her brothers don't want her around. What's wrong with her?

Misty: Nothing.

Jon: Good, because there's no information about her.

Misty: Right, right, right.

Jon: So, is there anything about this little girl that we can know from that?

Misty: No.

Jon: Ok. So, you get that.

Misty: Yes. It doesn't feel bad anymore.

WHEN SOMETHING IS TRAUMATIC, IT CONTINUES TO HAVE AN EFFECT EVEN THOUGH IT IS OVER. THIS IS BECAUSE THE INFORMATION PROCESSOR WITHIN THE MIND IS CONTINUING TO READ IT AS TAKING PLACE OR BECAUSE THE MEANING ASSOCIATED WITH IT HAS CONTINUED TO BE GETTING READ AS HAPPENING AND THAT SOMETHING NEEDS TO BE DONE ABOUT IT. THE MIND IS COMPLEX AND MULTI-FACETED. ONE COMPONENT CAN BE READING SOMETHING AS HAPPENING AND/OR MEANING SOMETHING EVEN WHEN ANOTHER PART OF THE MIND IS NOT READING IT THAT WAY. LOOKING BACK TO AN EARLIER EVENT FROM THE PRESENT PLACE OF CLARITY ADDRESSED THAT ISSUE. IT WASN'T ABOUT LETTING THE PAIN OUT, BUT, INSTEAD, ABOUT SHINING THE LIGHT ALL THE WAY THROUGH.

Jon: Yeah. Great job. So, then there was something that happened later. What happened when you were twelve?

Misty: Everyone turned on me.

Jon: They were mean to you?

Misty: Yes, but I feel like I caused it.

Jon: You were how old?

Misty: Twelve.

Jon: And what did this little twelve-year-old do?

I WANT HER TO EXPERIENCE BEING WITH ME NOW RATHER THAN HER AT TWELVE. BY ASKING, "WHAT DID THIS LITTLE TWELVE-YEAR-OLD DO?" RATHER THAN, "WHAT DID YOU DO?" FURTHER SEPARATES HER IDENTITY FROM THE EVENT.

Misty: I was a gossiper. I was kind of a bitch. I had a lot of friends, but I was a mean girl.

Jon: Is that right?

Misty: But I don't feel guilty. It's those other kids that I'm pissed at right now. They all ganged up on me. Everyone hated me. Every desk had something bad about me written on it.

Jon: Was it like carved into the desk?

Misty: Permanent marker and they couldn't get it off.

Jon: Do you think it could still be there? *(Said with alarm)*

BY ACTING ALARMED IN A SILLY WAY, I BRING HER BACK TO THE PRESENT AS SHE LAUGHS AT MY CONCERN THAT SOMETHING MIGHT STILL BE WRITTEN ON THE DESKS.

Misty: It could actually be. I'm not even kidding. *(Laughing)*

Jon: I mean they might not have replaced those.

Misty: I don't know. I think it's still there.

Jon: Let's go look together and see if we could find one of the actual desks.

I BRING HER INTO THE FANTASY OF IMAGINING TRAVELING TO HER SCHOOL, SEARCHING FOR THE DESKS. BECAUSE SHE IS EMOTIONALLY PRESENT WITH ME, WHAT HAS BEEN AWFUL HAS BECOME FUN.

Misty: I see it.

Jon: Would you like to buy it?

Misty: Yeah, I would actually. I would put it in my studio or maybe in the classroom.

Jon: Think back on what happened. Everyone was picking on you. How are you doing?

Misty: Good. I can think back on it and the hurt is gone. It's just something that happened.

HER MIND HAD BEEN READING THE INFORMATION ABOUT WHAT HAPPENED AT TWELVE EITHER AS SOMETHING THAT WAS STILL HAPPENING OR THAT SOMETHING LIKE IT WAS HAPPENING. PAINFUL FEELINGS WERE ASSOCIATED WITH THOSE EVENTS, SO THEY CONTINUED TO FUEL CONCERNS IN THE PRESENT. RECALLING THE MEMORY WHILE FEELING LIGHT AND AT EASE CAUSES HER TO EXPERIENCE THE PRESENT WITH MUCH MORE CLARITY.

Jon: Beautiful. And then something else happened. You were seventeen.

Misty: It was a rape.

Jon: Which moment shows up?

Misty: In the bedroom.

Jon: Before, during, after?

IT IS USUALLY MORE EFFECTIVE TO FOCUS ON SPECIFIC MOMENTS OF A DISTURBING EVENT. THE MIND CAN THEN GENERALIZE FROM THE SPECIFICS.

Misty: Before, there's a moment before, and there's a moment in the bedroom.

Jon: Ok, tell me about the moment before.

Misty: He had me sit on his lap and kept giving me drinks.

Jon: Good job. So, think back to that then and what are you thinking about her?

Misty: I used to feel guilty about that. I was sitting on his lap and I was drinking because he wanted me to. I was trying to be liked. Now it seems different. I was taken advantage of. He was a lot older. He was disgusting.

BECAUSE THE EVENTS AT SEVENTEEN ARE NO LONGER HAVING THE SAME EFFECT, SHE IS NO LONGER BLAMING HERSELF.

Jon: Then what happened, then, later?

Misty: I kept trying to put my underwear back on and he kept taking it back off, then he raped me. And it's clear that I had too much to drink and I didn't know what was going on.

Jon: You're angry with him.

Misty: Yes. He is a pig.

Jon: How old was he there?

Misty: Thirty-six.

FREQUENTLY INTERJECTING "THEN" AND "THERE" CREATES EVEN MORE DISTANCE FROM THE EVENT.

Jon: Would he pose a threat to you now? Could he take advantage of you?

Misty: No, no.

Jon: He poses absolutely no threat.

Misty: He poses absolutely no threat.

Jon: Are you angry?

Misty: I was. I guess not. *(She pauses and checks her feelings.)* No, I am not angry. Embarrassment, maybe? Shame.

ANGER IS A RESPONSE TO PERCEIVED THREAT. AS THE THREAT DISAPPEARED, SO DID THE ANGER.

Jon: You did great disappearing the threat and the anger. Let's look at the shame. Are you ashamed now of having been raped when you were just seventeen?

SHE GETS THE CREDIT FOR ALL CHANGES THAT HAPPEN.

Misty: Yeah, Maybe I led him on?

Jon: You were flirty?

Misty: Maybe.

Jon: So, if a girl's flirting she ought to get raped? *(Incredulous)*

Misty: I wanted him to like me.

Jon: She's seventeen-years-old and she wants to be liked. Is that a bad thing in your book?

Misty: *(Sigh)* No. It's normal.

THE NEGATIVE JUDGMENTS TOWARD HERSELF ARE DISAPPEARING.

Jon: And there's this older guy and she'd like to be liked by him. She's seventeen. He raped her. So, as we look at this girl who is seventeen years old and would like to be liked, is there anything to make us blame her for what happened?

Misty: No.

Jon: On any level?

Misty: No.

Jon: Ok. So, how are you with that?

Misty: Good.

Jon: Is it ok that she wanted to be liked?

Misty: Yeah, it's ok she wanted to be liked.

Jon: Yeah. And so, are you ashamed?

Misty: No. Not anymore. I just wish that wasn't the case that she wanted to be liked.

I THINK MOST PEOPLE WOULD STOP HERE. SHE DOESN'T SEEM UPSET, JUST WISHES THINGS HAD BEEN DIFFERENT. NO OTHER LIFE FORM WISHES THINGS WERE DIFFERENT BECAUSE IT ISN'T A GOOD USE OF ENERGY—NOT FOR ZEBRA AND NOT FOR MISTY.

Jon: Why would you rather not have wanted to be liked when you were seventeen?

Misty: Because I think I put too much emphasis on that.

Jon: Why wouldn't a seventeen-year-old girl want to be liked? That's completely normal. It was even more for her because of what happened with her brothers or that stuff with the kids writing on the desk. You really want her to be okay.

Misty: Yes, yes.

Jon: And I am looking for you to be all the way clear. No other life form ever wishes things had been different. The eagle is present. You are becoming clear and present. So, do you hate him?

Misty: Do I hate him? No. I don't care.

Jon: Very good. We got it. Got it. Got it. Good.

Misty: Yes, I'm okay. That's how things went and that's how I felt.

Jon: So, let's check the design you saw earlier. Remember? It had some zigzags and some diamonds. What are you seeing?

Misty: It's lighter. There's white in there now.

Jon: You are already moving things.

SHE GETS ALL THE CREDIT FOR THE CHANGES THAT ARE TAKING PLACE.

Misty: Yeah.

Jon: So, then later what happened?

Misty: I meet this guy when I was twenty-three.

Jon: Put your hand on top of mine, look there at that spot. Then, as slowly as you can, lift your hand and, if you're really strong, you can do it real slow. Do it grass-growing slow. That's right. And start to feel the energy from my hand against yours and then look at your hand. *(I move my hand over and imagine hooking my finger into the energy from her hand. I slowly move my hand and her hand follows it.)* Watch what happens when we hook the energy. There it goes. There it goes. Yes. Notice what's starting to happen with the fingers. *(Her fingers begin jumping and twitching on their own.)* Yes, yes, good. I'm going to tap your hand. Notice that it begins moving in towards you. There it goes, there it goes, in toward you. Close your eyes and wonder, as it's being drawn in closer and closer, wonder how it's going to keep moving. Guess. Well, you're already guessing and maybe it'll do just what you guess it's going to do, or maybe what you guess, it won't do. Or maybe that whole process stops, and you just fall and fall. *(Her body becomes limp and she falls forward.)* There it goes. That's it, that's it. Yes. Yes. So, look at that. See, what's going on is the rest of your mind becoming so very responsive and going with stuff.

THIS ALTERED STATE OF CONSCIOUSNESS CREATES PEACEFULNESS, SO HER MIND IS MORE RESPONSIVE AND CLEARS WITH MORE EASE. SHE EXPERIENCES THAT WHAT I SAY WILL HAPPEN DOES HAPPEN. THIS IMPLIES THAT WHAT WE ARE INTENDING WILL BE HAPPENING AS WELL.

Jon: And now back real slow. How was that?

Misty: Wonderful. I really feel good.

Jon: Look at the design. What's it look like now?

Misty: It's much lighter.

Jon: Good for you. You are learning quickly and well. You mentioned meeting a guy in your early twenties.

Misty: I feel really bad about this.

Jon: Tell me.

Misty: It's not as intense as it was. I can feel a difference even though I haven't even spoken to you about it yet.

Jon: Your mind is so smart it gets ahead of us. Let's clean it all the way.

Misty:	Yeah. I met a man when I was 23. It was great at first but, looking back, I can see the signs were obvious. I was just too head over heels to realize it. He had a temper and it showed up early in our relationship. I always made excuses for it. I wanted him to love me. We got married. He was abusive, and he cheated on me. I feel I let my family down.
Jon:	Really?
Misty:	No. So, looking back on it and seeing who I am today and seeing everything in my life, right now, I can look back at that younger me and say, "Look, yeah you're going to go through some shit to get here."
Jon:	Right.
Misty:	I know that. So, I get that. But, still, I feel that I've let people down. I want to make sure that I make the right decisions all the time from now on, make sure I'm a good person.
Jon:	You were letting somebody down?
Misty:	I was letting myself down.
Jon:	You let your parents down?
Misty:	Yeah, maybe my whole family. I got a feeling like I fucked up. I made a bad choice for myself.
Jon:	I'm wondering how you were letting them down.
Misty:	I mean, they paid for a huge wedding. That's a big deal. I just feel like I'm the only one in my family who's gone through a divorce and it's on me.
Jon:	It was a big deal for whom?
Misty:	Me. My mom so not me.
Jon:	Right. So, she got herself a big wedding.
Misty:	Yes. Yeah, you're right.
Jon:	How'd Mom do the second time?
Misty:	I told her to back the fuck off. This is my wedding.
Jon:	Did you let your mother down?
Misty:	She was disappointed and so was I, but I am not ashamed any longer. This is so neat.

Jon:	You spent time with someone you cared about. That's what you are supposed to do. **You didn't let anyone down.**
Misty:	No, no I didn't. You're right.
Jon:	So, you had an experience that wasn't as cool on the way to something better. It seems to me that it highlights the advantages of the one that you got.
Misty:	Yes.
Jon:	Doesn't it?
Misty:	Yes.
Jon:	I mean, I know you like him, but I think you like him even a little better than you would have if there wasn't the first one.
Misty:	Yes.
Jon:	So, that guy, your involvement with him enabled you to **feel more connection and love and excitement and appreciation for the person you are with now.**
Misty:	Yes.
Jon:	You've managed things financially in a way that puts you in better shape than most people your age. You get paid for doing something that you love to do.
Misty:	Yes.
Jon:	People are competitive, and they sometimes don't like people who are successful. And if you become even more successful, you'll have more people not like you.
Misty:	Right.
Jon:	As you become more successful, you will have more people not liking you. Does it make sense? Because, you know, the more you show up, the more you're going to show up in a way that somebody will say, "Who does she think she is? She doesn't even know what it's like to have to deal with the crap I have to deal with. She's successful and never had to do a thing in her life other than be catered to, the bitch." Some are going to think that. And so that person won't like you because they're like jealous or resentful or stuff like that. What about that? How are you going to deal with that?
Misty:	I'm not. I'm just going to turn to the people that I like and who like me.

Jon: Who doesn't like you isn't very interesting because, if you're in the game, if there's anything you care about that you move toward, then there's going to be people that just don't like you because you are making too big a splash in their pond.

Misty: Yeah.

Jon: Think of a fish tank. There is one part of the tank that interests us. Sometimes a fish swims into that part of the tank. Sometimes it even hangs out for a while. Sometimes there may be a few fish in that special place. Those are the fish that matter, and they only matter when they are there. These are the people that care about you and enjoy you and you also care about them. The only ones that matter are the fish in that section and they only matter while they are in it. That's the deal. That's how it is.

Misty: Yeah.

Jon: It doesn't matter how many are out of it.

Misty: Yeah.

Jon: If you're looking at that fish tank and someone says, "Wipe that smile off your face, gal. I'm going to tell you something really awful. There's an ocean. None of those fish are in this thing." It doesn't matter. People only matter when and if they are there.

Misty: Yes. I get it. I feel so much better.

Jon: So, check the design, what do you notice?

Misty: Less, less.

Jon: Check within you and let me know anything that is concerning.

Misty: Yeah, I guess it's the uncertainty that the friends I have are real friends.

Jon: So, sense that, but then, back in deeper, further back, under it. That's it. All the way under it. There it is. And there, what do you start to sense around you?

I GET HER TO FOLLOW THE FEELING BACK TO AN EARLIER TIME.

Misty: Grass.

Jon: Yes, yes. That's it. Be there. There you are, there's grass around. Yes? And how old do you feel, right there, in the grass?

Misty: Three. Very little.

Jon: What do you sense around you?

Misty: I am just alone.

Jon: What happens next?

Misty: I am not sure.

Jon: Just stay with it. What happens.

Misty: My brothers left. I was by myself. Mom's coming. I'm okay.

Jon: Yes, there were times you felt all alone. Things are always moving. What's going on here?

Misty: I am okay. I am really okay now.

Jon: And what's the sense? What's the feeling?

Misty: Peace

Jon: Check the design. What do you notice?

Misty: It's gone.

Jon: Yeah, and so check for the feeling? Here, let me help. People won't like you. Some people already don't like you. Go ahead and try to feel bad.

Misty: (*Laughing*) I can't…can't get it. It's not there.

Jon: I enjoyed talking with you.

Misty: Thank you. It was wonderful.

Follow-Up Commentary

I checked in with Misty six months later. She told me the insecurity she had lived with was no longer on her mind like it had been. There had been a conflict with her oldest brother's wife about planning for a holiday and she said that she found it aggravating, but it didn't preoccupy her like it would have. "I am sure she doesn't like me," she told me. But she then said, "I guess I don't like her either," and giggled.

Devon

One day, I picked up the phone and it was a friend and colleague who had an office nearby. He told me that he was meeting with a physician who, after a stroke, seemed to have lost his ability to recall important medical information. The career he had put so much energy toward was in jeopardy. My friend asked me to join them to see if I could get the doctor's memory to improve. I was close and got to my friend's office a few minutes later.

Jon: What should I know?

Devon: I have fourteen months left of my residency program and I'm done if I can complete it.

Jon: That's a wonderful accomplishment.

Devon: I guess it is, but now it seems like I won't make it. One thing that has been frustrating is that I was not being diagnosed as Attention-Deficit Disorder until recently.

Jon: Oh?

Devon: I've learned to adapt, I guess, because people with Attention-Deficit Disorder learn to adapt. Most people would study 2 hours and I would study 9 hours.

Jon: You really **stick to it.**

Devon: After I was diagnosed, I attended a course for physicians and medical students with Attention-Deficit Disorder and auditory processing problems. I'm clicking along and doing great through the course and then I had a massive cerebral bleed. It happened about a month before I had to take an important test. I got a horrible headache. I kept thinking, "I've never had a migraine. What is this?" My words were getting slurred and I wondered what's going on with me. After two days, I stopped going to class because I couldn't tolerate it any longer. I looked at my wife and asked if our life insurance was paid up. I said, "I'm going to die this weekend." She looked at me like I was crazy, but I was as serious as a heart attack. The headache got worse and I slept for about sixteen hours. It started on a Thursday. At 2 o'clock on Sunday morning, I just couldn't handle anymore. I've never had anything hurt so bad. I know it seems like a long time to wait, and it probably sounds funny, but I always hated going to doctors. My wife called a neighbor to watch the children and took me to the emergency room. They called in a neurologist. My head was x-rayed. The neurologist walked in with this large x-ray and set it up on a viewer. He sounded angry when he spoke to me. "Look here," he said, "Your brain is bleeding and there is nothing we can do to stop it. There are only two things that can happen. You will become paralyzed or die. This will happen within the next 24 hours." "I don't believe you are right," I told him. "I hope I am wrong," he said.

Jon: Obviously he was wrong.

Devon: Yes. With God's help, I recovered, but something happened to my ability to recall information. I've lost so much information. I haven't been able to access things that I've stuffed in my head all through medical school and residency, things I should know.

Jon: My intention for our meeting is that **you automatically access valuable information.**

I STATE THE INTENTION RIGHT AWAY. AS HE WAS DESCRIBING THE PROBLEM, I WAS LISTENING TO WHAT HE WAS SAYING, BUT I WAS ALSO SEEING HIS MIND WORKING IN A BETTER WAY. I BELIEVE THAT THE INTENTION I SET IN MY MIND IS THE MOST SIGNIFICANT PART OF WHAT I DO IN A MEETING. IT GUIDES EVERYTHING I SAY AND DO. I DON'T ALWAYS THINK IT IS OF VALUE TO SHARE THE INTENTION WITH THE PARTICIPANT AND CERTAINLY NOT THIS EARLY, BUT IT CAME TO ME TO SAY IT WITH DEVON.

Devon: Yes, that would be great.

Jon: **Useful information comes to your awareness** already and our intention is **this will increase.**

Devon: True.

Jon: You've been trying hard and it's been frustrating. You have been recalling and describing things to me since we began speaking. You couldn't have told me what you did if you couldn't recall information. You're looking for your mind to do more of this, particularly concerning medical information.

I ACKNOWLEDGE HIS FRUSTRATION YET TELL HIM HIS MIND IS ALREADY DOING WHAT HE HAS BEEN WANTING IT TO DO AND THAT I INTEND FOR THIS TO INCREASE. THIS IS AN EASIER PROJECT THAN TRYING TO GET HIS MIND TO DO SOMETHING IT HASN'T EVER DONE.

BECAUSE THIS PROBLEM BEGAN RIGHT AFTER THE MEDICAL ISSUE WITH HIS BRAIN, HE HAS BEEN CONNECTING THE TWO AND HAS BEEN EXPERIENCING THE ISSUE AS PHYSICAL. THIS HASN'T STOPPED HIM FROM LOOKING FOR A BETTER SOLUTION OUTSIDE OF MEDICINE, HOWEVER.

Devon: Oh, monumental!

Jon: Do you know how biofeedback works?

Devon: Some.

Jon: The biofeedback instrumentation doesn't do anything to a person's body. It gets him to notice things that are already going on so that they increase. Some biofeedback instrumentation reads things that go on in the body, but other instrumentation reads brainwaves. The machine causes people to notice what is already going on and that causes what is noticed to increase. There's an instrument utilized to increase the warmth in a part of his body and, as he is aware of the heat, it increases. As he becomes aware that it is increasing, it increases even more.

BIOFEEDBACK HAS SCIENTIFIC VALIDITY AND DEMONSTRATES MEASURABLE CHANGE. IT, THEREFORE, WILL VALIDATE MY POINT THAT NOTICING SOMETHING IS LIKELY TO INCREASE IT. I THOUGHT THE REFERENCE TO SOMETHING SCIENTIFIC AND MEASURABLE WOULD BEST DESCRIBE THE THEORY I AM SHARING AND MAKE IT CREDIBLE.

Devon: Yes.

Jon: The way to increase something is to notice it. It is even more powerful if you notice it appreciatively. Are you with me?

Devon: Yes.

BY POINTING OUT TO DEVON THAT THERE WERE THINGS WE CAN RECOGNIZE AND CHANGE THAT HAVE BEEN BLOCKING HIS RECALL, IT OPENS HIS MIND TO THE POSSIBILITY THAT, NOW THAT WE KNOW WHAT HAS BEEN WRONG, WE CAN FIX IT.

Jon: Two things have blocked your progress. Your subconscious left out negation. When you would think the words, "I don't want to have trouble with this," your mind heard the words, "have trouble with this."

Devon: And, therefore, it increased.

Jon: You were paying attention to the frustration of not remembering, therefore increasing it.

Devon: I understand. I was working against myself.

Jon: Well, no, it was just automatic. Because of the problem you had, you became afraid that your brain wasn't doing what you wanted. This interfered with your ability to recall.

Devon: This really makes sense. Because I couldn't recall the information I wanted, I feared my brain was no longer able to work the way I need it to in order to practice medicine.

Jon: Here's my intention. I see you in a medical situation recalling information, doing well on tests and providing excellent patient care. Let's both intend this, and it will guide what we do.

Devon: Yes. I've got it.

Jon:	As our intentions align, **our energy comes together,** and **your mind responds to this energy and moves toward what we intend.**
Devon:	That makes a lot of sense. I never thought of it this way. I always thought of it as, "Oh, I can't remember this. Why can't I remember this?" and the frustration would mount.
Jon:	If a hypnotist can convince someone that he can't open his eyes, he'll be unable to open them. If the thought of not being able to can interfere with something so simple, think of how it could interfere with something more complex.
Devon:	Tremendously.
Jon:	So, when you were telling me about what had happened, you said that you can't recall. "Can't" is future tense. The language of the thought took the problem from the past and pushed it into your future.
Devon:	Because it is future tense. That makes sense, but I never realized that.
Jon:	Yes, exactly. You are getting it. From now on, if you don't recall something, you will just think, "I'm not getting that at the moment."
Devon:	Instead of saying, "I can't get that."
Jon:	Exactly.
Devon:	The "I can't" thought was blocking information that now will come.
Jon:	Yes.
Devon:	And then, after the medical problem with my brain, my thoughts became even much more negative.
Jon:	It had to happen that way. Now, it is and will be different.
Devon:	Well, I basically have been crucifying myself.

DEVON HAS BEEN THREATENED BY HIS OWN THOUGHT PROCESSES. FOR ANIMALS, IF SOMETHING IS THREATENING, IT'S VERY IMPORTANT FOR THE ANIMAL TO NOTICE IT, BE ALERT TO IT AND REACT TO IT. UNLIKE HUMANS, HOWEVER, ANIMALS AREN'T THREATENED BY THEIR OWN THOUGHTS. WHEN A HUMAN BECOMES THREATENED BY WHAT HIS MIND IS DOING, HIS MIND NOTICES AND RESPONDS TO HIS OWN THOUGHT PROCESSES THE SAME WAY ANIMALS RESPOND TO A THREAT. IN HUMANS, WHAT INCREASES IS LOOKING FOR AND FINDING THE THREAT. THIS IS WHAT HAS BEEN HAPPENING FOR DEVON WITH HIS LACK OF RECALL.

Jon:	**Your subconscious is eager to provide what is beneficial.** Give me an example about a patient's history that would be useful to know.

Devon: Childhood measles. You have to be sure to check for certain crucial things in order to do a differential diagnosis.

Jon: Now, that's remarkable that came up to conscious awareness instantly.

I APPRECIATE HIS RECALL, WHICH INCREASES IT. I'M MODELING BEING APPRECIATIVE AND EXCITED BY WHAT HIS MIND IS DOING.

Devon: True.

Jon: You haven't been appreciating your mind even when it responded exactly as you wanted.

Devon: I took it for granted.

Jon: It wouldn't even get thanked for it.

Devon: No.

Jon: When your mind did what you wanted, you ignored it.

Devon: You're right!

Jon: And when it didn't, you kicked it.

Devon: You're right!

Jon: It's a good idea to say, "Thanks" when what you ask for is delivered.

I AM CHIDING DEVON FOR HIS PAST MENTAL BEHAVIOR, BUT IT IS ALL DONE WITH A SMILE.

Devon: Absolutely.

Jon: There has been no, "Thank you."

Devon: It's just been expected.

Jon: There has only been criticism.

Devon: You're exactly right!

Jon: If that were how you dealt with people in your life, you would notice a dramatic difference in the way you were served by them. You go into the same restaurant for lunch every day, never tip because it's the waiter's job to bring you the food. You never say, "Thank you," but yell at him every time it's not quick enough. What happens to the service? Go to the same place and be appreciative and the food is delivered faster and better. What should a doctor be aware of when treating someone for an injury?

Devon: Okay, hydraulic injuries are very bad. You have to keep that in the back of your mind all the time when treating certain conditions.

Jon: Wow, that's important.

Devon: Yes.

DEVON AND I ARE BOTH RESPONDING WITH APPRECIATION AS HIS MIND RECALLS INFORMATION. THIS IS PIVOTAL TO IMPROVING HOW HIS MIND PROCESSES INFORMATION.

Jon: And it came to your mind.

Devon: Yes, it did.

Jon: So, there's the information and there's appreciation. It's just that quick.

Devon: Yes.

Jon: Yeah, good. If you had an assistant handing you just what you need for the situation, like an operating room nurse, you need the knife, it's in your hand, you start to sweat, and your brow gets wiped. The difference is you're going to be saying, "Thanks! Great! I like that." You **appreciate recollection much more than you ever did.**

Devon: Okay.

Jon: If you don't recall something, the words, "at the moment" are going to be added.

Devon: Okay.

Jon: If I say, "I'm not getting it at the moment..."

Devon: It means that in the future I will get it.

Jon: Later might be two seconds later.

Devon: Yes.

Jon: Might be less.

Devon: Every time I said, "I can't do this," it blocked progress.

BY **IDENTIFYING SOMETHING AND TELLING** D**EVON** **THIS IS WHAT HAS BEEN BLOCKING HIS PROGRESS, HIS MIND UNDERSTANDS DESIRED CHANGE IS NOW POSSIBLE.** W**E HAVE IDENTIFIED WHAT HAS BEEN IN THE WAY AND WE ARE TAKING CARE OF IT.**

Jon: The words "at the moment" will be there whenever something isn't recalled. Devon, there is a room you haven't been in for a long time. Which room was it?

HAVING D**EVON RECALL A ROOM HE HASN'T BEEN IN FOR A LONG TIME WILL LEAD TO AN ALTERED STATE OF CONSCIOUSNESS AS HE WILL "BE THERE" IN ORDER TO RECALL IT.** T**HERE IS NO PRESSURE BECAUSE IT IS NOT ABOUT MEDICAL INFORMATION.** W**E WILL APPRECIATE WHAT HE DOES RECALL WHICH WILL, AGAIN, CAUSE HIM TO RECOGNIZE, APPRECIATE AND INCREASE HIS MIND'S ABILITY TO RECALL.**

Devon: The bedroom I shared with my brother when we were growing up.

Jon: How long since you were in that room?

Devon: About twenty-five years.

Jon: Close your eyes and you will recall details about the room. *(Devon's eyes close for little while. He appears quite pleased as he opens his eyes to tell me about his experience.)*

Devon: It was really funny and amazing how much I did recall. Our room was in the basement. You have to walk around the staircase to be able to get through the door. Over on the left-hand side, as soon as you enter, was a bookcase with two doors on it with gold handles that my father had made for my brother and me. My brother was on one side with a lock for his little door that he kept his snails in and his rocks and whatever else he had. Two double beds with a nightstand in the middle and my Dad's famous bell on the wall. He would wake you up by pushing this button beside his bed. He's an electrical engineer. So, he wired the house so when his alarm went off, he pushed our alarm and it was a fire bell.

Jon: Oh, gosh!

Devon: It would sound really loud. It could wake the dead. There was a little window and, because of how old the house was, the plumbing went through the roof, so you could hang your clothes up on the plumbing.

Jon: Yes.

Devon: The gas lines ran through the center of that room.

Jon: Yes.

Devon: Well, first, it was a tiled floor. Then, Dad put down a rug and he painted it this green I will never forget. He painted one wall green and paneled the other two walls. It was the most awful looking green. I'm just shocked that I am recalling all this.

Jon: Wonderful recall. Your brain works so well.

BEING SURPRISED AT HOW MUCH HE IS RECALLING CAUSES APPRECIATION AND ALSO CLEARS THE FEAR THAT THERE IS SOMETHING WRONG WITH HIS BRAIN.

Devon: Yes.

Jon: There was a time when you were outdoors in a setting that was very moving to you. It had some kind of magic.

ASKING FOR A SETTING THAT WAS VERY MOVING AND HAD SOME KIND OF MAGIC WILL AGAIN CAUSE AN ALTERED STATE OF CONSCIOUSNESS. HE WILL FEEL VERY GOOD AND HIS MIND WILL BECOME STILL MORE RESPONSIVE. AS IT RESPONDS TO THESE THINGS, IT IS RESPONDING TO WHAT WE ARE INTENDING FOR HIM WHICH IS THE EASY RECALL OF NECESSARY MEDICAL INFORMATION WHILE TREATING PATIENTS.

Devon: I was in Guatemala.

Jon: Tell me.

Devon: The mountains in Guatemala.

Jon: How long ago?

Devon: It was 15 years.

Jon: Go ahead.

Devon: It was very early in the morning, maybe 4:30 am. I got up and I just started to take a walk. By the time I got dressed and got out, it was just starting to get light. We were in the rain forest and the mist was blowing off the leaves of the trees and the air was very cool. It was damp, but not muggy damp. It was refreshingly damp. Nice cool breeze. As you looked down through the valley, the way the sun was hitting through the trees, it was like all those little specks of moisture on all those leaves were little crystals and it was like it exploded as soon as the light hit it.

Jon: Wow!

Devon: It was just absolutely breathtaking.

Jon: Isn't that something?

Devon: Yes, it is. I haven't thought about that for such a long time and I remember it in great detail.

Jon: **You have an extraordinary ability to recall.** Close your eyes. The only purpose this has is that it will give you the opportunity to hear me speak while your eyes are closed. Don't bother to try and do anything else. In fact, don't even bother trying to relax.

BY TELLING DEVON TO NOT TRY TO DO ANYTHING AND NOT TO EVEN BOTHER TO TRY RELAXING, IT IS MORE LIKELY THAT HE WILL RELAX. I STATE THE ONLY PURPOSE IS FOR HIM TO HEAR ME SPEAKING WITH HIS EYES CLOSED. IN SO DOING, THE POSSIBILITY OF FAILURE IS ELIMINATED.

Devon: Okay.

Jon: You're hearing not just the sound of my voice, but also many other sounds. You're hearing those sounds so clearly.

THE SOUNDS BECOME CLEARER AS I POINT OUT THAT HE IS HEARING THEM. HE IS EXPERIENCING WHAT I TELL HIM AND MY CREDIBILITY INCREASES.

Jon: Sensations in your shoulders...and in your hands. Finally, once again, you can open your eyes. What did you notice?

Devon: I think I heard a bird outside.

Jon: What else?

Devon: When you spoke of shoulders, I noticed my shoulders.

Jon: Yes.

Devon: When you spoke of hands, I noticed my hands.

Jon: Yes.

Devon: It felt like I really noticed my shoulders and I really noticed my hand. I don't know how to explain it.

HE NOT ONLY NOTICES HIS SHOULDERS, BUT HE "REALLY" NOTICES THEM. HE EXPERIENCES THAT WHAT I AM SAYING IS NOT ONLY "TRUE" BUT THAT IT IS OCCURRING BECAUSE I AM SAYING IT. THIS TIES IN WITH WHAT I HAVE BEEN AND WILL SAY ABOUT HIS ABILITY TO RECALL INFORMATION, CAUSING IT TO INCREASE.

Jon: That's what I was looking for. Close your eyes.

WHEN I SAY, "THAT'S WHAT I WAS LOOKING FOR," HE REALIZES THAT WHAT WE ARE DOING IS ON TRACK AND WORKING.

Jon: Rest your eyes. *(Pause)* You are aware of your left hand. Once again, your eyes can open.

Devon: It was like my left hand was bigger than my right hand.

AGAIN, HE HAS THE EXPERIENCE THAT WHAT I AM SAYING IS CAUSING THINGS TO HAPPEN.

Jon:	Excellent.

Devon:	It was amazing.

Jon: Okay. Look up...deep breath...exhale and your eyes close. That's it. **Your mind is wonderfully responsive**. Everything is happening perfectly. Nothing is required. Although you might find that **it's pleasant to relax or unwind,** it is not important. **Your mind is on your side and eager to respond.** I'll be silent for just a few moments…You can take your time until, once again, your eyes can open.

Devon: Wow!

Jon: What was your experience like?

Devon: It was so relaxing.

Jon: Is that right? Wonderful. Your eyes want to close. Yes. You've already noticed a surprising and delightful difference recalling detail. Fixtures in a room, droplets of water on a leaf. There is a record of the information that your mind has taken in. **When information is of benefit, it just pops up into conscious awareness. It pops right up.** Examining a patient, you look and listen and **what you need comes to mind. It's automatic. Your unconscious mind takes care of it,** and **it just pops.** *(I snap my fingers each time I say the word pop)* And **it pops,** and **it pops,** and **it pops.** You appreciate it and **it just pops even bigger** and **it pops even louder,** and **it pops even faster** as you notice it. *(Long pause)* Take your time. Find your way back to where your eyes can almost open. They can't quite get open. It will be fun to try and to learn they can't open yet. At three, your eyes can open. One, two, and three.

CAUSING DEVON TO HAVE THE EXPERIENCE OF NOT BEING ABLE TO OPEN HIS EYES IS A STRONGER CONVINCER THAT HIS MIND IS RESPONDING TO WHAT WE ARE INTENDING.

Devon: Where did I go?

Jon: Yes!

Devon: The recall got louder and faster and louder and more intense and more dramatic. It was like there was this influx of data.

Jon: Yes! That's wonderful!

HIS EXPERIENCE THAT THE INFORMATION COMING IN WAS LOUDER AND FASTER MEANS HE IS RESPONDING TO WHAT I AM DOING WITH HIM AND THAT THE NECESSARY INFORMATION IS AND WILL BE THERE.

Devon: And this lady on the table.

Jon: Yes.

HIS MIND HAS GONE TO A MEDICAL SITUATION IN WHICH HIS MIND IS WORKING JUST THE WAY HE WANTS.

Devon: And I was doing a thousand things at once.

Jon: Yes.

Devon: But I was really doing nothing. It was just there.

Jon: Right.

Devon: Looking, perceiving, picking up. That was it. That was great!

Jon: Yes.

Devon: I mean, it was great!

HE SAYS THAT HE WAS DOING A THOUSAND THINGS AT ONCE, BUT NOT REALLY DOING ANYTHING. THAT'S EXACTLY WHAT I AM INTENDING FOR HIM. ALL THE INFORMATION IS BEING PROCESSED AND CAUSING JUST THE RIGHT ACTIONS AUTOMATICALLY. WHEN HE SAYS THAT HE WASN'T DOING ANYTHING, IT IS THAT HE DIDN'T HAVE TO CONSCIOUSLY DO ANYTHING. IT WAS JUST AUTOMATIC.

Jon: Your awareness was drawn in toward your center where **you are always at peace. Your mind will vacuum in information and gain access to it when needed.**

IN THIS STATE OF INCREASED RESPONSIVENESS, I CAN TELL HIM THAT HIS MIND WILL VACUUM IN INFORMATION AND GAIN ACCESS TO IT WHEN NEEDED. AT THIS POINT, IT SEEMS LOGICAL TO EXPERIENCE THESE THINGS I AM SAYING AS TRUE. SELF-FULFILLING PROPHECY OFTEN REFERS TO SOMETHING NEGATIVE HAPPENING BECAUSE OF A NEGATIVE BELIEF. BUT HERE, THE POSITIVE OCCURRENCE WILL FOLLOW THE POSITIVE BELIEF.

Devon: At the same time, I was standing at the bed of this person and every time you would snap, the data would increase. I just kept realizing more and more.

Jon: Yes.

Devon: That was weird.

I, ONCE AGAIN, GUIDE HIM INTO AN ALTERED STATE OF CONSCIOUSNESS AND STILL GREATER RESPONSIVENESS.

Jon: Every time your eyes blink, they close. (*His eyes blink a few times and then rest closed.*) Enjoy going to still a deeper level where you benefit in ways that are incredible, amazing and extraordinary. Notice your right hand. You can wonder which finger will lift up. *(Pinky immediately lifts.)* The pinky. Which finger will follow it up? There it goes. The hand lifts itself up.

HIS HAND IS BEGINNING TO LIFT. IT LIFTS IN LITTLE TWITCHES THAT ARE NOT POSSIBLE TO MAKE HAPPEN CONSCIOUSLY. I KNOW THERE IS A RESPONSE FROM HIS UNCONSCIOUSNESS. HE IS NOT CONSCIOUSLY MAKING THIS HAPPEN AND THE FACT THAT IT IS HAPPENING MAKES HIM REALIZE THAT THE INTENTION WE HAVE IS MANIFESTING.

Jon: Your mind is not just powerful, but with its great power, it's also wonderfully responsive when treated with respect. **Your mind is eager to respond. The natural healing process that goes on all the time through your body and through your brain is going on now,** but **now it's going on more powerfully. It is happening many times more rapidly.** I'm going to put my hand near your forehead, and you will feel the energy that's around my hand. It enters your brain, increasing the healing process.

AS THE PROCESS OF HEALING IS POINTED OUT, IT INCREASES. THE SENSATION HE EXPERIENCES OF ENERGY WITH MY HAND NEAR HIS HEAD ADDS TO HIS EXPERIENCE THAT THIS IS HAPPENING.

Jon: **The wisdom of your own inner mind is directing the extraordinary healing energy. Your ability to recall pertinent information is wonderful. Useful medical information pops into your mind when it's valuable. Your recall is on the upswing, happening faster, bigger, more powerfully so that you appreciate it and there's more, and there's more to appreciate, and you appreciate it more, and there's more to appreciate, and you appreciate it more, and there's more, and more, and more, and more, and more, way beyond what you wanted, way beyond what you hoped for. You can now experience this level of deep peace and power on your own. Now, you can tap this power any time you like.** Here's how. Get the idea of how you want your mind operating. Conceive of it working that way. Create a way to symbolically represent your target. You might think of being completely focused on what you are learning as your mind takes in and absorbs the material. See or conceive of that happening. Find a way to symbolically represent it, whatever comes to mind as a symbol. Maybe it is a triangle of a particular size and color, maybe it is a pelican rising up from the water. Just pick a symbol because our minds are quite responsive to symbols. What would be a good way to symbolize focused attention and absorption?

SINCE EVERYTHING I HAVE SAID HAS HAPPENED, THEN EVERYTHING I SAY WILL HAPPEN. THE UNCONSCIOUS MIND IS VERY RESPONSIVE TO SYMBOLS AND SO WE ARE MAKING USE OF A SYMBOL SO THAT HE CAN TELL HIS MIND TO FOCUS WITHOUT SAYING LOTS OF WORDS.

Devon: A black and red arrow.

Jon: Decide to experience this state on your own for a minute. Next, focus on your symbol. Take a deep slow breath while focusing on your symbol and, as you exhale and your eyes close, hear numbers go down five to one. *(He takes a big breath, exhales slowly and his eyes close)* During this time, nothing is required. **Your mind is setting up in**

the way you intend. In just a moment, I'm going to bring you up. After I bring you up, you're going to go right back down on your own for a minute. You'll go right back down on your own and then you'll come up on your own. You can start coming up higher, more alert. I'll count up to three and, at three, your eyes will once again be able to open. One, two, three and your eyes open. Find a spot. Take a breath and, as you exhale, your eyes close. That's it. And you silently count down five, four, three, two and one. I'll be silent as your body is healing and your recall is supercharged. Then, you will come back on your own in a minute. (*His eyes close and remain closed for a minute and then they open.*) What does that feel like?

Devon: Like I slept for twenty hours.

Jon: Yes.

Devon: It feels great.

HE NOW CAN ACCESS THE STATE OF PEACE AND RESPONSIVENESS ON HIS OWN.

Jon: When you've been studying, Devon, how have you known when to stop?

Devon: Fatigue.

Jon: Have you ever noticed that sometimes it's hard to get started?

Devon: Oh, absolutely!

Jon: When you were studying, did you ever notice that there were thoughts about other things you might do instead?

Devon: Yes. Distracters.

Jon: Other thoughts were about how awful it would be if you flunked?

Devon: Oh, it's the louder voice.

Jon: Those voices continued to become louder as your studying continued, didn't they? The reason that happened was that every time you started to study, you continued until you were fatigued and depleted.

Devon: Yes, the longer I studied the more there was background noise in my head.

Jon: Your mind was suggesting the distractions in order to get you off of a track it knew was headed toward fatigue. There were other thoughts about how bad it would be if you did not succeed that were intended to keep you studying. How would it be to study with those voices silent and your mind clear and focused?

Devon: That would be a blessing.

Jon:	Before you begin to study, decide exactly when you're going to stop. Make sure, before deciding, that you are positive you will be able to reach that goal. Both voices will stop. There won't be any point to them. The voice that used to try to distract you won't bother because it won't do any good. It won't have to protect you from going too long because there is a stopping point. The second voice won't start because there is no reason for it. It won't be able to keep you studying past the pre-determined stopping point, so it wouldn't do any good.
Devon:	Yes.
Jon:	When it's time to stop, you stop. Now, stop might mean long enough to take a short walk. If you decide to begin again, that's okay. It's a new deal. Before you start, always know when you're going to stop. Let's say the task you have decided on is to read chapter four. You're sitting by your desk and you conceive of reading chapter four and being absolutely immersed in reading and learning. You're setting it up so that valuable information will be drawn right into your mind. Think "red and black arrow" as you inhale. As you exhale, your eyes will slowly close. Your eyes will close and remain closed for one minute. When your eyes open, you begin studying.
Devon:	I understand.
Jon:	You get to the end of the task and you stop. As soon as you stop, you will take another breath and again exhale slow and close your eyes. Your eyes will be closed again for one minute and, as you rest, your mind will organize the information you've just brought into it. Have you ever been inside the part of the post office where they sort the mail?
Devon:	Yes.
Jon:	As your eyes are closing, think "post office." **As your eyes rest, your brain will sort the material you have brought in.**
Devon:	What a joy.
Jon:	**You will be absorbed, involved and interested as you study and then mind will automatically organize the material.** (*There is a psychology book on the shelf. I open it and select a random chapter for him to read.*)
Jon:	I would like you to read this section.
Devon:	Okay.
Jon:	Before you read, take a deep breath and think "red and black arrow" as you exhale while hearing the numbers go down five to one. Your mind will prepare for learning. At the end of the minute, you will hear numbers go up one to five. You will then open your eyes. Then, read the section and then close the book. Take another deep breath

and close your eyes as you exhale, thinking "post office." Hear the numbers go down five to one. Your eyes rest for one minute as everything that has been brought in gets organized. Then, you hear the numbers go up, one to five, and open your eyes. Do you understand all the steps?

Devon: Yes. (*Devon does the process I described to him.*)

Jon: Tell me about what you read.

Devon: (*He describes it in such great detail that we are both surprised*) I can't believe I am sitting here reciting all this stuff. I usually have to write it out, you know.

IT IS BEST IF HE CAN ACHIEVE WHAT HE WANTS AND KNOW HE HAS IT WHILE HE IS STILL WITH ME. HE KNOWS HE CAN DO IT BECAUSE HE HAS JUST DONE IT.

Jon: Is there anything you would like to ask or tell me about before we end our conversation today?

Devon: Yes, why didn't I meet you when I first went to medical school?

Jon: It was a delight to get to spend some time with you.

Devon: I can't thank you enough, Jon.

Jon: It was a pleasure.

Follow-Up Commentary

Devon completed his residency and enjoys the practice of medicine. He has been in good health.

Abbie was 24 years old when we had this meeting.

Jon: I know there is something you wanted to speak with me about.

Abbie: I would like to be able to say what I like without worrying about what other people are going to think of me.

Jon: So, to **feel at ease as you say what you think**. What else should I know?

Abbie: I want to not be inhibited about what I want to do or what I think. I want to be able to say what I want. I don't know if I am making any sense here, but…

Jon: You make sense. So, to express yourself, speak easily and let people know what you think.

USING DRESSED COMMANDS AND DECLARATIVES, EMPHASIZED WITH AN INCREASE IN VOLUME, SLIGHT PAUSE AND DIRECT EYE CONTACT ENABLE SUBCONSCIOUS MIND TO ACCEPT THE STATEMENTS OF WHAT TO DO OR HOW THINGS ARE. "SO, TO" IS SAID SOFTER WITHOUT EYE CONTACT, PROCEEDED BY "EXPRESS YOURSELF, SPEAK EASILY, AND LET PEOPLE KNOW WHAT YOU THINK" IS SAID LOUDER AND USING EYE CONTACT.

Abbie: Right.

Jon: So, I've got it?

Abbie: Right, you do have it. It's true.

Jon: **You have a clear focus** on what you are looking for. What else?

Abbie: The other part of it, with my boyfriend, Jeff, is feeling afraid sometimes to tell him how much he means to me because I'll be too vulnerable with him.

Jon: So, to **talk to Jeff in a way that will be good for both of you.**

Abbie: Right.

ABBIE DOESN'T LIKE WITHHOLDING HOW SHE'S FEELING FROM JEFF YET IS FEARFUL THAT BEING OPEN ABOUT HER FEELINGS MIGHT MAKE HER TOO VULNERABLE. THAT DEMONSTRATES TO ME THAT THERE IS CONFLICT ABOUT WHAT TO SAY TO HIM. IF SOMEONE IS CONFLICTED AND YOU CHAMPION ONE SIDE OF THE CONFLICT, YOU MAY VERY WELL STRENGTHEN THE OTHER

SIDE. RATHER THAN COME DOWN PROMOTING EITHER SIDE OF THAT CONFLICT, I SAY, "SO, TO TALK TO JEFF IN WAYS THAT WILL BE GOOD FOR BOTH OF YOU."

Jon: Your subconscious will bring experiences to mind that troubled you at the time, but now will free energy that will fuel the transformation we intend. Something will come to mind for us to think about together. It might be something you haven't thought about for a while.

I UTILIZE WHAT I CALL AN "INCANTATION," ASKING HER MIND TO BRING TO HER ATTENTION SOMETHING THAT, AS WE SPEAK ABOUT IT, WILL FREE ENERGY AND FUEL THE TRANSFORMATION WE INTEND. IT IS CALL "INCANTATION," A TONGUE-IN-CHEEK REFERENCE TO SUMMONING THE GHOST. I'M ASKING THAT THIS EVENT COME TO HER AWARENESS AUTOMATICALLY. I DON'T ENGAGE HER CONSCIOUS MIND IN ASKING HER TO THINK ABOUT IT, BUT RATHER HER UNCONSCIOUS MIND. I AM LOOKING FOR IT TO JUST COME TO MIND. I'M NOT ASKING FOR SOMETHING THAT WOULD HELP US UNDERSTAND WHY THERE HAVE BEEN PROBLEMS, BUT, INSTEAD, SUGGESTING THAT THIS IS SOMETHING THAT, AS WE THINK ABOUT IT TOGETHER, WILL FREE ENERGY AND MOVE THINGS FORWARD.

THE EVENT THAT IS SELECTED IS ONE THAT HER MIND HAS CONTINUED TO READ AS HAPPENING AND SO REQUIRING A RESPONSE, CAUSING AN EMOTION THAT IS DISTURBING. SUCH EVENTS CAUSE AN UNCONSCIOUS PREOCCUPATION AND, HENCE, AN ENERGY DRAIN. AS THE SPECIFIC EXPERIENCE IS BROUGHT INTO THE LIGHT, IT WILL FREE UP ENERGY THAT WILL FUEL THE DESIRED SHIFT. WHEN MIND IS CLEARED, ENERGY IS FREED.

Abbie: This is something I haven't thought of in a long time. It's something that's kind of silly, but I grew up in Chicago and, in junior high, I rode the bus to school. I was really quiet and shy, of course, and didn't talk a lot. There were some older kids on the bus who were really scary, so I just stayed out of trouble and nobody ever bothered me. I got on the bus one day and had forgotten my lunch. My dad always worked a lot, so he wasn't around that much. But, for some reason, he was home, and so he brought my lunch to me. I was already on the bus and he stopped the bus to bring my lunch to me. He walked up on the bus and I saw him come in and he had my lunch and he said, "Abbie, here's your lunch." I was totally immobilized. There was no way I was going to get up and acknowledge that he was my father because I would have to be seen. You know, I was very good at not being seen. So, the bus driver just said to my dad, "Somebody isn't going to move." So, he just said, "Well, I'm just going to put it right here next to the bus driver." The bus driver looked at me and said, "Yes, it will be right here." It was no big deal. No one ever said anything, and it was just the older kids who were scary to me, but it was a big deal to me. What was even a bigger deal was that I felt so guilty and bad that I had done that to my father, that I had not acknowledged his presence. I just stared straight ahead. So, immediately, when I got to school, I went up to the principal's office and called my dad at work and thanked him for bringing my lunch. He said, "Oh, no big deal!" I don't think he was fazed by the whole thing, but I felt bad about it all day. I haven't thought about that for a very long time until just now.

THE THOUGHT THAT HER "PARALYSIS" CAUSED HER TO HURT SOMEONE SHE LOVED CONTINUED TO BE DISTURBING AND AN ENERGY DRAIN. ABBIE'S OWN MIND CHOSE THE BEST EVENT TO CLEAR.

Jon: It came to mind as something to talk about with me, so **there is an easy flow of thoughts and feelings as you express yourself.**

Abbie: Yes, I was thinking about being immobilized.

Jon: **You are compassionate and caring.** You like to **have a good and positive effect on people. You really care.** It wasn't just, "Oh gosh, maybe he won't bring me lunch next time." It was that you really care. Am I not correct?

Abbie: Oh, definitely, yes. I feel so bad about the effect on him.

Jon: How <u>did</u> <u>you think</u> it affected him?

I USED THE WORD "DID" RATHER THAN "DO" SO THAT IT WILL BE LEFT BEHIND AND DISAPPEAR. I USED THE WORDS "YOU THINK" SO IT BECOMES CLEAR THAT IT IS NOT REAL.

Abbie: Well, I had failed even to acknowledge his presence.

Jon: What <u>did</u> that <u>seem</u> to mean?

Abbie: I was a bad daughter, that I was bad.

Jon: A bad daughter? *(Said with surprise).*

Abbie: Yes.

Jon: And what else?

Abbie: Just that I was bad, and unappreciative and hurtful.

Jon: Even hurtful? *(Incredulous)*

Abbie: Yes, hurtful was the biggest.

I AM LOOKING TO EXPOSE THE MEANING HER MIND ATTACHED TO THE EVENT IN ORDER TO DESTROY THE BELIEF AND FACILITATE THE DESIRED CHANGE.

Jon: You <u>thought</u> you were hurtful, but this is what actually happened. **You were able to realize** the situation could have been dangerous. **You took appropriate action** by doing what there was to do in order not to be noticed. You <u>felt</u> troubled because you thought you had hurt your father. The more something is painful or hurtful, the more the meaning is distorted. Let's take another look at what happened that day. You got on the bus....

ABBIE BELIEVES SHE WAS HURTFUL. I DEMONSTRATE THAT I UNDERSTAND BUT ADD THE WORD "THOUGHT". I CALL THIS A "WEDGE". IT ISN'T DETECTED BY THE CONSCIOUS MIND BUT IS BY THE SUBCONSCIOUS. IN ADDITION TO ADDING THE WEDGE,

I ALSO CHANGE THE TENSE SO THAT THERE WAS AN INVISIBLE TENSE CHANGE AND A WEDGE. IT LETS HER MIND KNOW THAT IT WAS A THOUGHT RATHER THAN A REALITY AND THAT IT IS PAST RATHER THAN NOW.

Abbie: I got on the bus.

Jon: Without your lunch?

Abbie: Right, and my dad brought it to me.

Jon: You realized there could be danger on the bus.

Abbie: Right, because of all the noise from the back and the older kids that were there.

Jon: **That makes sense. You are smart** to have done that. **There was a good reason** you didn't feel safe.

Abbie: I think that was pretty accurate. I mean, it could be unsafe.

Jon: **You are smart** to have taken protective action the way you did.

Abbie: Right.

Jon: The protective action you took was to not be noticed.

Abbie: Right.

Jon: Was it true that you would be most safe not being noticed in that situation?

Abbie: Yes.

Jon: Was it true that people would more likely do hurtful things to someone who stood out and was noticed? You father was well intentioned, but didn't what he did, in fact, endanger you?

Abbie: Well, in my perception, yes.

Jon: He wants you okay. You **do the smart thing to be okay. You did what he actually wanted you to do.** Your father just made a mistake, but **you do the right thing**. And when you didn't get up, your father said?

Abbie: "I'll just leave it here."

Jon: He caught on to the fact that he had made you uncomfortable and did what he could to recover.

Abbie: I didn't realize that, but you are right.

Jon: You proceeded to school and called and expressed your concern and love.

Abbie: Right, I called my dad right away.

Jon: You didn't call and say, "What's the matter with you? Were you trying to get me killed?"

Abbie: (Giggles) Right, I didn't.

Jon: You didn't say anything like that. You said, "Hey, I'm sorry. I didn't mean to let you down." Even though you had been endangered by him, your immediate response was caring, and then you went on with your day.

Abbie: Yes.

As I LISTEN TO ABBIE DESCRIBE THE EVENTS THAT HAPPENED ON THE SCHOOL BUS, I SUGGEST THAT WHAT SHE DID MADE SENSE AND POINT OUT FEELINGS AND THOUGHTS THAT HAVEN'T BEEN TO HER BENEFIT, SUCH AS, "I WAS A BAD DAUGHTER," IN SUCH A WAY AS TO ELIMINATE THEM. THE EVENT ITSELF HAS NOT EVER BEEN WITHOUT THE DISTORTED MEANING ATTACHED, WHICH WAS THAT SHE HAD BEEN HURTFUL BECAUSE SHE HAD BEEN IMMOBILIZED. WITHOUT CHANGING THE EVENT, I CHANGE THE MEANING THAT CHANGES HER ENTIRE EXPERIENCE OF THE EVENT. NOW, SHE SEES THE WHOLE EVENT DIFFERENTLY. SHE SEES HERSELF AS HANDLING A CHALLENGING SITUATION EFFECTIVELY, AND EVEN COMPASSIONATELY, EVEN THOUGH HE HAD PUT HER IN DANGER. SHE ENDS UP WITH THE EXPERIENCE OF BEING HIGHLY EFFECTIVE IN THAT SITUATION BECAUSE SHE WAS QUIET AND STILL. HER ENTIRE RECOLLECTION OF THIS EVENT HAS BEEN FLIPPED.

Jon: Isn't that exactly what happened that day?

Abbie: That's exactly what happened, and it feels a lot better. It even feels good to know that I could have been angry about it. I wasn't, but it's nice to know that it would have been okay.

Jon: Yes, most people would have been angry.

Abbie: Yes, it feels different. It feels more neutral-like.

Jon: What does that mean about you?

Abbie: Well, nothing bad.

Jon: **You are appropriate, effective, compassionate and intelligent.** That's what it means. Try to get it to mean anything other than that.

Abbie: I can't. (*She is delighted*)

I CHALLENGE HER TO DISAGREE AND IT PUSHES THE AGREEMENT EVEN DEEPER INTO HER MIND. TRYING TO GET IT TO MEAN SOMETHING ELSE AND BEING UNABLE TO MAKES IT FEEL EVEN MORE TRUER.

Jon: You are here so that you can **express yourself with ease and confidence.** Your mind selected just the right experience to review. Now, another event will come to mind.

Abbie: There was another time when I was immobile. It was really different. There was a Peeping Tom in the bathroom window at our house when I was in the bathroom. I had gotten out of the shower, looked up at the window and there he was. I knew him. He was my neighbor and I felt immobilized at that moment. In fact, I felt like I was standing there immobilized for a while. I'm sure it was not that long, but it felt like forever before I could move to get out of the bathroom. What made me move was he had to pull himself up to the window because the window was so high, and then he dropped down and the noise of him dropping down on the ground is what made me move.

Jon: When he was no longer looking, you moved.

Abbie: Yes.

Jon: While he was looking, you were still.

Abbie: That's true.

Jon: He knew you saw him. He knew **you caught him and then he ran away.**

Abbie: Right.

Jon: You didn't move around in front of him.

Abbie: No.

Jon: You did the opposite of what a Peeping Tom is interested in. A Peeping Tom wants motion. The more someone moves, the better he likes it. He's not looking to see a statue.

LIKE THE FIRST INCIDENT, THIS ONE SHIFTS FROM ABBIE FEELING INEFFECTIVE TO EXPERIENCING HERSELF AS POWERFUL AND EFFECTIVE, THE ULTIMATE HEROINE.

Abbie: Yes, that's right.

Jon: How much do you think a Peeping Tom wants to be observed?

Abbie: Not a lot.

Jon: Zero!

Abbie: That's right.

Jon: Because it's not an interactive sport. You gave him the opposite of what he wanted. Try to improve on what you did.

Abbie: I can't! (laughing) I hadn't thought of it that way, but that's true, it makes sense.

BY ASKING HER TO TRY TO IMPROVE ON IT, I PROVE TO HER THAT THE WAY SHE HANDLED IT WAS PERFECT. IT CAN'T BE IMPROVED ON EVEN NOW. A SYMPATHETIC LISTENER OR COUNSELOR MIGHT TRY TO "NORMALIZE" ABBIE'S RESPONSE BY TELLING HER THAT IT WAS NATURAL TO BE FROZEN IN SHOCK WHEN HER PRIVACY HAS BEEN VIOLATED. I DIDN'T WANT TO BE SYMPATHETIC. THAT WOULD HAVE CAUSED HER TO FEEL VICTIMIZED. I PREFER SHE FEELS HEROIC AND BELIEVE SHE HANDLED THE SITUATION WITH POWER AND EXCELLENCE RATHER THAN FEEL THAT HER "PARALYSIS" WAS UNDERSTANDABLE.

Jon: You are on track toward how **you will express your thoughts easily and comfortably.** Another event will come to mind.

Abbie: What comes to mind is a bunch of sexual things that I feel bad about.

Jon: Oh boy, are you going to tell me about disgraceful sexual things? *(Said with humor and fun)*

Abbie: I was desperate or so needy or whatever.

Jon: Here comes the good part. So, what did you do?

BY SAYING, "HERE COMES THE GOOD PART," AND ACTING SILLY, I MAKE ABBIE LAUGH. HER SHAME IS SIGNIFICANTLY REDUCED.

Abbie: *(Laughing)* Actually, I just had sex.

Jon: You had sex with what?

AGAIN, SILLINESS REDUCES SHAME.

Abbie: A guy.

Jon: A guy. That's all you did?

Abbie: That's what's so bad!

Jon: What a disappointment. I was waiting for something strange and interesting.

INDICATING THAT HAVING SEX WITH A GUY IS SO NORMAL IT IS NOT WORTH ANY EMBARRASSMENT.

Abbie: This one particular guy.

Jon: That's all? You are going to tell me about a sexual experience with a guy. That's what it's about?

Abbie: *(Playful and exasperated)* Well, what did you think it was about?

Jon: I was hoping to hear about something really interesting.

Abbie: *(She rolls her eyes)* He was my boyfriend.

Jon: That's all it was? You had sex with your boyfriend?

Abbie: Yes, for a couple of years, maybe longer. Anyway, I broke up with him because I felt like I was a whore when I was with him. It was just too many things to go over, everything from going out and getting on the birth control pill myself at fifteen, you know, going to the doctor and doing the whole thing.

Jon: **You did all that for yourself?**

THE TONE OF MY QUESTION CAUSES IT TO BE EXPERIENCE AS SHE DID SOMETHING WELL AND IS BEING CONGRATULATED.

Abbie: And getting the prescription filled and all that stuff, and my family are Orthodox Jews.

Jon: Here comes the good part. Hurry up and tell me. What did you do?

AGAIN, THE QUESTION TURNS THE "CONFESSION" THAT ABBIE HAD BEEN EMBARRASSED BY TO LIGHT AND FUN.

Abbie: I was naked with him in the car, doing oral sex, when the police came up and saw us and yelled at us. They told us they were going to call our fathers. For days, every time the phone rang, I was afraid it was the police...calling to tell him...but they never did.

Jon: **They never did call, they never called.** Why <u>did</u> you feel like a whore?

I TELL HER, "THEY NEVER DID CALL," EVEN THOUGH SHE ALREADY KNOWS BECAUSE A FEAR CAN BE FROZEN THROUGH TIME AND I WANT ALL PARTS OF HER MIND TO GET THIS GOOD NEWS. HER FEELING LIKE A WHORE IS SAID IN PAST TENSE TO PUT IT BEHIND HER.

Abbie: I felt that way because he just wanted sex and he wanted it everywhere, even at my mom's house.

Jon: And a whore is what?

Abbie: Only there for sex. It was just that that's all I was worth, satisfying his needs. That was it.

Jon: So, that's what you <u>thought</u> it meant about you. What does it mean about him?

THE WORDS, "YOU THOUGHT," IS IN THE PAST TENSE AND STATES IT AS A THOUGHT RATHER THAN A REALITY.

ABBIE'S SITUATION WITH HER BOYFRIEND IS ANOTHER IDENTITY PIECE IMPACTING HER RELATIONSHIP WITH JEFF, HER FEELING ABOUT HERSELF AND HER FEELINGS ABOUT SEX. MEANINGS HER MIND ATTACHED TO INTIMACY STEMMED FROM THESE EARLIER SITUATIONS. AS ABBIE DESCRIBES FEELING BADLY ABOUT HER SEXUAL EXPERIENCES, I SHIFT THE MEANING OF HER BEING A "WHORE" TO HER BEING A LOVING, CARING GIRLFRIEND.

Abbie: He was pretty obsessed, real possessive. He was just...

Jon: Just what?

Abbie: A guy, I guess!

Jon: That's interesting. He's a guy, so you're a whore? What sense does that make? You were never a whore. You were with a guy you cared about. These cops came up to the car while you were naked and shined lights in the window and threatened you while wearing uniforms. I bet you thought that the world was a dangerous place for somebody like you, that if you were noticed it would zero-in on your badness.

I POINT OUT THE DOUBLE STANDARD OF A GAL BEING SEEN AS A "WHORE" WHILE THE GUY IS JUST A GUY. THEN SHE REALIZES THAT SELF-CONDEMNATION MAKES NO SENSE. THE EXPERIENCE OF POLICE OFFICERS STARING THROUGH THE WINDOW AT HER IS FLIPPED AROUND SO THAT THEY ARE SEEN AS ACTING IN A SILLY WAY.

Abbie: *(Laughing)* **Official!** *(She is now having fun with a story that used to be traumatizing.)*

Jon: Now we can see it clearly. This is what actually happened. You met a young man who you enjoyed, and you had warm and caring feelings for him.

Abbie: Right.

Jon: And he had affection for you, and you enjoyed pleasing him because you also had affection for him.

Abbie: Right.

Jon: He meant a great deal to you.

Abbie: Right.

Jon: And as you got closer to him and spent time with him, you let him kiss you, hold your hand and put his arm around you. You felt close, cared about and wanted. You also felt protective because he seemed vulnerable.

Abbie: Yes, that's just how it happened.

A HIGHER LEVEL OF CONNECTION AND CREDIBILITY IS ACHIEVED BY REALLY GETTING TO THE HEART OF THE MATTER BY DESCRIBING THINGS BACK THAT SHE HAD NOT ACTUALLY MENTIONED. THE MEANING HAS CHANGED FROM BEING USED BY

HIM TO PROTECTIVE TOWARD HIM. SHE CAN REMEMBER HERSELF BEING POWERFUL INSTEAD OF USED. THE FEELING OF BEING USED AND NOT STOPPING IT WAS SIMILAR IN STRUCTURE TO HER OTHER FEELINGS OF "PARALYSIS". NOW, THE HISTORY HAS CHANGED AND TO THE EFFECT IT HAS IS DIFFERENT.

Jon: You became protective.

Abbie: Yes.

Jon: And he became still more vulnerable and, of course, you didn't want to hurt him.

Abbie: Right, yes, I did not want to hurt him.

Jon: You did not want to hurt him and, therefore, you didn't want to reject him.

Abbie: Yes.

Jon: You didn't want him as much as he wanted you, particularly in sexual ways.

Abbie: Right.

Jon: When you did pull back, he was hurt.

Abbie: Yes.

Jon: You cared about him, you liked it better when he was happy, and then one day the police came and that felt terrible.

Abbie: Right, yes.

Jon: They even threatened to tell your dad, but it was an empty threat and they never did.

Abbie: Yes.

Jon: Now, what have I left out?

Abbie: Nothing.

Jon: What goes on for you now, as you consider it?

Abbie: It looks different than what it was before. I feel exhausted. I don't feel bad about it anymore, just kind of exhausted.

THE MEANING HAS BEEN TRANSFORMED. SHE IS A STRONG, LOVING AND PROTECTIVE WOMAN.

Jon: You are putting a real energy into this and it's all working.

WHEN SHE DESCRIBES EXHAUSTION, A NEGATIVE, I STATE SHE HAS PUT ENERGY OUT, A POSITIVE.

Abbie: Yes, I haven't told anyone about these things. I don't think I have even told myself!

THE DESTRUCTIVE MEANINGS HAVE BEEN BROUGHT TO LIGHT AND TRANSFORMED.

Jon: Excellent! Congratulations!

Abbie: Yes, I have never ever…I am surprised at what has come up. Very surprised.

Jon: Look back at that young girl on that bus where there was danger and see how she adapts and handles it. Watch her go through that and **feel admiration and respect for her.** Look back at what happened to you as a girl. See that young girl. **She caught that silly Peeping Tom** who climbed up to look through the bathroom window. **Watch how well she is handling it. Look at her with respect and with pride**.

Abbie: I've got it.

Jon: You don't do any silly girlish cover-up. You look right at him with nothing to hide, watching him. **You totally destroy his secrecy.** He is caught in the act as you look right at him and don't move until **you almost want to scream in triumph.**

Abbie: Yes, that was good.

Jon: Now, what about being with the boyfriend? Look at her. Does she seem okay to you now?

Abbie: No.

Jon: What are you seeing that you are putting her down for? In what way isn't she good enough for you?

I AM TEASING HER WITH THE QUESTION, "IN WHAT WAY IS SHE NOT GOOD ENOUGH FOR YOU?" IN ORDER TO CREATE AN OPENING TO GAIN HER FULL ACCEPTANCE OF HER "YOUNGER SELF."

Abbie: I guess it's just letting down my parents.

Jon: They weren't there!

Abbie: I know.

Jon: She is not with her parents. She is with her lover. What would you like your daughter to do for you when she is naked with her lover? Help with baking? What are people supposed to do for their mothers when naked with a lover?

JOKING WITH HER LIKE THIS AND ASKING HER WHAT SHE WOULD EXPECT FROM HER OWN DAUGHTER TURNS HER PERCEPTION AROUND.

Abbie: *(Laughing)* Not a thing.

Jon: Look at her in the car with police officers staring through the window like silly boys who have climbed up the window to look at her. They see her skin, but she sees grown men like little boys who have climbed a tree. They have whistles. Isn't it silly?

HER CATCHING THE PEEPING TOM AND HER BEING CAUGHT BY THE POLICE HAVE BOTH COME TOGETHER AND HAVE BEEN TRANSFORMED SO THAT SHE LOOKS GREAT AND THEY LOOK SILLY.

Abbie: Yes.

Jon: What is going on for you?

Abbie: I feel good. I feel really good!

Jon: Yes.

Abbie: Yes, yes, this is wonderful! I've got it!

Jon: I enjoyed talking with you.

Follow-Up Commentary

Six months later, Abbie reported being at ease and much less inhibited. She can express herself much more easily. She and Jeff are now engaged.

Phillip

Phillip heard a talk I gave and scheduled a meeting with me. He was 28 years old.

Jon: I know there was something that you wanted to discuss.

Phillip: I would like to put depression behind me.

I WOULD LIKE HIM TO THINK ABOUT DEPRESSION AS SOMETHING THAT IS HAPPENING RATHER THAN SOMETHING HE HAS. I WOULD LIKE HIM TO REALIZE THAT IT WAS INEVITABLE AND THAT IT CAN BE FINISHED. I LOOK TO SPEAK ABOUT THIS IN AN INTERESTING WAY AND KEEP HIM ENGAGED. WHEN HE IS INTERESTED AND ENGAGED, HE IS NOT SO LIKELY TO BE DEPRESSED.

Jon: You grew up in a culture in which there were some things that were never really said out loud but were definitely assumed by just about everybody you met. Here's what they were: that life is good and, if you are good, you will do well. If you do well, you will feel good. If you are not feeling well, it's because you haven't been doing well. If you haven't been doing well, it's important that you feel bad so that you will do better and feel good.

Phillip: *(Smiles with surprise)* I never thought of it that way.

Jon: You haven't heard anybody say this quite that way, but everybody you knew, everybody who raised you, every teacher you had, anybody who was in a parental or authority role all through your life believed it and acted from it. You were exposed to it from the time you were old enough to drool. There was no way to not be affected by it. Your mind began trying to make you feel bad, so you would be good and do well so that you would feel good. Here is how it goes. In order to feel good, you have to do good. In order to do good, you have to feel bad. That's why we try to help people feel bad when we want them to do better so that they can feel good. When people are worried that their kids are not getting good grades, they try to help them feel bad so that they'll do better, and then will feel good. It's all just so that they will feel good. I believe this has a great deal to do with what you call "depression". The intention behind what has been the cause of the depression has been to cheer you up.

I AM COVERING TWO IDEAS THAT CONVERGE. ONE IS THAT ONE SHOULD FEEL PRIDE OR SHAME REGARDING BEHAVIOR. THE OTHER IS THAT THERE WAS A CHOICE ABOUT BEHAVIOR. I AM INTERESTED IN ELIMINATING THESE BELIEFS TO FREE PHILLIP FROM FEELING DEPRESSED.

Phillip: What a way to do it!

Jon: Much of what causes depression is the belief that you shouldn't have done what you did. You shouldn't have done it the way you did it. You should have done it differently. You should have done it better. You shouldn't have done certain things, or you should have done other things you didn't do, and they should have been done in a better way. Other people also should have done what they didn't do and should not have done what they did do. Haven't you had those kinds of thoughts?

Phillip: Yes, I have often thought that about myself and others.

Jon: You have been thinking that you have made wrong choices. Am I wrong?

Phillip: No, you are not wrong. It's just weird to hear those words and to know that they have been true.

HAVING COVERED WHY CREDIT, BLAME, PRIDE AND SHAME ARE SILLY, I AM READY TO ATTACK THE BELIEF THAT THERE WAS EVER A CHOICE ABOUT THINGS THAT PHILLIP OR OTHERS DID. IF HE HAS HAD NO CHOICE ABOUT THE THINGS HE DID, THEN GUILT ISN'T POSSIBLE BECAUSE GUILT COMES FROM THE BELIEF THAT HE SHOULDN'T HAVE DONE WHAT HE DID AND/OR THAT HE SHOULD HAVE DONE WHAT HE DIDN'T DO. IF THERE WAS NO CHOICE, THEN IT IS RIDICULOUS TO THINK HE SHOULD HAVE DONE ANYTHING DIFFERENTLY. THEN, WHEN THE SAME PRINCIPLES ARE APPLIED TO OTHERS, RESENTMENT DISAPPEARS AS WELL. NO ONE ELSE COULD HAVE OR SHOULD HAVE DONE ANYTHING DIFFERENTLY.

Jon: Let's play with a different way of thinking about choice. Let's take a look at this thing about having done things poorly and having made bad choices. Let's take a look at a few choices you <u>thought</u> you made. For instance, do you *think* that you chose your shirt to wear today?

I ENGAGE PHILLIP WITH THE WORDS "LET'S PLAY" AND GO ON TO SAY, "A DIFFERENT WAY OF THINKING." THERE IS A LIGHTNESS AND SENSE OF FUN. I AM NOT SAYING I KNOW WHAT IS RIGHT, JUST THAT WE CAN PLAY WITH A DIFFERENT WAY TO THINK.

Phillip: Yes, of course. I chose to wear it.

Jon: You are <u>under the impression</u> that you chose the shirt you are wearing and that you could have worn something else.

SAYING THE WORDS "UNDER THE IMPRESSION" SUGGESTS THAT THIS IS A VIEW AND PERHAPS ONE THAT IS NOT ACCURATE.

Phillip: Of course.

Jon: What was going on just before you selected that shirt?

THE TONE OF THIS INTERCHANGE IS LIGHT AND FUN. IT ALL FOLLOWS, "LET'S PLAY."

Phillip: Well, I was looking in my closet and I didn't see anything I wanted to wear. I had a picture in my mind of this shirt and of these pants, and I knew they were clean because I washed them on the weekend.

Jon: OK. And then?

Phillip: Then I went out to the garage to the dryer and got them.

Jon: OK. Now, as you were there with this picture in your mind of that shirt and pants, and it was what you wanted, and it was OK to wear them, and it was possible to do.

Phillip: And possible to do, yeah.

Jon: How could you, therefore, with those thoughts about these clothes, have worn something other than what you are wearing?

Phillip: Well, I didn't think about wearing something else, so I didn't.

Jon: Right. Since there wasn't a thought to wear something else, how could you have? Even if there had been the thought to wear something else, you still had the thought you responded to. There wasn't any choice about what you wore today.

Phillip: *(Hesitant)* I guess not.

Jon: At first glance, as I asked you about it, it seemed to you that it was something you had chosen, but, as we examine it more carefully, there was nothing else you could have done.

Phillip: Yes, I guess that's true.

Jon: Now, the last time you had something liquid was how long ago?

Phillip: An hour ago.

Jon: What was it?

Phillip: It was a cup of tea.

Jon: And did you not think you chose it? Did you not think you had a choice?

Phillip: I'll say, yeah.

HE SAYS, "I'LL SAY, YEAH," BECAUSE HE IS ENGAGED IN THE SPIRIT OF PLAY.

Jon: You would have thought of it as a choice.

Phillip: Yeah.

Jon: But looking at it the same way, how much of it you drank, how rapidly you drank it, and how long you steeped it and the fact that it was tea at all weren't really choices.

There wasn't a time yesterday when you planned what you would be picturing this morning when it came time to get dressed.

Phillip: No.

Jon: There was no time yesterday when you said, "I think tomorrow morning when looking in my closet, I will picture this shirt and pants that are in the dryer in the garage." There was no time you planned that. There was no time you decided on that. You haven't been spending your mornings deciding what thoughts to have in the afternoon.

Phillip: No.

Jon: Can you tell me anything that you think you actually chose?

Phillip: In the sense we are talking about it, I chose nothing.

Jon: Guilt has come from thinking you shouldn't have done what you did, should have done what you didn't do, and should have done what you did better than you did it. It isn't designed to improve present or future performance. It is designed to cause what has happened to not have happened.

Phillip: Yes.

Jon: And the criticism has been from a later point in time.

WE HAVE COVERED ONE WAY OF THINKING, THAT NOTHING ELSE COULD HAVE HAPPENED. NEXT, I WILL ADD TO THAT WITH ANOTHER POINT. I WILL PROVE THAT IT IS SILLY TO THINK LATER THAT YOU SHOULD HAVE DONE SOMETHING DIFFERENTLY THAN YOU DID EARLIER.

Phillip: Yes, that's right.

Jon: See, it's sort of like this. We agree to meet at the races at 3 o'clock. I get there late, and Horse Number 3 is in the winner's circle. I criticize you for not having bet on that horse since it obviously won. I say, "Why didn't you?" You say, "It wasn't in the circle when I placed the bet." We could do that with Lotto. "Come on. Let's go get the money. Didn't you bet on these numbers?" "No, I didn't bet on those numbers." "Why not? They're published right here in the paper." "Well, they weren't in the paper when I bought the ticket." So, that's how it is when all that criticism comes from a different vantage point with other information available that wasn't available at the time. It's silly.

Phillip: It's silly, yes, and very easy to do. It has been for me.

Jon: Sure, it's been easy to do because everybody you ever heard who criticized themselves or anybody else did it that way. In other words, every criticism came from a different vantage point. It all is based on, "You should have done what you could have done had you seen what you didn't see. You should have done what you would have done if you knew what you didn't know."

Phillip: I see.

Jon: Why should I have done what I could have done if the situation was different than it was?

Phillip: I'm thinking about how very nice it would be to live the way you are suggesting.

Jon: Yes, very nice.

Phillip: A little scary.

Jon: How?

Phillip: Somehow, I have had some sense of safety with that. If I can judge the past, then, somehow, I'm going to be safer in the future.

Jon: Your future isn't made safer by condemning yourself for not having done what there wasn't an opportunity to do.

Phillip: I just have felt that way. That's been part of that whole package.

Jon: If anything, it would tend to decrease safety. The closer your perceptions are to what is actually there, the safer you will be.

Phillip: It's weird. I feel like I shouldn't listen to this.

Jon: How would it be better if you didn't?

Phillip: It's kind of a religious thing. If you see what you do wrong, then you can correct it.

IF I CAN SUGGEST A BETTER WAY OF ACCOMPLISHING THIS, HE WILL SEE THAT HE CAN HAVE EVEN MORE OF WHAT HE WANTS BY LOOKING AT IT THIS WAY.

Jon: You'll see what you did wrong better if you do it the way I am suggesting.

Phillip: How?

Jon: If you believe you shouldn't have done it wrong, there will be some reluctance to see it that way.

Phillip: Right.

Jon:	So, you are more likely to miss it.
Phillip:	And I have.
Jon:	If there isn't any condemnation, it will be easier to observe and correct.
Phillip:	I can see that.
Jon:	Yeah.
Phillip:	Can feel it, too.
Jon:	Any time you condemn yourself, the condemnation is stupid because it's saying that you should have handled this situation like you would have handled it if things were different or if you had experienced things differently.
Phillip:	It's just what I've done so much and thought it was good and thought it was safe.
Jon:	Yes, right.
Phillip:	Things are starting to change and rearrange in my thinking. There is one more piece that goes with what we were just talking about.
Jon:	Please.
Phillip:	It's related to religion. It's, "Don't let anybody talk you into anything that is bad."
Jon:	Yes.
Phillip:	So, I've had kind of a sentry, kind of a filterer of messages.
Jon:	While we have been talking?
Phillip:	Yeah and many other times, of course.
Jon:	Yes.
Phillip:	And I'm really glad that I'm talking about that.
Jon:	You bet!
Phillip:	Because that one is really important.
Jon:	What's wrong with not wanting people to talk you into what would be bad?
Phillip:	It's that one of the things that could be bad would be to stop condemning myself.

Jon: What would be bad about it? To no longer condemn yourself would mean that you could have more corrections of yourself.

Phillip: That is so strange.

Jon: And, therefore, more improvement.

I CONTINUE TO OFFER HIM A BETTER WAY TO ACCOMPLISH WHAT HE BELIEVES IS VALUABLE FROM THE RELIGIOUS POINT OF VIEW AND THE SELF-IMPROVEMENT POINT OF VIEW BY SUGGESTING THAT, THIS WAY, HE WILL HAVE MORE OF THOSE THINGS HE VALUES.

Phillip: *(Sighs)* That's one of my favorite things that you have said.

Jon: Good. I am glad you like it.

Phillip: *(Sighs)* Well, it's very Christian, too. It's very Jesus-like, which is even more important because He was always doing that with people. He was saying, "It's OK. It's OK. Don't condemn yourself." I always kind of thought, though, as a kid, and these are very basic things that we are dealing with today, from being a kid, I took it so seriously. I wanted to do it right.

Jon: For God?

Phillip: Yeah.

Jon: Yeah. Why?

Phillip: Because I was scared of Him.

PEOPLE OFTEN GROW UP HEARING ABOUT A GOD THAT WATCHES AND JUDGES AND THEN REWARDS OR PUNISHES. THE PUNISHMENTS ARE HUGE AND, SO, FEAR OF GOD IS WIDESPREAD.

Jon: You don't have to be scared of Him anymore because nothing that you have done will get me to feel condemning toward you.

Phillip: Well, that's good, but you are not God.

Jon: God is on at least as high a level as me. *(Laughs)*

Phillip: Yeah! *(Laughs)*

Jon: Since you are OK with me, you are OK with God. I'm not more understanding than God. I am not more compassionate than God. I am not more loving than God. If I am more compassionate, more understanding, and more loving than God, then God can go to church every weekend and worship me. God isn't going to do anything but love you and thank you and appreciate you. It's through you that energy is expressed. It's through you that God is manifest. It's through your eyes that God can see.

Phillip:	Wow!
Jon:	I understand why you were afraid of God. God has been portrayed as a maniac. Any guy who likes to catch young kids masturbating and then torture them is scary. So, God doesn't have His eye to some keyhole trying to catch some kid jerking off, so He can figure out how to burn him up! People have taken poor old God and turned him into a freak. Where does that put you?
Phillip:	It feels soft and easy.
Jon:	Good.
Phillip:	This is really very important because I've been trying to get this for a long time.
Jon:	Tell me what you mean.
Phillip:	The shifting of emphasis from condemnation to accepting as a way to actually grow spiritually.
Jon:	Let's make it still better. Let's deal with something that has caused guilt or shame.
Phillip:	Ready for a humdinger?
Jon:	Sure.
Phillip:	OK.
Jon:	I'll be delighted if it's really a humdinger. I'm usually disappointed.
Phillip:	When I was eighteen, I was seduced by my minister.
Jon:	You were sexually involved with each other.

THE WORD "SEDUCED" IS FILLED WITH MEANING AND JUDGMENT. SO, INSTEAD, I DESCRIBE IT MORE OBJECTIVELY.

Phillip:	Right.
Jon:	What have you been <u>taking that to mean</u>?
Phillip:	Well, for a long time, I took that to mean that I was gay. Now, I take it to mean that I am bi-sexual.
Jon:	You <u>took it to mean</u> something about your identity.
Phillip:	Right.

Jon: It is an activity. Many folks confuse activities with identities. It never had anything to do with who you are.

Phillip: Thinking that I was, I did it some more.

Jon: Yes. But I mean, it's like you read, right?

Phillip: Yes.

Jon: That doesn't make you a reader. It would be like looking at a caterpillar and thinking it's a crawler. I mean, it's what it's doing. It isn't what it is. You did some sexual things with guys.

Phillip: Yes.

Jon: And you did sexual things with women.

Phillip: Yes.

Jon: What does that mean?

Phillip: Well, from that point of view, it's just I did them both.

Jon: Exactly! Let's look at it this way for a while. Were you thinking that you were bad?

Phillip: Oh, yeah.

HUMANS HAVE SO MUCH MEANING AND JUDGMENT AROUND SEXUALITY. I BELIEVE THAT THIS IS ENVIRONMENTAL, NOT GENETIC EVEN THOUGH IT IS SO WIDESPREAD. THESE BELIEFS THEN AFFECT PEOPLE'S BELIEF ABOUT WHO THEY ARE AND WHETHER THEY ARE WORTHY AND LOVED BY GOD.

Jon: What was it you did that you thought was the worst thing?

Phillip: Well, that I did have sex with men.

Jon: And?

Phillip: Which, on three kinds of levels, was bad. The religious level, the societal level, and kind of a, "Well, that-means-I'm-not-a-full-man" level.

Jon: There has been a thought that you were bad.

I CALL IT A "THOUGHT" AND PUT IT IN THE PAST.

Phillip: Right.

Jon: *(Said decisively)* Your relationship with God isn't bad. It never was. God doesn't have a problem with you.

Phillip: I thought it was.

Jon: God isn't sitting around trying to figure out who is good and who is bad depending on who they have sex with or what they have sex with.

Phillip: Most of my life, I have thought so.

Jon: God is not warped like that.

I AM CHANGING HIS THOUGHTS ABOUT GOD AND I AM DEFENDING GOD AT THE SAME TIME.

Phillip: Yeah.

Jon: God isn't spying on people while they are having sex while planning on doing mean things to them. God is not a freak.

Phillip: Logically, as you say it, yeah, but I've still got a feeling, part of me that isn't sure.

Jon: At your center, where **you are wise**, at your center, where **you are at peace** and **secure**, at your soul, you certainly realize God isn't some kind of a weird pervert.

I AM NOT ATTACKING GOD, BUT, INSTEAD, DEFENDING HIM AGAINST THOSE WHO WOULD THINK OF HIM IN AN AWFUL WAY. BECAUSE GOD IS IMPORTANT TO PHILLIP, HE ALIGNS WITH ME.

Phillip: Yeah.

Jon: At the center, **you've got it.** On the surface, intellectually, **you've got it. At the center is the light of wisdom** and **at the surface is the light of knowledge.** Somewhere in the middle there have been some shadows. The shadow is surrounded with light. Distortion gives way to clarity. It's already happening. Can you imagine God on one of these "true confessions" daytime television shows saying, "Let me tell you what I've been doing lately! I sneak around trying to find out who's having sex with who, so I can hate them and plan ways to torture them!" God is not screwed up.

Phillip: One would hope.

Jon: Well, if He is, then He can go to church and worship us regularly and maybe He will get on better footing. But God is not in worse shape than we are. We can know this. So, spiritually or religiously, you certainly are not bad nor were you bad. Nobody feels angry without perceiving some kind of threat. Anybody who is angry about homosexuality is threatened by it. God is not threatened, so God is not angry. There are certainly people who are threatened by people making love to people of the same sex. You can find somebody who is going to be pretty threatened by most anything. A lot of people get threatened by guys being sexual with guys. So, what?

Phillip: Right.

Jon: The third thing was about being a man?

Phillip: I said to myself that I wasn't a full man.

Jon: Well, that's ridiculous. What is a full man, anyway, and who would even want to be one if there was such a thing? On no level does this connect with anything that makes any sense.

Phillip: No, but I have carried that specter and that ghost around.

Jon: Those are very good words for it, "ghost" and "specter" because they cannot live in the light. What is a full man? Some guy that goes to Wal-Mart, buys a rifle and camouflage clothes and joins a weekend army?

Phillip: *(A lot of laughter)*

Jon: Do you feel angry with the minister you said seduced you?

Phillip: Yes, some.

Jon: Is there anything about having been sexual with him that disturbs you now?

Phillip: *(He checks, looks confused, smiles)* No. There doesn't seem to be anything disturbing about it any longer. What happened? How did you do that? Actually, I realize that he was a good friend in many ways.

Jon: So, you seduced this nice minister, huh?

IT CONTINUES TO LIGHTEN. I CAN TEASE LIKE THIS BECAUSE THE PAIN IS GONE, AND THE TEASING DESTROYS THE LAST VESTIGES OF GUILT, SHAME AND RESENTMENT.

Phillip: *(Laughter)* Well, that's certainly another view!

Jon: *(Laughs)* If I can say that and get a laugh from you, then I know **you are past it.**

Phillip: I am.

Jon: Decide where you will have lunch today. You can choose things now. There was no choice and now there is. **Now, there is choice.**

Phillip: It is always the eternal now.

Jon: Yes, at least right now.

Phillip: True or not, useful because I no longer feel depressed.

Jon: Depression finds it hard to breathe in air that is poisoned with light, laughter and clarity.

Phillip: I feel very good.

Jon: If there is anything that you would want me to clarify before we end our conversation, I would be happy to do so.

Phillip: No. It feels complete.

Follow-Up Commentary

Five months later, Phillip told me he was guilt and shame free and much happier. He also told me that he had been dealing with headaches almost daily before our meeting and that they no longer occur.

I got a phone call late at night. The person on the phone was crying. I recognized her voice. She was a physician who had trained with me.

Jon: Tell me what has been going on.

Jodie: I can't. I can't because it's too weird. It's just too weird.

Jon: Tell me what has been going on.

Jodie: Last night, all of a sudden, I was just feeling really bad. I was afraid to go get in the pool because it just kind of felt like it would be okay if I died. This isn't me. So, you're going to tell me I need to go check myself into a psych ward, but it just felt like there was just something really dark in me. It's just not like me. It just felt like there was just something icky in me. So, anyway, I started crying. I was just crying, crying, crying. I sat down on the stairs and it was like I had some sort of past life thing going on, like, all of a sudden, my body was like on this ship and I was crying and there was a storm. And then I was in a different place, like a different lifetime, and there was a different sensation. I was, like, in a prison. This stuff doesn't happen to me and I don't even know. My wife, Sasha, finally started screaming at me because I was freaking her out. My body was so rigid it was almost like I was sort of catatonic. I was just sobbing, and Sasha is just screaming at me to stop acting crazy. She was screaming at me because she was so scared. I mean, I don't know, I don't know. I don't know. I don't feel right. Sasha made me call you. I didn't want to, because you will think I am crazy.

Jon: Something has been affecting you, but it isn't you.

IT DIDN'T SOUND LIKE SHE WAS RESPONDING TO ANYTHING THAT WAS AT ALL FAMILIAR OR THAT WAS WITHIN HER EXPERIENCE NOW OR AT ANY OTHER TIME. MY RESPONSE WAS QUITE UNUSUAL FOR ME, BUT IT'S WHAT CAME TO ME TO SAY.

Jodie: I don't know if it is. I don't know what's going on. I want it to stop. I'm scared.

Jon: You said it seems like a past life, a different lifetime. You kept saying, "That's not me. That's not how I am."

Jodie: I mean, this is not me. I am not new age. I am not woo woo. I am a doctor. I know people do strange stuff, speak in tongues, talk to spirits, but I have never experienced anything like that. I don't believe in those things. What's happening to me?

Jon: But you also said this doesn't feel like you and images that came to mind indicate that **it isn't really about you.** I don't know exactly what this is yet, but I know **it is not about you**.

Jodie: But, even if it's a past life, it is still me. I take me through each life if there are past lives, don't I? I don't even believe in past lives. What's happening to me?

Jon: It's not you in any way that we would know you to be. So, if it's past life, it's not you. The other possibility is that it's some kind of entity that got stuck in dealing with its own crap. **It's not your stuff.**

Jodie: Is that real? Past lives, entities? Do I need to be in a psych ward?

Jon: I don't even think about what's real. What I think about is how **we are going to get things better so you will be okay.**

Jodie: I don't want this anymore. I don't ever want to experience this ever again.

Jon: The thing that comes to me is that all those feelings this thing has had are coming from some sense that it needs to do something. You caught the emotion and the experience that something needs to be done.

Jodie: Yeah, like die. How do we know I'm not psychotic and I should be on some sort of meds?

Jon: There's nothing that sounds psychotic about you. There's nothing that you're saying that indicates psychosis.

Jodie: Have you heard of this stuff happening to people?

Jon: Sure.

Jodie: You said that it thinks something needs to be done. What does it want me to do?

Jon: It doesn't want you to do something. You have been picking up the emotion from it. **You are not on a ship. It is not on a ship. Nothing needs to be done about being on a ship. You are not in prison. It's not in prison. Nothing needs to be done about prison.**

Jodie: Right.

Jon: So, **you don't have to do anything** about being on the ship.

Jodie: Right.

Jon: **Be clear** on who you are and what you're up to.

Jodie: I'm who is here right now, right?

Jon: Yes. **We are very clear about** that. This other stuff doesn't matter, whether we call it an entity or a past life impression or whatever. Whatever **has been going on isn't you**. Let's wish it well. It's not trying to hurt you. That's the stuff it's been feeling, and you started feeling it too.

AS SHE THINKS OF IT AS HURT RATHER THAN TRYING TO HURT HER, THE THREAT DISAPPEARS. SHE CAN THEN JOIN ME IN BEING CLEAR, COMPASSIONATE AND WISHING IT WELL. WE WILL THEN BE IN A POSITION OF MUCH MORE POWER IN TERMS OF GETTING THINGS CLEANED UP AND CLEAR.

Jon: Let's think of it as an entity. **It's not trying to hurt you.** Let's say I was very empathic so that when somebody was with me who was hurt, I would feel hurt. Well, that wouldn't mean that the person was trying to hurt me. That's how to think of this. **It's not trying to hurt you**. It went through something traumatic. **We can take care of it. You and I can take care of it together.** Does that make sense?

Jodie: Yeah, I got it

Jon: It's been traumatized, and it doesn't yet realize **the traumatic experience is complete and finished** and, therefore, **nothing needs to be done about it.** It's experiencing a problem that actually isn't even in existence. I mean, whatever it is, is not lost on the ship at sea. If it thinks it is or has any sense of that, that's a traumatic response. It's like PTSD. The war is over, but it hasn't yet gotten that good news. Does that make sense?

Jodie: Yep.

Jon: This traumatized entity got attached to you. It's not you. It's not trying to hurt you. You were disturbed for a while, but it has been in constant turmoil. Think of how much it has been troubled if being near it was so troubling to you. **All you did was end up kind of like in the room with it for a while**. If we think of it that way, then it would be a good idea to **get this entity thing clear** from the trauma it has been troubled by.

Jodie: You're going to tell me what to do so this thing isn't around.

Jon: The thing to do for it to not be around, first of all, is to **wish it well** and understand it's not trying to hurt you. **Whatever it is that it's troubled by isn't something that actually exists. There is nothing it needs to do.**

Jodie: Why me?

Jon: You were just a convenient place to land.

Jodie: Why? Because I feel things a lot and it wants me to get something done for it?

Jon: I don't think it's that smart.

Jodie: Okay, I was just a sponge for it. How do I stop being like that?

JODIE IS LOOKING FOR WHAT THERE IS ABOUT HER THAT MAKES HER A LANDING PAD FOR TROUBLED ENTITIES. I DON'T THINK THIS IS ANYTHING TO PURSUE AT THIS TIME, SO I JUST MOVE PAST IT.

Jon: Let's just wish this thing safe travels. So, tell me something that took place while this was affecting you emotionally.

Jodie: Okay. So, I was sitting on the stairs and, all of a sudden, I just started physically feeling and experiencing like I was on a ship and it was a storm, and then, I was in the water and I was swimming and one of my kids, I don't know what kid, I couldn't find him, he had drowned. I was grieving. Then, that one was over. Then, I was holding on to the rails of the stairs and it was like I was in a jail that was like 2000 years ago and then, all of a sudden, my body just crumpled, and it was like I was crunched up.

Jon: Are those two different incidents?

Jodie: No, this was all one when I was sitting on the stairs. It was like four different lifetimes.

Jon: I don't mean different incidents for you. The entity is being affected by different events. The ship one was first, then being in the water, child drowned, in prison and being crunched up.

Jodie: Yeah.

Jon: Think of this thing, this entity, if you will, as sitting in a chair in front of you. It's been thinking that it's drowning and it's trying to--let's say it's a she-- and she's trying to save her child, but we know that she doesn't have to save her child. She doesn't have to save the child or herself or anything. She's not on a ship. She's not in the ocean. The child isn't in the ocean.

Jodie: Am I telling it that?

Jon: I'm telling you, but I am also telling it. You can tell it too, if you like. I'm telling it that it's all okay. When there is no longer worry about future or regret, what's left?

Jodie: Clear.

JODIE HAS BEEN MY STUDENT, SO SHE KNEW THE ANSWER TO THIS QUESTION RIGHT AWAY.

Jon: **And no one has to get present because everyone and everything is already present. Nothing has to be done because it has already been done**. And when that is completely understood and fully experienced, then what is felt?

Jodie: Light, light.

Jon Yes, peace and light. That is how the entity is as it realizes **that there isn't anything it needs to take care of because nothing needs to be done. It's fine. You are fine**. Does that make sense?

Jodie: I got it.

Jon: We know **it doesn't need to be taking care of anything in order to be fine. Get it that this thing is already fine. It is fine.** It's been this impression from past experiences, either real or imagined, but it doesn't matter. It's some kind of past data thing that it has <u>been</u> thinking it needs to do something about. It's <u>been</u> in turmoil, but **it can just rest and delight in its own existence.** It connects through you to me and I'm totally clear. I'm connecting through you to it and it opens to me. **There's nothing you need to do.** That message comes from me through you to it. There's nothing you need to do. Scary stuff <u>happened</u> but it is not happening, and **nothing needs to be done. You can simply be, and you are light, clear and there is peace.** What is its response?

Jodie: It's like there's a light in the middle. It's like it's opening up and there's just so much relief.

Jon: Feel loving toward the entity. Wish it well.

Jodie: It got it.

Jon: The other events all clear as well.

Jodie: Yes.

Jon: The in-prison thing?

Jodie: Yes, it got it, it got it.

Jon: Just **love it, wish it well**. Take a deep breath, exhale with eyes closed very slowly **as it just moves on into its existence of peace.**

Jodie: It's gone.

Jon: Yes.

Jodie: Oh my God, thank you.

Jon: It has been my pleasure.

Follow-Up Commentary

Jodie never had an experience like this again, but a year after we had this conversation, a child was brought to her by her parents who insisted that the illness was caused by an evil presence. Jodie told me that, somehow, she knew just what to say and do, and the child completely recovered. "We just had to love it," she told me.

Anne

Anne was 74 years old when we met. Her physician suggested she see me because she realized that Anne's emotional turmoil was exacerbating her medical issues.

Jon: Some people begin just by talking about what's been going on, and sometimes people begin by telling what they would like as a result of a meeting with me.

Anne: Well, it appears to me that my health is deteriorating rapidly in the last three or four months, and I have noticed it by not being able to function as well, when doing chores and things, and walking. I have three different kinds of arthritis, and I think that it may be from stress. I want to do something to reduce the stress that I have, and I know that a lot of it is on my part, but I'm not able to cut loose completely from trying to help or rescue those around me, even people not wanting to be rescued. My husband is very difficult to live with, the most difficult man I have ever seen in my life. Maybe it's me that's difficult, I'm not sure, but I try to help him, but he dodges it. He's not interested, and he's at the point now that he's 81 years old, he will not hear what I say, and he cuts me off completely. For instance, the other night, Friday night…

Jon: Before you go further, I'd like to tell you a little about what I'm going to do. My job is to understand you, and your job will be to make sure that I do.

I WANT ANNE TO BE ENGAGED WITH ME, NOT JUST TELLING ME, BUT ALSO COLLABORATING WITH ME TO MAKE SURE I GET IT. THIS CREATES A GREATER CONNECTION AND IS LIKELY TO PROVIDE A HIGHER QUALITY OF INFORMATION USEFUL IN CREATING A SHIFT. SINCE HER JOB IS TO MAKE SURE I DO MY JOB, IT HELPS TO BALANCE THE ONE-DOWN POSITION THE CLIENT IS IN WHEN THERE IS A PSYCHOTHERAPEUTIC RELATIONSHIP.

Anne: Yes, I want you to, surely.

Jon: I'll tell you what I've understood.

Anne: Ok.

Jon: You are bright and interested in what makes sense. You know that as things become clear, your health will improve.

BECAUSE SHE HAS STATED THAT THE PHYSICAL PROBLEMS ARE RELATED TO STRESS AND THAT SHE WANTS TO REDUCE IT, I AM ABLE TO AFFIRM THAT DOING WHAT SHE AND I ARE DOING TOGETHER WILL IMPROVE HER HEALTH. I AM COMPLIMENTING HER AT THE SAME TIME ON HOW MUCH SHE HAS BEEN ABLE TO REALIZE.

Jon: The relationship with your husband <u>has been</u> difficult, and yet you are able to **stay with it.** You care about people and you go out of your way. I know you were about to tell me about something that just happened, but I wanted to know, before you do, if there's anything that I've missed in what you've told me so far?

THIS QUESTION CREATES EVEN MORE CONNECTION. IT GIVES HER "PERMISSION" TO LET ME KNOW IF I SEEM TO HAVE NOT COMPLETELY GRASPED WHAT SHE HAS SAID. IT IS BETTER THAN ASKING HER FOR INFORMATION THAT SHE HAS NOT PROVIDED. OFTEN, THERAPISTS ASK QUESTIONS ABOUT THINGS THEIR CLIENT HAS NOT MENTIONED. I BELIEVE THAT THIS INTERRUPTS THE VALUABLE FLOW OF INFORMATION FROM THE CLIENT AND ALSO BREAKS CONNECTION.

Anne: You seem to have grasped it really good. I'd like to be able to not be overly good to him, and I want to do the right thing. Last Sunday, for instance, my husband walked off and left. He got a little perturbed at me telling him something. I was telling him to not be so abusive in certain ways. I don't remember what it was about. It is insignificant now, but I was telling him something and he walked away from the house. We live in a little country area and he walked over to his friend's house, about a mile or a mile and half away. I was not feeling well that day and had been sick with a cold. I hadn't started lunch or anything, so he walked away. I started fixing lunch when my brother called and asked me if I would like to go down to see Judy, our sister who had been in the hospital. I said I would, just to get away from the house, and I thought it would do me good just to get away. I went out to hunt for him, but I couldn't find him anywhere, and I came back about ten minutes later and told my brother I was going anyway. That's so unusual for me. It's seldom when I do that, go without telling him, but I left him a note and put the key out where he could find it when he came back to the house. I went that far, and that's beyond what I needed to do, because he didn't respect me enough to even leave a note. He didn't even respect me enough to tell me that he was going. He just does anything he wants.

Years ago, he used to go to his mother's house and eat dinner with them while I would sit home, fix and have dinner on the table. That's the kind of person I don't want to be any more and I leave him a note. I don't want to be that way anymore. I'm bad to myself. I blame myself for doing it. I go overboard trying to be good to him. I don't want to be. I don't want to give him the opportunity of saying I wasn't good to him. But I told him this when I came back home. I got home about four o'clock and I was going to fix dinner for him. He hadn't eaten lunch and it makes me mad because I do it all automatically in my life. I just feel it my duty to do it, so I do it. Anyway, he was at home when I got home. But I had left him a note, and he knew where I was. I told him, "You weren't here, and I didn't know where you were." He said, "I went over to Henry's." I said, "Well, I went out and looked for you a pretty good little bit and I couldn't understand why you would walk away without telling me." I said, "I think I'm due that respect, at least, to say I'm going over to so and so's," and he said, "Well, I just got away and I didn't think anything about it. I just went on." I said, "But you knew, when you walked away, you knew you were going. You should have at least, when you figured it out, come back and said, 'I'm going to so and so's'." Anyway, that was all that was said about it, but I felt ill at myself for leaving him a note, which he would never think about doing.

THERAPISTS OFTEN BELIEVE THAT IT IS THE CLIENT WHO SHOULD DETERMINE WHAT SHOULD BE ADDRESSED DURING THE VISIT. BECAUSE THE CLIENT IS NOT OPERATING FROM A PLACE OF CLARITY, MEANING FREE OF GUILT, FEAR, RESENTMENT AND ANGER, I DON'T BELIEVE THEY KNOW WHAT IS IN THEIR BEST INTEREST. THEREFORE, I DETERMINE WHAT IS INTENDED FOR HER AT THE HIGHEST LEVEL WHICH IS WHAT IS BEST FOR THE WHOLE WORLD, WHICH INCLUDES HER, EVEN IF IT IS DIFFERENT FROM WHAT SHE SAYS SHE WANTS. I MOVE FORWARD TO CHANGE HER MIND ON THIS SO THAT SHE WILL CONTINUE TO BE KIND AND CONSIDERATE TO HIM, BUT NO LONGER FEEL BADLY ABOUT IT.

Jon: You **follow your own nature** to **act in a kind, respectful fashion** and you have been disturbed about doing that.

I USE THE WORDS "HAVE BEEN" TO PUT IT BEHIND HER. THIS WON'T ELIMINATE THE DISTURBANCE, BUT IT DOES NOT SUPPORT OR REINFORCE IT. THE CHANGE IN TENSE IS DONE "INVISIBLY" BY SUBSTITUTING THE WORDS "HAVE BEEN" FOR THE WORD "ARE". IF IT HAD BEEN A VISIBLE TENSE CHANGE, I WOULD HAVE SAID, "IN THE PAST, YOU WERE DISTURBED" AND IT WOULD HAVE BEEN CONFUSING FOR HER. SHE WOULD HAVE VERBALLY OR NON-VERBALLY DISAGREED BECAUSE I WOULD HAVE BEEN CONTRADICTING WHAT SHE SAID.

Anne: He is due the same regard for me as I get from him!

Jon: *(Said with surprise)* You've <u>been</u> angry at yourself for doing things differently than him?

I USE HER ANGER AS A WAY TO SUGGEST THAT WHAT IS VALUABLE IS TO BE DIFFERENT THAN HIM. I WOULD LIKE HER TO CONTINUE TO BE CONSIDERATE EVEN THOUGH SHE BELIEVES HE HAS NOT BEEN.

Anne: I feel like I'm due the same respect I'm giving.

Jon: Yes, I hear that, but I get that you've <u>been</u> angry with yourself for not acting like him.

Anne: This is the part that makes me angry. I feel that I shouldn't have left the note. Not to be ugly to him, but if he's not... *(Here she pauses, looks puzzled and then there is a look of understanding)* ...I was upset because I wasn't acting disrespectful like I think he was.

Jon: Yes, I think so.

Anne: It just sounds so dumb. It doesn't sound like me to do that.

Jon: You <u>weren't</u> happy with the way he was acting, so there is no reason for you to act like him.

Anne: But I ask myself, "Why did you leave him a note? He didn't deserve leaving a note."

Jon: Because it's in your nature to be considerate.

Anne: *(She smiles and nods with understanding.)* Yeah, I know I'm trying to break my own nature.

Jon: Not only that, but you've been trying to break your own nature in order to get yourself to duplicate something you don't respect.

Anne: I guess I was.

Jon: And no wonder. How would you expect someone to break their own nature and change everything about themselves in order to model themselves after someone they don't want to be like?

Anne: Yes. You are right.

Jon: **Breathe a sigh of relief** and **follow your own nature by being kind,** no matter how you interpret his actions. In other words, **feel good** as you **follow your heart**.

Anne: You are making sense.

Jon: You were upset with yourself.

Anne: Right.

Jon: Do you still feel badly about leaving him the note?

Anne: Not anymore.

Jon: So, you can feel good about being considerate and leaving him a note.

Anne: It's wonderful. You're relieving me of the feeling I had after I left the note, and after I was kind to him. You're relieving the pressure of beating on myself for leaving him a note.

Jon: Tell me what sense it makes.

Anne: It makes perfect sense, because I feel that it's just me.

Jon: Yes, it's fine to be yourself.

Anne: It feels good. Half the pressure is off now because my actions were okay.

Jon: I am interested in how you think of things and how thoughts are structured.

I WANT TO CHANGE WHAT I AM ASKING HER TO DESCRIBE AND HOW I WOULD LIKE HER TO DO AND EXPERIENCE THINGS AS WE PROCEED. THIS EXPLANATION MAKES IT POSSIBLE FOR ME TO DO THIS. I AM LOOKING TO ACCESS A DIFFERENT EXPERIENCE AND UTILIZE THE FEELING FROM EXPERIENCING IT IN THE TRANSFORMATION THAT IS UNDERWAY. I JUSTIFY THE SHIFT BY TELLING HER I AM INTERESTED IN LEARNING ABOUT HOW HER THOUGHTS ARE STRUCTURED.

Anne: Yes, oh, good.

Jon: Tell me a place you saw that was beautiful. It doesn't matter when.

Anne: Well, we went to the mountains and the water was running down near the brook by the house, and there was snow on the ground and little particles of snow were just running down the stream.

Jon: What was the best part? What was the peak moment?

BY FOCUSING ON ONE PARTICULAR MOMENT, THE EXPERIENCE IS HEIGHTENED. THE SUBCONSCIOUS RESPONDS BEST TO SPECIFICS.

Anne: Yes, the birds. There was a bird in the morning right by the window and it was cool, but I could hear the brook. It was seven or eight years ago.

AS I SPEAK OF HER EXPERIENCE, I SPEAK OF IT IN PRESENT TENSE. I WANT HER TO HAVE THE EXPERIENCE AND THE FEELINGS NOW.

Jon: You know how it looks and how it sounds.

Anne: The birds chirping and the water running.

Jon: Please close your eyes. (*She does*) You know how it looks, how it sounds, even how it smells, and you know how you feel as the little particles of snow run down the stream. Take your own time with it.

THERE IS A SHIFT IN HER BREATHING AND THE MUSCLE TENSION RELEASES IN HER FACE AND SHOULDERS. I SEE A CHANGE IN SKIN COLOR. THESE ARE THE OUTWARD SIGNS OF A SHIFT IN HER EXPERIENCE, BOTH EMOTIONALLY AND PHYSICALLY. NOW I CAN MOVE AND SHIFT BELIEFS AND EXPERIENCES MUCH MORE EASILY.

Jon: Tell me about it.

Anne: I smelled the freshness of the air. It was crisp and felt beautiful and I could hear the birds chirping and the water running over the rocks and it was just a sound. It was so peaceful. There wasn't any conflict in my mind. It was just tranquil and peaceful.

Jon: Let's think together in this way. At that special moment, your awareness is drawn in to where, at your center, **you are peaceful and secure**. In a few moments, I'll talk to you while your eyes are closed.

I INVITE HER TO THINK WITH ME IN A PARTICULAR WAY. THIS IS MORE LIKELY TO GENERATE A WILLINGNESS TO DO SO. PSYCHOTHERAPISTS OFTEN ACCUSE THEIR CLIENTS OF BEING RESISTANT. I BELIEVE IT IS MY RESPONSIBILITY TO BE PERSUASIVE RATHER THAN HER RESPONSIBILITY TO AGREE WITH ME.

PEOPLE OFTEN SAY THAT THEY ARE THEIR OWN WORST ENEMIES, SO IT CAN FEEL LIKE THE DEEPER THEY GO WITHIN THEMSELVES, THE MORE PAINFUL THEIR EMOTIONS COULD BE. I AM CHANGING HER PERCEPTION OF WHAT I WILL REFER TO AS HER "INTERNAL GEOGRAPHY" BY TELLING HER THAT, AT HER CENTER, SHE IS PEACEFUL AND SECURE.

Anne: Okay.

Jon: What is going to happen will just happen.

Anne: Just listening to you.

Jon: Close your eyes. What happens just happens. Air...fresh and crisp...birds chirping... water running over rocks...so peaceful. You can open your eyes. What did you notice?

Anne: It's so nice. (*She smiles peacefully*)

Jon: Your awareness drifted in to where, at your center, **you are always at peace...you are fine...you are always fine**. Close your eyes...awareness drifting in to where **you are calm...you are peaceful**. Your eyes can open. What did you experience?

I EXPLAIN HER EXPERIENCE IN A VERY DIFFERENT WAY. SHE WOULD HAVE THOUGHT THAT A CERTAIN SETTING OR ENVIRONMENT CAUSED HER TO FEEL A PARTICULAR WAY. I AM SAYING THAT, IN THAT ENVIRONMENT, SHE WAS AT PEACE BECAUSE AT HER CENTER SHE IS ALWAYS AT PEACE. SHE FEELS PEACEFUL BECAUSE HER AWARENESS HAS MOVED TOWARD HER CENTER, TOWARD HER ESSENCE, TOWARD WHO SHE REALLY IS. IF, AT HER CENTER, SHE IS ALWAYS PEACEFUL, THEN SHE IS ALWAYS AT PEACE AND IT IS JUST HER AWARENESS OF BEING AT PEACE THAT MIGHT FLUCTUATE.

Anne: Very deep feeling of calm. Feeling wonderful. No pressure. No stress. Completely relieved.

PSYCHOTHERAPY IS OFTEN THOUGHT OF AS AN UNCOMFORTABLE PROCESS IN WHICH THE CLIENT WORKS ON HIMSELF IN ORDER TO FEEL BETTER AT SOME FUTURE TIME. I AM INTERESTED IN HER FEELING BETTER RIGHT AWAY, BOTH BECAUSE IT IS BETTER IN AND OF ITSELF AND BECAUSE IT MAKES THE TRANSFORMATION TAKE PLACE EVEN MORE EASILY.

Jon: It's interesting to notice what people identify with. So, if you say to someone, "Who are you?" What would he say? Someone would answer, "Well, I'm the owner of that house," or "I'm the owner of that car," or "I'm Billy's mother." It might be true that he owns a car, but it's not who he is. Our cars are not who we are. They are what we've got. We might like our cars. We might like our homes. You might like your sweater, but you know you can look at the sweater and say, "It's my favorite sweater," without thinking this sweater is yourself. People sometimes get confused between who they are and what they've been thinking and believing. "Who are you?" "I'm a Republican." Well, that's the way you're thinking about things or maybe what you have been doing, but that isn't your essence either. Some people confuse themselves with their emotions. Someone might say, "Oh, I'm sad." Well, that might be something he has been feeling, but that isn't who he is.

Anne: That's right.

Jon: And you know a lot of people confuse who they are with their occupation. "I'm a police officer," "I'm a baseball player." These are not good things to think of yourself as because at some point you stop doing them, and then where are you?

Anne: That's right.

Jon: Our hands are valuable. Our fingers are valuable and one of the most valuable fingers is the thumb. If somebody lost his thumb, if he came over to your house, you wouldn't say, "I'm glad you're here even though you're really not all here." Would you say that?

Anne: No. *(She laughs full and loud.)*

Jon: Because his thumb isn't him.

Anne: Right.

Jon: Sometimes people think they are their thoughts, but you are not your thoughts, and they aren't you. You're not your fingers, or your toes, or your nose, or your hands, or your feet, or your arms, or your emotions, or your beliefs, or what you've been doing.

Anne: That's right.

Jon: Let's think that the peace, excitement, clarity and wisdom at your center is who you are.

Anne: Yes.

Jon: And that the other stuff...

Anne: It's just stuff.

Jon: Who you are is what stays after the body falls off.

Anne: Yeah. It's the main you.

Jon: Who you are is wise...secure...calm...and at peace.

Anne: Yes.

Jon: **The light from who you are penetrates into where there were shadows.** Distorted meanings can't survive in the light.

Anne: They kind of leave or go away.

Jon: **Light always penetrates. Light wins.** It penetrates distorted impressions and meanings. Now, we can eliminate meanings that <u>caused</u> hurt.

Anne: Yes.

Jon: Does it make sense?

Anne: Yes, it does. You're very, very wonderful.

Jon: Thank you.

Anne: That is exactly what I need to hear; seeing what I was doing. Oh, it was just continuous. This is fabulous.

Jon: Your husband <u>has been</u> unhappy, and sometimes <u>has been</u> grumpy.

USING THE WORD "GRUMPY" MAKES IT LESS MALEVOLENT. HE HAS BECOME ONE OF THE SEVEN DWARFS.

Jon: Now, as **you are clear**...the brook...the birds...the smells...throwing open the window.

Anne: Fresh air.

Jon: Fresh air...he's grumbling...fresh air…the fresh air...he says words.

HER MIND HAS BEEN ATTACHING MEANING TO THE WORDS HE HAS BEEN SAYING AND THIS HAS BEEN CAUSING HER EMOTIONAL PAIN AND PERHAPS PHYSICAL PAIN AS WELL. I NOW DESCRIBE WHAT HE HAS BEEN DOING AS JUST SAYING WORDS. THIS TAKES THE STING OUT. THE FEELING OF PEACE DILUTES THE FEELING OF HURT AND BITTERNESS. THINK OF ADDING WATER TO ACID SO THAT IT CONTINUES TO DILUTE. DILUTE THE ACID UNTIL IT DISAPPEARS.

ALTHOUGH I AM DESCRIBING WHAT WILL BE HAPPENING, I DESCRIBE IT IN THE PRESENT. IT IS MORE POWERFUL FOR ME TO SPEAK IN PRESENT TENSE THAN TO USE WORDS LIKE "YOU WILL BE". IF I WERE TO SAY, "YOU WILL BE AT PEACE," IT CAN GENERATE DOUBT. SPEAKING OF THE PRESENT, SHE FEELS IT HERE AND NOW. IT IS HAPPENING AND THAT IS MORE POWERFUL AND SECURE THAN IT BEING SOMEWHERE IN THE FUTURE.

Jon: There are birds...there are words...there are birds...words...birds...words...so sometimes he says 13 words...sometimes he says 27 words...sometimes he may say about 8 words...sometimes he'll say maybe 300...400...500...600 words, but they are words...like there are birds...birds make sounds and words are sounds… birds and words and you throw the window open...there's fresh air...there he is and he's grumbling about this...goes on out the door...didn't think...out doing his thing...**you are light and easy...you follow your star. You are in tune with your nature...you are at peace with your own kindness.** The tone of the words... babbling of the brook...sounds of the birds...fresh air. Try to be troubled by it.

I AM TAKING THE MEANING OUT OF WORDS. I AM ALSO CAUSING PATTERNS OF ASSOCIATION TO DEVELOP SO THAT THINGS THAT USED TO TROUBLE HER BECOME MEANINGLESS AND THE WONDERFUL EXPERIENCE OF NATURE AND BEING WHO SHE IS OVERPOWERS AND ELIMINATES HURT AND ANGRY FEELINGS.

INSTEAD OF ASKING HER TO SEE IF SHE IS STILL TROUBLE BY THINKING OF HER HUSBAND BEING CRITICAL, I ASK HER TO TRY TO BE. BECAUSE "TO TRY" IMPLIES THE POSSIBILITY OF FAILURE, IT IS LESS LIKELY THAT SHE WILL SUCCEED IN FEELING BADLY. BECAUSE SHE DOES NOT SUCCEED IN FEELING BADLY, SHE NOTICES HOW MUCH SHE HAS ACCOMPLISHED. "TRY TO FEEL TROUBLED," IS A MORE POWERFUL STATEMENT THAN, "SEE IF YOU FEEL TROUBLED."

Anne: I can't even make it bother me. (*She is delighted.*)

PREVIOUSLY, SHE COULDN'T MAKE IT NOT BOTHER HER. THIS HIGHLIGHTS WHAT HAS BEEN ACCOMPLISHED.

Jon: You're home and he's not there. There is no note. You have the place to yourself until he pops up again. You don't know when that will be, and you **enjoy your time alone and free.** Going out...staying home...doing what you like...having something to eat...listening to something that you would enjoy...visiting a friend...making a call...totally free. He comes back in and he tells you how other people haven't been the way they were supposed to be.

Anne: Oh, yes. (*She smiles and laughs as she thinks of him complaining. It is a sweet laugh because she loves him and recognizes that this is his nature. Now, it's okay.*)

Jon: He has a lot of news to report. He's giving you this news bulletin.

CALLING WHAT HE IS SAYING A "NEWS BULLETIN" LIGHTENS IT AND TAKES THE STING OUT.

Jon: And it's about this person...and this news bulletin has about 78 words...this news bulletin has about 67 words...and this news bulletin has a bunch of other words.

WHEN I EMPHASIZE THE NUMBER OF THE WORDS, IT REPLACES THE MEANING OF THE WORDS. IT WAS THE MEANING HER MIND ATTACHED TO HIS WORDS THAT WAS CAUSING HER THE DISTRESS.

Jon: As you listen to the news bulletins and all the words...**your true nature**...**you are kind and loving**...guides what you do, and you do things your way. **You soothe him.**

I AM STATING THAT SOOTHING HER HUSBAND WHEN HE IS GRUMPY IS DOING THINGS HER OWN WAY.

Jon: And you say things like, "Gee, oh, really, no, he didn't...he did...is that right?"

HERE, I GIVE HER THE WORDS TO SAY TO HIM. SHE WON'T HAVE TO STRUGGLE TO FIND THEM BECAUSE, THIS WAY, THEY JUST FLOW.

Anne: They don't mean anything at all.

Jon: It's easy for your mouth to say words like that and there are more and more words.

BY SAYING THAT IT IS EASY FOR HER MOUTH TO SAY WORDS, IT BECOMES MORE AND MORE AUTOMATIC. IT IS MORE POWERFUL THAN TELLING HER THAT IT IS EASY FOR HER BECAUSE HER MOUTH IS THE ONE DOING IT AND SHE DOESN'T NEED TO EVEN GET CONSCIOUSLY INVOLVED IN IT. THINK OF BREATHING BEING AUTOMATIC. HABITS BECOME AUTOMATIC AND YOUR FOOT GOES TO THE BRAKE WHEN THE TAILLIGHTS OF THE CAR IN FRONT BRIGHTEN. THE WORDS ARE AUTOMATIC BECAUSE HER MOUTH IS DOING THE SAYING.

Anne: Just words.

Jon: Your mouth knows soothing things to say. Sometimes his words are loud, and sometimes they're softer. Different sounds. Different words. Different numbers of words and there are many different types of birds.

Anne: He's so critical, but I hear the birds.

HIS COMPLAINTS NOW TRIGGER THE EXPERIENCE SHE HAS ENJOYED IN NATURE.

Jon: All different kinds of things about how people are supposed to be and supposed to not be...and how they're supposed to think and act. He may say how he thinks you should act and even how you should think or feel. There will be lots of sounds like the sound of words and birds and an easy kind of flow.

A FEW MOMENTS GO BY AS ANNE IS AT PEACE AND HER MIND IS ABSORBING WHAT HAS BEEN SAID.

Jon: I learned so much from you.

PEOPLE WHO SEEK OUT PSYCHOTHERAPY BEGIN IN A ONE-DOWN POSITION. THEY HAVE PROBLEMS AND THE THERAPIST DOES NOT ACKNOWLEDGE THAT SHE DOES WELL. I BALANCE THINGS OUT BY SAYING I LEARNED SO MUCH FROM HER.

Jon: What it's like to hear the water...the birds...freshness...the smell...clear...light...joy...ease...birds...and words...like birds...flocks of birds...17 birds...35 words...secure...as **the healing within your body takes place, even much more rapidly...so much more powerfully...as there is energy...ease...and light. Health...and energy...healing...it's automatic...it just happens by itself...like a breeze.** Now, once again, your eyes can open. How does that leave you?

Anne: Real good.

Jon: Yes, you have such a kind spirit.

Anne: So, so light.

Jon: Wonderful.

Anne: I don't feel attached or that I have to respond to all the negative stuff. I can just respond like you said, you know, "Oh really", and stuff like that. I don't feel that I have to fight. I mean, it got to where it was a fight every morning when I got out of bed. I don't feel that anymore. I don't feel like it's necessary.

Jon: You've got it.

Anne: I just feel a lot better.

Jon: I'm delighted.

Follow-Up Commentary

A year after the meeting, Anne's son told me she had passed. He said that before that, time with her husband was peaceful. They became closer and she appreciated the life she had with him.

Peggy Sue

I conducted a training for mental health professionals and one of the folks who attended asked to speak with me. She told me she worked in a county mental health clinic and had been seeing a lady who seemed to be more and more troubled, isolated and spoke about wanting to die. The therapist was scheduled to see her and asked if I would come and meet with her, so I did. The heat had gone off in the clinic and it was very cold. Peggy Sue and I were both bundled up. She seemed quite despondent and it was hard to connect with her. The therapist had told her it was important to meet with me and I don't think she liked it but agreed. She was in her late thirties.

Jon: Tell me what has been happening for you.

Peggy Sue: It's all falling apart. *(softly)*

Jon: Things are not going well.

Peggy Sue: *(Nods)*

Jon: It has been very hard.

Peggy Sue: *(Nods)*

Jon: I want to understand.

Peggy Sue: Things just haven't been… *(voice hesitant, slow)* They're just not right. I'm nearly 37 years old, can't work, can't keep a job, and can't take care of my kids.

Jon: It has been hard to do what you want for your kids.

Peggy Sue: I can't keep a roof over their heads. They'll have to sleep in a cold house tonight. I can't do things for them, can't take them out to special places like kids like to do.

Jon: My job is to make sure I am following you. Your job is to make sure that I do, because I really do want to understand what's going on. What I'm understanding is that you're somebody who really loves her children.

SHE IS UPSET AND WITHDRAWN AS WE BEGIN. VERY LITTLE EYE CONTACT. I TELL HER I WANT TO UNDERSTAND. I ALSO SAY THAT WE BOTH HAVE JOBS TO DO. I AM CONCERNED ABOUT THE ONE-DOWN POSITION THAT THE CLIENT IS PUT IN AND SO, IN ORDER TO MOVE IT TOWARD MORE BALANCE, I PUT HER IN THE SUPERVISORY POSITION OF MAKING SURE I DO MY JOB.

Peggy Sue: *(Crying)* My kids are all I've got, and I can't even do for them.

Jon: You really **love your children** and you really want to **provide for them**.

I AM LOOKING TO DEMONSTRATE THAT I AM INTERESTED IN UNDERSTANDING AND THEN I AM LOOKING TO DEMONSTRATE THAT I HAVE UNDERSTOOD. IF I DO THAT BY REPEATING WHAT SHE HAS SAID, FOR INSTANCE, "YOU CAN'T EVEN DO FOR YOUR CHILDREN," THEN I HAVE SHOWN THAT I UNDERSTAND, BUT THE RESPONSE IS WHAT I CALL "POISONOUS." IT WOULD PUT SOMETHING INTO HER MIND THAT WOULD BE HURTFUL RATHER THAN HELPFUL. INSTEAD, I DEMONSTRATE MY UNDERSTANDING BY TELLING HER THAT SHE LOVES HER CHILDREN AND WANTS GOOD THINGS FOR THEM. SHE WILL AGREE WITH THIS AND IT DEMONSTRATES THAT I HAVE HEARD AND UNDERSTOOD, BUT IT DOESN'T POISON AND BRING HER DOWN.

Peggy Sue: They don't need to have fancy things. I don't mean that.

Jon: You want good things for them.

Peggy Sue: I want to be able to take them skating once in a while, take them swimming in the summertime, just little things like that, like the other kids. Their friends ask them to go do something with them and… *(her voice catches)* I don't have the money for them to do it.

Jon: You want them to have as much as you can give them that's going to be good for them, don't you? You **love them.** You're their mother. They're very important to you. *(Pause)* **You are the kind of mother that really cares**. Am I with you so far?

I DEMONSTRATE THAT I HAVE UNDERSTOOD WHAT SHE HAS SAID, AND I AM COMPLIMENTING HER AT THE SAME TIME.

Peggy Sue: Uh-huh

Jon: OK. I also understand, Peggy Sue, financially, things have been very difficult.

Peggy Sue: For a long time, it hasn't been good. I've had to depend a lot on my family to pay my bills.

Jon: Your family has given you support.

Peggy Sue: I just should be able to do it myself.

Jon: Why?

I DON'T AGREE THAT SHE SHOULD HAVE BEEN ABLE TO DO IT HERSELF. SOMETHING HAS CAUSED THE SITUATION TO BE AS IT IS AND, THEREFORE, IT DOESN'T MAKE SENSE TO SAY IT SHOULDN'T BE. IT IS TOO EARLY AND THERE IS NOT ENOUGH CONNECTION TO POINT THAT OUT TO PEGGY SUE, SO I JUST ASKED "WHY" WHICH, AT LEAST, INDICATES THAT I DIDN'T UNDERSTAND OR AGREE. IT WAS NOT AS OBVIOUS TO ME AS IT WAS TO HER.

Peggy Sue: 'Cause I'm the mommy.

Jon: **You care about them** and you want to **do what's best for them**.

Peggy Sue: I want them to have a normal life instead of them having to worry about Mama all the time.

Jon: They really love you, too.

THE CHILDREN WORRYING ABOUT HER SEEMS LIKE A BAD THING, BUT, IF THEY ARE WORRYING, THEY MUST LOVE AND CARE. SO, I DEMONSTRATE MY UNDERSTANDING BY POINTING THAT OUT.

Peggy Sue: I got good kids. I got really good kids.

Jon: You have really good children and love isn't a one-way street in your home.

Peggy Sue: No. I've got loving kids. My kids walk up to you and give you a hug. It doesn't matter who you are. They've had to take care of me several times.

Jon: You have raised children who are responsible and loving.

IF THEY TOOK CARE OF HER, THEY ARE RESPONSIBLE AND LOVING. AGAIN, I AM SHOWING THAT I AM HEARING HER. SHE HAS NOT DISAGREED WITH ME. WHAT I AM SAYING IS POSITIVE AND COMPLIMENTARY.

Peggy Sue: They have some friends that have real fancy clothes and things like that. I just want to be able to provide the necessities for them. We're not picky. We don't have to have fancy houses and clothes, cars, and stuff like that. Of course, they're kids. They want the toys. They are kids.

Jon: Sure. And you want them to have the best you can give them. In some ways, it seemed other kids have gotten more than your kids, just like in other ways **your kids have gotten more than other kids have gotten.**

Peggy Sue: I guess? *(Doubtfully or questioning)* I just want to be able to provide for them.

Jon: Now, just let me make sure that I understand. Keep making sure that I know what you're talking about. As I follow you so far, in some ways, other kids have had more stuff than your kids.

I HAVE REMINDED HER THAT SHE HAS A JOB TO DO AND HER JOB IS TO MONITOR HOW WELL I AM DOING MY JOB.

Peggy Sue: Yeah, they don't have to worry about...

I KNOW SHE IS ABOUT TO TELL ME THAT OTHER KIDS DON'T HAVE TO WORRY ABOUT THEIR MOTHERS. I INTERRUPT BECAUSE THAT WOULD NOT HAVE BEEN A USEFUL THING FOR HER TO HEAR FROM ME, SO IT ISN'T A USEFUL THING FOR HER TO SAY TO ME. WHAT'S SAID MAKES AN IMPRESSION JUST LIKE WHAT IS HEARD, PERHAPS EVEN MORE. INSIGHT-ORIENTED THERAPISTS ENCOURAGE PEOPLE TO SAY MORE AND MORE ABOUT FEELING BADLY. HEARING THESE TROUBLING THINGS FROM OTHERS WOULD BE DISTURBING AND SAYING THEM WOULD BE DISTURBING AS WELL. PEOPLE WHO ARE SPEAKING ARE ALSO HEARING WHAT THEY ARE SAYING.

Jon: Your kids have had less of some stuff than other kids and your kids have gotten more of some very valuable things than other kids get. So, your kids, in spite of having gone through not having as much stuff, or maybe because of it, are, in some ways, a cut above a lot of kids.

Peggy Sue: Yeah, how?

SHE WAS IN HER OWN WORLD WHEN I MET HER. SHE DIDN'T LOOK AT ME AND SPOKE SOFTLY. NOW, SHE IS INTERESTED, AND SHE EVEN ASKED ME A QUESTION.

Jon: **They are caring, mature, open and loving.** Those are things that have more value than designer sneakers.

Peggy Sue: Yeah.

NOW, THERE IS AGREEMENT ABOUT SOMETHING I SAID THAT IS POSITIVE ABOUT HER AS A MOTHER.

Jon: **You are successful** in the way **you provide what is important.**

Peggy Sue: That was the easy part.

Jon: And it's even been easy for you.

SAYING THAT IT IS THE EASY PART DEVALUES THE ACCOMPLISHMENT. I TURN THAT BY SAYING, "IT'S EVEN EASY FOR YOU," WHICH GIVES HER CREDIT. SHE DOESN'T DISAGREE. SHE IS LOOKING AT ME AND MUCH MORE CONNECTED. THE VOLUME OF HER VOICE HAS INCREASED.

Peggy Sue: Uh huh.

Jon: OK. I'm following you.

Peggy Sue: It should be for everybody!!

Jon: Well, that would be nice, wouldn't it?

SHE AND I SHARE THE SAME VALUE AND THE CONNECTION INCREASES.

Peggy Sue: I guess it's too much to ask for today.

Jon: Many kids aren't getting loved the way your kids are getting loved. In some ways, your kids have gotten less stuff than other kids, and, **in the way that is most important, your kids have their baskets filled to abundance.**

THE WORD "STUFF" IS SAID IN A TONE THAT DEVALUES ITS IMPORTANCE.

Peggy Sue: Yeah.

I WAS ABLE TO GIVE HER A BIG COMPLIMENT ON HER EFFECTIVENESS AS A MOTHER AND IT WAS ACCEPTED.

Jon: **You are caring and loving** and want even more.

Peggy Sue: I just don't want them to worry about whether they're going to have food to eat or they're going to have heat to stay warm or boots to wear if it goes to snowing tomorrow.

Jon: Right! You're caring and want what's going to work out in the best way for your children and in many ways, Peggy Sue, **you've provided them with much more than many children get,** and you want them to be comfortable and secure. Is there anything you've told me that I didn't pay attention to?

Peggy Sue: No.

Jon: Then what else should I know to really get it, because I want to really understand.

SHE STARTS TO CRY, BUT SHE IS MUCH MORE CONNECTED WITH ME THAN SHE WAS WHEN WE BEGAN.

Peggy Sue: I don't know.

Jon: *(Very gently) What's* going on for you?

Peggy Sue: *(Crying)* I got to be better.

Jon: Better at what?

SHE SAYS "BETTER" AS IF IT IS AN ATTRIBUTE. I ASK ABOUT IT AS IF IT WAS A BEHAVIOR. IT IS POSSIBLE TO CHANGE A BEHAVIOR, BUT NOT AN ATTRIBUTE. IT'S BETTER IF IT'S ABOUT SOMETHING SHE HAS BEEN DOING OR NOT DOING RATHER THAN ABOUT WHO SHE IS.

Peggy Sue: At all of it. *(Sobbing and looking away)*

Jon: Peggy Sue, let's stay in touch with each other while we're talking about this. I've got it that **you love them**, that **you care about them** and you are looking to **make things better**.

BY SAYING, "LET'S STAY IN TOUCH WITH EACH OTHER," I AM BRINGING HER BACK IN TO CONNECTION WITH ME.

Peggy Sue: *(Talking through tears)* I've got to be a better provider.

Jon: I understand what you are saying.

Peggy Sue: I got to be a better person. *(still crying)*

Jon: Peggy Sue, I understand your desire to give them more stuff, but there is more.

Peggy Sue: I don't know what it is! *(Talking through the tears--voice anxious)*

Jon: I don't know what you mean by being better as a person.

THE INNER MIND DOESN'T KNOW WHAT A BETTER PERSON IS, SO CAN'T PROVIDE IT. IT ISN'T SOMETHING THAT CAN BE DONE, AND IT ISN'T SOMETHING THAT NEEDS TO BE ACCOMPLISHED. IT ISN'T ANYTHING THAT EVEN EXISTS. I DON'T POINT THOSE THINGS OUT TO HER BECAUSE IT IS MORE BENEFICIAL FOR HER TO EXPERIENCE BEING REALLY LISTENED TO INSTEAD OF HAVING ME POINT OUT AN ERROR IN HER THOUGHTS.

Peggy Sue: I got...to...get...things...together! *(slow, loud, frustrated)*

Jon: Stay with me, Peggy Sue. Tell me. *(Pause)*

Peggy Sue: *(Crying)* I don't want to just tell my kids I love them; I want to feel it. When they tell me, they love me, I want to feel it.

Jon: Tell me.

Peggy Sue: There are times they come to hug me, or they come up and tell me, "I love you," and I just want to SCREAM.

Jon: Of course.

SHE IS SAYING THAT SHE HAS BEEN FEELING LIKE SHE DOESN'T ACTUALLY LOVE HER CHILDREN. THIS IS VERY PAINFUL FOR HER AND IT'S SOMETHING SHE HAS MOST LIKELY BEEN ALONE WITH. IT IS A HARD THING TO FEEL OR SAY BECAUSE MOTHERS ARE "SUPPOSED TO" LOVE THEIR CHILDREN. I AM GLAD SHE IS CONFIDING THIS IN ME SO THAT SHE IS NOT ALONE WITH IT AND SO THAT I HAVE THE OPPORTUNITY TO DO SOMETHING WITH IT. WHAT HAPPENED ABOVE PROVIDED ENOUGH OF A CONNECTION SO THAT THIS PAINFUL IDEA COULD BURST OUT OF HER. I WANT TO DO MORE, THOUGH, THAN OFFER CONNECTION AND "HEAR HER CONFESSION". I AM LOOKING TO TRANSFORM HER EXPERIENCE REGARDING WHAT SHE HAS BEEN FEELING AND HER EXPERIENCE OF WHO SHE IS.

Peggy Sue: Just scream at them, "DON'T TOUCH ME!" That's not fair to them. Sometimes, I feel like I'm giving so much out, but I don't have anything coming back in.

Jon: Sometimes, because of your love, there's <u>been</u> frustration at not <u>having been</u> able to do all that you want...Sometimes, so much frustration that you <u>wanted</u> stuff to just stop...Sometimes, so much frustration that you just <u>wanted</u> to scream, all because of the fact that there <u>is</u> so much love.

I USE PAST TENSE FOR THINGS I WOULD LEAVE BEHIND AND PRESENT TENSE FOR WHAT I AM <u>LOOKING</u> TO BRING FORWARD. CHECK THE UNDERLINED WORDS FOR THE TENSE I USE. "FRUSTRATION" IS IN PAST TENSE AND "THERE IS SO MUCH LOVE" IS IN PRESENT.

Peggy Sue: But why? *(Starting to tear)* Why can't I feel it? *(Sobbing)* I mean, when I get mad, I feel it.

Jon: Yes.

Peggy Sue: When I get sad, I feel it.

Jon: Yes.

Peggy Sue: Why can't I feel the other?

Jon: The sadness you've felt came from the love that's there within you. Sometimes it's been sad, sometimes it's been frustrating, angry or tense. Sometimes it's been like wanting just to disappear, all based on wanting to **be good**, wanting to **do well** because **you care about them** and **you care about your own well-being**. And there's been frustration. You've been focused on what **you would like to give to them** because **you love them**. You've been blinded to how **you provide them with what is of great value**, but **it can't be denied**.

Peggy Sue: You are right. I've fought my family over that *(resolutely, jaw set)* 'cause I've told them, "I've done a good job with my kids."

Jon: YES! And you know that.

Peggy Sue: I've got good kids.

Jon: And you know that. Right! Exactly!

Peggy Sue: Part of it is their own personalities, but part of it is because I was there.

Jon: You being there is what's central and essential.

Peggy Sue: I'm not perfect. I yell and scream at them too much, but I've even worked on that.

I NEVER ADDRESSED THE ISSUE OF NOT FEELING LOVE BECAUSE I FELT IT WAS A NON-ISSUE. IT WAS HER INTERPRETATION OF FEELING PRESSURED, DEPRESSED AND FEELING A NEED TO ISOLATE. I AM AFRAID THAT MANY THERAPISTS WOULD HAVE GONE DOWN THE RABBIT HOLE AND BEGUN EXPLORING WHY SHE DOESN'T LOVE HER CHILDREN. THEY WOULD HAVE AGREED WITH WHAT SHE SAID ABOUT NOT LOVING, PERHAPS NOT DIRECTLY, BUT BY LOOKING FOR THE SOURCE. I BELIEVE THE RESULTS OF THAT WOULD HAVE BEEN QUITE HARMFUL. INSTEAD, I TELL HER THAT SHE DOES LOVE HER CHILDREN AND THE FRUSTRATION THAT SHE HAS CONFUSED AS A LACK OF LOVE ACTUALLY COMES FROM LOVE. INSTEAD, SHE IS ACCEPTING AND AGREEING WITH MY COMMENTS THAT SHE HAS DONE A GOOD JOB WITH HER CHILDREN.

Jon: Good! And **you worked on all that!**

Peggy Sue: I don't always make it, but I've...

Jon: Yeah! Yeah! Good!

MOOD IS MUCH DIFFERENT NOW. SHE WAS EXPERIENCING DESPAIR AND NOW SHE IS APPRECIATING HER CHILDREN AND HERSELF.

Peggy Sue: I've got good kids.

Jon: Yes, **you are a good mom and you have great kids.** Does it seem that I'm understanding?

Peggy Sue: Yes.

I JUST TOLD HER THAT SHE IS A GOOD MOM AND THAT SHE HAS GREAT KIDS. SHE AGREED. THIS IS SO DIFFERENT THAN IT WAS WHEN WE BEGAN.

Jon: Good. *(Pause)*

Peggy Sue: It's just, I've got to get a job, *(voice soft, hesitant)* so I can pay the rent, pay the bills. When they need clothes, I can get them clothes. And maybe, every once in a while, we can go out and do something special.

SHE IS NOW LOOKING FORWARD AND MIND IS FOCUSED ON WHAT SHE COULD DO THAT WILL HAVE BOTH BENEFIT AND POSSIBILITY. PEOPLE FREQUENTLY TELL THEIR THERAPISTS THAT THEY LACK MOTIVATION AND THE THERAPIST IS LIKELY TO BEGIN EXPLORING WHY THAT IS SO. WHEN YOU LOOK FOR A REASON FOR SOMETHING, YOU ARE IMPLICITLY STATING THAT THE REASON YOU ARE LOOKING FOR ACTUALLY EXISTS. PEOPLE THINK OF MOTIVATION AS A QUALITY OR AS IF IT IS SOMETHING THAT DOES OR DOES NOT EXIST WITHIN SOMEONE. WHEN SOMEONE SEES WHAT COULD BE OF BENEFIT AND WOULD BE POSSIBLE AND THE MIND ATTACHES INTEREST AND APPEAL TO IT, THEN IT WILL MOTIVATE ACTION. IT ISN'T A QUALITY AND IT CERTAINLY SHOULDN'T BE UNDERSTOOD THROUGH THE USELESS LENS OF MORALISTIC JUDGMENT.

Jon: Uh huh. Uh huh. *(Voice soft, reassuring)*

Peggy Sue: Something special is having pizza delivered and just playing a game or just watching a show that we've all been wanting to see.

Jon: Yes, I understand.

Peggy Sue: It doesn't take a whole lot.

Jon: You give them a great deal of what is really important.

Peggy Sue: Right. I mean, sometimes, but you know for the last three Christmases I haven't even been able *(crying)* to buy them Christmas. For their birthdays, they didn't get anything but a birthday cake from me last year and they never complained, neither one of them.

Jon: It's because they are wonderful kids. They have a mother who is loving and effective.

I AGAIN COMPLIMENT HER ON HER CHILDREN AND ATTRIBUTE IT TO HER.

Peggy Sue: Uh huh.

Jon: Good mom.

Peggy Sue: Yes, I am.

SHE IS SEEING THINGS IN A MUCH MORE USEFUL WAY.

Jon: Absolutely. Absolutely. *(Pause)* Peggy Sue, tell me about a place that you remember being, maybe a place outdoors that was particularly beautiful.

I AM LOOKING TO CAUSE AN EXPERIENCE THAT WILL BE USEFUL IN SHIFTING HER EXPERIENCE AND TRANSFORMING HER SENSE OF WHO SHE IS.

Peggy Sue: I can give you a couple of places.

Jon: Give me one to start.

Peggy Sue: Out in the wheat fields with my daddy.

Jon: Uh huh.

Peggy Sue: Watching the combines cut the wheat, playing in the back of the grain trucks. *(She smiles.)*

Jon: The wheat fields with your daddy and playing in the back.

I USE PRESENT TENSE TO CAUSE HER TO HAVE THIS EXPERIENCE. SOME THERAPISTS TRY TO BRING PAINFUL EVENTS INTO THE PRESENT SO THAT THEIR CLIENTS WILL RE-LIVE THE EXPERIENCE IN A "SAFE PLACE" IN ORDER TO FEEL AND EXPRESS PAIN. I AM BRINGING A POSITIVE EXPERIENCE INTO THE PRESENT SO THAT THE FEELING FROM IT CAN BE USED TO PROMOTE THE DESIRED CHANGE.

Peggy Sue: The grain truck in the wheat. *(Eyes close, still smiling)*

Jon: Grain truck…wheat fields.

Peggy Sue: Wheat fields.

Jon: Yeah!

Peggy Sue: Way out in the open.

Jon: All *(pause)* open.

Peggy Sue: Nothing around, just the wheat fields.

Jon: And the sky, and the wheat, and playing in the back, and it's all open, and it stretches, FAR. And it's FAR…and to feel it, feels…

IT IS ALL PRESENT **TENSE**; IT'S ALL HAPPENING NOW. IT IS WORKING BECAUSE OF THE CONNECTION THAT HAS BEEN BUILDING SINCE WE MET. VARIOUS ASPECTS OF OUR MEETING COMBINE TO WHERE THE COMMAND "TELL ME ABOUT A PLACE THAT YOU REMEMBER BEING" RESULTS IN THIS PROFOUND EXPERIENCE.

Peggy Sue: Free.

Jon: Free.

Peggy Sue: And my daddy's there.

Jon: Uh huh. And FREE is like...light.

Peggy Sue: LIGHT!

Jon: Yeah!

Peggy Sue: Sun shining.

Jon: Sun shining.

Peggy Sue: Warm.

Jon: Warm sun against the skin, light on your eyes, and warmth on your skin. There's a smell. *(pause)*

INVOLVING THE OLFACTORY SENSE CAN MAKE THE EXPERIENCE STILL MUCH STRONGER.

Peggy Sue: Dirt. *(laughs)*

Jon: Uh huh.

Peggy Sue: Dust and chafe.

Jon: Uh huh. And the dust and the dirt…

Peggy Sue: And snakes *(laughing again)*.

Jon: Yeah. Yes. Exactly. And the earth...

Peggy Sue: It's just clean.

Jon: Right.

Peggy Sue: It's open and it's clean.

Jon: Yeah.

Peggy Sue: Birds...flying across the sky.

Jon: Right. Free...and there are birds...there's earth...**at your center, you are always secure and free**. In this experience, you experience your own center. You are experiencing **who you actually are**. Everything is open and there's dirt and wheat and sky, there's warmth on the skin and a cloud moves, automatically, and things come together. And, when you want to, you can open your eyes. *(After a while her eyes open.)*

SHE HAS THIS PROFOUND EXPERIENCE AND THE FEELINGS THAT IT GENERATES, AND I TELL HER THAT SHE IS EXPERIENCING HERSELF, HER ESSENCE, AND HER CENTER. I CONNECT THOSE THINGS HAPPENING IN THE ENVIRONMENT WITH WHO SHE IS AND WHAT I AM INTENDING FOR HER.

Peggy Sue: I am going to get a job, stand on my own two feet, pay my own bills and take care of my kids. I know I'm a good worker.

Jon: You are a good worker, a good mom, and a good person.

Peggy Sue: Sometimes, I think I get too picky...maybe that's part of the problem 'cause I know the type of job I want, and I know I'd be good at it.

Jon: You know what you can do.

Peggy Sue: I can't seem to get those abilities across to the interviewer.

Jon: You haven't seen opportunities.

Peggy Sue: I think I'm not motivated enough. I don't put enough energy in.

Jon: Motivation hasn't been the issue. It was about opportunity. When you see something that makes sense to you and is **possible, there will be plenty of motivation. You will begin to see opportunities. They will jump out at you.**

SHE HAS SAID THAT SHE CAN'T. I DON'T TELL HER SHE IS WRONG, BUT I OFFER A DIFFERENT VIEW. PEOPLE ARE FREQUENTLY ACCUSED OF NOT BEING MOTIVATED. THINKING OF IT IN THAT WAY IS NOT USEFUL. HOW WOULD THE IDEA OF NOT BEING MOTIVATED BE MOTIVATING? I DON'T TELL HER THAT THERE HAVEN'T BEEN OPPORTUNITIES BECAUSE THEN WE WOULD HAVE TO CHANGE HER ENVIRONMENT IN ORDER TO SHIFT THINGS. I TELL HER SHE HASN'T SEEN OPPORTUNITIES AND THEN I TELL HER THAT SHE WILL BEGIN TO SEE THEM. FOR SOMETHING TO BE AN OPPORTUNITY, IT WOULD HAVE TO BE BENEFICIAL, POSSIBLE AND INTERESTING. IT IS MY JOB TO GET HER MIND READY TO SEE OPPORTUNITY.

Peggy Sue: I'm lost.

Jon: I haven't been clear.

WHEN SHE SAYS SHE IS LOST, I PUT IT ON ME BY STATING THAT I HAVE NOT BEEN CLEAR. I TAKE RESPONSIBILITY FOR OUR FAILURES AND GIVE HER CREDIT FOR THE SUCCESSES.

Peggy Sue: I just wasn't seeing it?

Jon: Opportunities will be more obvious. It becomes clear what there is to do.

Peggy Sue: For right now, I may have to start at waitressing instead of continuing to look for the job that I want. I enjoy waitressing, meeting the people.

Jon: You enjoy meeting people.

Peggy Sue: I **love** working with people.

Jon: Meeting with people, working with people, being with people. You know how to be with people, and you like to work with people.

Peggy Sue: I like that part.

Jon: Yes!

SHE HAS BEGUN TO SEE OPPORTUNITY SO THAT SHE WILL MOVE FORWARD.

Peggy Sue: But waitressing is no challenge. I get bored.

Jon: As you are waitressing, there are people. You like contact, there is contact. You'd like even more of a challenge.

Peggy Sue: Yeah.

Jon: As you waitress, **you will be involved with people and you love that,** and **your eyes are open for other opportunities,** where there'll be more challenge and more interest.

Peggy Sue: Like on my days off, I can go look for something else. I just never make it out there to that something else.

"NEVER" IS PAST, PRESENT AND FUTURE. IT IS MY JOB TO GET "NEVER" OUT OF HER FUTURE.

Jon: You connect with people and **you can hear something, see something, find something, learn something.**

Peggy Sue: I can do this. I can do all of it. (*She speaks with strength and power.*)

DOING WHAT WILL HAVE VALUE HAS BECOME POSSIBLE AND INTERESTING.

Jon: You can waitress and you can connect with those people that you serve the food and talk to and, of course, your co-workers.

Peggy Sue: You only got to hear about one of the two places. We were out one day with friends, out there on the mountain.

SHE WANTS TO TELL ME ABOUT OTHER STUFF. HER MOOD HAS CHANGED. SHE IS TAKING CHARGE.

Jon: Yeah!

Peggy Sue: It's so pretty out there.

Jon: Yes.

Peggy Sue: And it's kind of funny because it's the exact opposite of the wheat fields. It's green, it's cool, snow all over, water flowing down the side of the mountain, trees all over the place. It's cold.

Jon: Your eyes may feel to close. *(Slowly, they do so.)* Trees all over the place. Cold snow. Cold. *(Pause)* Clear. *(Pause)* Trees. *(Pause)* To look, feel, touch the air there. To breathe…cold.

ALL OF THIS IS SAID IN PRESENT TENSE TO CONNECT HER EVEN MORE FULLY WITH THE EXPERIENCE. WHEN DESCRIBING AN EXPERIENCE SOMEONE HAS HAD, YOU NEED TO MAKE SURE NOT TO CONTRADICT ANYTHING THAT DID HAPPEN. I USE HER WORDS SO THAT I WON'T BE WRONG. IT WOULD BE A MISTAKE TO PARAPHRASE BECAUSE THAT WOULD BE DESCRIBING HER EXPERIENCE DIFFERENTLY THAN SHE DESCRIBED IT AND IT IS LIKELY TO BACKFIRE.

(Peggy Sue takes a deep breath.)

Jon: Yes…special place…you glide within and greener and more and further. Trees. And inside **things move together automatically**. Your mind is tuned up and cleared. You naturally understand and automatically follow through with those things that are in your long-term best interest. And the air, because **things just heal…and ease**. *(Pause)* Friends…snow…actual snow…actual snow. **At ease with yourself. Feeling good with your kids.** You find that you **do what makes sense**, you **spot opportunities, take the steps, stuff works out, short time, long run, all in between, falling together.** A special kind of air there…a special kind of clean…air…green. Tell me more about this place.

I CONNECT HER EXPERIENCE WITH THE INTENDED TRANSFORMATION.

Peggy Sue: Little animals…

Jon: Yes!

Peggy Sue: So cute and quick, sometimes almost still though, sometimes still.

Jon: Yeah…and then…what? And then still…

Peggy Sue: Walk through the trees.

Jon: Uh huh. *(Whispers)* You can hear things. *(Again whispers)* You can hear things.

I WHISPER TO HER AS IF WE ARE IN THE WOODS TOGETHER AND LISTENING FOR THE SOUNDS AND TRYING NOT TO ALARM THE ANIMALS.

Peggy Sue: A kind of rustling in the background.

Jon: Yes. *(Still whispering)*

Peggy Sue: The bushes.

Jon: Yes!

Peggy Sue: I can hear them, but it's all so quiet.

Jon: Yes.

Peggy Sue: We were...a family up there.

Jon: Family.

Peggy Sue: Yes. *(Emphatically)*

Jon: You really **connect and enjoy**, and **open up to things around you**, and **move into things**, and **see and respond to opportunities**.

Peggy Sue: Still got some dreams.

Jon: Dreams are clear and are good.

Peggy Sue: It'd be nice to have security.

Jon: Even sitting here, freezing cold room, **you are secure** as you **touch inside**, inside where **you are secure.**

Peggy Sue: *(Vague, relaxed)* I have to be careful of those spots. I have to be careful. I have to stay away from other things around it...but those were nice. *(Stretching)*

THERE WERE APPARENTLY EXPERIENCES THAT SHE HAS HAD THAT WERE QUITE DISTURBING. SHE SEEMS TO WANT TO AVOID THE MEMORY.

Jon: Things that **you have completely and totally survived...and finished** and absolutely can do you no harm. **You survived. The bad stuff is finished.** *(Pause)*

ALTHOUGH I DON'T KNOW WHAT "THE OTHER THINGS" WERE, THEY ARE NOT HAPPENING AT THE MOMENT, SO SHE HAS SURVIVED. I WANT HER ENTIRE MIND TO GET THAT GOOD NEWS. THEN, THERE WILL BE NOTHING SHE NEEDS TO STAY AWAY FROM.

Peggy Sue: I still hurt, but it's not as bad as it used to be.

BECAUSE OF WHERE WE ARE IN OUR VISIT, I DECIDE TO DEAL WITH THIS ISSUE WITHOUT ASKING QUESTIONS ABOUT THE SPECIFICS. I CAN SENSE WHAT TO SAY THAT WILL PROMOTE CLEARING WITHOUT ASKING HER FOR INFORMATION ABOUT THE EVENT THAT HAS COME TO MIND. THERE IS NO TIME DURING THIS MEETING TO GO FURTHER INTO THOSE EVENTS AND I AM CAREFUL NOT TO OPEN UP WHAT I DON'T HAVE TIME TO CLOSE.

Jon: It's done, and you've made it through, and that's over. It doesn't have to hurt anymore. You've finished with it. It can't hurt you again.

Peggy Sue: Thinking that...that...it doesn't have to hurt anymore *(voice soft, unfocused, pondering).*

Jon: **It doesn't have to hurt anymore.** *(Firm statement)*

IMPRESSIONS FROM PAST EVENTS ARE CLEARING.

Peggy Sue: I think sometimes I'm afraid that in some ways I might forget.

Jon: Ah! You will remember what you need.

Peggy Sue: But I don't want to forget any of it.

SOMETHING TOOK PLACE THAT IS IMPORTANT FOR HER TO REMEMBER, BUT I AM SUGGESTING THAT IT CAN BE REMEMBERED WITHOUT CAUSING HER PAIN.

Jon: You will remember whatever is important whenever it's important. You can remember and realize **it's done**. *(Pause)* Realize **it's done, all the way through, all the way down, all the way in, all the way out, up and down, and all the way through. Completely, totally, every part of you, knowing what's finished is finished** and you can remember **and know it's done** because everything you can remember has already happened. **You're in the present. Everything that can be remembered is past.**

Peggy Sue: I did it right.

Jon: Yes.

Peggy Sue: I do feel that I did it right.

Jon: There's much to feel that sense of pride and accomplishment about.

Peggy Sue: There is a sense of pride and accomplishment.

Jon: You did it right.

Peggy Sue: *(Deep breath)* Everything's OK. I did it right.

Jon: Tell me.

Peggy Sue: It helps to know...I'm not perfect, but I did what I thought was right at the time. And I never set out to hurt anybody else either. *(Pause)* They just can't understand that.

Jon: Because **there are things that are, and they just are, whether they're understood or not. Things are just the way they are,** just the way they are, and they are, and that's how it is, and that's it.

HER SENSE WAS THAT WHAT HAPPENED WASN'T FAIR AND THAT HAS MADE IT DIFFICULT TO ACCEPT. IN ADDITION, IT SEEMS LIKE OTHERS DISAPPROVE OF HER RESPONSE TO IT. MY GUESS IS THAT SOMETHING WAS DONE TO HER AND SHE REPORTED IT AND HER FAMILY DISAPPROVED OF HER ACTIONS, BUT, OF COURSE, THAT'S JUST A GUESS. IT WOULD NOT HAVE BEEN WRONG TO ASK HER FOR MORE INFORMATION, BUT IT WOULD HAVE OPENED SOMETHING ELSE UP AND I BELIEVED A LOT HAD BEEN ACCOMPLISHED ALREADY. IT WAS ALREADY LATE AND GETTING DARK. IT WAS STARTING TO SNOW AND THERE WAS NO HEAT IN THE ROOM WE OCCUPIED. IT IS TIME TO CLOSE THINGS DOWN RATHER THAN OPEN THEM UP.

Peggy Sue: I keep telling myself just because it's not fair doesn't mean it's going to change. Got to keep going.

Jon: And **you keep going,** and **you do keep going,** and it wasn't fair. **And you've done what made sense. It doesn't need to be understood because it just is.** Things **that you thought you had to get together are getting together automatically** while we're talking to each other. **Things shift, fall into place, so that it's automatic.** *(Pause)*

Peggy Sue: Come together. Take care of my kids. I've got good kids.

Jon: Oh, yes. You're doing fine with raising them to be good people and other things will open up and you'll see how to move, what to do. Other things can open later.

I AM ENCOURAGING HER TO MOVE AHEAD AND DO WHAT SHE CAN DO WHILE STAYING ALERT TO OTHER OPPORTUNITIES. THIS WAY, SHE IS NO LONGER STUCK.

Peggy Sue: I can wait *tables*.

Jon: Yes.

Peggy Sue: I can get that job and do what there is to do.

Jon: **You can get things done**. It's automatic to **do what makes sense. You'll just see it** and you **find yourself doing what really makes sense to do**. Yes, absolutely. On track, there's a shift, automatic.

Peggy Sue: *(Big smile)* I can't be too bad a person, can I?

Jon: **You are good, Peggy Sue, that's absolutely right.** I want you to drive very, very slow tonight. Real slow.

IT HAD BEEN SNOWING DURING OUR MEETING AND I WANT HER GETTING HOME SAFELY.

Peggy Sue: I always do *(smiling)*. People holler at me about my driving. "You're slower than Christmas." I just say, "I'm going to make it in my own time."

Jon: Good for you. I really, really enjoyed getting a chance to talk to you.

Peggy Sue: I haven't thought about those places for a long, long time.

Jon: You brought them to life for me. Thank you. I enjoyed being with you.

MY COMMENTS ON HOW I ENJOYED HER AND HOW SHE BROUGHT THINGS TO LIFE FOR ME BALANCE THE RELATIONSHIP THAT IS STRUCTURED TOWARD THE CLIENT BEING IN A ONE-DOWN POSITION.

Follow-up Commentary

Three months later, in a follow up discussion with the counselor who referred Peggy Sue, I learned that there has been no further incidence of suicidal thought. She has found work and feels much better about herself. The counselor who arranged our meeting still meets with her, but not nearly as often.

Bryan was 47 years old at the time of our meeting.

Jon: You believe that something has continued to affect you. I want to understand.

Bryan: Yes, when I was in about the fourth grade, the effect was probably anger at my parents. The long-term effect is that I'm not able to get close to animals. We have a dog, and I don't have any feelings toward this animal.

Jon: I would like you to think about a little puppy and notice what you experience.

Bryan: Okay.

Jon: What was it like?

Bryan: It was okay.

Jon: Did you imagine touching it?

Bryan: I petted it on the head.

Jon: Did it seem to feel affection for you?

Bryan: Yes, it kind of raised its head up.

Jon: What did you notice feeling?

Bryan: It wasn't uncomfortable, but I felt indifferent.

THIS PROCESS ESTABLISHED A BASELINE AND PROVIDES ME WITH A CLEARER UNDERSTANDING OF WHAT IT IS BRYAN EXPERIENCES. LATER, I CAN ASK HIM TO CHECK IT AGAIN SO THAT HE KNOWS THERE HAS BEEN AN IMPROVEMENT. I ENTER EVERY MEETING WITH THE BELIEF THAT THIS WILL BE MY ONE AND ONLY OPPORTUNITY TO MAKE A DIFFERENCE FOR THIS INDIVIDUAL. I DON'T WANT PEOPLE TO LEAVE ME HOPING THAT THINGS MAY CHANGE LATER. I WANT THE INDIVIDUAL TO LEAVE CERTAIN THAT ISSUES HAVE NOT ONLY BEEN ADDRESSED, BUT ALSO RESOLVED.

Jon: Before this thing happened, did you feel any affection toward animals?

Bryan: Yes, I had several pets as a child.

Jon: And you felt close?

Bryan: I felt close to these pets.

Jon: Do you recall an experience that seemed to change that?

Bryan: *(He shows a great deal of tension as he describes this event, but his voice remains soft and flat.)* I had a caramel-colored cat, and I couldn't find it one day. In fact, it was several days before I found it on the road, and a car had hit it. I decided I was going to bury it, so I put it into a shoebox. Then my parents got a movie camera and were filming this whole process and laughing, thinking it was cute. Then I buried it, and that was it.

Jon: You <u>did</u> not like the way your parents acted.

Bryan: I'd say that, for sure.

Jon: What did it mean when your cat died?

Bryan: It meant that another one of my animals had been run over. *(Frustrated)* This was not the first one. It seemed like every time I got another animal, it got run over.

Jon: I understand. That is a very hard thing for a child go through. And as you buried the cat?

Bryan: Well, it just seemed it didn't really matter that my cat had died, and it wasn't private. I felt embarrassed because the cat was already beginning to stink, and I was making faces, and the flies were all around us and I was trying to bat the flies away.

Jon: And your parents?

Bryan: They were invading my space. It was very intrusive.

Jon: I understand. That's what I needed to know. Thank you. Next, I would like to suggest a process in which you imagine that you are talking with yourself at an earlier age. Would that be all right?

Bryan: Sure.

THE WAY WE EXPERIENCE EVENTS IS LARGELY DUE TO THE MEANING OUR MIND ATTACHES TO THOSE EVENTS. THE MEANING IS RELATED TO PRIOR EVENTS AND THEIR MEANINGS. IN ORDER TO CHANGE THE MEANING OF THIS EVENT AND, THEREFORE, CHANGE THE EFFECT IT HAS HAD, I ENCOURAGE BRYAN TO MEET WITH HIS "YOUNGER SELF" AND, THROUGH A SERIES OF EXPERIENCES AND CONVERSATIONS, PREPARE HIM FOR A CHANGE IN THE MEANING AND, THEREFORE, THE IMPACT OF THE EVENT HE HAS JUST DESCRIBED. IN THIS WAY, HE EXPERIENCES A DIFFERENT HISTORY. I INVOLVE HIM IN THE PROCESS OF CHANGING THE EXPERIENCE OF WHAT HAPPENED TO HIM SO THAT HE EXPERIENCES THE POWER OF CREATING HOW HE FEELS FROM NOW ON BY CHANGING HIS REACTION TO THINGS THAT HAPPENED EARLIER IN HIS LIFE.

Jon: Conceive of the way you might have looked when you were, let's say, three years old. Imagine this three-year-old doing something fun.

Bryan: Okay.

Jon: Okay, what's he doing?

Bryan: He's playing with some blocks.

Jon: Good. I'm going to ask you in a moment to close your eyes and imagine you are going to enter the room where he's playing. Give him a smile. He will be glad to see you. Let him know you will be back, and when you are finished open your eyes.

Bryan: Okay.

I BEGIN WITH A FAST AND EASY TASK AND THEN CHECK ON HOW HE DID. THIS WILL BE LIKE WALKING UP A STAIRCASE BY MAKING STEADY, STEP-BY-STEP PROGRESS.

Jon: Good. What I'd like you to do now is to go back there and see him again, maybe a little later in that day. He'll recognize you and it'll be fun for him to see you again as you pop-in for the second time. You could show him something he can do with the blocks.

Bryan: I taught him to build a tower.

Jon: Let's imagine that you have been having regular contact with him, doing fun things with him for about a year, and he is now four years old. Tell him something fun that he'll learn from. I don't know whether you will tell him that when he looks at a tree, there is much hidden below the ground or how planets revolve around the sun. You make it fun and it is also educational. Close your eyes, take your time and when you are finished open your eyes.

BRYAN CAN PREPARE YOUNGER SELF TO DEAL WITH THE TROUBLING EXPERIENCE OF BURYING THE CAT BY SHOWING AND TEACHING HIM THINGS SO THAT WHEN THE EXPERIENCE OF BURYING THE CAT TAKES PLACE, HIS "YOUNGER SELF" WILL BE PREPARED.

Bryan: Okay.

Jon: Good, what did you teach him?

Bryan: Well, we started talking about the trees and everything. We had a bunch of pine trees in our yard, and I was showing him how tall some of them are. He got really curious about the pinecones.

Jon: Wonderful. Meet him again, let's say another year later, but let's imagine that you have been visiting together frequently. This time show him an ant farm or a beehive behind glass. *(Bryan closes his eyes and takes a few moments to complete this.)* And now, another year has passed. You have been together regularly. He'll have a complaint about something, it may be about some other kid he has to deal with, or it may be about something going on with his parents. I don't know what he's going to complain to you about but talk with him in a way that helps him move ahead toward better times.

Bryan: His parents had been arguing. Now, he knows things will be okay. This is good.

HE HAS THE EXPERIENCE OF HELPING HIS "YOUNGER SELF" DEAL WITH A PROBLEMATIC SITUATION IN PREPARATION FOR THE DAY OF THE CAT BURIAL.

Jon: Teach him about tadpoles and how they stop being tadpoles and become frogs. Teach him how caterpillars are transformed into butterflies.

I WANT TO OPEN UP THE POSSIBILITY THAT HE COULD SEE DEATH AS A TRANSITION RATHER THAN AS THE END.

Bryan: Okay. *(Minutes go by and finally his eyes open.)*

Jon: What happened?

Bryan: A lot of things. He was looking at each one. I guess I was trying to show him each little thing you told me. I was trying to show him that he's even going to change, and that he's constantly changing.

Jon: There are two girls, each playing with their own dollhouse. The first girl is playing with a small dollhouse and it's extraordinary and intricate. Each tiny piece has so much detail you would need a magnifying glass to fully appreciate it. The other girl has a much larger dollhouse, but it's crude. You have to use quite a bit of imagination to realize it is supposed to be a house. She likes it because it's big, and she makes fun of the girl who is playing with the smaller dollhouse because hers is bigger. This does not disturb the girl playing with the smaller dollhouse since she is into what she is doing. Discuss this with young Bryan and learn what he thinks about it. *(Pause)* What did he think of it?

Bryan: He was very intrigued with the miniature dollhouse and it interested him much more.

Jon: What did he think of the other girl?

Bryan: The mocking girl?

Jon: Yes.

Bryan: Well, he was not wanting to hurt her feelings, but he didn't think much of her dollhouse.

Jon: What about her behavior?

] with her behavior or her dollhouse.

ER ONE. I AM LOOKING TO CHANGE THAT PERCEPTION FOR BRYAN. SO, I HAVE
T NECESSARILY BETTER AND NEXT MOVE ON TO LONGER ISN'T BETTER EITHER.

)ne has a phonograph record that is very small, but has a very
three minutes in length; it's very short to listen to, but very
kid has a big scratchy record. It wasn't very good to listen to
itched, but it's a very big record. It can play scratchy tinny music
with the bigger record is making fun of the one with the smaller
s and see how he feels about it. There is a group of people
t gets higher in pitch until a human can't hear it. There is a dog
ear the sound, but the people think the sound has stopped
rry for the sound because they think it is gone. Show him this.
) have developed a great deal of affection for a caterpillar and,
as the caterpillar is transformed into a butterfly, they think it has disappeared. They feel sorry for it. Show him. Show him a little fish. When the body of the fish dies, there is transformation. He can't see it like he could with the butterfly, just as people couldn't hear the sound as it became too high in pitch. Teach him death is an illusion based on our limited senses.

I AM SUGGESTING THAT WHAT THE SENSES BRING IN IS NOT ALWAYS TRUE AND THAT, BECAUSE SOMETHING APPEARS TO NO LONGER EXIST, THAT THIS DOES NOT MEAN IT ISN'T ACTUALLY STILL THERE. GRIEF IS A RESPONSE TO PERCEIVING SOMETHING AS LOST. I AM LOOKING TO CHANGE HOW HE EXPERIENCES THE PASSING OF HIS ANIMALS AND OTHERS AS WELL.

Bryan: Yes, he understands. I understand as well now. It's different.

HE IS LEARNING AS HE IS TEACHING.

Jon: There's a girl who has a parakeet that she loves very much. The parakeet dies or, perhaps, is transformed. The girl is very sad for the parakeet. Young Bryan sees this, knowing the parakeet has been transformed. He feels compassion for the girl but knows that the bird has been transformed and the bird is fine. The girl will be fine as well.

Bryan: All right.

Jon: So, how's he doing?

Bryan: He's doing fine, and he was able to help her to feel better.

Jon: Tell me about a time when you felt thrilled.

Bryan: Hitting an ace in tennis, really being able to put the racket on it.

Jon: Take him into the future and show him what is in store for him. He's going to be impatient to do it. Tell him he will have to wait a little while.

DISTURBING EVENTS OFTEN SEEM LIKE THEY WILL NEVER END. IN ORDER TO CHANGE HIS EXPERIENCE OF A DISTURBING EVENT, I HAVE HIM CAUSE THE YOUNGER SELF TO BE AWARE THAT DURING A DISTURBING EVENT HE IS ON THE WAY TO SOMETHING WONDERFUL.

Bryan: *(Smiling)* He doesn't want to wait.

Jon: Good job. A little girl has a doll she is quite attached to and the doll gets broken. Her parents care about her and love her. She is upset, and they are touched by it. These parents are inept. They're loving, but buffoon-like. They photograph her while she is upset talking about how sweet she looks. They're kind of like a guy who's got a crush on a lady he wants to impress, but, while he thinks he is presenting her with a beautiful bouquet, it's actually a bunch of stinkweeds. Help young Bryan understand they are misguided rather than mean. *(His eyes close for a while.)*

Jon: Tell me.

Bryan: He was hurting for the little girl. He's telling the parents to put the camera down, that their daughter needs them to comfort her.

THIS EVENT WAS MUCH CLOSER IN PARALLELING BRYAN'S OWN EXPERIENCE. IN THIS SITUATION, HE WAS ACTIVE IN CONFRONTING THE PARENTS RATHER THAN STOIC AS HE WAS DURING THE EVENT THAT AFFECTED HIM. I AM DOING THIS TO CAUSE THE FEELING OF LOSS TO DISAPPEAR AND ALSO TO RESOLVE THE RESENTMENT TOWARD HIS PARENTS.

Jon: Let him see that the little girl will be fine. Show him there are wonderful things in store for her.

DISTURBING EXPERIENCES FEEL LIKE THEY WILL NEVER END AND MAY SLAM INTO THE INDIVIDUAL'S MIND AS AN EVENT THAT IS NEVER ENDING. EVEN THOUGH, INTELLECTUALLY, ONE REALIZES THAT THE EVENT ITSELF IS NO LONGER HAPPENING, THE MIND HAS TAKEN IT IN AS CONTINUING FOREVER AND THIS THEN INFLUENCES HOW MIND PERCEIVES LIFE EVENTS THAT HAVE A SIMILAR STRUCTURE. IMAGINE A HAND SLAMMING INTO SAND AND LEAVING A HANDPRINT. THE HAND IS NO LONGER THERE, BUT THE SAND THINKS IT STILL IS. IT SEEMS THAT BRYAN'S AFFECTION FOR THE CAT LED TO THE EVENT HE FOUND HUMILIATING AND SO HIS MIND HAS TURNED OFF THE FEELING OF AFFECTION TOWARD ANIMALS. PSYCHOTHERAPISTS WHO TRY TO FIND MEANING IN THINGS MIGHT SUGGEST THAT THE MIND TURNED FEELINGS OF AFFECTION OFF IN ORDER TO PROTECT HIM FROM FURTHER HURT. I HAD A SENSATION OF BURNING IN MY LEG ONE DAY, BUT I KEPT DOING WHAT I WAS DOING AND EVENTUALLY THAT PLACE ON MY LEG BECAME NUMB. I DON'T BELIEVE THAT THIS NUMBNESS OCCURRED IN ORDER TO PROTECT ME FROM FURTHER BURNING. OUR SUBCONSCIOUS MIND IS REACTIVE RATHER THAN PROACTIVE.

Jon: Show him a little boy who is sad about the death of a little rabbit. He will see it with wise eyes knowing that the rabbit is no more gone than the caterpillar. He will feel compassion for the little boy, but he knows things work out.

THE EXPERIENCE OF RABBIT DYING BECOMES LIKE THE EXPERIENCE OF A CATERPILLAR AS IT IS TRANSFORMED INTO BUTTERFLY. I AM IMPLYING THAT DEATH IS NOT AN END, BUT INSTEAD, A TRANSITION WHETHER WE CAN SEE IT LIKE WE DO WITH

CATERPILLAR OR CANNOT SEE IT AS WITH RABBIT. THE MUSICAL NOTE EXISTS EVEN WHEN THE HUMAN EAR CANNOT HEAR IT. THE RABBIT HAS TRANSITIONED JUST LIKE THE CATERPILLAR, EVEN THOUGH, IT CAN'T BE SEEN THROUGH THE SENSES.

Bryan: I was showing him, and I don't know why I was doing this, but I was showing him the future and some of the people he will get to be with.

Jon: Yes, exactly. When things <u>appear</u> to die, he understands that **what appears to have disappeared has been transformed and continues.** His concern is for the person that's out of hearing range rather than for the note he no longer hears. You can tell him that there will be pets he will love, and they will move out of the range of his senses. He's not concerned about how long things last. He'd rather listen to a really beautiful song for just five minutes than music he doesn't care for all day. Let him know about the quality of the animals he's going to be with. Let him know that the length of time before transformation will be short.

(His eyes rest closed for minutes. Sometimes he smiles. Then I continue speaking.)

Jon: There is a wedding and the couple getting married are excited with each other. There are a number of people watching the wedding. Some of them just think it's so sweet, but others think it's stupid. These two people are involved with each other. They are the players. The players may affect the audience, but the audience doesn't affect the players.

HIS PARENTS WERE THE AUDIENCE. THE AUDIENCE DOES NOT AFFECT THE PLAYERS. HE WILL NOT BE AFFECTED BY HIS PARENTS' BEHAVIOR WHEN HE BURIES THE CAT BECAUSE THEY ARE THE AUDIENCE. HE CAN AFFECT THEM, BUT THEY CAN'T AFFECT HIM.

Jon: He's on his way to wonderful experiences. He wants to see the best movie, not the longest. He is a player and not concerned about the audience. He is on his way to that tennis game. You're with him as he enjoys his cat and when the cat's body dies, its essence moves out of the range of his senses. He's with the cat's body on the road. He's burying the cat's body and has a knowledge of change and transformation. There are plants in the yard. His parents are in the yard, and trees are in the yard, and the job is done. He's playing tennis, he's feeling the thrill of really putting the racquet to it, and there's something else, there's something wonderful. What was that like for him?

I EMPHASIZE THAT THE JOB IS DONE SO THAT MIND STOPS EXPERIENCING THIS AS HAPPENING.

Bryan: Exciting.

I SURROUND THE PARENTS BEING THERE WITH TREES AND PLANTS BEING THERE SO THAT THE PARENTS BEING THERE LOSE ANY SPECIALNESS. I DESCRIBE THE EXPERIENCE OF FINDING AND BURYING THE CAT'S BODY AS A BRIEF INTERLUDE ON THE WAY TO SOMETHING WONDERFUL. THE MEANING OF THIS EVENT HAS CHANGED, AND IT GOES BY QUICKLY.

Jon: Please close your eyes again and find the little three-year-old you first met. Feel your consciousness move into the child and look out through the child's eyes. You are three and looking up at a friendly man who's smiling at you. He speaks with you and shows you such interesting things: pinecones, butterflies, frogs, dollhouses, musical notes, pets, tennis and up to the present to look ahead with wisdom and ease. Take your time and, when you feel ready, your eyes will open. How's that?

Bryan: That was amazing. I feel so much better. I can go to the scenes, especially where the cat's death was, and not feel like crying or anything like that. I am able to experience things for what they are and move on. It feels natural.

Jon: Yes. Close your eyes. Think about a little puppy licking your fingers. You can open your eyes.

Bryan: That feels really good.

Jon: They're fun and sweet, aren't they?

Bryan: Yes. I just feel like they're wanting to be petted and wanting some attention. It feels good. I would like to do that.

Jon: I enjoyed our time.

Follow-up Commentary

Bryan's wife got in touch a few months later. She told me that he had formed a closer relationship with both of his parents, but particularly his father. Their dog, who used to keep its distance from Bryan, now follows him around.

Janet was referred by her gynecologist. She told me that Janet had been traumatized when she miscarried and that she experiences physical and psychological symptoms.

Jon: I know your doctor suggested me and I am looking to be valuable to you. What should I understand?

Janet: I miscarried two and a half years ago and, since then, I haven't been able to get pregnant. It's not a matter of not really being able to. It's more that I'm afraid to. When I'm ovulating, I can't go through with it. I'm blocking it, I guess, in my own way.

Jon: If I understand what you're saying, you haven't been having sex at times you might get pregnant.

Janet: I want to, but I can't. It's very frustrating for me. For a while there, everything, my body even, started telling me I was pregnant. I would go through these ups and then find out that I wasn't. I used to be very regular and then I started getting a week late. That's never happened before except the one time I was pregnant. Now, it happens often. I also get other symptoms that make me think I am pregnant when I'm not. That is why my doctor says I should see you.

Jon: It seems, on one level, you would like to **get pregnant and have a baby.**

BECAUSE OF THE FEAR, THERE IS CONFLICT.

Janet: Yes, but I didn't handle it well when I miscarried. I'm not sure how I would handle it if it happened again.

SHE HAS BEEN IN CONFLICT. SHE WANTS TO HAVE A BABY BUT THE LAST TIME SHE TRIED WAS VERY BAD FOR HER. WHAT MADE IT SO PAINFUL WAS THE WAY HER MIND RESPONDED TO WHAT HAPPENED. HER MIND PROCESSES DATA OUTSIDE OF CONSCIOUS AWARENESS. THE DATA INCLUDES INFORMATION INCOMING THROUGH HER SENSES BUT ALSO THE MEANINGS THAT HER MIND ATTACHED TO THE DATA. SHE IS ALSO BEING AFFECTED BY DATA FROM PRIOR EXPERIENCES AS WELL AS DATA THAT HER MIND CREATED. HER MIND HAS BEEN CAUSING EMOTION AND THOUGHT IN ORDER FOR HER TO ACT AND DEAL WITH THINGS THAT ARE NOT EVEN IN EXISTENCE. IF I ADJUST THE WAY HER MIND IS RESPONDING TO WHAT HAPPENED, THE CONFLICT THAT HAS BEEN SO DISTURBING WILL RESOLVE AND SHE WILL BE READY TO MOVE FORWARD.

Jon: When you were pregnant, it didn't work out and you felt a great deal of emotional pain.

Janet: I was very depressed and upset about it. I kind of flipped out there for a while.

Jon: What about the miscarriage was most disturbing to you?

PEOPLE DON'T USUALLY ASK QUESTIONS LIKE THAT. INSTEAD, THEY TRY TO UNDERSTAND OTHER PEOPLE BY TRYING TO UNDERSTAND HOW THEY THEMSELVES WOULD RESPOND IN A SIMILAR SITUATION. THIS IS WHAT THEY CALL "EMPATHY". I AM INTERESTED IN WHAT SHE HAS BEEN EXPERIENCING AND SHE IS THE BEST ONE TO TELL ME ABOUT THAT.

Janet: I guess because I don't know if there was something I did that caused it.

Jon: Why?

Janet: I'm an athlete and I was playing volleyball after I found out I was pregnant. The doctor said that it would be all right that I continued doing things that I was already doing, but he did suggest that I not dive. I've played pretty serious ball. I went right over a chair that I didn't know was there. I was playing in the sand. It was a white chair and it blended right in.

Jon: *(Incredulous)* You have been blaming yourself? For what?

Janet: Well, he told me not to dive and I obviously wasn't following the doctor's orders.

PEOPLE GROW UP EXPOSED TO A MORALISTIC VIEWPOINT SUGGESTING THAT, IF THEY ARE GOOD, THINGS WILL GO WELL. IF THINGS DON'T GO WELL, MANY PEOPLE BLAME THEMSELVES OR BLAME OTHER PEOPLE. SOME PEOPLE BLAME GOD. I DON'T BELIEVE THAT GUILT OR ANY BLAME IS PRODUCTIVE. SO, I AM LOOKING TO MAKE IT DISAPPEAR FOR JANET.

Jon: He said, "don't dive." He didn't say don't trip.

Janet: *(Laughter)* No. This was just a thought.

Jon: It's thoughts that <u>have been</u> so disturbing. Does that make sense?

Janet: Yeah, definitely.

Jon: It's been like a soundtrack.

Janet: It just kind of happens.

Jon: The feeling just kind of happened when certain thoughts...

PEOPLE ARE OFTEN TOLD THAT THEY NEED TO STOP CONDEMNING THEMSELVES AND TO, INSTEAD, THINK MORE POSITIVELY. I THINK THE THEORY IS IF YOU CAN CONVINCE PEOPLE THEY ARE RESPONSIBLE FOR THEIR THOUGHTS THAN THEY CAN CHANGE THEIR THOUGHTS. I DON'T THINK PEOPLE ARE CHOOSING THEIR THOUGHTS AND I THINK THAT TO SUGGEST THAT A PERSON HAS CHOSEN THE WRONG THOUGHTS CAN LEAD THEM TO THINK THAT THIS IS NOW SOMETHING ELSE THEY HAVE DONE WRONG. INSTEAD, I SUGGEST TO JANET THAT THE THOUGHTS HAVE JUST BEEN HAPPENING. I SUGGEST WE THINK OF THEM AS A SOUNDTRACK PLAYING IN THE BACKGROUND, BUT NOT ONE THAT WAS CHOSEN.

Janet: Right.

Jon: Kind of happened?

Janet: Yeah. *(Laughter)* I would think, "God, how could you have screwed this one up?"

Jon: You think God screwed it up? *(I purposely misunderstand her last comment.)*

Janet: No. I think I screwed it up.

Jon: You said, "God, how could you have screwed this up?" Were you referring to yourself as God? *(Light and fun)*

Janet: *(Laughing hard)* Oh, no. Oh, no.

Jon: Was it a prayer?

I AM BEING LIGHT AND PLAYFUL, AND SHE IS CONNECTING WITH ME. HUMOR CAN BE VERY USEFUL BOTH IN CREATING THE FEELING OF CONNECTION AND BONDING AS WELL AS CHANGING PERSPECTIVE. I WATCH FOR HER RESPONSE TO LEARN IF HUMOR WITH HER IS USEFUL AND, IF SO, WHAT WILL WORK.

Janet: Good grief! *(Laughter)* Just stop it! You know what I am trying to say.

Jon: Have you ever been outdoors? *(This is a silly question, but I definitely have her attention and the atmosphere is light and fun.)*

Janet: Yes, of course.

I AM LOOKING FOR HER TO ACCESS THE FEELING THAT CAME WITH A VERY SPECIAL MOMENT AND THEN TO UTILIZE THAT FEELING TO CREATE A SHIFT.

Jon: Tell me about a place that was wonderful.

Janet: The woods!

Jon: I'd like you to think of a particular moment, a wonderful moment, and tell me about it.

Janet: When I was a little girl, probably about seven years old, I was camping with my parents and I woke up. There were these sounds.

Jon: What were the sounds?

Janet: Ker plunk. Ker plunk.

Jon: Yes.

Janet: The birds were singing. The light was just coming up and I jumped up immediately, as quietly as possible. Very quietly, I unzipped the door of the tent. When I stuck my head out, I was growled at. *(Laughter)* So, I jumped back in really quickly.

Jon: What was growling?

Janet: It was a raccoon. *(Laughter)*

Jon: Was it the raccoon making the "ker plunk"?

Janet: No. There was also a deer.

Jon: What was the best part of that?

Janet: That I was a part of it.

Jon: Yes, you are peaceful and excited.

Janet: Oh, yeah!

Jon: Let's think the beauty that surrounded you caused your awareness to move in toward your center where **you are always excited and at peace.**

ALTHOUGH THIS IS DIFFERENT THAN THE WAY MOST PEOPLE THINK AND DIFFERENT THAN THE WAY SHE HAS BEEN THINKING, THERE IS ENOUGH CONNECTION THAT SHE BUYS-IN IMMEDIATELY. I AM ALSO GETTING A BUY-IN BECAUSE I USE THE WORDS "LET'S THINK". I AM ASKING HER TO THINK IN A PARTICULAR WAY. I AM NOT ASKING HER TO CHANGE HER BELIEF ABOUT WHAT IS TRUE.

Janet: Cool.

Jon: I'm going to take you through a short process. The only purpose is for you to acquire the experience of hearing me speak while your eyes are closed.

Janet: Okay.

Jon: Don't even bother to try to relax.

Janet: All right.

Jon: Just close your eyes. Now your eyes are closed and I'm talking to you. And therefore, you're having the experience of hearing me speak to you while your eyes are closed. Once again, you can go ahead and open your eyes. I'm interested in what you noticed within you during those few moments.

Janet: I just felt fine. I was comfortable.

WHEN GOING THROUGH A PROCESS AND ASKING THE CLIENT TO CLOSE HER EYES, IT MAKES SENSE TO CHECK QUICKLY ON HER EXPERIENCE. IF SOMEONE IS UNCOMFORTABLE, THE SOONER I REALIZE IT THE BETTER.

Jon: Close your eyes again and we'll do a little more. I mentioned to you that it wasn't necessary to put any effort into trying to do anything. It isn't even necessary for you to put any kind of effort into trying to relax *(slower)* and yet, you mentioned **feeling fine, feeling comfortable** and so it comes to mind to tell you that **feeling comfortable can be pleasant** and yet it's not required. In terms of what we are here to accomplish, it's not important. *(pause)* Once again, you can open your eyes. Tell me what you were noticing.

IT CAN BE HARD FOR PEOPLE TO RELAX WHEN THEY FEEL IT IS IMPORTANT TO DO SO. THIS PROCESS ENCOURAGES RELAXATION BY TELLING THE PARTICIPANT THAT RELAXATION IS NOT IMPORTANT.

Janet: *(Pause)* I felt relaxed, very relaxed.

Jon: Let's think that you become aware of your center where **you are always at peace**. People think it is important to feel good. Would you agree?

Janet: Sure.

Jon: People believe that doing well is important in order to feel good. They also believe it is useful to make people feel badly so they will do better when they are not doing well. It's how the school system works. That's why they give people detention. It's how the prison system works and that doesn't work at all. Millions of dollars go into it trying to get people to feel badly so they act better. It's everywhere. You can't breathe the air in this culture without catching that notion. It's important to feel good, it's important to do good in order to feel good and people make other people feel bad in order to get them to do better. Our own minds make us feel bad in order to get us to do better. Am I making any sense?

Janet: You're making sense. It's sad, but you're making sense.

Jon: Feelings are not inside you. The feelings that have troubled you come from thoughts. Some of these thoughts were conscious and others were outside of awareness, but you didn't decide to have the thoughts. Think of the thoughts that have been disturbing as a soundtrack. You just sort of heard them inside. So, what's on the soundtrack? It basically says something like, "You've screwed up again!" It takes it for granted that you would screw up and, yet, it manages to be shocked, nonetheless.

BY DESCRIBING HER EXPERIENCE OF "THE SOUNDTRACK" BOTH ACCURATELY AND HUMOROUSLY, I STRENGTHEN THE EXPERIENCE OF CONNECTION AND PRESENT AN OPENING FOR CHANGE. I WANT HER TO EXPERIENCE WHAT HAS BEEN CAUSING HER DISTRESS AS WELL INTENTIONED, BUT NOT WELL FUNCTIONING. I WANT HER TO REALIZE IT HAS COME FROM OUTSIDE OF AWARENESS. SHE DIDN'T DO IT ON PURPOSE, AND SHE COULDN'T HAVE NOT DONE IT.

Janet: That's exactly what happens. *(Laughter)*

Jon:	Guess what it's trying to do.
Janet:	Trying to make me feel bad.
Jon:	So that you will…?
Janet:	Learn or something. I don't know.
Jon:	It's trying to make you feel bad so that you'll do well so that you will…?

I PAUSE HERE TO GIVE HER A MOMENT TO FIGURE IT OUT. THIS HELPS KEEP HER ENGAGED.

Janet:	(*Exasperated*) So that I'll feel good?
Jon:	Yes, it's trying to cheer you up.
Janet:	Good grief!
Jon:	Right. The purpose of the soundtrack is and has been to cheer you up. The way it attempts to cheer you up is by telling you one of two things. It sometimes tells you you're bad, and sometimes it tells you you're inept.
Janet:	It usually tells me both.
Jon:	Yes, it does and that proves it makes no sense. You can't be both.
Janet:	Why not?
Jon:	If someone means to do harm, we could call that "evil". If someone does something wrong accidentally, then we could call it "inept". It seems like it would have to be one or the other.
Janet:	I guess that's right.

INSTEAD OF TELLING HER SHE IS TELLING HERSELF THESE THINGS, I ATTRIBUTE IT TO THE SOUNDTRACK. THEN, I BEGIN DESTROYING THE CREDIBILITY OF THE SOUNDTRACK. I DO THAT FIRST BY SUGGESTING THAT IT HAS BEEN TELLING HER TWO DIFFERENT THINGS AND THAT THOSE THINGS CONTRADICT EACH OTHER. THEN, I WILL GO ON TO SUGGEST THAT THE SOUNDTRACK IS INEPT BY TRYING TO MAKE HER FEEL BAD IN ORDER TO GET HER TO DO WELL AND FEEL GOOD. AS ITS CREDIBILITY DISAPPEARS, IT NO LONGER HAS THE SAME EFFECT. AS THE EFFECT IS DIMINISHED, THE SOUNDTRACK WILL FADE AWAY.

Jon:	Listen to it and notice what it's trying to accomplish. Listen to it while keeping in mind that it's attempting to cheer you up. (*Pause*) What happens as you hear it that way?
Janet:	It's always telling me I should have done better or been more careful or tried harder.

Jon: It is trying to cheer you up by telling you you're inept. It's inept and nothing it says makes sense.

Janet: Right. Exactly. You don't tear someone down to build them up.

Jon: What does the soundtrack want you to feel?

Janet: If I look at it the way you have explained it to me, the soundtrack wants me to feel good.

Jon: Imagine feeling like the soundtrack really wants you to feel, like in the woods feeling excited and peaceful. Hear it and imagine feeling the way it wants you to feel.

SINCE THERE IS NOW AGREEMENT THAT THE SELF-CRITICAL VOICE OR "SOUNDTRACK" IS TRYING TO GET HER TO FEEL GOOD, WE BRING ITS INTENTION INTO BEING BY RELIVING THE EXPERIENCE IN WHICH SHE FELT VERY GOOD. I THEN POINT OUT THAT THIS WILL IMPROVE PERFORMANCE SO THE SOUNDTRACK, WHICH IS HER MIND TRYING TO IMPROVE HER ACTIONS, LEARNS A BETTER WAY.

Janet: I feel better. I don't feel scared.

THE CREDIBILITY AND POWER OF THE SELF-CRITICAL VOICE IS DIMINISHED, AND SHE IMMEDIATELY FEELS BETTER. IT WASN'T THE STUFF THAT DID HAPPEN OR THAT MIGHT HAPPEN THAT HAS BEEN CAUSING THE PAINFUL FEELINGS. IT WAS THE FEELING THAT HER MIND CREATED WITHIN HER.

Jon: As **you do things, feeling peaceful and excited,** you do them at least as well and probably much better than you would have done them feeling scared. Isn't that so?

Janet: Yes.

Jon: Your mind actually wants you to **enjoy the experience of excitement and peace,** which you have gravitated toward and have shown a deep appreciation for in a number of ways. It was approaching this the way it was because of the beliefs and experiences that happened to you. ***Your beliefs were because of things that happened and things you were told. So, your beliefs actually happened to you just like your experiences happened to you.***

PSYCHOTHERAPISTS MOST OFTEN TRY TO MAKE THEIR CLIENTS TAKE RESPONSIBILITY FOR THEIR THOUGHTS, FEELINGS AND ACTIONS. I AM DOING THE EXACT OPPOSITE. THERAPISTS ACCUSE PEOPLE OF CARRYING THEIR BELIEFS AND SUGGEST THAT THEY LET THE BELIEF GO. I AM SAYING THAT THE BELIEF HAPPENED TO HER IN A SIMILAR WAY THAT THE WEATHER HAPPENS TO PEOPLE

Janet: That makes sense.

Jon: You now know what motivates the soundtrack. You can embrace what it's attempting to do. Do you know what I mean?

Janet: Yes.

Jon: The soundtrack wants you to be happy. The more desperate it has gotten to secure your happiness, the more inept and useless its attempts have been. It wanted you to be happy in pregnancy and in giving birth, but in order to try to get you to feel good, it has been making you feel badly and sometimes freakin' awful.

I WANT JANET TO KNOW THAT I HEARD HER EARLIER WHEN SHE SPOKE ABOUT HOW TERRIBLE SHE FELT WHEN THE PREGNANCY ENDED. SHE NEEDS TO KNOW THAT I GET IT IN ORDER FOR HER TO ACCEPT THE THINGS I AM TELLING HER. I NEED HER TO UNDERSTAND THAT I UNDERSTAND HOW PAINFUL THIS HAS BEEN.

Janet: I felt I was to blame. I felt like a terrible person.

Jon: When someone trips, it has nothing to do with being bad. You and I grew up in a culture in which people got yelled at for making mistakes. People end up feeling guilty and getting depressed. Raccoons and deer don't do that. That is one of the things that draw you to them.

I UTILIZE HER OWN EXPERIENCE IN NATURE TO AFFIRM WHAT I AM SAYING AND IMPLY THAT SHE IS ALREADY DRAWN TOWARD THIS WAY OF BEING. IT'S IMPLIED THAT THERE IS AN OPENNESS TO THIS WITHIN HER. PSYCHOTHERAPISTS ARE LIKELY TO BRING INTEREST AND CURIOSITY TO WHAT THEY WANT LESS OF. BIOFEEDBACK IS EFFECTIVE BECAUSE IT CAUSES THE CLIENT TO NOTICE WHAT WOULD BE GOOD TO INCREASE. I AM DOING THE SAME THING AS I EXPLAIN THAT SHE IS ALREADY AWARE OF WHAT I AM SAYING AND THAT IS WHY SHE IS PLEASED WITH NATURE. I AM USING THE EXPERIENCE SHE HAD IN THE WOODS TO PROVE MY POINT.

Janet: Wow! Yes, of course.

Jon: They don't get embarrassed.

Janet: Right. They just are.

Jon: They have something to teach us, these animals. You know that. You wanted to complete the pregnancy and give birth. It didn't happen and that's it. That's how it would be for any other life form. But our human minds are more complicated and, hence, much more prone to error. Let's take a closer look because our looking at it together will destroy distortion and bring clarity. Does that sound okay?

Janet: Yes, that makes sense. Even though people care about me and, of course, my husband cares, I feel like I have been alone with this.

Jon: Okay, here we go. What about the miscarriage has been disturbing?

Janet: I guess it's the disappointment.

JANET'S REACTION WAS SO HUGE THAT I SENSE THAT IT IS BEYOND JUST THAT. I PUSH A BIT FURTHER, SO I CAN UNDERSTAND AND REMEDY WHATEVER IS GOING ON.

Jon: There has been more to it. What else?

Janet: I feel I caused the baby harm or that I caused it to feel pain.

Jon: Do you think the baby's in pain now?

Janet: I don't know. I don't know what I think.

HER MIND HAS BEEN CAUSING INTENSE AND ONGOING EMOTION AND THAT IS WHAT HAS BEEN CAUSING HER PAIN. THE MIND CAUSES EMOTION IN ORDER TO CAUSE AN ACTION. HER MIND HAS BEEN ATTEMPTING TO GET HER TO DO SOMETHING TO PROTECT HER BABY FROM PAIN THAT SHE BELIEVES HER ACTIONS CAUSED. THE EMOTION SHE HAS BEEN FEELING HAS NOT BEEN DESIGNED TO MAKE HER FEEL BAD, BUT, RATHER, TO GET HER TO DO SOMETHING. IT HAS BEEN TRYING TO GET HER TO DO SOMETHING THAT CAN'T BE DONE AND DOESN'T NEED TO BE DONE BECAUSE WHAT IT IS TRYING TO GET HER TO DO IS ABOUT SOMETHING THAT DOES NOT EXIST. THIS IS AN EXAMPLE OF HOW COMPLICATED AND DYSFUNCTIONAL THE HUMAN MIND IS.

Jon: Have you been thinking it's possible that the child is in pain now?

Janet: It might be in hell. *(Said with fear and horror.)*

Jon: In hell?

Janet: Yeah.

Jon: How would it get into hell? *(Incredulous)*

Janet: I don't know.

SHE WAS RAISED WITH THE BELIEF THAT THERE IS A PUNISHING GOD WHO WILL PUNISH IF HE DOESN'T GET HIS OWN WAY, THAT GOD HAS ALL OF THE WORST QUALITIES OF HUMAN BEINGS AND THEN SOME.

Jon: Even people who are crazy enough to think that there's a hell don't think that babies end up there.

I AM SENSING THAT THE CONNECTION IS STRONG ENOUGH AND THAT I HAVE ENOUGH CREDIBILITY TO GO AT THIS HEAD-ON. WITHOUT THAT, HER BELIEF IN HELL MIGHT HAVE COST ME CONNECTION AND CREDIBILITY WHEN I COMMENTED THAT IT WAS CRAZY.

Janet: *(Laughter)* Okay.

Jon: Would you punch a baby?

Janet: No! Of course not.

Jon: Well, neither would God. God doesn't punch babies and he doesn't put them in hell. Your child is not in hell. The baby is in a lot better shape than you have been in. The baby is fine.

COMPARING GOD PUTTING HER BABY IN HELL WITH HER PUNCHING A BABY COMPLETELY ELIMINATES HER CONCERN ABOUT THAT. BY STATING THAT THE BABY IS IN BETTER SHAPE THAN SHE HAS BEEN IN DRIVES THE SENSE THAT THE BABY IS FINE INTO HER MIND. A SIGNIFICANT CAUSE OF JANET'S DISTRESS WAS THE BELIEF THAT HER BABY MIGHT BE SUFFERING. ANOTHER SOURCE OF DISTRESS WAS THAT SHE CAUSED THE BABY'S SUFFERING. THIS WAS PLAYING THROUGH HER SUBCONSCIOUS AND, SOMETIMES, HER CONSCIOUS MIND. JANET'S MIND IS NOT TRYING TO GET HER TO SUFFER. IT IS TRYING TO GET HER TO PROTECT THE CHILD. OF COURSE, SHE LOGICALLY HAS KNOWN ALL ALONG THAT THIS IS NOT POSSIBLE OR NECESSARY. HOWEVER, BECAUSE SHE WISHED THAT SHE HAD DONE IT, HER MIND BELIEVES SHE CAN DO IT. HER MIND HAS BEEN PRODUCING THE EMOTION, NOT TO MAKE HER FEEL BAD, BUT TO GET HER TO PROTECT HER BABY.

Janet: No shit.

Jon: Your child is saying, "Blaming yourself and feeling badly is stupid. Cut it out."

HAVING HER BABY CALLING HER STUPID ADDS BOTH HUMOR AND POWER TO THE POINT I AM MAKING.

Janet: I feel so good. Calm and good. Everything is different. I enjoyed your sense of humor. I feel different, completely different.

Jon: You are such a fast learner.

Follow-up Commentary

I spoke with Janet a year later and learned that the depression that had been dominating her mood level before our meeting has never returned. She and her husband now have a son.

Cheri

Cheri was 29 years old when we had this conversation. A friend had attended a talk I did and encouraged her to make an appointment. She was unhappy with her relationship and unhappy with herself.

Jon: I know you have some things for us to think about together.

Cheri: Men have taken advantage of me emotionally and I basically don't trust them. It keeps me from having a good relationship and I appear to be attracted to men who are, in some way, on the cruel side.

Jon: I want to understand.

Cheri: In the relationship that I am in now, when there is an argument, he insults me. The other night he said, "You don't need a boyfriend, you need a psychiatrist." He blames his moodiness on me.

Jon: Sounds like he's not clicking on all cylinders.

Cheri: And I'm not good at standing up for myself.

Jon: So, to **feel okay** even when he's silly.

CHERI SEEMS TO FEEL THAT HER BOYFRIEND IS POWERFUL AND THAT SHE HAS BEEN VICTIMIZED. I AM BEGINNING TO ALTER THAT BY STATING THAT HE IS NOT CLICKING ON ALL CYLINDERS AND THAT HE IS SILLY. BY THINKING OF HIM AS SILLY INSTEAD OF HIM BEING POWERFUL AND HER BEING DEPENDENT, THE FEELING OF BEING THREATENED WILL BEGIN TO DISAPPEAR. SILLY IS CHILDISH AND, THEREFORE, NOT POWERFUL.

Cheri: Yes, and not have such great anxiety. I get so much anxiety when Tom pulls away. When he withdraws from me or is angry with me, then it makes me do whatever I need to do to try to turn him around and get him to come back and like me again.

Jon: I sense you know what might work better.

IT IS BETTER FOR HER TO BE TELLING ME THEN IF I WERE TO TELL HER. IT PREVENTS ME FROM TELLING HER THINGS SHE ALREADY KNOWS. DOING SO WOULD INTERFERE WITH CAUSING THE EXPERIENCE OF CONNECTION THAT I WOULD LIKE HER TO HAVE WITH ME.

Cheri: I would just not approach him because approaching him never works anyway. It just makes him worse. Then, I could just leave him in his withdrawn state, go on about my business, do other things and not have that great anxiety.

Jon: You are looking to **enjoy independence.**

Cheri: Yes, like, if you want to be withdrawn, be withdrawn, and let me know when you want to come out of it.

Jon: Sounds great. Would that be okay with you?

Cheri: What makes it not okay is when he withdraws, and I am usually not sure why he has because he won't tell me. I am always concerned that I did something wrong, and that he will leave.

I AM ASKING HER IF IT WOULD BE OKAY TO BE ALRIGHT IN THE FUTURE, BUT BECAUSE CHERI HAS BEEN "STUCK," HER MIND GOES TO THE PAST AND SHE TELLS ME HOW IT HAD BEEN.

Jon: Would he be more likely to leave with you being okay even when **he is silly**?

Cheri: No. I think it would decrease it. I think he would have more respect for me.

Jon: So, then, it's okay?

Cheri: Yes, if I could be independent and go on. But when he is withdrawn, it controls everything that happens.

ONCE AGAIN, ASKING ABOUT THE FUTURE CAUSES HER TO DESCRIBE THE PAST. WHEN THE FUTURE IS NO LONGER THE PAST, SHE WILL NO LONGER BE STUCK.

Jon: Conceive of how it would be to **function independently**.

Cheri: I could just say, "Ah, he's done it again. Okay, well, I will just do this, or I'll do that."

Jon: How would that be?

Cheri: I would feel independent. I wouldn't feel like he is jerking me around or that he was in charge of my emotions. Right now, I feel like he is.

Jon: What thoughts were causing you to feel anxious when he would be distant or angry with you?

Cheri: I would think that this might be the time that he really does leave and, if he leaves, it will make me feel so anxious and so depressed. I would think, "What if I can't do everyday things?"

Jon: Anxious and depressed about what?

Cheri: Being alone. Somehow, being alone, I couldn't handle that.

WHEN PEOPLE THINK OF A RELATIONSHIP ENDING, IT CAN FEEL LIKE THEY WILL BE ALONE FOREVER. I AM GOING TO BREAK THIS INTO PIECES SO THAT, AS SHE CONSIDERS BEING WITHOUT TOM, IT IS NO LONGER OVERWHELMING.

Jon: If you had to make it through this evening without Tom, would there be a problem with that?

Cheri: If he was just going out with friends or something, I would be fine. There is no anger involved.

Jon: Okay, so **there is no problem being without Tom** tonight.

Cheri: Right, if anger is not involved.

Jon: If you were going on a trip to Hawaii, would you be able to handle not seeing Tom's face for a whole week?

Cheri: Oh, yes.

Jon: What if it was a European tour and it was two whole weeks in different cities?

Cheri: I could handle that as long as he wasn't mad.

Jon: What has been disturbing, Cheri, was thinking that you would be alone forever. That will never happen to you.

Cheri: (*She becomes thoughtful and sits in silence for a few moments.*) I felt the same way about a number of men and I'm fine without them.

Jon: That's right.

Cheri: After a period of adjustment, and that period of adjustment is really hard…

RATHER THAN EXPLORE THE RECOLLECTION OF PAINFUL ADJUSTMENTS, I AGAIN LET HER KNOW SHE WOULD BE FINE. THERAPISTS THINK FEELINGS ARE IMPORTANT AND ARE MORE LIKELY TO BE INTERESTED IN EXPLORING PAINFUL FEELINGS THAN PLEASING FEELINGS, CAUSING THEIR PATIENTS TO BE VERY CONCERNED AND INTERESTED IN THEIR EMOTIONAL RESPONSES. MOST PEOPLE SEEKING PSYCHOTHERAPY ARE ALREADY TOO CONCERNED ABOUT THEIR EMOTIONS. THERAPISTS ALSO HAVING GREAT INTEREST IN THEIR EMOTIONS ARE LIKELY TO MAKE THEM EVEN STILL MORE CONCERNED. PEOPLE WHO BELIEVE THEIR EMOTIONS ARE IMPORTANT ARE LIKELY TO DO THINGS BASED ON HOW THEY FEEL RATHER THAN WHAT MIGHT BE GOOD FOR THEM.

Jon: You would be fine without Tom tonight, not just tonight, but tomorrow, not just tomorrow, but for a week, not just a week, but also a month. You can be fine without him.

Cheri: Yeah, I really could.

Jon: You are fine without him. You don't need any particular man to be just fine.

BECAUSE THERE IS CONNECTION AND CREDIBILITY, WHAT I AM SAYING IS BEING TAKEN IN AND ABSORBED AND IS CHANGING HER THOUGHTS AND HER EMOTIONAL RESPONSE.

Cheri: Yes, you are right. It's really very insignificant. I have handled everything in my life.

Jon: Yes, **you can really handle things.** I would like you to close your eyes while I talk with you for a while. Good, that's it. As your eyes rest closed, nothing at all is required. Everything is happening perfectly. Take your time 'til, once again, your eyes can open. Good, Cheri. Tell me what you were noticing within you.

HER EYES ARE CLOSED, AND SHE IS BEING TOLD THAT EVERYTHING IS HAPPENING PERFECTLY AND THAT NOTHING IS REQUIRED. THIS CAUSES HER TO BECOME CALM AND AT EASE.

Cheri: A real calm feeling.

NEXT, I WILL SUGGEST THAT THERE IS ALWAYS CALM AT HER CENTER. TO GET THIS DONE, I NEEDED TO CAUSE HER TO EXPERIENCE A PEACEFUL STATE AND TELL HER THAT THE PEACE WAS THERE BECAUSE SHE WAS DRAWN TOWARD HER CENTER.

Jon: Your eyes are closing. You're calm because you are drawn toward your center where **you are secure.** You are drawn to where **you are always at peace** because **you are always secure**. We have been talking together about **secure, independent, free.** Once again, your eyes can open.

Cheri: I feel very calm.

Jon: Something will come to mind for us to look at together. It was something that has been impacting your mind in a negative way. As we look at together, it clears and resolves, and energy is freed and directed toward improving your life in many ways.

Cheri: Last Wednesday night, Tom had really withdrawn from me and I was tired. I wanted to go to bed. So, I went to bed, but I couldn't sleep. He was out on the couch and I thought he was upset, but he denied it.

Jon: Yes.

Cheri: I got up and tried to talk to him, but he was mean to me.

Jon: Mean to you in what way?

Cheri: He said, "You are acting like an idiot." I felt insecure and wanted his attention. I went out and sat next him and said, "How about if I sit here with you for a while? Would that bother you or would you rather be alone?" He didn't really say anything. He kept watching TV and I kind of just teasingly put my face in front of him and he turned towards the TV and wouldn't respond to me. Then, he said I was acting like an idiot.

Jon: You were ready to play, and he was insecure, stiff and guarded, kind of like a child who is sulking.

Cheri: Yes.

"READY TO PLAY" REFERENCES HER SEXUAL MATURITY. RATHER THAN TOM BEING SEEN AS A POWERFUL GUY WHO MIGHT REJECT HER, HE IS NOW VIEWED AS A SULKY CHILD.

Cheri: I have been feeling like I was acting childish, but what you say makes sense. He does act like a sulky little boy sometimes.

Jon: You are beginning to **see things as they really are.** Something else will come to mind, something from a long time ago. As we think about it, mind will update, and energy is freed.

Cheri: Yes.

Jon: What is it?

Cheri: (*She seems troubled*) In the first grade.

Jon: What's wrong?

Cheri: It hurts.

CHERI BECOMES TEARY AND BEGINS TO RE-EXPERIENCE THIS TROUBLING EVENT. I WANT HER TO EXPERIENCE THE CONNECTION WITH ME, BUT SHE IS EXPERIENCING THE PAIN FROM BACK THEN. THIS IS HAPPENING BECAUSE I DIDN'T ADEQUATELY PREPARE HER TO DEAL WITH THIS MEMORY. IF I HAD, I BELIEVE THE EMOTIONAL PAIN SHE WENT THROUGH IN DEALING WITH THIS COULD HAVE BEEN AVOIDED.

Jon: Hey, stay with me. What's wrong? What's going on?

I DON'T BELIEVE THAT FEELING PAIN FROM HER PAST IS NECESSARY IN ORDER TO PROVIDE RESOLUTION AND CLARITY. I AM DOING WHAT I CAN TO BRING HER BACK TO ME.

Cheri: I'm so embarrassed!

Jon: Embarrassed? You didn't even say anything yet! I mean, if you are going to be embarrassed, let me in on it so that I can enjoy it.

(Cheri begins to laugh.)

Jon: That's better. Just tell me about it, don't re-live it.

Cheri: I can just look at the event and not feel this feeling again. Is that what you are saying?

Jon: You might have met people who told you that there was sadness, anger or fear inside you, that it had been repressed and that it is important that it be expressed so you can let go of it.

Cheri: Therapists have told me that. Every one of them.

Jon: I am sure they meant well, but **there are no bad feelings inside you. You are not in first grade**. What happened when you were?

Cheri: My parents, or at least my mother, made it very clear to me that if I ever did anything wrong that the teacher had permission to paddle me. The only stipulation was that she was to tell my parents right away because I would get it twice as hard when I get home.

Jon: Good grief! *(I express shock that anyone would say something so stupid.)*

Cheri: And in the first grade, there was a Ralph Johnson sitting next to me. He dropped his pencil. I picked it up and, initially it was politeness in me, but then he dropped it again and I picked it up. Then he dropped it another time and I picked it up. The teacher, whose name was Mrs. Brown, said, *"Cheri and Ralph, go out in the hall."* I was humiliated, frightened and scared to death. I hated him. I hated him because I didn't know what was going to happen and I felt I had done something that I never should have done. I should have known not to do it. When I went home that night, I didn't know how bad it would be. I was afraid I would get this awful punishment. I started crying walking up the sidewalk. I was afraid to tell my mother, but I told her because I figured the teacher would tell her if she hadn't told her already. I cried so hard that I couldn't go to my piano lesson that night. I was so upset.

Jon: Did they beat you?

Cheri: I thought I would really be beaten.

THE THOUGHT THAT SHE WOULD BE BEATEN SLAMMED INTO HER MIND AND LEFT THE ONGOING IMPRESSION THAT IT IS STILL ABOUT TO HAPPEN.

Jon: Did they beat you?

Cheri:	They didn't.
Jon:	No.
Cheri:	They didn't do anything.
Jon:	Yes, you didn't get beaten. No beating will happen.
Cheri:	No, I guess not. I was afraid just remembering it, but you're right, of course. It never happened.
Jon:	That's great, Cheri. Now, tell me what was embarrassing.
Cheri:	That I did something wrong.
Jon:	Picking up a pencil?
Cheri:	That it was such a stupid thing to do. Why did I go along with that?
Jon:	Why did you pick up the pencil? (*Sounds incredulous*)
Cheri:	Yeah. Why didn't I realize?
Jon:	Cheri, wait a minute. Are you telling me that you are embarrassed because you picked up a pencil back when you were in first grade?
Cheri:	Yes, I still feel embarrassed. I was sent out in the hall.
Jon:	Are you embarrassed that you picked up a pencil when you were in first grade?
Cheri:	No, it's not embarrassment. Maybe it's just fear.
Jon:	Are you afraid that you picked up a pencil when you were in first grade?
Cheri:	It's more of a humiliation.
Jon:	Are you humiliated now that you picked up a pencil in first grade? (*Incredulous*)
Cheri:	Yes.
Jon:	Why?
Cheri:	I should have known what I was doing.
Jon:	Maybe you should go to confession.

THERAPISTS TRY TO CREATE A "SAFE PLACE" WHERE THEIR CLIENTS ARE ENCOURAGED TO FEEL THEIR FEELINGS AND TO GET THEM OUT. THERE ARE NO FEELINGS STUCK IN PEOPLE THAT NEED TO COME OUT. INSTEAD, I AM LOOKING TO UPDATE HER MIND SO THAT IT STOPS PRODUCING EMOTIONS IN RESPONSE TO A SITUATION THAT IS NO LONGER TAKING PLACE. THE HUMOR FINALLY SNAPS HER COMPLETELY OUT OF THE FEELING. EVERY FACET OF MIND FINALLY REALIZES THAT IT IS NOT HAPPENING AND THAT IT DOES NOT MEAN A THING.

Cheri: *(Laughter)* Father, I was sent to the hall in first grade for picking up a pencil!

Jon: Good job, Cheri! Picture the little girl that you were, earlier in the day, before the pencil dropped. Whisper in her ear. Tell her she can hear you and that nobody else can. She is going to think it's really neat. Then, whisper something that will make her smile. Tell her that you are having fun whispering to her and then, tell her something else to make her giggle. Tell her you are doing something magical and fun. First, something silly will happen. Tell her what it is and make sure she knows her parents will not punish her later and that it will all amount to nothing. Tell her she is going to be put out in the hall after she picks up the pencil, but that you are going to be with her and will talk with her. She will look forward to going into the hall to meet you. Go wait for her in the hall. Here she comes. Say things that make her smile. Hang out with her. Take your time coming back to me and open your eyes.

Cheri: That was so nice!

CHANGING HOW SHE PREVIOUSLY EXPERIENCED THINGS WILL SHIFT THE WAY SHE WILL EXPERIENCE TOM'S DISAPPROVAL AND ANYONE ELSE'S DISAPPROVAL AS WELL.

Jon: See that little girl just before you whispered to her. Your consciousness moves into her. You hear the whisper in your ear. It makes you smile. He drops the pencil. You pick it up. You know you will get to go out to the hall and meet your friend from the future. Pick it up again. Do it again and again. Soon, you can be with your wonderful new friend. She is telling you to go out in the hall. You're in the hall. It's fun! You **grow up light, bright and easy. You are peaceful, secure, positive and independent. When he is silly, angry, sulky or withdrawn, you see him as a sulky little boy. You are a grown up. You are independent and secure.**

Cheri: I feel so much better! In fact, the headache that I have had for the past eighteen hours is gone.

Jon: You've changed the atmosphere in your own brain and body. Men are plentiful. They are found in great abundance. They are like wildflowers. They will always be around. It's pleasant to experience them and yet, you're certainly fine without them.

CHANGING HOW SHE PREVIOUSLY EXPERIENCED THINGS WILL SHIFT THE WAY SHE WILL EXPERIENCE TOM'S DISAPPROVAL AND ANYONE ELSE'S DISAPPROVAL AS WELL.

Cheri: Yes, I feel lighter.

Jon: Good. Now conceive of Tom sulking. What comes up?

Cheri: What can I do to enjoy myself while he is like this? At that point, I can't enjoy myself with him, so I'll do something that I enjoy without him. It's a good chance to take time to do things that I like to do alone.

Jon: <u>Try</u> to be afraid of not being with him.

TO TRY IS TO FAIL.

Cheri: I can't be afraid. I would have fun doing something else and being with someone else. I just don't feel anything. I don't feel any anxiety. It's more like, "Oh, well."

Jon: **Men are to be enjoyed moment by moment**. If it doesn't continue with Tom, you are fine.

Cheri: Because I was doing what I wanted to do at the time, without concern for the future. I have been thinking about the future instead of enjoying now.

Jon: If he leaves tonight, **there is no way that yesterday could be a mistake.**

Cheri: *(Excited)* That's a brand-new way to think and feel.

Jon: It wasn't a mistake to have dinner with him, to kiss him or to make love to him or to live with him. He can leave, but he can't take the experiences you have already acquired.

Cheri: Yes. It feels so good. Thank you.

Jon: I enjoyed meeting you.

Follow-up Commentary

I heard from Cheri a year later. She had ended the relationship with Tom and was dating a new guy. He sulks, but not as much as Tom.

Sally

Sally was 44 when we had this conversation. She was referred by a friend from her church who she had confided in about her sadness and guilt regarding her mother.

Jon: What's been going on for you?

Sally: Sadness when I think about my mother and the guilt of not knowing if I made the right decision.

Jon: I want to understand.

Sally: When I was taking care of my mother, I was the sole caregiver when she was going through cancer. I was making a lot of decisions and, as I started to say, I'm not sure if I made the right decisions.

Jon: Help me understand.

Sally: When my mother first came down here, she lived with me. She worked so hard all her life and then thought, at this point, she would have the opportunity to spend the winters down here with me, and the summers up state with my sister. It seems she was healthy up north, but, as soon as she came down here, two months later, a little tumor showed up in her neck. We thought it was a salivary gland. It was clogged or something, so we took her to an ear, nose and throat doctor. For three months after that, they were treating a salivary gland problem and didn't even consider that it could have been cancer. When they opened her up to take the salivary gland out, they found she was just full of cancer. The tumor had grown, and it just metastasized. I'm wondering if I had brought her to an internist first, maybe they would have gotten her to a doctor sooner to solve the problem.

Jon: Rather than to what?

Sally: Taking her to an ear, nose and throat doctor, which a friend of ours recommended.

Jon: When you <u>have been thinking</u> of it that way, what has the feeling been like?

Sally   The feeling is, did I make the right decision, and did I investigate enough?

Jon: Do you think you could have done it differently than you did it?

Sally: Well, I guess I could have gone to an internist and he may have…

Jon: You did exactly what there was to do. The ENT doctor is a physician with a great deal of extra training. That was the best possible decision.

Sally: *(Speaking very softly and her voice beginning to crack)* I don't know. I don't know because all she was touching was her neck, you know. We went to a doctor that we thought would guide us.

Jon: Do you think you could have done it any differently than you did it?

Sally No, not with what I…No, I wasn't a medical practitioner. *(Sniffling)*

Jon: Do you feel guilty for having done it the way you did?

Sally No, because I didn't have any information.

IT IS FINALLY CLEAR TO SALLY THAT THERE IS NOTHING ELSE SHE SHOULD HAVE DONE. IT WAS AFFECTING HER NEGATIVELY, BUT THE DISTORTED BELIEF COULDN'T SURVIVE WITH SHE AND I LOOKING AT IT TOGETHER WITH LOGIC AND CLARITY. I WILL, NEXT, UTILIZE A SHORT PROCESS TO SHIFT HER AWARENESS.

Jon: OK, I'd like you to close your eyes a moment and I'd like you to just breathe slower and deeper than you normally would. That's all that's necessary. You don't have to do anything else. You don't have to **calm your mind** or **focus your attention** or **relax** or anything. All you need to do is exactly what you are doing at the moment which is to consciously make an alteration in your breathing. Again, you can open your eyes. OK, good job. Think back on what happened with Mom and what does it feel like now? What comes to mind now?

Sally: I can see it as if I'm just looking at a picture or a movie.

Jon: OK, good job.

SHE NOW HAS CLARITY AND OBJECTIVITY. SHE IS NO LONGER ALONE WITH THE DISTORTED MEANING HER MIND HAD ATTACHED TO THE EVENT. SHE HAS ALSO BECOME QUITE RELAXED THROUGH THE PROCESS OF CLOSING HER EYES AND BEING ASSURED THAT THERE IS NOTHING SHE NEEDS TO DO.

Sally: Yeah, even when she got upset in the hospital and she got all emotional, *(long pause)* it was hard, but *(pause)* it happened *(taking a deep breath)*.

ALTHOUGH SALLY IS STILL SOMEWHAT EMOTIONAL WHEN RECALLING WHAT HAPPENED, IT IS NO LONGER BECAUSE OF A SENSE OF NOT HAVING DONE WHAT SHE SHOULD HAVE.

Jon: What do you believe happens when people die?

I THINK THAT IT IS A SIGNIFICANT QUESTION. SHE IS UPSET AS SHE THINKS ABOUT HER MOTHER HAVING DIED. I AM LOOKING TO UNDERSTAND THE SOURCE OF THE UPSET. THE GUILT IS NO LONGER THERE, BUT SHE IS STILL UNHAPPY. IT'S NO LONGER THE SAME GUILT, SO I WANT TO UNDERSTAND WHAT IT IS.

Sally: They go to heaven *(she starts to cry)* and they look out over you.

Jon: I want to understand.

Sally: *(Continues crying)* She is looking over me, but I wish she were here with me.

Jon: Tell me about heaven. What is she doing?

Sally: She is in heaven and looking down and being happy, but...

NOW, WITH THE GUILT FINALLY GONE, WE CAN DEAL WITH THE ISSUE OF MISSING HER MOTHER. HER BELIEF ABOUT HEAVEN HAS NOT ELIMINATED HER MISSING HER BELOVED MOTHER.

Jon: Heaven seems very far away. Is that right?

Sally: Very far away. *(Sobbing)*

I DON'T TRY TO STOP HER TEARS, BUT I DON'T GET DERAILED BY THEM. WE JUST KEEP GOING.

Jon: OK. Help me understand <u>your notion</u> that <u>heaven is pretty far from here</u>. Where did you get <u>that sense</u> that it was far?

HEAVEN BEING FAR AWAY IS A BELIEF AND I AM MAKING THAT CLEAR TO SALLY. UP TO NOW, SHE WAS THINKING OF IT AS A STATEMENT OF FACT DESCRIBING HOW THINGS ARE.

Sally: I don't know, I don't know where I got it.

Jon: Someone could have told you it was up in the sky.

Sally: Up in the sky, my parents always said up in the sky.

Jon: And the sky is...

Sally: Far away.

Jon: Yeah, so that's where <u>that sense</u> of "far away" came from.

Sally: *(Laughing through her tears and sounding relieved)* Interesting...

Jon: Yes. <u>Knowing</u> **Mom is happy** is a relief, but <u>the thought</u> of her being far away <u>has been</u> sad.

MOM BEING HAPPY IS SAID AS A KNOWING AND IS IN THE PRESENT TENSE. FAR AWAY IS REFERRED TO AS A THOUGHT OR SENSE AND IS SAID IN THE PAST TENSE.

Sally: Right.

I WANT TO BRING SALLY'S EXPERIENCE OF HER MOM CLOSER SO THAT SHE EXPERIENCES ONGOING CONNECTION INSTEAD OF LOSS. IN ORDER TO DO THIS, I HAVE TO OVERCOME HER SENSE THAT HER MOM COULDN'T BE CLOSE BECAUSE SHE NO LONGER SEES OR HEARS HER. I BEGIN BY GETTING HER TO REALIZE THAT OUR SENSES OFTEN GIVE US INFORMATION THAT IS NOT ACCURATE SO THAT SHE IS OPEN TO THE EXPERIENCE THAT MOM IS STILL WITH HER EVEN THOUGH SHE DOES NOT SEE OR HEAR HER LIKE SHE USED TO. MY INTENTION IS THAT SHE EXPERIENCE MOM AS CLOSE AND CONNECTED.

Jon: Some of the information our senses give us is useful. Like, my senses tell me that you're sitting here with me.

Sally: Right.

Jon: And that's a useful thing and I believe it's pretty accurate.

Sally: *(Laughing)* Yeah, it's accurate.

Jon: My senses also tell me that the earth is flat. When I look out, it doesn't look at all like a ball.

Sally: OK.

Jon: Right? When you look at the earth and you look at a cornfield, does it look like a ball or does it look like it's flat?

Sally: No, it looks like it's flat.

Jon: There's a situation in which my senses are giving me information, but it's not really accurate.

Sally: Right.

Jon: When I look out, I notice that the sun is revolving around the earth because I see it go up and then I see it go down. So, it certainly looks like it's going around.

Sally: Around, right.

Jon: And that's what my senses would give me. But you would point out that I shouldn't bank on it.

IN ORDER TO CAUSE A DIFFERENT EXPERIENCE, I AM LOOKING TO CAUSE A CHANGE IN BELIEF. PEOPLE OFTEN THINK OF THEIR BELIEFS AS TRUTHS. SINCE VERY BRIGHT PEOPLE OFTEN DISAGREE ON WHAT IS "TRUE," I PREFER TO BELIEVE THAT A BELIEF IS A WAY OF THINKING. I BELIEVE THAT THE BELIEF ORGANIZES INFORMATION IN A PARTICULAR WAY AND A DIFFERENT BELIEF MIGHT ORGANIZE IT IN ANOTHER WAY. PEOPLE CAN SEE VERY DIFFERENT THINGS WHEN LOOKING AT, HEARING OR TASTING THE SAME THING.

IN ORDER TO OFFER DIFFERENT BELIEFS, I REFERENCE THINGS THAT THE INDIVIDUAL IS ALREADY FAMILIAR WITH, LIKE THE "FACT" THAT THE EARTH IS ROUND AND THAT IT SPINS AND REVOLVES AROUND THE SUN. THE CHALLENGE IS TO BRING THIS

TO THE INDIVIDUAL'S AWARENESS WITHOUT HER FEELING SHE IS BEING TALKED DOWN TO BECAUSE I AM DESCRIBING THINGS SHE ALREADY KNOWS. FOR INSTANCE, I SAID, "YOU WOULD POINT OUT THAT I SHOULDN'T BANK ON IT." I HAVE HER TELLING ME HOW THINGS ARE RATHER THAN ME TELLING HER.

Sally: Right.

Jon: Because it isn't accurate. If you and I and a dog were sitting here, and we were listening to musical sound and commenting on it, and the sound continued to get higher and higher in pitch until I said, "The sound is gone," you would realize the dog is still hearing the sound and the sound is in existence even though we can't hear it.

I SAY THAT SHE WOULD REALIZE IT. IF I JUST TELL HER, IT IMPLIES THAT SHE LACKS UNDERSTANDING WHICH COULD BE EXPERIENCED AS CONDESCENDING.

Sally: Yes, exactly.

Jon: So, is the sound there? Of course. If I think it's silent, am I correct? No. My thought is based on what my senses are telling me.

Sally: Right.

Jon: Our senses give us information that might be accurate and, sometimes, might not be. The fact that it comes to me in a sensory way doesn't prove it. Am I making sense?

Sally: Yep!

Jon: OK. If it was somebody from another planet, and you were showing him around, you might show him some ice in a glass, then you might take him for a walk and, when you come back, the ice isn't there in the glass. Then this guy says to you, "Look at that. The ice that was here before has vanished. It has disintegrated into nothingness." You point out that the ice has been transformed into some water in the glass.

ONCE AGAIN, IT IS BETTER FOR ME TO SAY, "YOU POINT OUT" BECAUSE THIS WAY SHE IS ONE-UP. SHE IS THE TEACHER.

Sally: Right, right.

Jon: Let's say he believes you and now you take him for another walk. At the end of this walk, the glass is dry. He says, "Now, the water has disappeared." Then, you say, "No, it hasn't disappeared. It just changed again and it's still there. It's as much there as when it was water. It's just as much there as when it was ice." And he says, "I don't see it." You let him know it's still there. You point out that things can change and lead us, through our senses, to the illusion that they aren't--the high-pitched note, the ice, the water. Am I making sense?

Sally: Yes!

Jon: Ok, so when **your mom vacated her body**, which was about how long ago?

MANY PEOPLE SAY THE WORDS "PASSED ON" SO THEY DON'T MAKE MUCH OF AN IMPRESSION, BUT THE WORDS I USED ARE UNUSUAL AND IT IS MORE LIKELY THAT THEY MAKE AN IMPRESSION. MOM LEFT HER BODY, BUT MOM IS FINE.

Sally: About four years ago.

WHAT FOLLOWS IS ABOUT CHANGING SALLY'S EXPERIENCE OF HER MOM. IT IS NOT ABOUT CONVEYING INFORMATION, BUT ABOUT CREATING AN EXPERIENCE. THINK OF A DRAMATIC STORYTELLER TELLING A STORY TO CHILDREN. THE CHILDREN ARE EXPERIENCING WHAT IS BEING SAID AS HAPPENING. IT IS AFFECTING THEM EMOTIONALLY. ONE DIFFERENCE, HOWEVER, IS THAT THIS IS BEING PRESENTED AS HOW THINGS ARE RATHER THAN AS A STORY. THE "STORY" FOR SALLY IS REAL AND THE SEPARATION FROM HER BELOVED MOTHER DISAPPEARS INTO THE JOY OF REUNION.

Jon: Ok, about four years ago. The way that she <u>had been showing up</u> for you changed so dramatically that it <u>was</u> quite shocking and then there <u>was</u> a bunch of other stuff going on for you stemming from shock and distortion around self-recrimination concerning whether you had been negligent in the doctor thing. It was distraction and a distortion. That distraction, distortion and pain, blocked your awareness of your ongoing connection with her.

Sally: Her spirit.

Jon: No, her.

Sally: Her, in general? Her physical being?

Jon: The sun doesn't go around the earth, the earth is not flat, and Mom's body was never who she was.

I START BY STATING SOMETHING THAT SHE HAS TO AGREE WITH AND FINISH BY STATING SOMETHING I WANT HER TO AGREE WITH. I STACK WHAT SHE WILL AGREE WITH SO THAT WHAT I WANT HER TO AGREE WITH SLIPS IN WITH IT. I NEEDED TO GET INTO A STORAGE FACILITY, BUT I DIDN'T HAVE THE PASS CODE NEEDED TO ENTER THE GATE. I JUST TAILGATED THE CAR IN FRONT OF ME SO THAT I COULD PASS THROUGH THE GATE WHILE IT WAS UP.

Jon: Sally, tell me about a time that you were outdoors in a natural setting. You saw something, and it was just beyond beautiful. You might have thought "awesome." What is it?

I COMPLETELY CHANGE THE NATURE OF OUR DISCUSSION AND, SINCE SHE IS EXPERIENCING A DEEP CONNECTION WITH ME, SHE GOES RIGHT WITH IT. THIS PROCESS WILL USE THE MEMORY OF A PRIOR EXPERIENCE TO CAUSE A STATE OF MIND THAT I WILL THEN SAY IS COMING FROM WHO SHE REALLY IS AT HER CENTER.

Sally: Mount Washington with snowcaps on it with the sun setting around it. It was all pink and beautiful...it was at sunset.

Jon: There was peace and excitement.

Sally: Yeah.

Jon: This guy had seen a beautiful bird flying above and had similar feelings to those you just described. If the man from another planet overheard him talk about those feelings, he might think that the bird dropped the feelings into the guy. But you don't believe that birds drop feelings into people. You might, instead think, the feeling he is experiencing is going on at his "center," and his awareness was drawn in as he looked up at the bird. His awareness moved closer to his "center." Peace and excitement are there as you become aware of your own essence. Some people engage in practices in which they tap into the peace, excitement and clarity that is that is there at one's essence.

I ARGUE FOR A PARTICULAR POINT OF VIEW BY MAKING THE OTHER POINT OF VIEW SILLY. OF COURSE, A BIRD DIDN'T DROP THE FEELING IN. WHEN PEOPLE THINK OF BIRD DROPPINGS, THEY DON'T THINK "PEACE AND EXCITEMENT." THEY THINK OF BIRD POOP.

Sally: I see.

Jon: Imagine that I have a lit candle in my left hand, and I take my right hand and start bringing it toward the flame. Then I say to you, "Goodness, the flame here keep's getting hotter."

ONCE AGAIN, THE OTHER POINT OF VIEW IS MADE SILLY.

Jon: You would say, "You're just getting more aware of the heat."

Sally: *(Laughter)*

Jon: You know the flame is not any cooler or hotter. What happened was, as he saw that bird, as you looked at that mountain, awareness was drawn in closer to your center, excitement, peace and clarity. You experienced the real you.

WHEN CONVEYING INFORMATION, THE PERSON HEARING IT IS IN A ONE-DOWN POSITION. THE SPEAKER KNOWS STUFF AND THE LISTENER HAS TO LEARN IT. BY SAYING "YOU KNOW" OR "YOU WOULD SAY" OR "YOU UNDERSTAND" OR "YOU REALIZE", YOU PUT THE LISTENER IN THE KNOW AND IT IS NO LONGER A ONE-DOWN POSITION.

Sally: Yes.

I SAY THINGS SHE HAS TO AGREE WITH AND CONNECT THESE THINGS TO THINGS I AM LOOKING FOR HER TO AGREE WITH. THE WAY THINGS ARE DESCRIBED CAUSE HER TO NOT ONLY UNDERSTAND, BUT TO EXPERIENCE WHAT I AM SAYING--LIKE WHEN I SPEAK ABOUT BEING AWARE OF THE HEAT OF THE CANDLE FLAME OR THE EXPERIENCE OF MT. WASHINGTON AND THE FEELINGS THAT CAME WITH BEING THERE. THIS INVOLVES NOT ONLY HER INTELLECT, BUT THE REST OF HER MIND AND MAKES A STRONGER AND DEEPER IMPRESSION.

Jon: As you look around and see, hear and smell, your senses bring in information about your environment which is organized by your mind and you can look and know what is around. With your senses and your intellect, you have this knowledge. You have heard people talk about the light of knowledge, have you not? At you center, there is an even brighter light. Let's call this the "light of wisdom."

Sally: OK

Jon: I remember talking to a gal about this. She spoke about a feeling of deep shame. As a little girl, she had a pet hamster and it died. Her brother told her it was her fault and it happened because she gave it the wrong food. Because I knew the whole family, I knew that wasn't what her brother actually thought happened. He believed she had killed her hamster and blamed it on her, so she would not only grieve, but also feel guilty.

After she and I talked about this the way you and I are, I asked her, "If there's this light of wisdom at your center and a light of knowledge on the surface, where is the shame? Where is the guilt? Was the shame on the surface?" "No," she said, "it is not on the surface. It is not intellectual." I asked her if the shame could be at her center where there is wisdom. She responded, "No, it can't live in that light." I said, "Then, where is the shame?" She realized that it was hiding in a shadow and that it was surrounded by light. **Light penetrates. Shadows disappear. Guilt is eliminated. Shame is gone.**

I AM GIVING SALLY INFORMATION BY TELLING HER ABOUT SOMEONE ELSE. THIS HAS THE ADVANTAGE OF BALANCING THE LEARNER'S ONE-DOWN POSITION AND IT ALSO MAKES THE INFORMATION MORE INTERESTING. SHE IS NOT JUST LISTENING TO SOMEONE GIVE HER A POINT OF VIEW BUT GETS TO OVERHEAR A CONVERSATION BETWEEN A THERAPIST AND A CLIENT, AND THAT IS SOMEWHAT MORE INTERESTING. HER MIND APPLIES THESE PRINCIPLES TO HER EXPERIENCE OF GUILT REGARDING THE CHOICE OF HER MOTHER'S DOCTOR AND THIS FURTHER OBLITERATES ANY REMAINING GUILT.

Jon: There's light of wisdom and there is light of knowledge. The shame *was* hiding in the shadows between them, but, **as the light comes in, the shadow disappears.**

PEOPLE WHO ARE DEALING WITH EMOTIONAL TURMOIL FEEL THAT THERE IS PAIN WITHIN THEMSELVES AND, THE DEEPER THEY GO WITHIN, THE MORE PAIN THEY WILL FEEL. I AM OFFERING SALLY A VERY DIFFERENT VIEW OF THIS. DEEP INSIDE, THERE IS LIGHT, NOT PAIN. THE PAIN HAS BEEN HIDING FROM THE LIGHT IN THE SHADOW. LIGHT DESTROYS THE SHADOW. LIGHT WINS. I CALL THIS PROCESS "CHANGING INTERNAL GEOGRAPHY."

Sally (Delighted) It just disappears. It has been lit and cleared away.

Jon: Right, right.

Sally: Wow!

Jon: At your center, there is this wonderful light of wisdom. On the surface, there is a light of knowledge. However, in between, there's been distortion where guilt and grief have been hiding.

Sally: There was a shadow.

Jon: Destroyed by the light.

Sally: Right.

NEXT, I BEGIN TO SHIFT THE SENSE OF WHO PEOPLE REALLY ARE. WHO MOM IS, THEREFORE, IS FINE. MOM IS FINE. SHE DIDN'T GO AWAY. SHE ISN'T LOOKING DOWN. SHE NEVER LEFT. THERE IS NO LOSS.

Jon: These two ladies had attended a wake and they were admiring what a good job the undertaker had done with the body. "Look what a good job they did," one of them said. The other agreed and said it was just remarkable. Then, the first one said that even though they did a very good job, it was like something was missing. What was missing was the guy whose body it was. Now, if you look at somebody who is alive and then you look at a dead body, it's pretty clear that there's something different

Sally: *(Begins laughing)*

Jon: One might say that there is something missing.

Sally: *(Laughing even more)* Right, right.

Jon: What is missing is that person.

Sally: Right, right.

Jon: If I look at a dead body, I am not seeing the person. His body might remind me of him, just like I might be reminded by looking at a jacket he wore. Does it make sense?

Sally: It does.

Jon: When your mom vacated that dwelling, there <u>was</u> the illusion of separation. The shock of the transformation blocked your awareness of your ongoing connection with mother. You were told things meant to be a comfort, but actually were not comforting. You were told, "Mom is very far, far away, looking down." However, **Mom is right here with you**. She's right here, participating, involved and excited about our conversation. Your love for her is as strong as it was ten years ago. Her love for you is amazing.

I SAY, "MOM VACATED THE DWELLING" RATHER THAN "DIED" OR "PASSED". IT IS AN UNUSUAL WAY OF SPEAKING, SO IT IS LIKELY TO GRAB HER ATTENTION AND IT CONVEYS THIS NEW AND DIFFERENT PERSPECTIVE.

Sally: *(With deep emotion) Yes*, yes!

Jon: **Your connection with Mom has never been stronger**.

Sally: (*Crying with great relief*) Yes!

Jon: She's right here.

Sally: (*Crying tears of relief*)

Jon: She's not looking down like some bird on a perch. She's right here.

I AM OFFERING A SPIRITUAL PERSPECTIVE MIXED WITH HUMOR TO KEEP HER LIGHT AND INTERESTED.

Sally: (*Crying and laughing at the same time*)

I HAVE ENOUGH CONNECTION AND ENOUGH BUY-IN THAT I CAN TELL HER WITH TOTAL CREDIBILITY WHAT HER MOM IS THINKING AND FEELING.

Jon: She's excited that you're doing this, and she likes the fact that now **you know she is here with you.**

Sally: (*Very relieved and taking a deep breath*) Yes!

Jon: You will continue to experience her presence in a way that's rich, fulfilling and close.

RATHER THAN ENCOURAGING HER TO ACCEPT THE LOSS AND GO THROUGH THE SUPPOSED STEPS OF THE GRIEVING PROCESS, I AM CREATING THE EXPERIENCE OF REUNION.

Sally: Right.

Jon: She is as close as the air. Mom is as close as your breath.

Sally: Yes!

CHANGE HAPPENS AS SHE THINKS DIFFERENTLY AND HAS NEW EXPERIENCES.

Jon: Good. Close your eyes and, again, just breathe. During the time you're breathing, just like you are now, there isn't anything else that you need to be doing. There isn't anything else that you need to not be doing. **Things are just working inside, naturally, automatically, exactly the way they're supposed to. Things are just happening just the way they should**…again…when you're ready, you can open your eyes. Good. Think about mom and tell me what comes up.

Sally: She was a beautiful, joyous person who just loved life. And she would want me to go out there and do whatever I could and be happy.

Jon: Tell me the same thing again but keep it in present tense. It begins with, "Mom is…"

Sally:	Mom is a very wonderful, happy person and she'd do anything for anyone. She was an angel.
Jon:	Yes. Tell me. She is here. Tell me.
Sally:	*(Said with deep conviction)* Mom is a wonderful person. She's here for everyone and she's with me and she'd do anything for the family or anyone.
Jon:	Yes, good. Close your eyes and slowly release your breath. **A wonderful and joyous person is with you, loving you, encouraging you, supporting you and is as close as your own breath and she's so happy that you're getting it. She's so happy for you.** When you're ready, you can open your eyes. Tell me what's going on for you now.
Sally:	She's happy that I finally went to straighten my head out.
Jon:	She's vibrant, she's excited and she's really good with what's going on right now.
Sally:	I can feel it, too.

ALTERED STATE OF CONSCIOUSNESS, CREDIBILITY AND CONNECTION TRANSFORM FEELING AND THOUGHT. THE EXPERIENCE OF CONNECTION HAS REPLACED THE FEELING OF LOSS.

Jon:	What happens as you think of Mom, now?
Sally:	She's by my side and everything's going to be OK. Everything is OK.
Jon:	Mom is by your side.
Sally:	She's right here. *(Sighing and breathing deeply)*
Jon:	That's right.
Sally:	Has she been sad about the way I've been feeling all these years?

HER CONCERN SPEAKS TO HER SENSE THAT MOM IS WITH HER.

Jon:	She's glad to know that you're good now.
Sally:	*(Both excited and relieved)* Cool!!!
Jon:	I enjoyed visiting with you.
Sally:	It was wonderful. Thank you.

Follow-Up Commentary

Sally contacted me a year later and told me her vibrant connection with her mother has continued. She told me that a close friend's son died, and she said she was able to comfort her friend in a way she never would have.

Kevin

Kevin was a 47-year-old police detective when we met. He was dealing with emotional and physical issues and had been pre-occupied with pain, guilt and resentment.

Jon: I know there were some things you wanted to talk with me about.

Kevin: I have troubles with my stomach and neck. I am frequently nervous. I have trouble sleeping.

MOST PEOPLE REALIZE THAT SOMETHING THAT HAS A NEGATIVE EFFECT ON THE BODY WILL NEGATIVELY AFFECT THE EMOTIONS AND THOUGHTS, WHICH, OVER TIME, MAY NEGATIVELY AFFECT THE BODY. LIKEWISE, THERE ARE THINGS THAT CAN POSITIVELY AFFECT THE BODY THAT WILL POSITIVELY AFFECT THE MIND, SUCH AS EXERCISING OR GETTING A MASSAGE. IT IS NOT AS WELL KNOWN, HOWEVER, THAT HAVING A POSITIVE EFFECT ON THE MIND WILL ALSO POSITIVELY AFFECT THE BODY. INDIVIDUALS WHO THINK ABOUT MIND-BODY CONNECTIONS ARE MORE PRONE TO BE LOOKING FOR AND ENCOURAGING AN INTROSPECTIVE UNDERSTANDING OF THE PSYCHOLOGICAL CAUSE OF A MEDICAL ISSUE. I PREFER TO ASK THE MIND TO SELECT SOMETHING THAT, AS IT IS CLEARED, WILL PROMOTE ADDITIONAL HEALTH. BOTH QUESTIONS MAY ELICIT THE SAME ANSWER. BUT THE WAY THAT THE ANSWER IS VIEWED BY THE MIND WILL BE SIGNIFICANTLY DIFFERENT. ONE EXPLAINS THE CAUSE AND THE OTHER ORGANIZES THE MIND TOWARD THE SOLUTION.

Jon: You would like to **sleep easily, feel calm** and **be healthy, comfortable and at ease**.

IN SAYING, "SLEEP EASILY, FEEL CALM, AND BE HEALTHY, COMFORTABLE AND AT EASE," I'M DEMONSTRATING MY UNDERSTANDING OF WHAT HE HAS SHARED WITH ME AND I'M DOING IT IN A WAY THAT ENABLES ME TO DRESS COMMANDS TO HIS UNCONSCIOUS MIND.

Kevin: That's exactly what I want.

Jon: Our time together will be driven by what we together intend for you. Something will come to mind for us to speak about. It will be an experience you had that was troubling. As we think about it together, energy will be released to fuel the changes and improvements that we are both intending for you.

I SAY, "OUR TIME TOGETHER WILL BE DRIVEN BY THESE THINGS," MEANING THAT OUR TIME WILL BE SPENT AIMING AT THE TARGET OF HIM SLEEPING EASY, FEELING CALM, BEING HEALTHY, COMFORTABLE AND AT EASE. I MENTION THAT, AS WE THINK ABOUT THINGS TOGETHER, ENERGY WILL BE RELEASED TO FUEL CHANGES AND IMPROVEMENTS. WHAT WE WILL DO TOGETHER IS DESIGNED TO SHIFT HIS MIND AS OPPOSED TO PRODUCE AN UNDERSTANDING. SIMPLY HAVING AN UNDERSTANDING DOESN'T CAUSE CHANGE.

SAYING, "SOMETHING WILL COME TO MIND," SUGGESTS THAT AN EVENT WILL COME TO HIS MIND BASED ON OUR INTENTION THAT HE BE HEALTHY AND COMFORTABLE. I SAY THAT THE EVENT WILL COME TO HIS MIND RATHER THAN HAVING HIM FIGURE OUT WHAT EVENT WE SHOULD DISCUSS SO THAT WHAT DOES COME TO HIS MIND SEEMS TO COME TO CONSCIOUSNESS AUTOMATICALLY.

Kevin: What I'm going back to is my freshman year in college. I know that my neck pain started somewhere in there. I think it was spring semester. I had been involved in a youth group before college and got involved in what I thought was a similar group in college. It was very condemning. It's like somebody controls your beliefs about God and existence in the world. It was really scary. At the time, I blamed myself. I was very critical of myself. It was my entire fault.

Jon: What was?

Kevin: I wasn't good enough. I wasn't a good enough Christian.

Jon: I want to be clear on what you're saying.

Kevin: Somehow, I felt like I was supposed to be strong and trusting and faithful. I had questions and doubts. Later, intellectually, I thought, "Good thing." I tossed out the whole mess. But, at the time, I remember, for instance, they would have their meetings on Friday night. When everybody else would be going out with their friends, I would go to the group meetings and then to the chapel. I would go, and I would just almost sob. I just really kind of beat myself up emotionally. They made me feel guilty about everything.

Jon: Tell me.

Kevin: I just kind of look back at me sitting on this stone-cold floor of that chapel and the kind of grief, remorse and sadness that I felt at the time…and the guilt.

Jon: What about it bothers you now?

Kevin: It bothers me that I let myself get taken over.

WHEN A PERSON DESCRIBES AND EXPLAINS AN EXPERIENCE, IF THE LISTENER IS EMPATHETIC, THERE IS A TENDENCY TO BELIEVE THAT WHAT IS SAID IS ACTUALLY WHAT HAPPENED. KEVIN SAYS, "IT BOTHERS ME THAT I LET MYSELF GET TAKEN OVER." HIS MIND HAS ATTACHED MEANING BASED ON HIS PRIOR EXPERIENCES AND PRIOR WAYS OF THINKING. I HEAR WHAT KEVIN IS SAYING AS ONLY A PERSPECTIVE RATHER THAN A REALITY. I DON'T BELIEVE HE LET HIMSELF GET TAKEN OVER.

Jon: They were very influential people and you were a young man.

Kevin: They took something that had been good in my life, twisted it and made it a bad thing.

Jon: **You have an open mind.** Those ignorant people were certain they were correct, and they outnumbered you. I understand what you are telling me.

Kevin: I hate that anyone could have that kind of influence on me.

Jon: They have no influence over you. They never will. You are much stronger than you were and surviving it makes you stronger still.

WHEN KEVIN SAYS, "THEY TOOK SOMETHING THAT HAD BEEN GOOD IN MY LIFE, TWISTED IT AND MADE IT A BAD THING," I MENTION THAT THE PEOPLE WHO DID THIS ACTED OUT OF IGNORANCE INSTEAD OF EVIL BECAUSE, IN THAT WAY, THE ANGER BEGINS TO FADE. AS HE SAYS THAT HE HATES THAT ANYONE COULD HAVE THAT KIND OF INFLUENCE ON HIM, THE ANGER IS REFERRED TO IN THE PRESENT TENSE, AS IF IT'S HAPPENING NOW. TO ME, THIS MEANS THAT THE THREAT THAT HE COULD BE INFLUENCED AND TAKEN OVER IS BEING EXPERIENCED NOW. BY SAYING, "THEY HAVE NO INFLUENCE OVER YOU. THEY NEVER WILL," THE THREAT DISAPPEARS, AND HE HAS A DIFFERENT PICTURE OF WHAT HAPPENED.

Kevin: Right.

Jon: So, as you think about it, what comes up?

Kevin: I have a different picture.

Jon: Tell me.

Kevin: I look down seeing myself and that self is no longer knotted up. It's more relaxed.

Jon: Yes, you have a more complete recollection.

Kevin: That's right.

BY HAVING THE THREAT ELIMINATED, HE IS THEN ABLE TO ACCESS A POSITIVE MEMORY, ONE OF FEELING SECURE.

Jon: What do you notice as you think about that?

Kevin: It's not as powerful.

Jon: Does it disturb you at all?

Kevin: I don't feel the disturbance.

Jon: Are you able to be angry about things that don't threaten or disturb you?

I BELIEVE ANGER IS A RESPONSE TO A PERCEIVED THREAT. HENCE, WHEN I SAY, "ARE YOU ABLE TO BE ANGRY ABOUT THINGS THAT DON'T THREATEN OR DISTURB YOU?" MY INTENT IS TO SET IT UP SO THAT THE ANGER DISAPPEARS. I CONTINUE BY SAYING THAT THE GROUP WHO HAD CAUSED THIS HURT TO HIM WERE DOING SO BECAUSE OF THE WAY THAT THEIR MINDS VIEWED THINGS, AND THAT THEIR ACTIONS, IN SPITE OF BEING HARMFUL, WERE POSITIVELY INTENDED AND EVEN MADE SENSE WITHIN THEIR BELIEF SYSTEM. THE ANGER IS ELIMINATED BECAUSE THEY POSE NO THREAT AND NEVER WILL AND BECAUSE THEY WERE WELL MEANING.

Kevin: No, I don't think so.

Jon: What was their motivation?

Kevin: Well, that was their version of witnessing and saving people.

Jon: Did they think that they were saving people from eternal damnation?

Kevin: Something along those lines, yeah.

Jon: They thought it was best for you.

Kevin: Yeah. I think, in their own way, they did.

Jon: Tell me.

Kevin: Well, they did that without asking me.

Jon: They didn't think you knew.

Kevin: Right. They just imposed.

Jon: Right. Did they think it was the best thing for you?

Kevin: Yes, they did.

Jon: Didn't they think you were way off track?

Kevin: Yes.

Jon: Didn't they think it would be best for you to get you on track?

Kevin: Uh huh.

Jon: Did they think you should have been consulted about what to do to be on track?

Kevin: No.

Jon: They didn't think you would know.

Kevin: Right.

Jon: Did they do what they thought would be the best thing in order to save, not your life, but something they considered far more precious?

Kevin: Yeah.

Jon: Can you be angry with them for that now?

Kevin: No, it's amazing that my picture of them shifted.

Jon: Try to be angry with them.

Kevin: I can't.

Jon: This means that, on some very deep levels, you now realize **you got away.**

AS I TELL HIM TO TRY TO BE ANGRY AND HE FAILS IN BEING ABLE TO DO SO, IT DRIVES IN THAT A TRANSFORMATION HAS TAKEN PLACE. THE UNDERSTANDING THAT THERE IS NO THREAT NOW IS FURTHER AFFIRMED BY THE DECLARATIVE, "YOU GOT AWAY." THIS SHIFTS HIS BODY'S RESPONSE FROM DEFENDING AGAINST A THREAT TO HEALING. THIS SHOULD IMPROVE THE PHYSICAL COMPLAINTS HE DESCRIBED WHEN WE MET.

Kevin: Wow. I just want to breathe. It feels like there's openness.

KEVIN SAYS THAT HE USUALLY FEELS LIKE HE CAN'T GET ENOUGH AIR. WHEN THE BRAIN PERCEIVES THREAT AND TRIGGERS SYMPATHETIC NERVOUS SYSTEM ACTIVITY, THE BRAIN CAUSES THE BODY TO BRING MORE OXYGEN AND MORE GLUCOSE INTO THE BLOODSTREAM AND CAUSES THE HEART TO BEAT MORE RAPIDLY IN ORDER TO INCREASE WHAT'S BEING DELIVERED TO THE CELLS. BREATHING IS SPED UP SO THAT THERE IS MORE OXYGEN. BUT, AS BREATHING SPEEDS UP, THE AMOUNT OF CARBON DIOXIDE BEING RELEASED WILL ALSO INCREASE AND THIS AFFECTS THE pH LEVEL OF THE BLOOD STREAM AND, IRONICALLY, CAUSES THE FEELING THAT ONE IS NOT GETTING ENOUGH OXYGEN.

Jon: Now, **you are open.**

Kevin: It goes all the way down.

Jon: Yes.

Kevin: I can really breathe fully. It usually feels like I'm trying to get enough air.

Jon: You made it. You're on solid ground.

Kevin: It feels like I could just continue opening up.

Jon: Absolutely. Do you think that someone could convince you that feeling horrible about yourself is the best way to spiritually be in a good place?

Kevin: No.

Jon: What if someone repeated it over and over?

Kevin: It wouldn't matter. I can never again be convinced of that.

Jon: Knowledge is power, and you are an expert.

Kevin: That's right.

Jon: What do you think?

Kevin: I have grown from it in a lot of ways. I can move forward and use it as a tool rather than a liability.

I'M CONTINUING TO TELL KEVIN THINGS THAT CONSCIOUSLY HE HAS ALREADY BEEN AWARE OF, BUT NOW HIS SUBCONSCIOUS MIND ALSO HEARS THESE THINGS. I GO ON TO PROVE THAT THIS CAN NEVER HAPPEN AGAIN BY ASKING IF ANYONE COULD CONVINCE HIM NOW OF THE THINGS HE HAD BEEN PERSUADED BY THEN. THE PERCEIVED WEAKNESS HAS NOW TRANSFORMED INTO THE EXPERIENCE OF STRENGTH. HE ACKNOWLEDGES THIS BY SAYING, "I HAVE GROWN FROM THIS IN MANY WAYS AND CAN USE IT AS A TOOL RATHER THAN A LIABILITY."

Jon: Yes. You're right. Something else will come to mind that, as we think of it together and it clears, it will lead to **health, well-being and clarity.**

Kevin: Well, here we go into a can of worms again--my whole existential awareness. I had this security before then, of knowing that I had this belief of this kind of good God. Then, good God became punishing God. I've had trouble getting that perception out of my mind even though I don't intellectually agree with it, especially since I just lost my dad. That really brought it back. I think it's brought about questions, the questions you ask when somebody dies, about where are they now. Is he okay?

Jon: Have you been <u>thinking</u> he's not okay?

THE WORD "THINKING" ENABLES ME TO DEMONSTRATE MY UNDERSTANDING WITHOUT A BUY-IN.

Kevin: Well, you know, you always have your worst fears.

Jon: Like?

Kevin: I think my worst fear would be ultimate aloneness, non-existence.

Jon: One can't be alone and also not in existence.

KEVIN BELIEVES THAT THE IDEA THAT THERE WAS A PUNISHING GOD FURTHER EXACERBATED THE TURMOIL SURROUNDING HIS FATHER'S PASSING. I BEGIN WITH KEVIN'S EXPERIENCE OF WHAT HE BELIEVES IS GOING ON FOR HIS FATHER PRESENTLY, AND HE MENTIONS, "...ULTIMATE ALONENESS...NON-EXISTENCE...FOREVER GONE." UNFORTUNATELY, THE WAY HUMAN MINDS ATTEMPT TO UNDERSTAND IS TO ATTACH MEANING TO EVENTS. THE MEANING ATTACHED TO EVENTS THAT HAVE BEEN PAINFUL OFTEN MAKES THESE EVENTS EVEN MORE PAINFUL.

Kevin: Okay, that's true, but it's that "forever gone" thing.

Jon: Forever is not a real thing. It is a concept.

Kevin: Yes, I guess. *(Looking away)*

Jon: I'm not sure you're convinced of that.

Kevin: I'm not.

Jon: Well, then don't "Yes" me. *(Smiling)*

Kevin: It makes some sense.

Jon: Don't patronize me. *(Smiling)*

Kevin: I'm not. What you're saying could be true. I'll give you that.

I SAY, "FOREVER IS NOT A REAL THING. IT IS NOT ANYTHING THAT COULD BE FOUND ANYWHERE." KEVIN ISN'T FULLY CONVINCED OF THAT. THEREFORE, I MAKE THE SHARP STATEMENT, "WELL, THEN DON'T 'YES' ME." IT'S SAID WITH A SMILE AND IN A LIGHTHEARTED MANNER. IT ENGAGES HIM IN WHAT WE ARE DOING RIGHT NOW AND AWAY FROM THE THEORETICAL. I SAY, "DON'T PATRONIZE ME," WHICH IS LIGHT AND UNEXPECTED FOR THE ROLES THAT WE ARE IN. THEREFORE, IT IS ATTENTION GRABBING AND AMUSING.

Jon: Your father is not suffering.

Kevin: I miss some connection to something beyond. It's like I threw out everything and I haven't got anything.

Jon: You discarded what you've been able to determine doesn't have value for you, and nobody can sell you on a punishing God. You're not afraid of that, so **you are open to connection with a loving God or other spiritual perspectives.**

KEVIN MISSES THE EXPERIENCE OF CONNECTION WITH A LOVING GOD. NOW, HE IS NO LONGER ON GUARD AGAINST THE BELIEF ABOUT A PUNISHING GOD. SO, HE CAN AGAIN BECOME OPEN TO A FEELING OF CONNECTION WITH A LOVING GOD.

Kevin: Yes, I think that's what's been holding me back in a way. I've been hyper-critical. I want to be open without being hurt.

Jon: Yes, the critical was good for a while, wasn't it?

Kevin: That protected me.

Jon: Yes. And as you think of it now?

Kevin: I don't have to be on guard.

Jon: That's right. What comes to mind about your father?

Kevin: The last day, the pain, the agitation and the bad part. I want to tell you.

Jon: Go ahead.

Kevin: He was suffering, and he was having delusions and hallucinations that day. The day before, he had some normal thoughts. We knew it was in the brain. He was really agitated. He was asking me to give him medication and I was trying to draw it, but my hand was shaking, and I couldn't. Then, just before I gave him the injection, he said, "No, it'll kill me." I went ahead anyway. He had been irrational. I gave him the morphine and some valium. Those were his last words.

Jon: What have you been thinking about that?

Kevin: Well, I felt like he wasn't ready to go and that I...

Jon: Yes?

Kevin: I killed him.

Jon: *(Immediate and decisive)* **You didn't kill him.**

Kevin: The doctor said I could give as much medication as I thought he needed. I was so scared he would wake up and be out of control and knowing there was no good end in sight. It was just getting worse. He was just getting more agitated.

Jon: It is done. His body has stopped.

Kevin: I liked when you said that it was his body that had stopped because his body had become a bad thing.

Jon: That's right, Kevin. What's <u>been</u> troubling you about this?

Kevin: It goes back kind of to the thing the group was imposing on me— something I didn't want. If that was a conscious choice of his to refuse the medication because he wanted to live, then I violated his rights and chose for him. It was hard to tell because he wasn't rational anymore. He hadn't been rational all day. Maybe telling me not to give him the medication was his rational moment.

Jon: No, Kevin. If he were rational, he wouldn't have said not to.

Kevin: If he was rational, he would probably have said, "I'm dying. Let me go."

Jon: That's right. You gave medication to relieve his suffering. That was the right thing to do. It was the loving thing for you to do for your father.

Kevin: Yes, I see that now. I remember the day of his memorial service. That day was a celebration of his life. I had calls and letters from people for weeks after, saying that it was the most inspirational thing and "that was just what your father wanted". Even though he wasn't there, it was like we really caught his spirit. He wasn't that person that Sunday night. He was just so much more free and alive.

BECAUSE I HAVE PLAYFULLY REENGAGED CONNECTION AND CREDIBILITY, THE STATEMENT, "YOUR FATHER IS NOT SUFFERING," IS ACCEPTED, EVEN THOUGH IT RUNS CONTRARY TO OTHER LONG-STANDING BELIEFS. KEVIN'S BEEN LIVING WITH THE FEELING THAT HE KILLED HIS OWN FATHER, AND THAT WHAT HE DID TO HIS FATHER WAS AS HURTFUL AS WHAT WAS DONE TO HIM.

KEVIN'S BRAIN HAD BEEN PERPETUALLY AND URGENTLY YELLING OUT, "STOP MAKING YOUR FATHER DEAD," AND "STOP DOING TO YOUR FATHER WHAT WAS DONE TO YOU." THERE IS LITTLE WONDER THAT HIS BODY HAS BEEN HURTING.

IN ADDITION, SINCE INTELLIGENT HUMANS ARE LIKELY TO FIND SIMILARITY EVEN IN THINGS THAT ARE VERY DIFFERENT, HIS MIND THEN BROUGHT THE IDEA OF "SIMILAR" TO "SAME". KEVIN'S MIND BEGAN TO SEE HIS GIVING HIS FATHER THAT INJECTION AS THE SAME AS WHAT THE GROUP OF PEOPLE THAT KEVIN FOUND SO OPPRESSIVE DID. WITH CREDIBILITY AND CONNECTION, WHAT I SAY IS ACCEPTED AS WHAT IS, EVEN WHEN IT CONTRADICTS PRIOR BELIEFS. THEREFORE, WHEN I SAY, "YOU GAVE MEDICATION TO RELIEVE HIS SUFFERING. THAT WAS THE RIGHT THING TO DO. IT WAS THE LOVING THING FOR YOU TO DO FOR YOUR FATHER," KEVIN'S MIND TAKES THIS IN, AND HE NOTICES AN IMMEDIATE, AND RATHER DRAMATIC, SHIFT IN THE WAY HIS BODY FEELS.

WHEN HE REALIZES THAT HE WASN'T DOING ANYTHING TO HIS FATHER LIKE WHAT WAS DONE TO HIM AND THAT HE WAS ACTUALLY RESPONDING TO HIS FATHER'S WISHES, THE PRE-OCCUPATION STOPS. WITH ENERGY FREED, HIS BODY CAN BECOME MORE COMFORTABLE.

Jon: What's that like?

Kevin: It's better.

Jon: Try to feel guilty.

Kevin: There is no guilt, none at all.

Jon: Try to be afraid.

Kevin: I don't have anything to be afraid of.

Jon: Check out your breathing.

Kevin: It's better.

Jon: Check out your stomach.

Kevin: It's better, yeah, much better. It's really easy to breathe. My neck is better. I feel lighter.

Jon: You did a great job today. Does it feel complete?

Kevin: Yes. Thank you. This has been wonderful.

Follow-Up Commentary

At the time of the six-month follow up interview, Kevin shared that his state of mind had greatly improved and the problems with his neck and stomach had not returned. He said he feels that he has become spiritual rather than religious and this works in a satisfying way for him.

Diane was 29 years old when we had this conversation. She called and told me that she knew I dealt with people who had real trauma and that she was afraid what she wanted to see me about would seem silly to me. "It might seem silly, but I am really upset," she said.

Jon: I know something upset you.

Diane: Thursday night, my fiancé Marc and I sat down. We were sitting there having a drink and we were talking about our upcoming wedding, which happens in four months. All of a sudden, we had this conflict come up. We were talking about who we were going to have marry us. I have this fundamentalist Christian upbringing in my history that has resulted in my desire to avoid traditional religions. You know, scared about churches and ministers and things like that. Marc, on the other hand, didn't really have this. He had just a regular religious background and it's been a real positive thing for him. He really wants a traditional wedding with a traditional service and a minister and all that.

So, I was saying that if we do that, we are going to have to do it very carefully and approach it carefully. We went to bed with these kinds of weird feelings. Friday morning, I don't know why, but I got really emotional. I started thinking of getting married in a church. I got really angry. I got so upset that I ended up sobbing really hard. Then last night, Marc and I were talking, and I found myself talking about my mother. I have another issue that has always followed me, which is that I was born into a very impoverished family and setting. I have always kind of felt cheated in a way. Not only that, but it's like this poverty follows me. I can't get away from it. It's like I have been a real independent survivor, went out and got myself a grant and a loan and a scholarship to go to college. I got myself a career that I could depend on. I am a dental hygienist. I make fairly good money and I like what I do, but it's like I can't hold on to it. It's like something always happens where the money slips out of my hands. Sometimes it seems like it's some freak accident and then sometimes it's a mistake that I made. But then, last night when I was crying, I realized that it's all connected with this religion stuff somehow. I started saying, "I'm mad! I have had it with this! I don't want this!"

I started thinking about my mother and how pitiful she is. I started thinking about when I used to go visit her and I would hear her cry. Well, not cry. She never cries. Hearing her make a remark that she always wished that she had a beautiful bathroom or something like that, that would just make me feel…I have always had trouble identifying this feeling. It's like feeling like she is so pitiful, and she can't help herself. I know that there is no way that she can and that's sad. It makes me sad for my mother and it makes me angry. So, I just think that maybe you can help me see this thing. I know that was really lengthy, but that's the way it feels to me.

Jon: You were able to break away from religious stuff. **It took a lot and you did it**.

Diane: I did.

Jon: You are going to get married.

Diane: Yeah.

Jon: You have a man that you love. There is some stuff that <u>has</u> bothered you.

Diane: I'm tired of it.

Jon: Pissed off!

Diane: I am! I am really sick of this!

Jon: Stuff with money, religion, family, Marc. I want to get it.

Diane: I am pissed off that I cannot hold on to money.

Jon: And your mother doesn't like her bathroom.

Diane: You wouldn't either. It's scary.

Jon: It's an ugly bathroom?

Diane: Not only ugly, it's scary. *(Laughs)*

Jon: Has it got snakes?

Diane: No, it doesn't have snakes. It's got plumbing that the "Three Stooges" put in, and a toilet that is held up by a 2x4 and a big crack up the wall. The house that she lives in is sort of falling apart. She is turning 60 in a few days.

Jon: Wow!

Diane: Just the thought of her living in this house, you know, by herself, way out in the middle of nowhere, is scary. That's her choice. That's what she wants to do.

AT THE BEGINNING OF OUR MEETING, SHE DESCRIBED HER MOTHER AS PITIFUL, YET I ALSO HEAR HER SAY THAT HER MOTHER MAKES CHOICES AND DOES WHAT SHE WANTS. DIANE VIEWS HERSELF AS DEFECTIVE AS SHE DESCRIBES HER INABILITY TO HOLD ON TO MONEY. IN ORDER TO CHANGE THE VIEW SHE HAS OF HERSELF, I WILL START WITH HER THOUGHTS ABOUT HER MOM.

Jon:	Mom is a rugged, independent, tough-stuff lady. She has a lot of power.
Diane:	Definitely! She is a wonderful woman.
Jon:	You come from rugged people.
Diane:	Yes. I have good genes.

BY NOTICING WHAT DIANE HAS TOLD ME ABOUT HER MOTHER, I REALIZED THAT I COULD SAY DIFFERENT THINGS AND YET GET A BUY IN. I EMPHASIZED HER MOTHER'S STRENGTHS AND, IN SO DOING, BUILT HER EXPERIENCE OF HER OWN STRENGTH.

Jon:	OK. I'm starting to get it a little.
Diane:	Yeah.
Jon:	The religious thing. It didn't make sense to you?
Diane:	At a very early age.
Jon:	See it as it is knowing what you know.
Diane:	It's absurd.
Jon:	OK. What is that like? Tell me a little more.
Diane:	Gross.
Jon:	How are you doing?
Diane:	Fine.
Jon:	You can **look at it and be fine.**
Diane:	Yes.
Jon:	Stained glass.
Diane:	I felt a little sinking in my stomach when you said that.
Jon:	Well, let's see. Stained glass. Stained glass! *(Laughs)*
Diane:	*(Laughs)*
Jon:	What's going on?
Diane:	It's glass with color in it, all so silly.

Jon: What are Marc's thoughts about religion?

Diane: Marc will say, "It's important to me to have some kind of religious element to our wedding or I won't feel married."

Jon: Wow! Sounds like you better pay attention to that. It's important for him to feel some kind of religious element or he won't feel married.

Diane: *(Laughter)* Well, it's important to me that he feels married.

Jon: Bring on the Pope, huh?

Diane: Right. Yeah.

Jon: Whatever will work?

Diane: Yeah.

Jon: You want him feeling married, yes?

Diane: Well, I do feel that way, but I want it to be the most beautiful thing for myself that I can imagine. Some of my family are coming; some of his family are coming. I don't want any of this absurd stuff. I don't need any new age stuff. I don't need that. I just want some kind of ritual, something we can both be ok with, like a minister that we both like.

Jon: Oh?

Diane: I can like ministers. That is possible.

Jon: You are looking for a double win on this one, are you not?

Diane: I'm sure we can find something. I know we can.

DIANE WAS RAISED WITH VERY RELIGIOUS PARENTS AND REJECTED THOSE BELIEFS AT AN EARLY AGE. SHE BECAME UPSET THAT RELIGION MIGHT BE A PART OF HER MARITAL CEREMONY. AS THE FEELING OF THREAT AND TURMOIL DISAPPEARS, SHE IS READY TO LOOK FOR A WIN/WIN ARRANGEMENT TO MAKE THE CEREMONY PLEASING TO BOTH OF THEM.

Jon: What else?

Diane: Well, Marc appeared to be pretty surprised that I would have this reaction the other night. I was concerned that he was surprised I would react that way.

Jon: Why?

Diane: Because it makes me think that maybe he doesn't really know me.

Jon: You are a woman. You are not to be known. You are a mystery to be forever discovered. It is beautiful.

TELLING HER THAT SHE IS TO BE DISCOVERED RATHER THAN KNOWN ELIMINATES HER HURT AT MARC NOT KNOWING HER BETTER.

Diane: *(Smiling)* Oh, that is nice. Marc and I have such different backgrounds. He was brought up in a very rich family. I was brought up in this poverty family. I've had this fear that if he really knew who I was, he may not want to be with me.

DIANE HAS BEEN VIEWING HER UPBRINGING "IN POVERTY" AS CAUSING HER TO NOT HAVE VALUE AS A WIFE FOR MARC. I WANT TO DESTROY THAT BELIEF.

Jon: You <u>think</u> you were brought up in poverty?

Diane: My dad never did make much money. There were nine children.

Jon: I want to understand about poverty.

Diane: Well, there was always food.

Jon: Ah!

Diane: I was never hungry.

Jon: There <u>is</u> always food. You <u>are</u> never hungry. **You have a mother who is rugged and strong.**

Diane: There was no money for music lessons or dance lessons.

Jon: Poverty is going without dance lessons? *(Light and challenging)*

Diane: There was no transportation to participate in after school extracurricular activities.

Jon: Poverty is not participating in after school activities? *(Light and challenging)*

Diane: It affected me socially in sophistication, worldliness, education and travel.

IF I TRY TO POINT OUT EXCEPTIONS TO WHAT SHE IS SAYING, I WILL BE ARGUING WITH HER, BREAKING CONNECTION AND IT WILL BE A WEAK APPROACH TO CHANGING HER MIND. INSTEAD, I AGREE AND INCREASE WHAT SHE HAS SAID SO SHE IS FORCED TO ARGUE WITH ME FROM THE OTHER SIDE. I CAN DO THIS WITH DIANE BECAUSE HER BELIEFS ABOUT HERSELF ARE IN CONFLICT WITH EACH OTHER.

Jon: You don't know much, and you can't do much.

Diane: I know a lot. I can do lots of things.

Jon: Poverty developed knowledge and skill?

Diane: Yes, I guess that is true.

Jon: Well, then, how was poverty?

Diane: I like that. It's a whole new way of looking at it.

Jon: So, did you grow up impoverished?

Diane: No.

Jon: **You haven't known poverty. You have been richly prepared**.

Diane: I feel like crying. (*She is relieved and emotional.*)

Jon: You haven't experienced poverty.

Diane: No, I haven't. *(Crying)*

Jon: What are you feeling?

Diane: Relief and gratefulness.

Jon: You are grateful for your blessings.

Diane: I have many.

Jon: You are grateful and blessed.

I USED THE WORD "BLESSED" IN ORDER TO FURTHER REDUCE HER ADVERSE REACTION TO RELIGION.

Diane: Wow, I feel so powerful right now. I really do.

Jon: Yes.

Diane: I feel like I need a substitute word now.

Jon: What word comes to mind?

Diane: I'm thinking of enrichment.

Jon: Rich.

Diane: Oh, my God! Oh, my God! I can't believe I just said that! This is just incredible!

Jon: Yes!

Diane: It really is!

Jon: Now, those things that had concerned you, tell me.

Diane: It was somewhat disturbing that Marc was surprised that I would be this way about traditional religion.

Jon: Marc doesn't know you.

Diane: Right.

Jon: Get that.

Diane: All right. I got it. It's still evolving. He really will never know me totally because he can't know me. He can experience me. That's actually better. It feels sexier to be discovered than to be known. I like it. I'm still growing anyway. I'm not even complete!

Jon: Good job. What else has been disturbing?

Diane: I was afraid that if he knew who I really was that he wouldn't like me, that he wouldn't want to marry me.

Jon: Particularly if he knew you were…

Diane: From a poverty background.

Jon: Was it poverty?

Diane: No, it really wasn't.

Jon: What do you think?

Diane: It's all changed.

Jon: And what is it now?

Diane: Now, it's to my advantage.

Jon: And what is to your advantage?

Diane: That I had the experience that I did when I was young.

Jon: Which we call what?

Diane: Enrichment.

Jon: OK.

Diane: And, really, that's what he loves about me, that I am creative and the way I look at things, the way I commit and follow through and all those things. He thinks I have integrity and I couldn't have gotten that from an impoverished background.

Jon: No.

Diane: That can only come from a very rich background.

Jon: **You grew up rich.**

Diane: Yeah, I really did.

Jon: **And lucky.**

Diane: That's funny! I mean, really, it feels so good to think of it that way.

Jon: Look at the wall in front of you. The stillness and solidity are illusions. What looks still is moving, what seemed solid is filled with space. Your eyes close. *(pause)* **You are light. You shine. You penetrate. You illuminate. You brighten. You shine through**. *(Her eyes begin to tear)* Light. Breath. Tears. Joy. Cleansing. Shining. Bright. Fresh. Wisdom. Excitement! Energy! Take your time to open your eyes.

THINGS ARE MOVING RATHER THAN STUCK. RATHER THAN BEING INADEQUATE, SHE IS LIGHT. SHE PENETRATES, AND SHE SHINES.

Diane: Oh, God! You won't believe what happened.

Jon: Try me!

Diane: Oh, God! I was Jesus. Jesus! I had those biblical clothes on, and I had all these animals around me, like little sheep and deer and raccoon and they were just climbing all over me. It was really fun! It wasn't bad at all. It was good! It was good to be Jesus! Then, all of a sudden, I was me. I just feel really resolved. *(Giggles)* I do!

Jon: I am glad we got to visit today.

Diane: I am too. Thank you so much.

Follow-Up Commentary

Six months later, Diane told me that she very much enjoyed her wedding and is happy in her marriage.

Jenny

Jenny was thirty-two years old when we met. She was living with emotional turmoil and had never had a sexual relationship. Yet, she was a successful artist and made a great income doing something she really loves.

Jon: I have seen your artwork and I love what you do. It is a great pleasure to meet you. I know there are things you want to tell me about.

Jenny: Thank you. I am lucky to be doing something I really enjoy. I hope you can help me. I had an experience with hypnotherapy that was very troubling.

Jon: Oh?

Jenny: It brought up material I wasn't aware of and it was very disturbing. I would like to tell you about it.

Jon: Okay.

Jenny: It happened about two years ago. I'd been in therapy for a long time and my therapist kept saying he was pretty sure that I had been sexually abused. He decided to hypnotize me in order to learn why I was afraid of becoming intimate, and it flashed on something that may have happened when I was two or three years old. The therapist could tell I was getting disturbed, so he brought me out of it and that was it. I was kind of left with this knowledge that I wasn't really ready for.

IT IS HARMFUL FOR THERAPISTS TO MAKE INTERPRETIVE GUESSES AS TO WHAT MIGHT HAVE HAPPENED IN THE PAST THAT MIGHT HAVE CAUSED A CURRENT PROBLEM. SUGGESTING THAT THERE WAS A PRIOR TRAUMA THAT NEEDS TO BE UNDERSTOOD AND PROCESSED MAY CAUSE AN INDIVIDUAL'S MIND TO MAKE UP AN EVENT. MUCH HAS BEEN DOCUMENTED ON THE DEVASTATION TO CLIENTS AND THEIR FAMILIES WITH WHAT IS CALLED "FALSE MEMORY SYNDROME." JUST AS I BELIEVE THERE ARE PHYSICIAN-CAUSED, OR IATROGENIC ILLNESSES, I THINK THERE ARE IATROGENIC MENTAL HEALTH ISSUES CAUSED BY WELL-INTENTIONED BUT POORLY TRAINED PSYCHOTHERAPISTS.

THERAPISTS CAN DO HARM IF THEY BRING THEIR CLIENT'S AWARENESS TO A PRIOR DISTURBING EXPERIENCE WITHOUT THE SKILL TO RESOLVE THE EXPERIENCE AND ELIMINATE ITS DISTURBING EFFECT. JENNY'S THERAPIST TOOK HER TO SOMETHING DISTURBING AND THEN, WHEN HE SAW THAT SHE WAS TROUBLED, HE BROUGHT HER BACK OUT OF IT. THIS CREATES THE EXPERIENCE THAT EVEN THE THERAPIST IS FRIGHTENED OF DEALING WITH WHAT HAPPENED TO HER AS A CHILD.

Jon: Knowledge about what?

Jenny: What I saw in that trance was me having oral sex with somebody. The body was big and white, like a light was shining on it. It was really black in the background. What came to my mind was that this had been filmed.

Jon: Filmed?

Jenny: Yes. *(She looks down and speaks softly.)* There were other events that I had a negative reaction to that this would explain. My mother told me that when I was very young, she took me to have a picture taken. She told me that I became hysterical. Also, at Christmas time, when my mother took me to see a store Santa Claus, I got upset.

Jon: It seems to be upsetting to tell me about this.

Jenny: Yes, I guess it is. I cry when I think of it, but I don't know for sure if it happened.

Jon: Let's think about it as if it did happen. By looking at it this way, we can clear things that have happened or even thoughts about things that might have happened. Whether it happened or not, it doesn't currently exist. So, what we are resolving is the way mind is processing information. We don't need to be detectives and try to figure out what actually took place.

THIS FREES JENNY'S MIND FROM FEELING THE NEED TO DISCOVER IF IT WAS AN ACTUAL EVENT THAT TOOK PLACE. WITHOUT THIS PRESSURE, WE CAN MOVE FORWARD MORE EASILY. IF SOMEONE IS PRE- OCCUPIED ABOUT WHETHER OR NOT AN EVENT ACTUALLY DID HAPPEN, IT IS LIKELY TO CREATE TROUBLING FEELINGS AND DRAIN ENERGY. THIS IS SOMETHING THAT MAY HAPPEN WHEN AN INDIVIDUAL IS ENGAGED IN AN INSIGHT-ORIENTED PSYCHOTHERAPEUTIC PROCESS IN WHICH THE CLIENT IS ENCOURAGED TO REMEMBER PAST EVENTS IN ORDER TO UNDERSTAND THE ORIGIN OF CURRENT PROBLEMS.

Jenny: Okay.

Jon: What about it bothers you?

Jenny: Well, I'm still a virgin. I am afraid to be intimate.

I ASK JENNY WHAT ABOUT THIS "MEMORY" IS DISTURBING AND THAT SHE DESCRIBE THE EFFECT SHE BELIEVES IT HAS CONTINUED TO HAVE. IF SHE FINDS THE EVENT TROUBLING BECAUSE OF THE EFFECT THAT IT HAS HAD AND IF IT IS HAVING THE EFFECT BECAUSE IT IS TROUBLING, WE ARE STUCK, LIKE TRYING TO PICK UP MERCURY. IT KEEPS SLIPPING AWAY. I NEED TO SEPARATE THE EVENT ITSELF FROM THE EFFECT IT CONTINUES TO HAVE IN ORDER FOR IT TO RESOLVE.

Jon: What about remembering the event is disturbing?

Jenny: I've lived with shame my whole life.

JENNY WANTS TO TALK ABOUT THE SHAME SHE HAS HAD HER WHOLE LIFE BECAUSE OF WHAT HAPPENED TO HER AT THE AGE OF TWO. IN ORDER TO ADDRESS THE SHAME, HOWEVER, I NEED TO ADDRESS THE EVENT. SHE HAS BEEN EXPERIENCING THE EVENT AS UPSETTING BECAUSE OF THE SHAME, AND THE SHAME IS HAPPENING BECAUSE OF WHAT HAPPENED. IF I DEAL WITH

THE SHAME BUT MISS THE EVENT, THE SHAME WILL CONTINUE. HENCE, I ACKNOWLEDGE THAT BECAUSE THE EFFECT OF THE SHAME IS SO IMPORTANT, WE WILL ADDRESS THE EVENT AND DEAL WITH ITS EFFECT LATER.

Jon: Let's stay with what happened when you were a child rather than the effect it has had on you. The earlier event deserves our full attention. We can think about how it affected you later.

Jenny: I don't know why I'm crying.

Jon: Things will **clear and release.**

Jenny: I think there's fear there.

Jon: Tell me.

Jenny: I don't think I thought I was going to live through it.

THE CONVERSATION WITH JENNY GOT AWAY FROM ME. EVERYTHING WENT SO QUICKLY. IT WAS LIKE LOOKING AT A LAKE AND THEN BEING UNDER WATER IN THE MIDDLE. I DIDN'T HAVE HER CONNECTED ENOUGH WITH ME TO RESOLVE THIS EXPERIENCE WITHOUT IT PULLING HER INTO AN ABREACTION. NOW, I HAVE NO WAY TO GET HER OUT BECAUSE I DIDN'T DO A GOOD JOB KEEPING HER FROM FALLING IN.

JENNY IS SAYING THAT SHE IS CRYING BECAUSE OF FEAR AND THE FEAR IS THAT SHE WOULDN'T LIVE THROUGH SOMETHING THAT SHE DID, IN FACT, SURVIVE. I WANT TO MAKE IT CLEAR TO HER THAT THERE IS NO CAUSE FOR FEAR NOW. IT IS IMPOSSIBLE NOW TO NOT SURVIVE WHAT HAPPENED THEN.

Jon: You did live through it.

Jenny: Nobody was with me. It's a terrible feeling.

Jon: Stay with me. What is it?

Jenny: *(She sounds like a little girl.)* Because I don't know what to do.

Jon: What to do about what?

Jenny: About that feeling.

JENNY IS EXPERIENCING AN ABREACTION. SHE IS NOT JUST REMEMBERING WHAT TOOK PLACE BUT FEELING LIKE IT IS TAKING PLACE. OFTEN, THERAPISTS PROMOTE THE BELIEF THAT THE INDIVIDUAL IS GETTING THE FEELING OUT BY FEELING AND EXPRESSING IT. CLIENTS WHO ARE EXPOSED TO THIS TYPE OF TREATMENT FIND THE EXPERIENCE OF THERAPY TO BE EXTREMELY PAINFUL AND LENGTHY. FEELINGS DO NOT NEED TO BE LET OUT. THE PROBLEM IS WITH THE WAY THE MIND IS PROCESSING INFORMATION. IT IS READING THE INFORMATION ABOUT SOMETHING THAT DID HAPPEN OR THE MEANING THE MIND HAS ATTACHED TO WHAT HAPPENED AS IF IT IS HAPPENING. THIS CAN BE THE CASE EVEN IF THE EVENT IS ONLY

Jon: **You know what to do**, and you're doing it right now by addressing it with me so that it can clear.

I TELL HER SHE DOES KNOW WHAT TO DO REFERRING TO "NOW" AND THAT WHAT TO DO "NOW" IS EXACTLY WHAT SHE IS DOING "NOW". I AM TRYING TO GET HER OUT OF RELIVING A PRIOR EXPERIENCE AS IF IT IS HAPPENING NOW.

Jenny: Okay.

Jon: **You are doing fine**, Jenny.

Jenny: They hurt me, and I couldn't do anything about it.

Jon: What bothers you about that now?

Jenny: Because they can do whatever they want to.

JENNY'S MIND CONTINUES TO READ THE INFORMATION ABOUT THE EVENT AS WELL AS THE MEANING HER MIND ATTACHED TO THE EVENT AS HAPPENING. I CONTINUE DOING WHAT I CAN TO GET HER EMOTIONALLY CONNECTED TO WHAT IS HAPPENING NOW.

Jon: When you were young, someone hurt you and you couldn't do anything. What would you do now if some guy in a Santa Claus outfit walked over to you and started unbuttoning your blouse?

Jenny: *(Laughing)* I would belt him.

Jon: Right.

Jenny: I would very definitely do something.

EARLIER, JENNY HAD SPOKEN ABOUT BEING UPSET WHEN SHE SAW SANTA AS A YOUNG GIRL. SHE BELIEVES SHE MAY HAVE BEEN FORCED TO GIVE ORAL SEX TO A MAN AND THE EVENT HAD BEEN FILMED. TO YANK HER OUT OF THE ABREACTION, I AM LOOKING TO MAKE HER REALIZE THAT THIS IS NOW, AND SHE IS FAR FROM HELPLESS. IN ORDER TO DO THAT, I ASK THE QUESTION ABOUT WHAT SHE WOULD DO IF SOMEONE DRESSED LIKE SANTA BEGAN UNBUTTONING HER BLOUSE. HER LAUGHTER SHOWS ME THAT, FINALLY, I HAVE SUCCEEDED IN GETTING HER EMOTIONALLY PRESENT.

Jon: There was a time when you couldn't do anything about it on the way to where **you can defend yourself**. You used to be small on the way to **now you're big**. What has been troubling you?

SAYING THE WORDS "YOU'RE BIG" IS SOMETHING ONE MIGHT SAY TO A CHILD. I AM DIRECTING IT TO WHERE HER MIND HAS BEEN STUCK AND USING WORDS A CHILD WOULD UNDERSTAND AND RESPOND TO BECAUSE THAT'S WHERE SHE HAS BEEN STUCK.

Jenny: Well, it's that feeling of helplessness. It's just that feeling that I can be hurt.

Jon: You were hurt when you were small.

Jenny: I don't know if I'm finished with that.

HER VOICE IS NOW A GROWNUP VOICE AND SHE IS NO LONGER EMOTIONAL. YET, SHE SAYS THAT SHE IS NOT SURE SHE IS FINISHED WITH IT. WHAT HER MIND IS DOING IS JOINING HAVING BEEN HELPLESS BACK THEN WITH BEING HELPLESS NOW BECAUSE BEING HELPLESS THEN HAS CONTINUED TO HAVE AN EFFECT ON HER FEELINGS, THOUGHTS AND ACTIONS. THERE IS MORE TO BE DONE TO GET HER CLEAR. I GO BACK TO THE "SANTA NOW" TO BRING HER TO THE PRESENT.

Jon: So, if Santa Claus started to unbutton your blouse, are you finished enough with it to push his hand away?"

WHEN I SAY, "WHAT IF SOME GUY IN A SANTA SUIT STARTED UNBUTTONING YOUR BLOUSE?" IT BRINGS HER INTO THE MOMENT, DEMONSTRATING THAT THIS IS NOW AND THAT WAS THEN, AND IT GRABS HER ATTENTION. IT ALSO INCREASES THE REALIZATION THAT NOW SHE'S A STRONG WOMAN. IT'S GRAPHIC ENOUGH TO FORCE HER ATTENTION TOWARD WHAT IS HAPPENING NOW, HENCE, UPDATING AND CLEARING HER MIND.

Jenny: I'm finished with it unless I choose it.

"IT," MEANING HAVING SEXUAL EXPERIENCES.

Jon: I don't think you will choose it with somebody wearing a Santa Claus suit.

Jenny: *(Laughing)* No, or a photographer.

Jon: This thing happened. **You finished with it.**

Jenny: *(Once again her voice becomes childlike)* But they still keep reaching out.

Jon: No one is reaching out. **Nobody's hurting you.**

Jenny: I feel like they are.

Jon: **No one is hurting you now.** Check it out.

I SAY, "NOBODY IS HURTING YOU," TO PULL HER INTO THE PRESENT. SOMEONE WHO HAS BEEN HURT IS MORE LIKELY TO BE PRE-OCCUPIED WITH GETTING HURT. THEY MAY FEEL THAT THEY ARE MORE LIKELY TO BE HURT AGAIN. IF SOMEONE WHO HAS BEEN HURT IS EMOTIONALLY CLEAR, HOWEVER, THEY ARE LESS LIKELY TO BE HURT AGAIN.

Jenny: I'll just live like a nun or something.

THERE IS STILL A TANGLE IN HER MIND BETWEEN THE EVENT AND THE EFFECT IT HAS HAD. THE EVENT IS TROUBLING HER, AND IT CONTINUES TO AFFECT HER BECAUSE SHE IS TROUBLED BY IT. IT ISN'T AS TANGLED AS IT WAS BECAUSE HER VOICE IS NO LONGER LITTLE GIRL EMOTIONAL, BUT THERE IS MORE TO CLEAR.

Jon: Nobody can grab you as a two-year-old.

Jenny: Because I'm not two now.

Jon: Yes. **You're big. You're a grown-up. You're a woman.**

Jenny: Yeah, I really know that. It would be different at this point.

Jon: Yes.

Jenny: I have sexual feelings, but I haven't let anyone get to me. But now, it's like the feelings are very powerful.

Jon: Yes, **you are a grown-up, you are a woman.** When you were little, someone may have put his penis in your mouth.

Jenny: That's all I know that may have happened.

SHE WONDERS IF HE DID OTHER SEXUAL THINGS TO HER AS WELL.

Jon: Well, let's start with that. Maybe somebody put his penis in your mouth, and you were little, and you couldn't do anything about it because you were little.

Jenny: Yeah.

Jon: Could that happen now?

Jenny: I don't know.

Jon: Well, which is stronger, you or a penis?

I SAY, "WHICH IS STRONGER, YOU OR A PENIS?" WHICH IS PROVOCATIVE, KEEPS HER ENGAGED, AND IS ENTERTAINING. HUMOR BRINGS HER INTO THE PRESENT. IF SHE IS EXPERIENCING DELIGHT, AMUSEMENT, AND INTEREST, THE SHIFT TO MIND CLEAR IS ACCELERATED.

Jenny: I'm stronger.

Jon: Can you imagine that there was a war between you and this very fragile little thing?

Jenny: *(Big smile)* I bet I would win that war.

Jon: Which do you think would win the war between a breast and penis?

Jenny: The breast would win.

SHE IS STRONGER THAN A PENIS. EVEN HER BREAST IS STRONGER THAN A PENIS.

Jon: Wouldn't it be crazy for someone to stick their fragile penis near you unless you really want it there?

Jenny: That wouldn't be a good idea.

Jenny: No.

Jon: When you were two, there were things you couldn't do.

THE WORDS, "WHEN YOU WERE TWO, THERE WERE THINGS YOU COULDN'T DO," RHYME AND REVERBERATE WHERE HER CHILD MIND CAN UNDERSTAND IT. I TELL HER THAT NOW SHE IS "BIG AND STRONG" AND THAT SHE'S ALSO "...DANGEROUS WITH TEETH" BECAUSE IT UPDATES HER MIND IN A WAY THAT IS POWERFUL, EFFECTIVE AND FUNNY.

Jenny: Yeah.

Jon: You can do lots of things.

Jenny: Yeah.

Jon: When you were little you were little. Now, **you are big, strong and dangerous**. It wouldn't be smart for someone to stick his unwanted penis near something big, strong and dangerous, something with teeth.

Jenny: No.

Jon: It would be like putting his penis in a power mower.

Jenny: *(Laughing hard)* That wouldn't be a good idea.

Jon: What else?

Jenny: The picture. What if someday I find that? What if he is keeping it on film for eternity or something.

SHE FINALLY COMPLETELY REALIZES THAT THIS EVENT IS FINISHED. NOW, I CAN TACKLE THE NEXT ISSUE WHICH IS HER SHAME ABOUT BEING PHOTOGRAPHED WHILE SHE WAS BEING MOLESTED.

Jon: A photograph is just a piece of paper with a representation of what something looked like.

Jenny: I like that thought.

Jon: Yeah, I'll show you something. Let's see if I can find it here. *(I hand her my driver's license)* Do you think that's me?

JENNY FELT AS IF THE PICTURE OF WHAT HAPPENED WHEN SHE WAS A CHILD WAS CAUSING HER TO BE FOREVER EXPOSED AND VULNERABLE. BY HUMOROUSLY SHOWING HER MY PHOTO ON MY DRIVER'S LICENSE, IT BECOMES CLEAR THAT A PHOTOGRAPH ISN'T HER. IF I HAD USED ONLY AN INTELLECTUAL OR LOGICAL EXPLANATION OF THAT FACT, IT WOULD HAVE REACHED ONLY THE SURFACE OF HER MIND AND WOULD NOT HAVE BEEN ACCEPTED BY OR RESPONDED TO ON A DEEPER LEVEL OF HER MIND WHICH IS WHERE HER FEELING OF EXPOSURE AND VULNERABILITY WAS COMING FROM. ALSO, IT WOULD HAVE SEEMED LIKE I WAS EXPLAINING THE OBVIOUS AND, THEREFORE, WOULD HAVE LIKELY BEEN EXPERIENCED AS CONDESCENDING. USING MY PHOTOGRAPH MAKES IT HUMOROUS AND IS MULTI- LEVEL COMMUNICATION THAT IS RESPONDED TO BY HER DEEPER MIND. WHAT I AM SAYING IS ADDRESSING JENNY'S CONCERN ABOUT THE PICTURE, BUT THE WAY I AM TALKING ABOUT IT IS SILLY AND SHE IS GIGGLY AND ENTERTAINED.

Jenny: Well, it is a representation of you. It's just an image of you.

Jon: Good. Because I don't want you to think of me as one inch tall and flat.

Jenny: *(Jenny is having fun. She is smiling and laughing)* Okay. I won't.

Jon: And you're absolutely sure that's not me, aren't you?

Jenny: I'm absolutely sure that's not you.

Jon: Somebody may have taken a picture of you when you were two years old. It doesn't even look like you look now. No one can recognize you and the picture means nothing. Does that bother you now?

Jenny: I'm not crying.

Jon: You're laughing.

Jenny: It bothers me a little bit, but not as much.

Jon: What disturbs you?

Jenny: Just the helplessness.

Jon: It's true that you <u>were</u> helpless back then.

I AM CHANGING WORDS AND TENSES TO ELIMINATE IT FROM HER PRESENT.

Jenny: Yeah.

Jon: Is there something about having been helpless then that troubles you now?

Jenny: I don't like to be helpless.

Jon: Is there something about <u>having been helpless back then</u> that's troubling now?

Jenny: Less and less. It feels like it's moving back.

Jon: You're finished with it. It's over. You survived. You are powerful. You are dangerous. You are strong.

Jenny: Right.

Jon: What do you think of that?

Jenny: Now is not then.

Jon: Right. Now is not then.

Jenny: Now is not then. I think that was what was confusing me.

Jon: Would your mouth be a safe place for an uninvited penis?

Jenny: No, it wouldn't be. I do have power and it won't ever be like that again.

Jon: No.

Jenny: I know that now.

Jon: Isn't that nice?

Jenny: It's very good to know that.

WHEN THERE WAS FEAR EARLIER IN OUR MEETING, THE DATA ABOUT WHAT HAD HAPPENED AND WHAT IT MEANT WAS BEING READ BY HER MIND AS IF IT WAS HAPPENING. NOW, JENNY HAS A BREAKTHROUGH REALIZATION ON A DEEPER LEVEL THAT THE PAST ISN'T HAPPENING, AND, IF IT ISN'T HAPPENING, THEN IT DOESN'T EXIST.

Jon: Where is the past? You can recall that it happened, but it's not to be found. It isn't anywhere.

Jenny: It's not there.

Jon: Right. Yeah. It's not there.

Jenny: It can't bother me now. It can't be disturbing my life now. I have a great feeling of freedom. I'm a little bit confused, though. I mean, my identity was based on that.

Jon: Your identity was not based on the fact that some guy may have put his penis in your mouth when you were little.

Jenny: It upsets me that I lived according to that perception.

Jon: Why?

Jenny: I believed something was wrong with me.

Jon: This is where you are. Where you were wasn't as good as where you are. Are you sad that you were where you were before you got to where you are?

Jenny: I couldn't be here if I wasn't there.

Jon: What's going on now for you?

Jenny: Something deep inside is happening. It isn't there.

Jon: Since the past does not exist, the experience does not exist.

Jenny: That is kind of strange.

Jon: The past is just a concept. It is not a real thing like this chair or that table.

Jenny: That feels very good. I can breathe better. Now, I can breathe.

Jon: If we disrupted some misunderstanding about identity, that's fine because anything we can kick out of the way gets you closer to the exciting realization of who you are. And who you are is not a sex abuse victim. You aren't a sex abuse anything.

Jenny: No. I am not a victim or a survivor. That is not my identity.

Jon: No, you're not any of that.

Jenny: I don't know who I am exactly.

Jon: Who you are is the energy you experience as you are absolutely clear.   Everything else is falling off. Anything else has been distortion.

JENNY IS NOW SO OPEN AND CONNECTED THAT I JUST CONTINUE MOVING THE BALL DOWN THE FIELD. THE EFFECTS FROM WHATEVER HAPPENED TO HER AS A CHILD AS WELL AS THOSE FROM THE PREVIOUS THERAPY ARE NOW CLEAR, HAVING BEEN PUT IN A CLOSED FILE IN HER MIND. SHE IS OPEN, AND I CONTINUE WITH THE ISSUE OF IDENTITY TO SUGGEST THAT HER BODY IS NOT HER IDENTITY EITHER. I SUGGEST THAT HER BODY IS TEMPORARY, AND, AT SOME POINT, SHE WILL DROP IT AND BE JUST FINE.

Jenny: This thing just kind of leaped inside of me, you know, and I don't have to do anything to make it fall off. It's just happening.

Jon: Yes, illusion is falling away.

Jenny: This is so good!

Jon: And, someday, your body will fall off. Some people who have identified with their body find the idea of it falling off to be quite disturbing. Say that you thought you were your blouse and then you started to unbutton it. You'd say, "Damn, this is the scariest thing I ever did in my life. What am I with it unbuttoned? What am I when it drops?" When it drops and you're still there, you get a little closer to who you are.

Jenny: I mean, it isn't me. I can see me differently.

Jon: **So many things have become clear** to you **it just sets off a chain reaction.**

Jenny: Right. It takes away the underpinnings of a lot of stuff that was troubling.

Jon: There you go.

Jenny: I could feel something shifting.

Jon: Yes.

Jenny: I have had so much psychotherapy. It went on for years without things getting resolved. It wouldn't have gotten to the same result I got tonight, I don't think, ever. I really feel like boulders moving or something. It's a big shift.

Jon: I'm very excited for you.

Jenny: Me, too.

Jon: It's right on time because the time is now, and that's what matters.

Jenny: That's right.

Jon: It makes no sense to regret the past. Can you imagine a leopard drinking water that is fresh and clean while being depressed about being thirsty in the past?

Jenny: No. No. That's right. This is really neat. Oh, gosh. It's really neat. Thank you.

Jon: I enjoyed being with you.

Follow-Up Commentary

Six months later, I spoke with Jenny. She is enjoying a satisfying romantic and sexual relationship. The anxiety and pre-occupation are gone.

Nina

Jon:	What would you like our meeting to address?
Nina:	I have been in therapy for five years now and I'm ready for something to come to closure, somehow or another, and, you know, my anxiety is there. The weight problem is one of the things that I've worked on throughout therapy, but then it seems like other things come into play, marital problems, the divorce, custody, and things like that, and so it just seems like I am continually...there's nothing closing. Nothing.
Jon:	You are invested in what is best for yourself.
Nina:	That's right.
Jon:	And **now, you are ready for closure**.
Nina:	On some things, yeah.
Jon:	Now, **you are ready for closure** on some things.
Nina:	The feelings, yes, that if I don't get closure on some aspect...maybe not closure, but if I don't get control of some aspect, control of my personal life or control of work or control of the weight problem, I just keep hoping, in other words, and…
Jon:	So, to **focus your power.**
Nina:	Right, rather than "Oops!" This problem is coming in the way, so now we have to throw this other one over here for a while, and I mean, you know, I started therapy for one reason, and then it just seems like, that it kept getting interrupted with other things.
Jon:	You dealt with some things that came up and now is the time to **focus your power and get what you want**.
Nina:	Right. I have had some growth and I have had some movement, and I have had some backtracking.
Jon:	You are looking to **do what will make life better.** Am I with you so far?
Nina:	Yes.
Jon:	For you, the thing is to **move ahead** and enjoy that sense of **"you are doing it".**

Nina: It's mine, for me. It's not, you know, for people at work or it's not for my ex-husband. It's not for the public in general.

Jon: It's for yourself.

Nina: Yes.

IN LISTENING TO NINA, I HEAR THAT SHE HAS BEEN STUCK. I UNDERSTAND THIS STUCK-NESS AS HAVING TWO QUALITIES. FIRST IS THAT SHE IS CONSIDERING MANY THINGS SIMULTANEOUSLY AND EACH THING IS BEING CONSIDERED IN A WAY THAT COULDN'T PRODUCE ANY POSITIVE ACTION. THE WAY SHE HAS BEEN THINKING IS NOT A WAY THAT HER INNER MIND COULD TRANSLATE INTO A SPECIFIC ACTION. SECOND, AS SHE CONSIDERS WHAT IS TROUBLING, HER MIND MOST OFTEN THINKS ABOUT WHAT NOT TO DO RATHER THAN WHAT TO DO. SINCE THE UNCONSCIOUS DOESN'T UNDERSTAND AND RESPOND TO NEGATION, PARTICULARLY WHEN IT'S USED IN DESCRIBING A DESIRED OUTCOME, THE THINGS SHE DESIRES ARE HEARD ALMOST IN REVERSE. IF I ASK YOU TO NOT THINK ABOUT AN ANGRY MERMAID, THE MIND CREATES A PICTURE OF AN ANGRY MERMAID. THIS HAS NOTHING TO DO WITH RESISTANCE OR A DESIRE TO FAIL, BUT RATHER THAT THE INNER MIND DOESN'T UNDERSTAND NEGATION AND, THEREFORE, LEAVES IT OUT. IN DEMONSTRATING MY UNDERSTANDING OF WHAT NINA HAS SAID, I MENTION WHAT THERE IS TO DO RATHER THAN WHAT HAS BEEN GOING WRONG.

THE COMMAND, "FOCUS YOUR POWER," IS PREFACED BY THE WORDS, "SO TO," WHICH CAUSES HER TO HEAR THE COMMAND AS A CLARIFICATION OF WHAT SHE JUST TOLD ME, BUT IT TELLS HER WHAT TO DO ON A LEVEL BELOW CONSCIOUS AWARENESS. IN ADDITION, I LOOK STRAIGHT INTO HER EYES WHILE SAYING THE WORDS TO ADD EMPHASIS. I REPEAT IT TWICE TO DEMONSTRATE AN UNDERSTANDING OF BOTH WHAT HAS BEEN GOING WRONG AND WHAT TO DO ABOUT IT. THIS CONTINUES AS I SAY, "DO WHAT WILL MAKE LIFE BETTER." AS NINA DESCRIBES WHAT'S BEEN HAPPENING, I EXPRESS THAT I UNDERSTAND BY SAYING, "NOW, YOU ARE READY FOR CLOSURE." I USE HER WORDS TO STATE THE SOLUTION.

I SAY, "MOVE AHEAD AND ENJOY THE SENSE OF YOU ARE DOING IT." I CAN TELL THAT I HAVE A BUY-IN FROM NINA BECAUSE SHE RESPONDS, "IT'S MINE, FOR ME." HERE AGAIN, ALTHOUGH I'M TELLING HER WHAT TO DO, SHE EXPERIENCES BEING HEARD AND UNDERSTOOD.

Jon: So, tell me what you want.

Nina: Well, of course, I want to physically look better and feel better. One of the things is I found out that I do have this syndrome that makes it very difficult to lose weight. I have a hormonal imbalance, but I still also know that I have behaviors that trigger my eating, not excessively anymore, not to the gorging point or that type of thing but eating unhealthily. You know, driving by the burger place and being emotionally stressed or something, and going in and getting maybe two hamburgers. But still, that's, like I said, that's not an excess, but it's the wrong kind of food.

Jon: You are looking to **eat healthy food** that will make you **look good and feel good and get accomplishment and power.**

Nina: I recently received a promotion at work. I'm a hard worker. At one time, I had been turned down for a job and the statement that was made was that fat people can't be motivated. I fought that at the time and won, but I still didn't feel like I accomplished anything because I was still fat, you know.

Jon: You work hard. You know how to fight and now is your time to do this for you.

Nina: One of my aspects of being a hard worker is I give and give and give and give. I'm not ready to quit giving, but I'm ready to start taking. I guess this is the way to explain it.

Jon: You know how to give and how to **take this for yourself,** so you **feel better** and **move toward what you want immediately.**

Nina: Yes. Like I said, I need some kind of closure of some kind. You are terming it "focus" which may be a more appropriate word than "closure". I have certainly learned from all my experiences and mistakes. I don't really want to just forget it, but I am ready to move on.

Jon: You have learned, and now it's your time to **move ahead** and **do what you really want.**

NINA ISN'T RESPONDING TO MOST OF WHAT I SAY, BUT THE WORDS I EMPHASIZE ARE REACHING HER INNER MIND AND SHIFTING HER MIND'S PROCESSING SO THAT CHANGE IS POSSIBLE.

Nina: I have some problems with thinking it's a little selfish and that type of thing, but then, you know…

Jon: Eating healthy foods is selfish. Eating fattening foods is generous.

Nina: Well, I never looked at it that way. Taking time for myself is selfish.

Jon: Taking the time to eat healthy is selfish and eating poorly is kind?

Nina: Not to me, no.

Jon: No, you're right.

NINA ALREADY KNOWS EATING UNHEALTHILY ISN'T ADVANTAGEOUS. HENCE, I RESPOND BY ACKNOWLEDGING, NOT WHAT WAS SAID, BUT WHAT WAS MEANT. I SAY, "SO, TO EAT HEALTHY FOOD THAT WILL MAKE YOU LOOK GOOD AND FEEL GOOD AND GET ACCOMPLISHMENT AND POWER." I HAVE GIVEN HER COMMANDS AT THE LEVEL BELOW CONSCIOUS AWARENESS FOR WHAT SHE ALREADY AGREES IS A BETTER COURSE OF ACTION. HOWEVER, HER EXPERIENCE IS THAT I'M ACKNOWLEDGING WHAT SHE JUST SAID TO ME.

NINA TELLS ME WHAT HAPPENED CONCERNING HER PROMOTION AND I RESPOND WITH WORDS THAT ARE POSITIVE AND WITH WHICH SHE WOULD AGREE. FOR EXAMPLE, "YOU WORK HARD, YOU KNOW HOW TO FIGHT, AND NOW IS YOUR TIME TO DO THIS FOR YOU." I NOTICE AND, THEREFORE, ENHANCE TWO THINGS THAT SHE AGREES WITH AND FEELS GOOD ABOUT, WHICH STARTED A PATTERN OF AGREEMENT. THE FIRST IS POSITIVE AND AGREED WITH, THE SECOND IS POSITIVE AND AGREED WITH

AND THE THIRD STATEMENT IS POSITIVE. I'M LOOKING FOR AGREEMENT. HER MIND GETS USED TO SAYING, "YES," WHICH MAKES IT MORE LIKELY THAT SHE WILL AGREE WITH THE THIRD STATEMENT.

NINA HAS MENTIONED A NUMBER OF ISSUES, BUT I CONTINUE TO ADDRESS ONE THING WITH HER, WHICH IS LOSING WEIGHT AND BEING HEALTHIER. MORE SPECIFICALLY, EATING IN A HEALTHY WAY, EXERCISING IN A HEALTHY WAY, LOOKING GOOD AND FEELING GOOD. BECAUSE NINA STATES HER EFFORTS HAVE BEEN SCATTERED AND UNSUCCESSFUL, I INTEND TO CAUSE SUCCESS IN ONE SPECIFIC AREA AND FOCUS ON THAT.

NINA HAS BEEN THINKING THAT, ALTHOUGH SHE'D LIKE TO EAT HEALTHY, IT'S SELFISH. I DON'T DISAGREE DIRECTLY WITH HER BECAUSE THAT MIGHT NOT ERASE HER BELIEF. INSTEAD, I EXAGGERATE HER OWN REASONS WHY SHE THINKS SHE CAN'T DO IT SO THAT SHE WILL THEN DISAGREE. I SAY, "EATING HEALTHY FOODS IS SELFISH AND EATING FATTENING FOODS IS GENEROUS." SHE DISAGREES WITH ME BUT GOES ON TO SAY THAT TAKING THE NECESSARY TIME IS SELFISH.

PEOPLE TYPICALLY EXPERIENCE THEIR BELIEFS AS REAL AND TRUE. I HEAR WHAT NINA IS REPORTING AS HER BELIEFS, HER PERSPECTIVE AND HER EXPERIENCE, BUT NOT AS REALITY. THIS PROVIDES ME WITH THE OPPORTUNITY TO ALTER WHAT SHE EXPERIENCES, WHICH, IN TURN, OPENS UP OTHER POSSIBILITIES AND, THEREFORE, THE POTENTIAL FOR SUCCESS.

Nina: Eating healthy is good and it's right, but it's not always convenient and it's not always available and its hard work to make it available, you know.

Jon: Are you sure?

Nina: Well, no.

Jon: So, not really sure? Yes! **It's your time** to **do it.**

Nina: Yes.

Jon: You work hard. You've shown that. You are caring and now is the time for closure and to **move ahead** and **do this, get the results, enjoy the benefits** and **be energized**. Is that it?

Nina: Yeah, I mean, that's what I want up here. *(She points to her forehead)*

Jon: Yes, so, here, *(pointing to my forehead)* **you do get it.**

Nina: Yeah, the reservation again is am I going to be able to deal with the guilt feelings or whatever? Is it going to take away time from other things that I enjoy doing or have been doing and that type of thing?

Jon: You should be guilty if you eat foods that are good for you.

Nina: No, not if I eat the foods that are good for me--if I take that time to, or what I see as the time to do that.

Jon: You know **now is your time** to **take for you** and **move ahead and accomplish what you want**. Am I with you?

Nina: Yes.

Jon: And you know that. You know that now. Yes?

Nina: Yes.

Jon: That's what you know. Am I with you so far?

Nina: Yes, you are.

I AM GETTING NINA TO FOLLOW ME WHILE TELLING HER THAT I AM CHECKING TO MAKE SURE I AM FOLLOWING HER.

NINA SAYS, "EATING HEALTHY IS HARD WORK," BECAUSE HER MIND HAS BEEN SEEING EATING HEALTHY AS ONE HUGE, COMPLEX TASK. PURCHASING A BAG OF SPINACH IN THE GROCERY STORE ISN'T DIFFICULT, HOWEVER, AND TAKING THE SALAD OUT OF THE BAG ISN'T COMPLEX. I CHALLENGE HER WAY OF THINKING BY ASKING, "ARE YOU SURE IT'S DIFFICULT?" WHICH CREATES DOUBT AND THE PERCEIVED OBSTACLE LOSES SOME SUBSTANCE. THEN, I PAUSE BEFORE I SAY, "NOW SINCE IT'S YOUR TIME, YOU DO IT," WHICH IS A COMMAND THAT TELLS HER MIND ON THE LEVEL BELOW AWARENESS WHAT TO DO.

WHEN NINA SAYS, "I WANT IT UP HERE," THE WAY THAT SHE SAYS IT DISCOUNTS IT. IN ORDER TO INCREASE IT, I AFFIRM THAT BY SAYING, "YES, SO RIGHT HERE YOU DO GET IT," WHICH IS ALSO A DECLARATIVE TO HER MIND ON THE LEVEL BELOW CONSCIOUS AWARENESS.

Jon: Close your eyes for a few moments. What I want to accomplish as you let your eyes rest is to give you a chance to begin getting used to hearing me speak to you while you rest your eyes closed. That's all we're going for, that's all I'm looking to accomplish is that you have a few moments and get used to hearing me speak with your eyes closed. Notice that, in addition to hearing me speaking, you are hearing other sounds and hearing those sounds quite clearly. And then, you can open your eyes. I would like to know what you were noticing within yourself while your eyes were closed.

Nina: Well, initially, the jaw was really tight, but then the car door slammed and it just kind of went away.

Jon: You **quickly release tension** and then **you relax.**

Nina: Yes.

Jon: Close your eyes again. Well, I'm certainly delighted to learn how quickly, how readily you're able to really experience how it just goes away, and let me remind you that, while hearing those other sounds drifting in from outside, that there is nothing that's required from you. Rather, this is just about acquiring the experience of hearing me speak while resting your eyes. Nothing is required because **everything that needs to happen will simply happen automatically.** It was good to hear that already you've been able to **notice an easing,** and yet, even though **you've already begun relaxing and letting go**, it isn't necessary to put any kind of effort into that at all. It's nice, but it's not necessary. It's not important. Again, find your way back to here 'til your eyes can open. And again, I would like to know what was happening for you, what you're noticing within you.

Nina: My mind got really busy, which it does frequently.

Jon: Oh?

Nina: But then, without even really thinking or whatever, it just cleared up.

Jon: Yes! Your mind can be clear. It happens by itself. It follows what we intend, and our intention is clear.

Nina: Yeah, then they just cleared as quickly as they came in. They all cleared.

Jon: Great.

Nina: That's something that consciously I'm trying to work on, especially like at night when I'm ready to go to bed, to clear and I haven't been able to really accomplish it.

Jon: So, **you've been able to really accomplish something today** without any effort. You **get clear** and you **feel good**.

Nina: Yes, I feel good.

IN DEMONSTRATING MY UNDERSTANDING, THERE ARE COMMANDS AND DECLARATIVES. I TELL HER, "YOU KNOW HOW TO FIGHT," AND, "NOW IS YOUR TIME...DO THIS FOR YOU." I ASK NINA TO CLOSE HER EYES FOR A FEW MINUTES. I WANT TO CAUSE EXPERIENCES THAT ARE NEW AND DIFFERENT FOR HER. SHE FEELS STUCK AND FEELS THAT NOTHING HAS BEEN WORKING SO FAR. I DO SOMETHING DIFFERENT, NOT TO REPEAT THE SAME OLD THING. WHAT I ASK NINA TO DO IS DESIGNED TO BE FAIL PROOF. I'M LOOKING FOR NINA TO HAVE AN EXPERIENCE OF SUCCESS AND LOOKING FOR HER TO AGREE WITH WHAT I'M SAYING. SO, I'M SAYING THINGS THAT ARE IMPOSSIBLE TO DISAGREE WITH. FOR INSTANCE, "YOU WILL ACCOMPLISH ACQUIRING THE EXPERIENCE OF HEARING ME SPEAKING WITH YOUR EYES CLOSED," AND THIS STATEMENT, "AS YOU'RE HEARING ME SPEAK, YOU'RE HEARING OTHER SOUNDS AS WELL," AND THIS STATEMENT, "YOU QUICKLY RELEASE AND RELAX." WHAT I SAY TO HER IS ALL PRESENT TENSE AND, THEREFORE, COMMANDS THAT CAN BE FOLLOWED.

CAUSING NINA TO HAVE A NEW AND DIFFERENT EXPERIENCE OPENS HER MIND TO THE POSSIBILITY OF DOING THINGS DIFFERENTLY. NINA'S NEW EXPERIENCE IS FAIL-PROOF, EFFORTLESS AND AUTOMATIC--LIKE BEING ON A PLANE OR AN ELEVATOR. SHE MOVES TOWARD HER DESTINATION, BUT THERE IS NOTHING SHE HAS TO DO.

NINA HEARS A CAR DOOR SLAM IN THE PARKING LOT AND SAYS THAT HER JAW BECAME LOOSER. I PICK UP ON THIS BEING A SKILL AND ABILITY, AND NOTICE IT BY SAYING, "YOU QUICKLY RELEASE TENSION AND THEN YOU RELAX." IT HAS BEEN APPRECIATED; THEREFORE, IT WILL INCREASE. I HEAR WHAT SHE SAYS, APPRECIATE WHAT SHE ACCOMPLISHED, AND TELL HER WHAT TO DO.

RATHER THAN MAKE IT IMPORTANT FOR NINA TO TRY TO MAKE RELAXATION HAPPEN WHICH PREVENTS IT, I MAKE IT UNIMPORTANT AND IT HAPPENS AUTOMATICALLY.

"THINGS CLEAR," IS STATED AS HAPPENING NOW AND IN THE FUTURE. I SHIFT FROM PRESENT TO PAST TENSE IF I INTEND TO ERASE SOMETHING, BUT PAST TO PRESENT IF I INTEND FOR SOMETHING TO INCREASE.

Jon: You've come here to really **accomplish something. You have accomplished something already.** Do you know how you want to be eating?

Nina: I want to be eating healthy.

Jon: Do you know what that is, eating healthy?

Nina: Intellectually, yes.

Jon: Okay.

Nina: I read it in a book.

Jon: Yes. That is good learning. Learning to **eat in a healthy way**.

Nina: Yes.

Jon: Now, to **enjoy immediate gratification as you eat in a healthy way.**

Nina: Immediate gratification?

Jon: Yes, immediate gratification--knowing **you are on your way** and **it's immediately and profoundly gratifying** to know **you're really doing it.** Close your eyes. We're ahead of schedule. Everything is going on perfectly. You have already begun to **relax, release tension** and even **experience the clearing. Enjoy the immediate gratification of eating healthy** because **it's your time.** Find your way back. What's come up for you?

Nina: The image of a beach. I hate the color pink or at least I thought I did. Anyway, I saw myself in a fluorescent pink two-piece. I kept going back and forth between a nice-looking person, and it was me, like a blown-up version, and they kept changing places. Then it went back to the nice-looking one.

Jon: The **immediate gratification** of **being on your way** and that whole experience of **really doing it. Focus** and **enjoy that instant...delightful, satisfying, lasting, control, the power that's immediately yours.** Close your eyes. You thought you hated the color...**and now immediate gratification. Right now, gratification. Instant closure...**realizing **you're on your way. You're in charge. You're doing it** and **things are different.** You thought you hated it. **Things are different. The signs are abundantly clear.** And again, your eyes can open. And what else will you be doing as **you're doing it** and as **you do it** you really know **you are on your way; you are in charge. You've turned the corner; you're on a new path.** What else will you be doing that's a clear sign **you're on a different journey** and **it's a much better trip?**

Nina: I think probably just being happy.

I ASK NINA TO CLOSE HER EYES ONCE AGAIN AND CAUSE THE EXPERIENCE THAT THINGS ARE BEING ACCOMPLISHED BUT ACCOMPLISHED EFFORTLESSLY. SHE EXPERIENCES A SENSE OF PEACEFULNESS AS HER MIND BECOMES CLEAR. INITIALLY IN SPEAKING WITH NINA, THERE WERE SO MANY JUMBLED AND RAPID THOUGHTS AND IN A FORM THAT WAS CAUSING HER TO BE IMMOBILIZED RATHER THAN SERVING AS A CALL TO ACTION. NOW, HER THOUGHTS ARE CLEARING AND WHEN SHE MENTIONS HAVING TRIED TO CLEAR HER MIND AT NIGHT UNSUCCESSFULLY, I'M ABLE TO SAY, "YOU'VE BEEN ABLE TO ACCOMPLISH SOMETHING ALREADY." SHE IS ACCOMPLISHING SOMETHING IN TERMS OF MOVING FORWARD IN TERMS OF EATING HEALTHIER AND HEALTHIER ACTIVITY.

PEOPLE OFTEN THINK OF EATING HEALTHY AND IMMEDIATE GRATIFICATION AS POLAR OPPOSITES. I'M SUGGESTING THAT SHE ENJOY THE IMMEDIATE GRATIFICATION THAT IS HERS AS SHE EATS IN A HEALTHY WAY. I AM RESOLVING THE CONFLICT BETWEEN THESE TWO.

SHE SEES HERSELF IN THE FLUORESCENT PINK BIKINI AND IS SURPRISED BECAUSE SHE DIDN'T THINK SHE LIKED THAT COLOR. I USE THIS AS PROOF THAT THERE HAS ALREADY BEEN A SIGNIFICANT CHANGE AND THAT SHE IS ALREADY ON HER WAY.

Jon: What else would you be doing that you're doing and, since **you're doing it**, **it's a clear sign** that **you're doing this. The corner's been turned. It's a new journey** and **a better journey. It's clear**, **you're on your way. It's clear, you're doing it.** What else will you be doing?

Nina: Participating in doing something physical.

Jon: What would you be doing physically, **immediately, participating, involved in, a clear sign, excitement, beginning it right away, sure you're doing it, it's clear, it's involving,** no question about it. What?

Nina: There are so many things.

Jon: Yes. What?

Nina: I'd probably do...the easiest or quickest with me would be walking.

Jon: Yes. **Fast, quick, easy,** sure, certain **it's a clear and definite sign.**

Nina: I really went around the corner, didn't I?

Jon: Yeah, **totally different ground**. Close your eyes. That's clear. That's sure. **Around the corner. A new trip. It's yours.** And you used to think you didn't even like that color. Once again, open your eyes. Good. Is there anything else that I should know about, that we haven't spoken about yet, that I should know about in order to get where you're at now that **the corner's been turned and you're on this new trip?**

Nina: Oh, probably, although I have been heavy all the time and, again, there is some physical reason for it, but I had several episodes of sexual abuse.

Jon: Let me be clear in my question. Is there anything I should know in order to get where you're at and what you're doing right now, that **the corner has been turned and you're on this trip? I really want to know whatever I should know to really understand what you're doing right now.**

Nina: Now?

Jon: Yes.

Nina: Nothing that I can think of.

Jon: Close your eyes. So, we have covered everything that is necessary. **You've turned the corner, the change, the immediate, delightful, satisfying change you have made. The signal, you enjoy those walks, you are clearly doing it. Eating healthy** and **walking provides immediate, definite gratification. You enjoy, right now. Nothing else needs to be learned. Now, it's clear.** Now, open your eyes. Anything else you would want to ask or tell me?

Nina: As I'm turning the corner, I am going from the "now" to the "thin" person.

WHEN NINA IS ASKED WHAT SHE WOULD LIKE TO BE DOING PHYSICALLY, SHE SAYS, "MANY THINGS." THE UNCONSCIOUS MIND, HOWEVER, CAN'T RESPOND WELL TO, "MANY THINGS." I PUSH FORWARD UNTIL SHE SAYS, "WALKING," THEN I TAKE THE IDEA OF WALKING AND ACCELERATE IT, SHARPEN IT AND PUSH IT FORWARD, BOTH AS A RIGOROUS ACTIVITY AND AS A VERY CLEAR SIGN. WHEN NINA SAYS, "I REALLY WENT AROUND THE CORNER, DIDN'T I?" THAT'S A DELIGHTFUL SIGN THAT SHE REALIZES THIS SHIFT THAT HAS TAKEN PLACE.

NOW, HER MIND WILL FULLY ACCEPT THEM. "YOU'VE TURNED A CORNER, YOU'RE ON THIS TRIP," ARE POSITIVE, AFFIRMATIVE AND APPRECIATIVE STATEMENTS THAT I SAY WITH BOTH ENERGY AND POWER BECAUSE I INTEND TO MOVE HER INTO MY ENERGY.

I ASK NINA IF THERE'S ANYTHING I SHOULD KNOW NOW, AND SHE MENTIONS PAST SEXUAL ABUSE. INSTEAD OF EXPLORING THAT MORE DEEPLY, I JUST AGAIN REPEAT THE QUESTION, BUT EMPHASIZE THE WORD, "NOW," AND SHE RESPONDS WITH THE WORD, "NOTHING." SO, THERE'S NOTHING NOW IN THE WAY. THEN I ASK NINA TO CLOSE HER EYES AGAIN, AND THIS TIME I CONTINUE TO DEEPEN, CELEBRATE, SHARPEN THE SHIFT THAT HAS TAKEN PLACE.

THROUGHOUT THIS ENTIRE CONVERSATION, I HAVE BEEN DELIVERING HER OWN WORDS BACK TO HER BECAUSE HER WORDS ALREADY RESONATE WITHIN HER AND ARE, THEREFORE, MORE POWERFUL. FOR EXAMPLE, "YOU REALLY TURNED THE CORNER," AND "YOU DIDN'T THINK YOU LIKED THAT COLOR."

WHEN NINA TALKS ABOUT WALKING, I SAY, "FAST, QUICK, EASY, SURE, CERTAIN IT'S A CLEAR AND DEFINITE SIGN." NOW, WHEN SHE WALKS, SHE WILL BE GETTING THE MESSAGE, "YOU ARE ON TRACK." CONNECTING THE ACTIVITY OF WALKING TO A MESSAGE OF EXCITEMENT AND AFFIRMATION WILL INCREASE THE ACTIVITY.

Jon: Close your eyes. It is now and now you're doing it. It is now. Now, you are doing. Each walk a clear, bright sign that it's now. Now, you've got it. **Each taste of healthy food you enjoy, anticipating, slowly savoring, remembering, yes, remembering the taste of healthy food, and the satisfaction, knowing you're doing it. You've got it, it's now and it's satisfying.** And you can open your eyes. So, is there anything else you would want to know from me or that I should know about the fact that you're really doing this now?

Nina: No.

Jon: It's clear. Yes?

Nina: Yes. Previously, I kept going the other way.

Jon: But now it's different and there are clear and definite signs.

Nina: Yeah.

Jon: Good.

Nina: I mean, even a few minutes ago, I kept going back the other way, around the corner.

Jon: But not any longer.

Nina: That's right.

Jon: It was delightful to get to spend some time with you. I enjoyed it and we're done!

Nina: We're done?

Jon: We're done.

Nina: Yes.

Jon: No question about it. It was fun to be with you.

Nina: Thanks.

WHEN NINA NOTICES HOW SOMETHING IS DIFFERENT, I SAY, IN EFFECT, "YES, THAT'S HOW THINGS WERE, AND THIS IS HOW THEY ARE." I CREATE A FUTURE IN HER MIND THAT IS SEPARATE FROM WHAT SHE RECALLS IN THE PAST AND NOTICE, COMMENT AND EXPAND ON THINGS THAT FEEL PUZZLING TO HER. THE EXPERIENCE OF HER VISUALLY SCANNING BACK AND FORTH BETWEEN HERSELF OVERWEIGHT AND HERSELF TRIM AND FIT IN A PINK BIKINI, WONDERING WHY SHE NOW LIKES THE

COLOR PINK, IS USED AS PROOF THAT SOMETHING IS HAPPENING. I TELL HER, "THINGS ARE DIFFERENT...YOU THOUGHT YOU HATED THE COLOR."

THROUGHOUT THE CONVERSATION, I HAVE BEEN LOOKING FOR WAYS TO APPRECIATE HER UNCONSCIOUS AND APPRECIATE HER. WHEN SOMETHING COMES UP THAT CAUSES HER TO EXPERIENCE SOMETHING AS UNUSUAL, THEREFORE, I USE IT AS AN INDICATION THAT TRANSFORMATION IS OCCURRING BELOW THE LEVEL OF CONSCIOUS AWARENESS. I USE HER OWN LANGUAGE TO MAKE THE EXPERIENCE MORE POWERFUL FOR HER. FOR EXAMPLE, SHE SAYS, "I GUESS I SHOULD WALK," AND I SAY, "YES, FAST, LONG, HARD AND MOVING YOUR ARMS AND LEGS."

Follow-Up Commentary

In a follow up interview, a year after her visit with me, Nina said that she realized she had previously been overly dependent on her therapist, calling her several times a week. Since our session, she has not felt the urge to call. Her therapy sessions have decreased to once a month. Nina reports more self-confidence, the ability to deal with stress and significant weight loss as well as an increase in energy. She further states that she is taking more risks, both in her personal and professional life. She is more spontaneous where in the past she used to "plan and plot

Pamela

Jon: What would you like our meeting to address or accomplish?

Pamela: A miracle. I want to be able to move forward in my life in a positive direction. I want the skills, the ability, whatever it takes, to do that as pain-free as possible.

Jon: That makes sense to me. You are looking to **move forward and do what makes sense.**

Pamela: I am real compulsive, though. I have a real addictive personality towards people.

PAMELA SAYS THAT SHE IS COMPULSIVE AND THAT SHE HAS AN ADDICTIVE PERSONALITY. IF SOMEONE BELIEVES THE FEELINGS, THOUGHTS OR BEHAVIORS THAT HAVE BEEN PROBLEMATIC ARE SOMETHING THEY HAVE OR WHO THEY ARE, IT CEMENTS THE EXPERIENCE OF BEING STUCK. THESE ARE BELIEFS PROMOTED BY MENTAL HEALTH PROFESSIONALS.

Jon: Tell me.

Pamela: For most of my life, I think I have been addicted to people and certain situations. I think my dependency stems from being abandoned from birth.

Jon: You mentioned compulsive and addictive. I understand that you are intelligent and insightful and that you are willing to really take a look at things. In spite of feeling kind of stuck on some things, it's clear that you are energized and motivated. **You have the ability to survive. You have proven that.**

AS SOMETHING IS NOTICED APPRECIATIVELY, IT INCREASES. PAMELA SAYS THAT SHE IS ADDICTED AND IS COMPULSIVE. SHE MENTIONS BEING ABANDONED AT BIRTH. I RESPOND BY SAYING SHE HAS PROVEN THAT SHE HAS THE ABILITY TO SURVIVE SO THAT BOTH HER ABILITY AND HER APPRECIATION OF HER ABILITY INCREASE.

Pamela: Yes, I guess that's right. I am motivated, and I am very willing to look at these things.

PAMELA'S COMMENT THAT SHE GUESSES THAT WHAT I SAID WAS RIGHT MEANS THAT THE APPRECIATION I OFFERED WAS NOT NEGATED.

Jon: What else should I know to really get it?

Pamela: *(Sighs)* That I am basically stuck in a pattern of doing the same destructive behavior over and over and over, knowing better and then still doing it.

ALTHOUGH OUR HUMAN MINDS ARE MORE ADVANCED THAN OTHER LIFE FORMS, THE COMPONENTS ARE NOT INTEGRATED AND OFTEN DON'T WORK TOGETHER. IN ADDITION, PEOPLE ARE NOT GIVEN USEFUL INSTRUCTIONS TO GET INTERNAL

CONFLICTS RESOLVED BUT, INSTEAD, ARE PRESENTED WITH MORALISTIC PLATITUDES THAT, MORE OFTEN THAN NOT, FURTHER FUEL INNER TURMOIL.

Jon: **You know what makes sense**. You are looking to **do what you know makes sense**.

Pamela: Use my mind rather than my emotions, instead of reacting on an emotional level.

HER INTELLECT HAS NOT BEEN INTEGRATED WITH THE MORE PRIMITIVE FACETS OF MIND. THE PRIMITIVE MIND USES EMOTION TO CAUSE BEHAVIOR AND THE ABILITY TO BE LOGICAL DECREASES AS THE EMOTIONS INCREASE.

Jon: You already realize that **what you do is more important than what you feel**. This gives us a significant head start. You are looking to **put your knowledge into action** and that is why you are with me today. **Turn your back on feelings** and then they will go running after you trying to be nice. You want to **do what makes sense and feel good about it** so that **good feelings follow constructive actions**.

PSYCHOTHERAPISTS ARE LIKELY TO ACT AS IF EMOTIONS ARE IMPORTANT. THE TYPICAL THERAPEUTIC QUESTION IS, "WHAT ARE YOU FEELING?" THERAPY IS A PLACE WHERE CLIENTS ARE ENCOURAGED TO FEEL THEIR FEELINGS AND TO FEEL THEM EVEN MORE DEEPLY THEN THEY USUALLY DO. WHAT I AM SAYING TO PAMELA IS REALLY THE OPPOSITE. I TELL HER TO TURN HER BACK ON HER FEELINGS RATHER THAN FEEL THEM.

PURSUING COMFORT, PARTICULARLY IMMEDIATE COMFORT, CAN LEAD TO DISCOMFORT. IT WILL BE BETTER FOR PAMELA TO DO THINGS THAT PROMOTE LONG-TERM WELLBEING, BUT THE EMOTIONS HAVE BEEN SO INTENSE THAT THEY HAVE BEEN IN CONTROL.

Pamela: That's exactly what I want to do, but I don't do what's in my best interest. God really blessed me with a lot of emotional feelings or something! It has been just real self-destructive.

AS I DESCRIBE WHAT IS INTENDED, SHE TELLS ME HOW IT HAS BEEN. SHE DESCRIBES WHAT SHE HAS BEEN FEELING AND DOING AS IF THOSE THINGS WERE ATTRIBUTES THAT ARE PART OF HER. I WILL NEED TO SEPARATE WHAT SHE INTENDS FROM WHAT SHE REMEMBERS AND SEPARATE WHO SHE IS FROM WHAT SHE HAS BEEN FEELING AND DOING.

Jon: You weren't trying to destroy yourself. You were trying to feel better.

THE NOTION THAT PEOPLE ARE SELF-DESTRUCTIVE WORKS AGAINST THEM. IF A PART OF YOUR BEING IS LOOKING TO DESTROY YOU, THERE IS NO WAY TO INFLUENCE OR MAKE PEACE WITH IT. TELLING SOMEONE THAT HE IS SELF-DESTRUCTIVE IS DESTRUCTIVE. I TELL PAMELA THAT, EVEN THOUGH THE BEHAVIOR MIGHT NOT HAVE WORKED OUT TO HER ADVANTAGE, THAT IT WAS NOT DESIGNED TO CAUSE HER HARM. IF THE MOTIVATION FOR THE BEHAVIOR IS VIEWED AS WELL MEANING, THEN IT BECOMES MORE POSSIBLE TO MAKE IMPROVEMENTS. INSTEAD OF TRYING TO DEAL WITH AN ENEMY, WE ARE JUST MAKING ADJUSTMENTS SO THAT HER INTEREST IN DOING WELL FOR HERSELF IS MORE EASILY ACCOMPLISHED.

Pamela: I was trying to feel better quick. It's like a drug.

Jon: Like a drug?

Pamela: Right, I was in a desperate state. I would do anything.

Jon: Yes, you know that it makes sense to **take a breath**, **be calm** and **put your intellect in charge**.

BECAUSE SHE IS CRITICAL OF HOW SHE HAD REACTED TO FEELINGS, I RESPOND BY TELLING HER WHAT TO DO INSTEAD. I CREDIT HER WITH THE IDEA BY SAYING THAT SHE KNOWS WHAT MAKES SENSE.

Pamela: I really loved being married. I really love the family unit. I really loved having a partner. I am grieving that loss on a real severe level.

Jon: You are a woman who has the ability to love and connect and be gratified and enjoy.

BECAUSE SHE TELLS ME THAT SHE IS GRIEVING THE LOSS ON A SEVERE LEVEL, I KNOW SHE HAS THE ABILITY TO LOVE, CONNECT AND ENJOY. SHE KNOWS I HAVE HEARD WHAT SHE SAID. INSTEAD OF RESPONDING TO HER GRIEF, I APPRECIATE HER STRENGTHS AND ABILITIES. PSYCHOTHERAPISTS RESPOND TO GRIEF BY ENCOURAGING PEOPLE TO FEEL IT MORE DEEPLY. I DON'T BELIEVE THAT FEELING WORSE IS ON THE WAY TO FEELING BETTER.

Pamela: Yes, but I have always, inevitably, picked somebody who is going to abandon me.

Jon: Relationships haven't lasted as long as you would like.

I RESTATE WHAT SHE HAS SAID BUT LEAVE THE MEANING OUT. PSYCHOTHERAPISTS LOOK TO FIND MEANING WHICH I THINK OF AS ADDING MEANING. I BELIEVE THAT MEANING IS DISTORTION AND I WOULD RATHER TAKE IT AWAY.

IF A CHILD IS LEFT WITHOUT CARE, IT CAN'T SURVIVE. THE POWERFUL EMOTIONS THAT PAMELA HAS EXPERIENCED ARE CREATED BY A PART OF HER MIND OUTSIDE OF AWARENESS. THEY FEEL SO POWERFUL BECAUSE THEY ARE CONNECTING TO AN ISSUE AROUND SURVIVAL. ABANDONMENT IS FATAL SINCE IT IMPLIES LEAVING ANOTHER PERSON, USUALLY AN INFANT, WITHOUT THE CARE NECESSARY FOR SURVIVAL. THE WORD IS APPROPRIATELY USED, THEREFORE, IF PARENTS LEAVE AN INFANT IN THE WOODS AND IT DIES. I DON'T CONFRONT PAMELA AND TELL HER SHE IS USING THE WORD INCORRECTLY, BUT I DO REWORD WHAT SHE HAS SAID IN A WAY THAT MAKES IT MORE ACCURATE AND THAT BRINGS THE EMOTIONAL TONE DOWN.

Pamela: My ex-husband could be and is the nicest, most charming, do-anything-in-the-world-for-you kind of a guy and, at the same time, the most abusive S.O.B. you have ever met in your whole life. I mean, it's like two people in one.

PAMELA MENTIONED ABUSIVE AS ONE OF HER EX-HUSBAND'S ATTRIBUTES. I PUT THE BRAKES ON THAT AND RESPOND JUST TO THE WORD "ABUSE". IT'S A BIG DEAL. IT ISN'T ONE OF A NUMBER OF CHARACTERISTICS. IT IS SOMETHING I WANT HER TO BE EXTREMELY AWARE OF AND NOT BE TOLERANT OF.

Jon: Abusing you is no longer allowed.

Pamela: Well, I allow it.

SHE PUT THE IDEA OF ALLOWING ABUSE INTO THE PRESENT BY THE WAY IT WAS VERBALIZED. PEOPLE WHO ARE STUCK, EXPERIENCE TROUBLING THINGS THAT HAVE HAPPENED AS IF THEY ARE EVENTS THAT WILL BE AS MUCH IN THE FUTURE AS THEY WERE IN THE PAST.

Jon: **No longer will that be allowed**. You will **have zero tolerance** for that.

Pamela: That's my goal.

Jon: Do you travel where they have those signs, "ZERO TOLERANCE FOR DRUGS"? You now have **"ZERO TOLERANCE FOR ABUSE"**.

Pamela: Right. That's what I want.

Jon: Written all over you.

Pamela: Yeah. Wouldn't that be nice? *(Laughs)* I seem to attract people that are abusive. I came from a real abusive home, so it's familiar to me.

THE POSITIVE STATEMENTS I AM MAKING ARE JUST BOUNCING OFF. SHE AGREES WITH THE ADVANTAGE BUT DOESN'T BUY INTO POSSIBILITY. SHE THINKS THAT BECAUSE IT HAS HAPPENED, IT MEANS SOMETHING ABOUT HER AND THAT, THEREFORE, SINCE IT HAS HAPPENED, THAT IT WILL CONTINUE TO HAPPEN. I AM TRYING TO SEPARATE THE PAST FROM FUTURE, BUT I AM NOT DOING A GOOD JOB. IF SOMETHING DOESN'T SEEM POSSIBLE, EVEN THE ADVANTAGES ARE NOT MOTIVATIONAL.

Jon: That's finished. **People won't abuse you when there is zero tolerance.**

Pamela: Right.

Jon: Do you know what I mean?

Pamela: Oh yeah! I know. I allowed it. I was bad.

MY ATTEMPTS AT MOVING THINGS FORWARD BACKFIRED. IN ORDER TO MAKE AN IMPRESSION THAT WOULD LEAD TO TRANSFORMATION, I NEED TO NOT ONLY SAY THINGS THAT ARE POSITIVE, BUT TO SAY THINGS THAT ARE ACCEPTED. ALL PAMELA SEEMS TO BE EXPERIENCING FROM WHAT I AM SAYING IS THAT SHE WAS BAD FOR ALLOWING HERSELF TO BE ABUSED. IF THERE IS A BURNING HOUSE, YOU MIGHT WANT TO GRAB AHOLD OF THE PERSON AND PULL THEM OUT. I TRIED TO PULL HER OUT, BUT I ENDED UP OUTSIDE THE HOUSE AND LOST HER IN THE PROCESS. SHE IS STILL IN THE HOUSE BURNING BECAUSE I DIDN'T HAVE A GOOD ENOUGH GRIP. I HAVE HEARD THERAPISTS ACCUSE THEIR CLIENTS WITH BEING RESISTANT. IF I THOUGHT OF PAMELA AS RESISTANT, THEN THE POWER IS OUTSIDE OF ME AND I CAN FEEL VICTIMIZED BY IT. I WOULD RATHER TAKE RESPONSIBILITY AND REALIZE THAT SHE WAS DISAGREEING WITH ME BECAUSE I HAD NOT BEEN ABLE TO CAUSE THE NECESSARY CONNECTION AND I WASN'T PERSUASIVE ENOUGH TO GET THE JOB DONE. SINCE THIS IS HOW I VIEW IT, THEN THE PROBLEM WASN'T WITH HER BUT INSTEAD WITH THE WAY I WAS COMMUNICATING WITH HER. BY BELIEVING THIS WAY, I HAVE THE POWER TO ADJUST MY COMMUNICATION IN ORDER TO GET THE RESULTS I AM LOOKING FOR.

Jon: No, you were NOT bad. You were abused. From now on, things will be different. **It's written all over you. ZERO TOLERANCE. ZERO TOLERANCE. That is what**

shines through. That's what shows. If somebody is inclined to do some abusing, you are not who to start with.

Pamela: That's what I want--zero tolerance.

SHE CONTINUES TO WANT, AND I HAVE TO GET HER TO EXPERIENCE HERSELF IN THIS NEW WAY.

Jon: Make up a woman who has no tolerance for being abused. Just create a character in your mind. She is your creation.

Pamela: I get the concept. I can do it.

Jon: Excellent! Close your eyes. Step into her. See out of her eyes. Take a ride in her. Try it on.

Pamela: It's very powerful, very powerful.

FINALLY, I HAVE PHRASED THINGS EFFECTIVELY AND SHE IS EXPERIENCING THE POWERFUL PERSON SHE HAS WANTED TO BE.

Jon: **You are also very attractive that way.** *(Snaps fingers)* **That power works on you.**

Pamela: That's true.

Jon: **Looks good on you. Looks sexy. Do it.**

Pamela: I like that. I like that. I can do that.

I HAVE ATTACHED BEING SEXY AND ATTRACTIVE TO BEING POWERFUL, MAKING IT EVEN MORE INTERESTING. IT ALSO FITS WITH THE NOTION OF TRYING IT ON. TRY THIS ON BECAUSE IT LOOKS SEXY.

Jon: Yes, you can. You are a woman who has zero tolerance for abuse.

Pamela: From anybody?

Jon: Yeah, from anybody.

Pamela: Oh good! *(Laughs)*

Jon: **You have zero tolerance for abuse from anybody.**

Pamela: It feels good.

TO WANT IS TO EXPERIENCE LACK. THE PLANT LACKS FOR WATER. IF DESIRE IS COMBINED WITH POSSIBILITY, IT MOTIVATES ACTION. PROLONGED WANT WITH NO ACTION CAUSES WHAT IS WANTED TO LOSE EVEN MORE POSSIBILITY. WHEN DESIRE COMBINES WITH POSSIBILITY AND PRODUCES AN ACTION, IT LEADS TO SATISFACTION AND INCREASES THE FEELING THAT WHAT IS WANTED IS POSSIBLE. THIS IS WHAT PEOPLE REFER TO AS "CONFIDENCE". WHEN THERE IS WANTING, BUT NOT

SEEING POSSIBILITY, IT THWARTS ACTION. PROLONGED WANTING CAUSES A SENSE OF DEPRIVATION AND POWERLESSNESS. WHEN WANTING LEADS TO NO ACTION AND FINALLY TURNS OFF, WHAT IS LEFT IS DEPRESSION. INITIALLY, PAMELA EXPERIENCED MY INTERVENTION AS INCREASING OR ATTEMPTING TO INCREASE WANT OR DESIRE. IT DID NOT CREATE THE EXPERIENCE OF POSSIBILITY, SO SHE WAS STILL STUCK. THIS FINALLY CHANGED WHEN I GOT HER TO TRY IT ON. SHE GOT IT BY EXPERIENCING IT, BY ACTING INSTEAD OF BY WANTING. HER EXPERIENCE OF WHAT SHE CAN DO IS CHANGING.

Jon: It feels good. It feels powerful. It looks sexy. You look good.

Pamela: Yes. I feel it. I can actually feel it! How can we get it to last?

SOMETIMES, PEOPLE HAVE EXPERIENCES THAT LEAVE A NEGATIVE IMPRESSION. IT IS OFTEN THE MEANING THAT THE MIND HAS ATTACHED TO AN EXPERIENCE THAT CONTINUES TO HAVE A TROUBLING INFLUENCE. OUR HUMAN MINDS AUTOMATICALLY ATTACH MEANING TO THINGS BASED ON PRIOR EXPERIENCES. PEOPLE DON'T CHOOSE MEANINGS. WHAT SOMETHING MEANS IS NEVER THE PERSON'S FAULT, BUT PSYCHOTHERAPISTS OFFER BLAMING INTERPRETATIONS BY SAYING THINGS LIKE, "YOU NEED TO STOP CARRYING THAT."

OUR MINDS MAY BE READING THE IMPRESSION FROM THE EVENT AS IF THE EVENT IS ONGOING. THESE MOMENTS OF PAINFUL EXPERIENCES HAVE BECOME FROZEN IN TIME. PART OF THE MIND MAY REALIZE THAT THE EVENT IS FINISHED, BUT OTHER PARTS READ THE EXPERIENCE AS IF IT IS CONTINUING.

Jon: To look at something with me is very different from being alone with it. As we look together, it becomes clear to all facets of the mind that **the troubling event is finished** and, therefore, does not exist. The meanings that our minds attach to events are distorted and, the more troubling the event, the more there is distorted meaning. Meanings may be about oneself or perhaps other things. These distorted meanings will disappear. Energy that has been stuck will then be freed and this **additional energy provides power to fuel positive change. Terrible experiences become an ongoing source of power and energy.**

An experience will come to mind that will be useful to speak with me about. It left an impression that has been keeping you feeling stuck. The impression it left is just an impression and, therefore, it will change as we look at it together. Looking at the event with me will be different. **As we look together, light will dissolve the shadow.**

I DON'T TELL HER TO SELECT WHAT WE WILL ADDRESS BECAUSE THAT WOULD INVOLVE LOGIC. I TELL HER AN EVENT WILL COME TO MIND, IMPLYING IT WILL COME FROM HER SUBCONSCIOUS.

Pamela: The event that led up to my now ex-husband actually packing his things and leaving.

Jon: Tell me.

Pamela: I felt like, after a lot of years of a bad marriage, we finally got into a place that we were comfortable with each other and could trust each other and could confront each other in a civilized way without feeling threatened. I confronted him, and he left.

Jon: What do you think about that?

I DON'T ASK HER HOW IT MAKES HER FEEL. HER FEELINGS ARE PAINFUL AND TO DESCRIBE THEM IS LIKELY TO INCREASE THEM.

Pamela: The reality of how this person could control me, number one, because he knew about my fear of abandonment and that was used as a form of control.

Jon: What do you think now as you recall it?

Pamela: Rather than the shock, now I feel really used. That's clear.

Jon: No more shock. **Yes, clear**.

Pamela: Clear.

Jon: The shock is gone and **now you are clear.**

Pamela: Right.

Jon: Tell me about clear.

Pamela: I feel something being lifted.

Jon: Yeah!

Pamela: That it was OK. It is OK that we are not together.

THIS IS A NEW THOUGHT AND SHE IS FINALLY EXPERIENCING THAT IT IS OKAY. WHEN SHE WAS EXPERIENCING IT AS NOT OKAY, HER MIND WAS PRE-OCCUPIED. SOMETIMES THE PRE-OCCUPATION WAS CONSCIOUS AND THEN IT WAS A DISTRACTION, BUT EVEN WHEN SHE WAS THINKING ABOUT SOMETHING ELSE IT WAS RUNNING IN THE BACKGROUND AND DRAINING ENERGY. THE ENERGY SPENT ON THE EXPERIENCE OF IT NOT BEING OKAY WAS ENERGY ON SOMETHING THAT COULD NEVER HAVE RESPONDED TO THAT ENERGY. ENERGY DIRECTED TOWARD SOMETHING THAT DOES NOT RESPOND TO IT CAUSES FRUSTRATION AND A FEELING OF HELPLESSNESS.

Jon: **You're OK**. By the way, **that stuff was NOT your fault.**

Pamela: No.

Jon: **None of that was your fault. The shock is over.**

Pamela: The scary part is the future for me.

SHE HAS BEEN EXPERIENCING REGRET ABOUT PAST EVENTS AND FEAR ABOUT FUTURE EVENTS. THERE IS NO POWER TO DO ANYTHING IN THE PAST OR IN THE FUTURE. SO, THE PRE-OCCUPATION FED THE FEELING OF FRUSTRATION AND HELPLESSNESS.

Jon:	Have you ever looked at your watch and it said, "future"? **It's always now. Future doesn't happen**. People spend a lot of time worrying about it.
Pamela:	Right.
Jon:	**You feel powerful being present** because that is where the power is.
Pamela:	We're divorced. He is going to have either a person or different people in his life. I have a fear of how I am going to deal with that.
Jon:	**You will deal with it much better than you thought.**
Pamela:	You might want to stick around to be a witness to this!

SHE IS NOT CONVINCED THAT I AM RIGHT WHEN I PROCLAIM THAT SHE WILL DEAL WITH HER EX-HUSBAND'S INVOLVEMENT WITH ANOTHER WOMAN BETTER THAN SHE THOUGHT, BUT SHE IS NOT CONVINCED THAT I AM WRONG EITHER. SAYING WHAT I SAID WITH CONVICTION HAS OPENED HER MIND TO THIS NEW POSSIBILITY. I PUT THIS IDEA INTO HER MIND AND THEN CHANGE THE TOPIC TO SOMETHING COMPLETELY DIFFERENT. IT IS A POWERFUL IDEA AND CONTINUES TO WORK WITHIN HER.

Jon:	Tell me about a place you have been that was pleasant.
Pamela:	My yard.
Jon:	Your yard?
Pamela:	*(Laughs)* Yeah, I love my yard.
Jon:	Yes?
Pamela:	Oh, yeah. I mean, I get great pleasure.
Jon:	Close your eyes and experience being there. Notice things you might see, hear, feel and smell. Take your time and, when you are finished, open your eyes. Do it now. *(Pamela closes her eyes and becomes very still. After several moments, she opens her eyes and smiles.)*

SHE FEELS AT EASE AS SHE IMAGINES THE EXPERIENCE OF BEING IN HER YARD AND HER MIND BECOMES MORE OPEN AND RESPONSIVE. I THEN USE THE EXPERIENCE TO TELL HER A VERY DIFFERENT WAY OF EXPERIENCING WHO SHE IS. BECAUSE OF THE CONNECTION, BECAUSE OF THE CREDIBILITY AND BECAUSE OF THE OPENNESS THE EXPERIENCE OF IMAGINING HER YARD HAS CAUSED, THERE IS A BUY-IN TO THIS CHANGE IN HER PERCEIVED IDENTITY.

Jon:	Tell me what you experienced as you did that.
Pamela:	I just love my yard.
Jon:	Tell me.

Pamela:	The peace and serenity that I am able to draw from just being, even if I'm inside and looking out at my yard.
Jon:	Tell me about peace and the serenity.
Pamela:	It's a safe feeling. It's real safe.
Jon:	Your awareness moves within, toward where **you are secure, and you have been secure**.
Pamela:	Yeah.
Jon:	You have the wisdom there to know you are secure and you are fine. You are close to something forever lasting and it is within you all the time. This is who you are. At your center, you are fine.
Pamela:	Right.
Jon:	At your very essence, **you've got it**. **You've got everything you need.**
Pamela:	Yes.
Jon:	On the inside, you've **got it**. On the outside, intellectually, **you have the knowledge** to **know you are fine**.
Pamela:	Yes.
Jon:	At the surface, **you are now secure**. At your center, **you are secure**. Make sense?
Pamela:	I am with you.
Jon:	**You have it surrounded**. That stuff, that quaky, shaky…
Pamela:	I know that stuff!
Jon:	**It's surrounded** because, at your center, **you've got the wisdom**. On the surface, **you've got the knowledge**. The shaky stuff is from impressions left by particular experiences you have had. **Impressions can and will change. Impressions that have troubled you can change like that**. *(Snaps fingers)* The **light shines through**. *(Snaps fingers)* So, let's clear up impressions and **let the light shine through**. Let's clear something that left a negative impression on you.
Pamela:	This will be a hard one for you! *(Laughs)* This will be a real hard one.
Jon:	I am ready.

Pamela: I found out that my son--I have a 16-year-old son--used my ex-husband's calling card to call his girlfriend in Germany. The bill was eight hundred and some odd dollars!

Jon: Wow! I guess he must really like her. *(Laughs)*

Pamela: So, he doesn't think anything about it.

Jon: Kids will be kids! *(Laughs)*

Pamela: Well, I find that out and I'm going, "Oh, my God! Oh, my God!" I get in my car. First, I went home and confronted him. Within ten minutes, I have a car accident. It's my fault.

Jon: OK.

Pamela: Fender-bender, pouring down rain. I go to the store; my ex-husband owns this electronic store. He said, "What are you going to do about this bill?" I said, "I don't know." I just couldn't think of what to do about it.

Jon: Right.

Pamela: He was busy, so I went to Hardee's, pulled up there. You can get free refills on Diet Coke at Hardee's many times a day. I went back to my husband's store. When I got there, he told me I had tried to run over or hit or do something to some girls that work at his store when I was at Hardee's. He told me that there was a police report made. I was just shocked as all get out! He said, "Go get a copy of the police report and then you can see what you did!" I'm thinking, "Hell, maybe I really DID do something." So, I went to the police station and there was no police report. I went back to Hardee's. They said, "No, nothing happened."

Jon: Got it.

Pamela: I went back to tell him nobody knows anything about what he was talking about. He had undercover policemen in the store, plainclothes like you and I are wearing. The first thing he does is stand like half in the door and half out of his office and says, "I want you out of the store and I want you out now!" And I said, "Bill, you just told me to go get the police report. We've got this phone bill to deal with. What are you doing?" Then, a cop in plain-clothes flips out his badge and says, "I believe he just told you to leave." I walked out really quick, you know. Then I was surrounded by the patrol cars. They were asking me my name, address, height. I'm so shook, I can't even give it to them. I just finally hand them my driver's license and say, "Take it off the driver's license." They gave me a trespass warning.

Jon: Right.

Pamela:	Now, that was a traumatic experience. I mean, do you think that would be a traumatic experience?
Jon:	I believe you. What did you take it to mean?
Pamela:	Well, a lot of things.
Jon:	What?
Pamela:	I was set up, which is something I allowed to happen to myself.

IN ORDER TO HELP HER, PEOPLE HAVE TOLD HER THAT SHE HAS BEEN ALLOWING THINGS LIKE THIS TO HAPPEN AND SHE HAS BOUGHT INTO THAT. ALLOWING IT IS SOMETHING PEOPLE SAY FREQUENTLY AND BELIEVE ACTUALLY EXISTS, BUT I BELIEVE IT IS A THEORY RATHER THAN A TRUTH AND, FURTHERMORE, I BELIEVE IT IS INACCURATE. THERE WAS NO MOMENT DURING THE EVENT THAT PAMELA DESCRIBED IN WHICH SHE DID SOME ACT WE CAN TERM "ALLOWING". MORE ACCURATELY, THERE WAS A SITUATION AND THERE WAS A RESPONSE.

Jon:	What did it mean about you?
Pamela:	I felt like a bad person.
Jon:	What else did you think it meant?
Pamela:	Real shameful.
Jon:	What did it mean about you that there was all that shame?
Pamela:	I was very inadequate, very unworthy.
Jon:	A bad person, unworthy person. You <u>thought</u> it meant all that stuff?

I COMPLETELY EXPOSE THE DISTORTED, TROUBLING MEANING.

Pamela:	Right. And then, you know, I worried, is this going to happen in every relationship I am in? I am so compulsive that I would go to a place knowing that he is capable of doing just what he did. It didn't enter my mind that he would do it then. But I knew that that's his style. He loves to call the police for, I mean, for anything, he would call the police. That's just who he is. Putting myself in that situation, knowing something could have happened, never dreaming it would be that extreme, every negative feeling about myself. When I finally got to work, I get this lecture from my boss. She has gotten really aggravated with me for letting myself get into this stuff. She was very angry and said things like, "How stupid are you? How many times do you have to be slapped in the face? You bring it on yourself and deserve everything you get."

HER BOSS HAS APPARENTLY BEEN TRYING TO GET HER TO STAND UP TO HER HUSBAND AND HAS GOTTEN FRUSTRATED BECAUSE SHE HAS NOT BEEN ABLE TO DO SO. BECAUSE OF MORALISTIC THINKING, IT IS NOT UNLIKELY FOR PEOPLE TO MAKE THEMSELVES AND OTHERS FEEL BADLY IN ORDER TO TRY TO IMPROVE BEHAVIOR, BUT PEOPLE DON'T USUALLY DO BETTER BECAUSE THEY FEEL BADLY.

233

Jon: What do you think about that?

Pamela: To be honest about the entire situation, I used the phone bill to give me a reason to go to the store so that I could see my husband because I missed him so much. I thought that maybe I could pull off some miracle so that he wouldn't be mad at me and the problem will be fixed. I was such a jerk to try.

SHE IS ASHAMED THAT SHE MISSED HER EX-HUSBAND AND WENT TO SEE HIM. IT'S GOOD THAT THIS BELIEF HAS BEEN SHARED BECAUSE NOW SHE KNOWS THAT I HAVE HEARD WHAT SHE EXPERIENCED, AND THIS WILL GIVE ME MORE CREDIBILITY AND A DEEPER CONNECTION AS I LOOK TO SHIFT HER EXPERIENCE.

Jon: When something is disturbing, our minds attach meanings and the meanings are always distorted. The more disturbing the event is, the more distortion there is. There are two ways the mind distorts the information. One, it can read the information about a previous event as if the event was still happening. It can read it as if it is happening now. Two, it can also attach meanings that are extremely distorted but read by the mind as if the meaning was real. Let's take another look and shed some light on what actually took place. What actually happened? Let's stick with the facts.

Pamela: I went to my ex-husband's store.

Jon: You went to the store to talk to your son's father.

SHE SAID TO "EX-HUSBAND" AND I SAID TO "SON'S FATHER". REFERRING TO HIM AS "SON'S FATHER" MAKES SPEAKING TO HIM ABOUT THE ISSUE THAT INVOLVED HER SON REASONABLE AND POSITIVE AND PUTS HER IN A BETTER LIGHT THAN REFERRING TO HIM AS "EX-HUSBAND". I ALWAYS HAVE THE EFFECT I AM LOOKING TO HAVE IN MIND AND THAT CAUSES MY MIND TO SELECT LANGUAGE THAT WOULD BE USEFUL IN FACILITATING THE CHANGES I INTEND FOR HER.

Pamela: Yes.

Jon: You went to the store to talk to him about your son's behavior. This was an issue of mutual concern and shared responsibility.

Pamela: Right.

Jon: He was busy, so you left for a while and got a cold drink. When you came back, he told you that you had been accused of causing a problem and that a report had been made to the police. You, of course, went to check that out. It makes sense to do that.

Pamela: That's right.

SHE HAS BEEN FEELING THAT WHAT SHE DID WASN'T SENSIBLE AND WAS BECAUSE SHE WAS WEAK AND NEEDY. WHAT SHE DID MADE SENSE TO HER AT THE TIME AND I AM GOING OVER IT IN A WAY THAT CAUSES HER TO RECALL IT AS SOMETHING THAT DID MAKE SENSE. THIS IMPROVES HER EXPERIENCE OF WHO SHE IS.

Jon:	After you checked it out, you went back to the store to tell him none of this had taken place. Again, this is logical and **what you did makes perfect sense.** He told you that something concerning happened and, yet, there was no record of it. It made sense, of course, to check. There was a police officer in the store.
Pamela:	Right. This plain-clothed fellow.
Jon:	And he did what?
Pamela:	All that cop did was say, "I think he told you that you were instructed to leave the store immediately."
Jon:	And you left.
Pamela:	Yes, I did.
Jon:	You do what makes sense.
Pamela:	Oh, definitely. He's already had me sit in jail once.
Jon:	You did what made sense. It was the right thing to do.

I CONTINUE TO AFFIRM THAT WHAT SHE DID WAS SENSIBLE AND CORRECT. HER EXPERIENCE OF WHO SHE IS CONTINUES TO IMPROVE.

Pamela:	Yes, and then I was surrounded by the police cars.
Jon:	You handled that well.
Pamela:	I was very calm.
Jon:	You answered their questions.
Pamela:	Right. I did.
Jon:	And then?
Pamela:	I left.
Jon:	So, that's what happened. What do you think it meant?
Pamela:	I should have had the sense not to go to his store is what it means!

SHE CONTINUES TO BLAME HERSELF AND THINKS OF HERSELF AS A WEAK PERSON THAT DOES STUFF THAT MAKES NO SENSE. THIS IS NOT SOMETHING SHE IS CONSCIOUSLY OR PURPOSELY DOING, SO SHE CANNOT MAKE IT STOP BY HERSELF. IT HAS BEEN A DEEPLY ENTRENCHED BELIEF AND I NEED TO GUIDE HER THINKING IN A WAY THAT ELIMINATES IT. BELIEFS ARE OFTEN

CONFUSED WITH TRUTHS. PEOPLE ARE TOLD TO THINK MORE POSITIVELY, BUT HOW CAN SOMEONE DO THAT WHEN THEIR MIND HAS ATTACHED A NEGATIVE MEANING TO THINGS? TELLING PEOPLE THEY SHOULD BE THINKING MORE POSITIVELY IMPLIES THAT THEY ARE AT FAULT AND USUALLY MAKES THEM FEEL WORSE.

Jon: What does it mean about somebody if they go to a store to talk to their child's father about an issue of some concern?

Pamela: It's very normal.

Jon: So, what does all this mean about you?

Pamela: Very little about me.

Jon: It means you are sensible and responsible.

Pamela: I really wanted to see him. I used the credit card billing as an excuse to go in there.

PAMELA WAS MISSING HER EX-HUSBAND AND TELLS ME THAT SHE USED WHAT HAPPENED WITH HER SON TO CONNECT WITH HIM. I WANT TO ELIMINATE THE IMPORTANCE OF THIS SINCE IT HAS LED TO SELF-CRITICISM. I DO IT SIMPLY BY TELLING HER THAT IT DOESN'T MATTER AND DISMISSING IT.

Jon: That doesn't matter. **What you did makes sense.** When you heard information, you checked it out. When the situation became difficult and strange, **you handled it effectively**.

Pamela: Yes.

Jon: It means **you check things out and handle things effectively.** Isn't that exactly what that means?

Pamela: Yes.

Jon: What does that feel like?

Pamela: Actually, I feel much better about it. I don't feel ashamed of myself the way I did before. It was a terrible experience to go through.

FINALLY, THE SHAME HAS DISAPPEARED. THE MEMORY OF THIS EVENT NO LONGER CAUSES PAMELA TO THINK NEGATIVELY ABOUT HERSELF. HER CONCEPT OF WHO SHE IS CONTINUES TO BE TRANSFORMED.

Jon: Well, it was a challenging situation and **you handled it effectively.** Another situation will come to mind.

Pamela: I just remembered something else.

Jon: OK.

| **Pamela:** | I knew he was going to be at a function, and I went to the function because it was something that we were both involved in. I walked in the door and began socializing with a few people. I looked up and saw him running out the door. |
| **Jon:** | Is that right? |

| **Pamela:** | In a way that would make people notice and make me feel embarrassed that I couldn't be at the same event that he was without him having to run out the door. I don't know what came over me. My whatever-illness came over me like a feeling of rage and I went after him. We had words in the parking lot. I don't know what they were, but they were not good. He left in his car and I went after him. At the traffic light, I put my car in reverse and hit his car. That's what I did. |

PAMELA USED THE WORD "ILLNESS" AND SAID IT "CAME OVER" HER. I AM INTERESTED IN CHANGING HER EXPERIENCE OF HERSELF FROM A MENTALLY ILL, DEPENDENT PERSON TO A SELF-CONCEPT THAT WILL ENABLE HER TO LIVE A MUCH HAPPIER LIFE.

Jon:	Let's take a look at what happened.
Pamela:	OK.
Jon:	You went to this function and you saw your husband run.
Pamela:	Leave in a fast manner.
Jon:	Okay, you saw him leave in a fast manner. It certainly seemed like an insult and you felt it made you look bad.
Pamela:	Yes.
Jon:	Right. You were feeling angry and hurt. You did something that wasn't useful when you were upset. What does that mean about you?
Pamela:	I don't know. Tell me! *(Laughs)*
Jon:	If I said to you, there's someone who did something that wasn't useful when she was upset, what would you know about her? Do you know anything about her from that?
Pamela:	Not really, no.
Jon:	It means nothing about you.
Pamela:	That's a relief.

PAMELA WAS INCORPORATING BEHAVIORS SHE ENGAGED IN AND FEELINGS THAT SHE HAS HAD INTO HER SELF-CONCEPT. THE PROCESS WE ARE ENGAGING IN ELIMINATES THIS NEGATIVE SELF-IMAGE. IT'S NECESSARY THAT I HAVE CREDIBILITY WITH HER

AND THAT I DEMONSTRATE UNDERSTANDING OF HER EXPERIENCE, BUT I DO NOT HAVE TO BE SYMPATHETIC. IF I WAS SYMPATHETIC, I WOULD BE AGREEING WITH HER THAT SHE SHOULD BE FEELING BADLY.

Jon: **Things are clearing up.** I am going to ask you to close your eyes. Then I am going to talk to you with your eyes closed for about a minute. The purpose of this is for you to acquire the experience of hearing me speak with your eyes closed. That's all it is about. Don't try to do anything else. Close your eyes. That's it. And let me just remind you that, as your eyes rest closed, nothing is required. You don't need to do anything. In fact, you can remember that I mentioned that you don't even need to bother to put any kind of effort into relaxing. This is simply about acquiring an experience and the experience you are acquiring is of hearing me speak as your eyes rest closed. That's what we have set out to do and that is what we are doing. Notice you are hearing, not just my voice, but lots of other sounds, and notice that, in hearing other sounds, you are hearing quite clearly now. Then again, open your eyes. Tell me what you were noticing within yourself while your eyes were closed.

SHE CAN RELAX BECAUSE SHE DOESN'T HAVE TO DO ANYTHING. IT IS FAIL-PROOF BECAUSE SHE CAN'T HELP BUT EXPERIENCE WHAT I MENTIONED. SAYING WHAT I AM ABOUT TO DO AND DOING WHAT I SAY BUILDS CREDIBILITY. IT EASES INTO A HYPNOTIC EXPERIENCE THAT IS NOT ALARMING.

Pamela: I was hearing the fish tank.

Jon: And…

Pamela: I felt really at peace.

Jon: At peace, yes.

Pamela: I mean, I really felt…you were saying don't relax, but I was relaxed. And then I was trying to think how NOT to relax!

IT WASN'T MY INTENTION TO CAUSE HER TO THINK THAT SHE SHOULDN'T RELAX, BUT THAT'S WHAT HAPPENED. THE PROCESS WAS SHORT, HOWEVER, AND SO THE MISUNDERSTANDING DID NOT EXIST FOR LONG. IT IS BEST TO BEGIN WITH A VERY SHORT PROCESS WHEN ASKING SOMEONE TO CLOSE THEIR EYES AS YOU SPEAK TO THEM. THE BEST WAY TO LEARN HOW SOMEONE IS DOING IS TO ASK THEM. IF THERE IS ANYTHING CONCERNING, IT WOULD BE BEST TO ADDRESS IT SOONER RATHER THAN LATER.

Jon: I said you didn't have to, not that you shouldn't. It was fine that you did, and it was wonderful that you did it so quickly. Let's do a little more. *(Speaking softly)* Close your eyes again. That's it. And once again, I want to remind you that nothing is required. You are doing this perfectly. What we have set out to do is for you to acquire the experience of hearing me speak, even as your eyes rest closed. You are hearing me speak while your eyes are closed and that's what we set out to do and that's what you are doing. It's interesting to hear that already **you have begun relaxing** and, yet, I want to remind you that it's not required. It's fine to relax, but it isn't required. **You will benefit** because of the way **you respond automatically to things I say** to you. **You benefit automatically. What's happening is happening perfectly. Things are**

falling into place exactly as they should. Once again, you can open your eyes. Tell me what you were experiencing within you.

Pamela: I was really relaxed. I wasn't having a lot of thought processes.

Jon: You learn very quickly at this deep level. We are going quickly because you are a fast learner.

Pamela: I was really trying to focus on everything that you were saying.

NEXT, I WILL TELL HER THAT, WITHIN HER, THERE IS A PLACE THAT SHE IS ALWAYS RELAXED. SHE CAN'T DISAGREE BECAUSE I SAY IT IS WITHIN AND, THEREFORE, OUTSIDE OF CONSCIOUS AWARENESS. THERE IS DEEP CONNECTION AND TOTAL CREDIBILITY, AND SHE IS EXPERIENCING AN ALTERED STATE OF CONSCIOUSNESS WHERE THE THINGS I SAY ARE ABSORBED AND INTEGRATED. THINGS BEGIN TO HAPPEN THAT ARE UNUSUAL. HER BODY BEGINS TO DO THINGS THAT SHE IS NOT CONSCIOUSLY CAUSING. THIS INCREASES CREDIBILITY SO THAT WHAT IS PUT INTO HER MIND IS ABSORBED STILL MORE DEEPLY.

Jon: You don't even have to do that. Within you, there is a place where **you are relaxed. You are at peace. You are totally secure. You have wisdom and it's who you really are. That's where the light is,** and **you are where the light is** and there is no shame because it can't live in the light. **Things become clear and light** so that you **do what makes sense.** Close your eyes. And as your eyes remain closed, you begin to notice the sensations there through your left hand and fingers and you become aware of how those sensations are changing and you may notice some of the movements happening through that left hand, the movements happening through your hand without you doing anything consciously in order to direct movements to happen in your hand *(Her hand begins to jump and jerk)* so that, although you could, of course, move your hand on your own any time you choose, if you move it consciously, there would be a smooth flowing motion. But the way your hand is moving is with little jumps, jerks, twitches, fits and starts and movements that are so different from conscious movements because those movements are being directed by a different part of your mind. They are being directed by the part of your mind that isn't conscious, being directed by your subconscious mind. And your subconscious mind is moving your hand in a way that you couldn't consciously move it. Maybe you will picture it as moving the way you feel it moving, with those little tiny jumps, quivers, twitches, and then, that's right, that's it, so that the fingers as you picture them, you picture them lifting. That's it. *(beginning to speak louder)* And notice that they are lifting, but not only are your fingers lifting up, Pamela, your fingers are lifting up perfectly in exactly the way they should. Lifting up, that's it, up, that's it, with just those little twitches. You can remember I said it, little jumps, jerks, fits and starts, movements lifting your fingers. That's it, up, higher, that's right, and more movements happening, not through the direction of your conscious mind, but lifting your hand up in a way that you couldn't consciously lift it. It's happening even now and it's happening because it's really happening for you through the direction of your subconscious mind, your inner mind!

Your mind is wonderfully responsive when treated with respect and with your mind's wisdom (speaking softer), **with its power, it deserves our respect.** Lifting your hand up. Everything is happening perfectly, exactly, perfectly, exactly as it should. That's right. That's right. And **each time I tell you that your eyes are closing, they close.** And each time they close, **you go even further**. Imagine how deep you would be and how good you would feel and how relaxed you would become if you were to realize you have gone so deep that it's no longer possible to open your eyes. And if you were to realize that as you tried to open your eyes, the harder you tried, the more they'd shut so you would **go even deeper still**. Just imagine that, how deep you would go. You can't open your eyes. Go ahead, try and realize you cannot and **enjoy even still more warmth, even still more peace, even still more security** because **there can be no doubt it's happening for you now. Things are falling into place.** That's it, **further, towards even more peace and security,** moving within Pamela to where you really are, right down to where the light is. Now, again your eyes can open. Now they can. Yeah. And again, tell me a little about what you are noticing within you.

Pamela: Everything is just right in here. (She points to her ches.t)

Jon: Yeah, everything is just right within you.

Pamela: It's where the whole is. It's warm.

Jon: It's warm and **you are whole, at peace, secure, wise and powerful**.

Pamela: Right, and powerful.

Jon: You direct what happens.

Pamela: I want to be powerful. I want to have power.

I REPEAT WHAT SHE HAS SAID, LEAVING OUT THE WORD "WANT". "WANT" INDICATES "LACK". I DON'T CHALLENGE IT BUT, INSTEAD, JUST LEAVE IT OUT.

Jon: DO powerful. **Be powerful** (snapping fingers) and **do what it is that makes sense because it makes sense.** Something else will come to mind. This time it will be something that happened even earlier in your life.

Pamela: I was about 15 or 16.

Jon: What happened?

Pamela: My mother, she used to run away a lot. She ran away and, this time, we didn't know where she was. I was acting out as a teen-ager, you know, pretty bad and my father was an alcoholic. He tricked me. He took me to the psychiatric ward and left me there on a closed ward for six months.

Jon:	Six months?
Pamela:	I can remember being so depressed. I was given heavy anti-psychotic medication. I never was able to communicate because I was just out.
Jon:	You are amazing. You have survived such horrible stuff. What does it mean?
Pamela:	I was in a bad situation that I had no control over.
Jon:	Does that mean anything bad about you?
Pamela:	Nothing.

HER MIND IS NOW TRAINED TO NOT ATTACH MEANINGS TO HER UNLESS THEY ARE POSITIVE.

Pamela:	I was kind of at that stage of my life where I was uncontrollable.
Jon:	You are into doing what you want.
Pamela:	Right, right.
Jon:	**Being free, having power, having fun.** And then you got brought somewhere and they kept you and they drugged you and **you survive.** What bad thing does that mean about you?
Pamela:	Nothing! *(Laughs)* Really nothing!
Jon:	**You learn so quickly. You learn quickly on many levels**. *(Snapping fingers)*
Pamela:	It meant nothing. This is good. This is really good.

OUR PRIOR CONVERSATIONS ABOUT EVENTS AND THE ALTERED STATE OF CONSCIOUSNESS AND THE DEEP CONNECTION THAT HAS BEEN FORMED HAVE ALTERED THE WAY HER BRAIN PROCESSES INFORMATION. IT NO LONGER CREATES MEANINGS OF BEING DEFICIENT OR INADEQUATE OR BAD IN ORDER TO EXPLAIN EVENTS. PEOPLE WHO ARE THERE TO HELP OTHERS OFTEN PRIORITIZE MAKING LIFE MORE MEANINGFUL. I LIKE THINGS BEING MEANINGLESS AND THAT IS WHAT HAS BEEN ACHIEVED.

Jon:	Another event will come to mind. It will be even earlier.
Pamela:	I believe I was, like, in the first grade. I know this is a really silly thing, but I thought it was really creative. I took, you know how you bundle your socks up? Clean socks?
Jon:	Yeah?
Pamela:	I put them in my underwear all the way around because that was the style to make your skirt stick out real far. It made me seem lumpy, but it made my dress stick out real far and my mother beat me bloody for doing that. I didn't understand what was so bad, you know. I think of that experience every time I pull on underwear.

Jon: Got it. Now, so, what does it mean about you?

Pamela: I was just a kid.

Jon: You are a fun and creative person.

Pamela: Right! That I found a way to make my skirt stand out!

Jon: And what about your mom? What does it mean about her?

Pamela: *(Sighs)* She was angry about something that had nothing to do with me.

Jon: She wasn't playing with a full deck. You survived very difficult things. What a strong little girl! It is amazing that you survived.

ANYTHING BAD THAT SHE HAS COMPLETED IS TO HER CREDIT. I DON'T SYMPATHIZE BUT, INSTEAD, CREDIT HER WITH SURVIVING THOSE THINGS.

Pamela: I guess I was. It was horrible. I couldn't go to school. I feel like that was a stupid thing to do. I feel a lot of shame from that experience.

Jon: **You are a creative, smart person who does what makes sense.** Close your eyes and be back there as that little girl but take me with you.

HER CONNECTION TO ME PROVIDES CLARITY SO THE LITTLE GIRL IS CLEAR AND, HENCE, GROWS UP CLEAR.

Jon: Clarity. *(Snapping fingers)* See it for what it really is. I'm with you. *(Snapping fingers)* **Clear. All the way through and out the other end of it.** Whoosh! *(Snapping fingers)* Good. And then open your eyes.

Pamela: It's gone.

Jon: Yeah, it's gone. And what was it like to go through it?

Pamela: There was some pain, but just for a moment.

Jon: And?

Pamela: It was gone.

THIS TRAUMATIC EVENT CONTINUED TO COLOR THE WAY HER MIND PROCESSED INFORMATION UNTIL THIS MOMENT. THIS DISTORTION IS NO MORE. SHE IS CLEAR.

Jon: OK. Close your eyes. You are that little girl again, but things are clear. Now, grow up clear. Grow all the way up to here with me. Look ahead and see how it's clear up ahead. Good. Open your eyes.

Pamela: Really nice! It's really nice!

Jon: Picture your husband with another woman. Clear! *(Snapping fingers)*

Pamela: Actually, I feel sorry for her! She's his next victim!

I WENT RIGHT FOR WHAT SHE WAS ANTICIPATING WITH SUCH DREAD AND WE WERE BOTH DELIGHTED WITH HER RESPONSE. I DID THAT TO CONFIRM AND DRIVE IN WHAT SHE HAS ACCOMPLISHED.

Jon: Close your eyes and you see him with his arm around this lady. *(Snapping fingers)* **See it clear**. *(Snapping fingers several times)* You **are clear with it**. There it is. And **you're clear**. And **you're clear**. Open your eyes.

THE WORD "CLEAR" AND THE FINGER SNAP ARE STRONGLY ASSOCIATED WITH CLARITY OF MIND. WHEN I ASK HER TO SEE HER HUSBAND WITH ANOTHER WOMAN, I SNAP AND SAY "CLEAR" TO BRING CLARITY TO THE ANTICIPATED SITUATION THAT USED TO BE SO DISTURBING.

Pamela: I'm glad it's her and not me!

Jon: Yeah, you bet you are!

Pamela: I moved ahead.

Jon: OK. Close your eyes again. Watch it. Just look. He puts his arm around her, and you breathe a sigh of relief. Do it. *(Snapping fingers)* Clear. Easy. Whoosh! *(Snapping fingers)* Got it. Good. Eyes open. Made it through. OK. Now, there were a number of events that we cleared. There are a number of other events we didn't touch on. But what I am going to ask your subconscious to do--you don't have to consciously get involved with this at all--I am going to ask your subconscious to tag those events. It doesn't have to tell you about them or me about them, but I want your subconscious to go through your whole life and tag every event that left an impression that hasn't been useful. So, you don't know it, I don't know it, we don't know what is tagged, but every one of them has got like a little label on it. Put your arms like I have mine, hands forward, your hands drop, your eyes close. Now, as those movements continue through your hands, those tags are being placed on all those events that took place. And your subconscious can do that all so rapidly, tagging each one, each one that will be cleared. When they have been tagged, your subconscious can signal me by lifting one of the fingers up on that left hand. *(finger jumps)* Thank you.

The events have been tagged. I am going to find out how many events have been tagged. You let your arms just drop like they were, like that, that's perfect. I am going to say numbers and when I get into the range of the number that it was, the number of events that have been tagged--I might say, like, for instance, "Between 1 and 5, that's the number of events that have been tagged" --that's when I am going to get the signal. When I get to that range, your subconscious is going to signal me. You're not. Your subconscious is. What you will experience is a "jump" in that right hand.

A jump. It won't be that you are doing it, your subconscious is doing it, letting me know that we are in that range. I want to know if it was ten events or less that have been tagged. Ten or fewer. Between 20 or less? Under 30? Under 50 such events? 100 or less? (*Her hand jumps*) Thank you. 90 or less? (*Her hand jumps*) Is it 80 or less? (*Her hand jumps*) Is it 70 or less? (*Her hand is still*) When I get to the right number, it jumps. 80. 81. 82. 83. 84. 85. 86. (*Her hand jumps*) Thank you. Eighty-six separate events have been identified by your subconscious mind. All of them left impressions that caused distortion and drained energy, but you have survived every one of them so that, in just moments, what you have survived becomes a source of wisdom and power. Your subconscious mind now knows how to clear them up because they mean nothing bad, but surviving demonstrates your amazing power, flexibility and wisdom. Isn't that so? (*Her hand jumps*) Your subconscious is going to replace those useless impressions with (*snapping fingers*) **clarity. Strong, no tolerance** for abuse. NOW (*Snapping fingers and speaking softly.*) And you can just drift while it's happening because it's big, eighty-six impressions are cleared all at once. **Light destroys the shadows that have caused pain.** (*Pauses*) When **they are clear**, (*snapping fingers*) your subconscious will signal me. *(10 second pause. Her hand jumps. I speak louder.)* It's done. (*Snapping fingers*) It's **clear now.** (*Snapping fingers*) That's it. **You are strong, powerful, flexible, compassionate, clear and in touch with your true identity. Wisdom, light, energy, excitement, peace, clarity. Your true self.**

Now, notice a shaking in hands that moves up your arms and, with every movement, **it gets better and better and better for you.** (*Snapping fingers*) Clear. (*Her hands begin to shake and quiver*) **Clear.** (*I snap my fingers. Her arms begin to shake as well.*) More. More. More. That's it. That's it. That's it. (*Arms and hands shaking hard*) It's big. (*Speaking louder*) It's big. Your arms begin to reach now, up, UP, UP. All the way. (*Her arms are stretched up over her head. Her hands and arms are jumping and shaking. I snap my fingers.*) **Clear.** (*Snap* Big. **Brand new. Strong.** (*Speaking softer*) **You feel good, you look good, you like your body, and you like yourself. Zero Tolerance for abuse. Compassionate. Fun-loving. Easy. Clear. Enjoyment. Alive. Proud of yourself. Courageous. You made it through.** (*Snapping fingers*) *Clear.* (*Snap*) **Easy.** (*Snap*) **Whole. Strong. Bright. Light. All the way through.** (*Snap*) **YES**! (*Snap*) Stretch. **Flexible. Powerful. Strong**. *(I speak louder, and Pamela's hands and arms continue to shake)* **Feel it! It gets bigger. It gets bigger. It gets bigger. What's happened to you tonight is big. You can't stop it.** (*Snap*) **It's big. It's got you. It's a whole new you. It's so much better than it's ever been before! Bigger than you thought about, better than you wanted, more than you ever dreamed! Feel it!** (*Snap*) **Bigger. Now. And it takes you strong, light, and bright. That light from inside.** (*Whoosh!*) **Shining!** (*Whoosh!*) **Vibrant. Alive. Positive. Excited. Clear. Strong.** (*Softer*) **It's all new.** (*Whoosh!*) **Colors are brighter. Now you know who you are. And you're free. Yes.** Once again, your eyes can open.

SHE IS HAVING THE EXPERIENCE OF EVERY TRAUMATIC EVENT BEING ELIMINATED SIMULTANEOUSLY. IT IS POWERFUL AND DRAMATIC AND WILL BE LIFE-CHANGING.

Pamela: I feel like an earthquake or something. I really don't feel like I could be penetrated. I just don't, like, now I don't feel I can be penetrated. It's just right through the center of my body, just right through from even my heart. A lot of things were happening with my heart. A lot was happening with my heart! Just right through the floor, just like I was, it felt like a channel. I noticed things leaving my body. I don't really want to use the word "bad" but the things that were destructive, you know, I could feel it leaving. I could, I mean, I could actually, physically feel it leaving.

I noticed, for one thing, that I have had a desperate feeling like I've got to go out here and join this dating service. I don't feel that at all anymore. I don't even feel it the least little bit. I'm OK with myself. I feel really comfortable with myself and I feel really fine about it. I mean, I am even excited about going home and there is nobody there.

PREVIOUSLY, THERE WAS A PRESSURE TO MEET AND BE INVOLVED WITH SOMEONE IN ORDER TO PREPARE FOR THE EX-HUSBAND GETTING INVOLVED. IT NO LONGER MATTERS. THE PRESSURE IS GONE. THE PRESSURE WOULD MOST LIKELY HAVE CAUSED HER TO BECOME INVOLVED WITH SOMEONE THAT WOULD NOT HAVE BEEN GOOD FOR HER OR TO HER.

Jon: **It's nice to have your home to yourself**, isn't it?

Pamela: I feel really happy! I feel happy as all get out! It's good.

Jon: Yes.

Pamela: Thank you.

Jon: Is there anything while we are still together that you would want to either ask or tell me about?

IT IS EXPECTED THAT, AS SHE ANTICIPATES LEAVING THE MEETING, THERE WILL BE SOME FEAR. I WANT TO MANAGE THAT IN THE BEST WAY FOR HER.

Pamela: I'm a fearful kind of a person and I am afraid, as good as I feel right now and as powerful as I feel right now, I am afraid it's going to leave me, and I will revert back to my usual patterns, and I don't want to do that.

OUR TIME TOGETHER IS ALMOST OVER, AND SHE KNOWS THAT. SHE FEELS GREAT, BUT THERE IS STILL APPREHENSION.

Jon: Check out where you are right now and ask yourself if you are a fearful person.

Pamela: I'm not.

Jon: Now, you're not.

Pamela: No.

Jon: Right. And you have learned many things and re-done all kinds of things. So, you have got it now that there were many difficult things and you got through them. **You are strong, free and clear.** *(Snap)*

Pamela: I got it.

Jon: Good! I think we're done.

Pamela: I felt like I did a lot of work!

Jon: Yeah. You did great.

Follow-up Commentary

Six months after our conversation, Pamela stated she is feeling more at peace than she had been before our meeting. She is no longer taking psychotropic medications. She no longer experiences panic attacks and is sleeping much more easily at night. She has a new boyfriend and has been experiencing a new joy in living. She also got a different job and tells me she enjoys it.

Tammy

Jon: What I'm interested in is making a difference in your life. The way I look at things, the way minds are processing information is what is affecting the way people feel, think and act. This often has to do with things that have happened. I can't affect what has happened, but I can affect the way your mind responds to what has happened.

I think that a computer needs to be adjusted more than a hammer because it's more complicated. I think that our minds are even more complicated than our computers and, hence, our minds are instruments that would benefit from an expert tune-up so that they are in the best possible working order. What I want to do today is get the way your mind processes information adjusted to your best advantage. What should I know in order to be useful?

Tammy: I've been traumatized quite a bit with molestation.

Jon: Help me understand.

Tammy: From five years old until I was fifteen, so about ten years of that. It was a family member. And then again when I was twenty-two. After that, it has been pretty hard to have a normal relationship.

Jon: **You have survived some extremely difficult stuff.** I am looking to make significant improvements in how your mind responds to those events.

I DON'T SYMPATHIZE, BUT, INSTEAD, GIVE HER CREDIT FOR SURVIVAL. I STATE MY INTENTION OF CHANGING HER MIND'S RESPONSE TO THOSE THINGS.

Tammy: That would be great. That would be wonderful.

Jon: I would like to start by finding a way to represent the way that your mind has been processing the information. This is how things have been. This is our starting point. Let's represent it with a design. When I think "design," I think something that I can see in my mind, but something that doesn't have recognizable content. So, it might be dark or bright. I think of something somebody might make with crayons or finger paints. It might be smooth or jagged. If we create such a design representing the way mind has been functioning, would it be more like a dark thing or a bright thing? Harsh or dim?

Tammy: I would have to say dark.

Jon: And is it more like jagged or smooth?

Tammy: I would have to say, jagged.

THIS VISUAL BASELINE CAN LATER BE CHECKED SO THAT SHE HAS IMMEDIATE CONFIRMATION THAT THE SHIFT WE INTENDED HAS ALREADY TAKEN PLACE. THE BASELINE REPRESENTS THE WAY THAT HER MIND HAS BEEN PROCESSING INFORMATION RATHER THAN HER ACTUAL FEELINGS, THOUGHTS OR BEHAVIORS. IT IS THE WAY HER MIND HAS BEEN PROCESSING DATA THAT HAS CAUSED THE PROBLEMATIC RESPONSE. THIS IS WHAT IS ON THE TABLE FOR US TO ADJUST.

Jon: Ok, perfect. We are done with that. Let's imagine this gal who has also gone through some really rough stuff, not as rough as you, but stuff you would consider rough, nonetheless. Her response to it was even worse than your response to what you've gone through. Her mind has been tuned and cleared to her advantage so that we find her now with her mind working *(snap)* in just the way we would want. She is fully present, and she is sourced from her own center. She is clear. Her mind is automatically bringing to her attention those things that are both beneficial and possible. Hence, her experience is, "I can do that. I can get there. I can do that." As she is putting energy out, she is ending up with more than she spent. Does that sound like that would be ok?

THE WOMAN I DESCRIBE HAS GONE THROUGH STUFF, BUT NOT STUFF AS BAD AS WHAT TAMMY HAS GONE THROUGH. HER REACTION HAS BEEN EVEN WORSE. THIS CREDITS TAMMY FOR HAVING GONE THROUGH THINGS THAT WERE EVEN WORSE, BUT NOT HAVING AS BAD A RESPONSE. IT MAY BE HARD FOR TAMMY TO IMAGINE FEELING MUCH BETTER AT THE END OF OUR MEETING, SO I REFERENCE SOMEONE ELSE WHO WAS IN EVEN WORSE SHAPE GETTING ALL THE WAY BETTER, SO THIS BECOMES A MODEL FOR WHAT WE ARE LOOKING TO GET DONE.

Tammy: Yes.

Jon: That would be ok for you?

Tammy: Yes.

Jon: I am seeing what I intend our meeting today to do and where I intend for it to take you. And, since our minds are so responsive to symbols, which is why countries use flags, let's find a way to symbolically represent our intention--a wild bird, a wild animal, something from nature or the sky will symbolize what we are intending for you. What is it?

Tammy: A flower.

Jon: Beautiful, I like that. Tell me the color.

Tammy: I want to say bright yellow.

Jon: Beautiful, beautiful. That's going to work just fine. You see, I could come up with a symbol, but, even though I probably could come up with a good one, yours isn't a good one. Yours is perfect.

Tammy: Oh, yeah?

Jon: The lock for itself creates the perfect key and this means your mind created a way to symbolically represent to itself what it is that we intend. You've got the concept and, in checking your response to what I have described, it was clear to me that that is ok with you. So, what we are representing with flower is what we intend for you. Make sense?

Tammy: Yes.

Jon: Ok, perfect. Just to have it there is on the way. I am all about that happening for you. I am fully intending it and you're here with me intending it also. When we add intention like that, it's not one and one; now we have two. It is expanding. **What's expanding is the energy and the power that is fueling the transformation** that is desired--to create what we both have in mind as we bring that together. I feel that going on even as we are getting started here. I am going to offer you information about different things and ways of thinking about things. I would like you to take a look through these lenses, interested in what would be the effect of thinking this way. I am not saying it's the only way to think, by any means. I'm just interested in, if we looked at it that way, what would that do? So, I'll present a way to look at things that's a view of what we can share as we get things accomplished for you. There was a time when you were outdoors in a natural setting and you see something that is beyond beautiful. It's like, "Whoa! Awesome!" What is it that comes to mind as I say that?

I TELL TAMMY THAT I AM OFFERING A WAY OF THINKING AND THIS MAKES IT MUCH EASIER FOR HER TO JOIN WITH ME IN THESE VIEWS RATHER THAN IF I SUGGESTED THAT I WAS TELLING HER THE TRUTH ABOUT HOW THINGS ARE. I ASK HER TO RECALL A VERY SPECIAL EXPERIENCE, SO I CAN USE THE FEELING THAT WAS GENERATED DURING IT TO CREATE A NEW WAY OF VIEWING THINGS.

Tammy: Several different things. I find beauty in most anything, especially outdoors.

Jon: Well, I would like you to pick one particular moment that was over the top.

Tammy: Ok, looking straight up into one of the largest red woods.

Jon: Yeah, yeah.

Tammy: That almost makes you dizzy. It's a big "wow" factor.

Jon: Yeah, yeah…and breathing that air that those beautiful trees exhale.

Tammy: Yes, that clean oxygen.

Jon: It's amazing, isn't it?

Tammy: Yeah.

Jon: So, as you see that, there is peacefulness and excitement together.

Tammy: Yes.

Jon: Let's think this way. As you see the giant tree, your awareness is drawn in toward where, at your center, **you are at peace, you are excited**. There were other moments that you **feel at peace** and moments when **you are excited**. There have also been times your awareness was far from excitement or peace.

I have a lit candle here and I bring my hand closer to the flame. "This flame is getting hotter," I say. You say, "You know what, guy, you're just getting more aware of the heat. At that moment, your awareness was moving in toward where **you are at peace and you are excited**." Let's think of it that way.

Tammy: Ok.

Jon: Let's think that the **peace, excitement, light, and wisdom is who you really are** and that your body is yours, but not you. Does that make sense?

Tammy: Yes.

Jon: This is silly, but it brings this awareness in to the rest of your mind. I'd like you to repeat these words. I have a foot.

Tammy: I have a foot.

Jon: I am not a foot.

Tammy: I am not a foot.

Jon: And I never introduce myself as a foot.

Tammy: And I never introduce myself as a foot.

Jon: I have an ass.

Tammy: I have an ass. *(Laughter)*

Jon: You can figure the rest of that one out, right?

Tammy: *(Laughter)* Ok.

Jon: So, you have a body and it's absolutely yours. Every cell has been replaced over and over again, so it's very different than it was when you were in the womb and very different than it was when you were three weeks old. So, cells keep getting replaced, the body keeps changing. What I am suggesting is who you are is who you are even as that thing is going on. You have a foot, but you are not your foot. You have a body, but you are not your body. Who you actually are is what you become aware of as you are looking up at a red wood tree. So, **that excitement, that peace, that wisdom, that clarity, that energy, then, isn't yours, but, instead, it is you. It is who you are.**

Tammy: Ok.

Jon: So, we are kind of just looking at identity in a little different way and, I think, a useful way. Make some sense?

Tammy: Yeah.

Jon: When Rabbit sees approaching Wolf, her body becomes strong, particularly her legs. So, if Rabbit is thinking about carrots, as soon as she sees Wolf, there are no carrots. There is nothing but Wolf. Rabbit's mind is not thinking about what she will be doing later when she's done with the wolf. It's not, "Hey, when I get done with the wolf maybe I'll have another carrot." At that moment, it's Wolf without end. It's perpetual Wolf. When something is traumatic, meaning weird, confusing, disturbing, scary, yucky, awful, it slams into awareness. What is slamming into awareness is just that moment and, at that moment, there is no future. It's Wolf without end.

Think of a hand slamming into the sand at the beach. The hand leaves an impression that remains after the hand leaves. The impression is not a slamming hand. The impression is from the event, but the human mind, particularly on the deeper levels, may confuse the impression with what caused it. It's as if the sand doesn't know that the slamming hand is no longer there.

Some guy is talking to us about having been mugged. Someone held a knife to his throat, and you notice, as this guy is talking to us, that his face is starting to turn white and he's starting to shake. You interrupt him and say, "Hey, man, there is no knife to your throat. You're here with us. You made it." And he goes, "Yeah, yeah, thanks." You tell him that even though, obviously, he must know that. You realize that although he knows that, it's kind of like some part of his mind hasn't gotten the good news. The part of his mind that hasn't gotten the good news is the part that is controlling his circulatory system, which is why his face has changed colors. On the surface, he realizes that the knife is no longer threatening him, but because of the impression that was left, the rest of his mind hasn't gotten that good news.

Sometimes people know they are being affected by a prior event because they are thinking about it and the thoughts cause troubling feelings. But people can be affected by the impressions from prior experiences even if these experiences are not consciously thought of. I want to get in there and clean stuff up so that energy is released and available for the desired transformation.
You know, people's minds are always looking for meaning. When something really awful happens, the mind attaches a meaning to it and, damn, if the meaning isn't

worse than the thing, even when the thing totally sucks. The more disturbing the event was, the more distorted the meaning.

A woman was walking to her car in a parking lot near where she works. It was about 6 o'clock at night. She had stayed a little bit later to clean some things up on her desk and she was on the way out to her car. A guy drove by and threw a huge rock out the window and it hit her in the back of the head. As she told me this story, she said, "I'm just so upset with myself for putting myself in danger like that." And I thought to myself, "That's what the rest of us call 'walking to the car'." The meaning that her mind attached to it attached so well that it's what she actually thought happened. It's not what you would have thought by watching it. You wouldn't have said, "Oh, gee, interesting. A gal seems to be putting herself in danger." You would say, "Wow, some maniac just threw a rock at a lady while she's walking to her car."

Tammy: Right.

Jon: But you see what I mean about meaning. Then our minds notice things that have structural similarity to the earlier event that was troubling. The combat veteran dives behind the couch when he hears a firecracker. If she is experiencing it as she put herself in danger, she may also get nervous if something happens that has some similarity. If the guy that threw the rock was in a blue Volkswagen, she may get nervous around blue Volkswagens, even though she consciously realizes that throwing the rock had nothing to do with the color or make of the car.

Our minds are built that way because Mother Nature would prefer that the rabbit jump unnecessarily away from a harmless snake than not jump when the dangerous snake is there. This can continue until the mind has been cleared and that usually doesn't happen by itself. That is why I utilize this process to get people's minds to clear. The process of clearing can be painless and even enjoyable. It doesn't require letting painful feelings out. It involves spreading the good news so that all facets of the mind realize that the disturbing event is no longer in existence and that nothing, therefore, needs to be done about it.

Jon: How many times have you heard somebody say, "Well, that's in the past"? We hear that so much that we start to believe it. Most people are thinking that there is a past and stuff is in it, but, actually, when you turn the lights on, there is no such thing. This is a process that will enable your unconscious mind to begin understanding that there is no past and there is nothing bad happening in the past. So, for instance, you remember getting dressed this morning?

Tammy: Sure.

Jon: You remember putting your pants on?

Tammy: Yeah.

Jon: You have info about it, like, you could tell me where you were. You might even be able to tell me which leg you put in first.

Tammy: Left one first.

Jon: There you go. That's info, that's not putting on your pants. So, where are you putting on your pants?

Tammy: In my room?

Jon: No, it's not in existence. Info is available, but if I say, "So, where is it?" the real answer is, it doesn't exist.

Tammy: Right.

Jon: Of course, it did, and yes, we have info, but mind confuses the info about the event with the event until we turn the lights on like we are doing right now.

Tammy: Ok.

Jon: And there are some things I don't want my mind thinking are still in existence just because I have info on them.

Tammy: Yeah. Ok.

Jon: So, there are fixes. I will show you one around the issue we just spoke about. This is very easy, and it makes our minds very sharp, so bear with me, and it only takes a minute and it turns a bunch of lights on. So, here's what we do. You remember putting your pants on. As you remember it, I'm going to say to you, "Hey, stop putting your pants on!" You answer me by saying, "I am not putting my pants on." So, remember putting your pants on? Hey, stop putting your pants on.

Tammy: I am not putting my pants on.

Jon: Good. Next, I am going to say, "Make me stop putting my pants on." And you go, "You're not putting your pants on." Make me stop putting my pants on.

Tammy: You're not putting your pants on.

Jon: Perfect. And then I'll say, "Well, then, where is it?" And we both say, "It doesn't exist." Here, we are going to do it again. Think about putting your pants on. Stop putting your pants on!

Tammy: I'm not putting my pants on.

Jon: Well, make me stop putting my pants on.

Tammy: You're not putting your pants on.

Jon: Where is it?

Tammy: It doesn't exist.

Jon: There you go. That lights some lights in the mind. Think of this big skyscraper. It's dark out and the top floor has a few lights on. Second to the top has a light on, but most of its dark. Something really good has happened, but only where the lights are on did they find out. And, now, *(snap)* another light goes on and it's like, "Wow! That guy just woke up and got some good news." So, the good news has already happened. The good news is the stuff that really sucked is not happening. The lights turn on when the mind, on different levels, gets that good news.

When I was a kid, I liked to play basketball. When I was eleven years old, not only did I like to play basketball, I had my own basketball court. How good is that when you're eleven-years-old? Except, my idiot father used to park his car in the middle of the court. I was a smart kid, so I realized what to do about that. I ran in, got the car keys and moved his car off of my basketball court. He didn't find that amusing. He responded with a punch to my face. I can tell you exactly what his face looked like. I can tell you what his shirt looked like. I can tell you all about that and I have a lot of info about it, yet I am emotionally here. You know why? Two reasons. One is, this is a lot better.

Tammy: *(Laughter)* Way!

Jon: Two is, this is happening. But there was a time when I couldn't have told you that story. I would have gotten a little bit through it but couldn't think about it. My heart would beat really fast and I would get choked up and freaked out and all kinds of stuff. My mind was confusing the data about what happened with what happened. My mind hadn't realized that it doesn't exist, that it is completed, that it is defeated.

I saw this kid wearing a t-shirt that had a picture of a tornado on it, like a print, and then he was wearing a political button, but his button said, "I won." So, t-shirt, tornado print, "I won" button. I went up to him and said, "What is all that?" He said, "Do you see any tornados?" And I said, "Of course, I don't see a tornado. It's a nice day." And he said, "Do you see me?" I said, "Sure, I see you." And he said, "There you go! There's no tornado." There was a moment in which he didn't know that would be. He exists and there is no tornado. That tornado is completed. He exists, and it does not exist, so it's defeated.

That's why people have bumper stickers and license plates that say, "Former Prisoner of War." I mean, they didn't join the service to get captured. Why are they putting this thing on the back of the car? Because they beat it, they defeated it. All you have to do to get one of those is make it to the place where they give out the license plates because they, sure as heck, don't give them out in the Prisoner of War camp. They figure, you got here, you get a plate. If you made it to here, then you won. We want to get that good news all the way through.

Think about these two gals sitting by this gorgeous, beautiful fountain. They are drinking water and they are splashing each other, and they are laughing and reminiscing. They are reminiscing about having crossed the desert together and how incredibly dry and parched and awful it was. And, as they splash and giggle and sip the water, they know that there are other people there at the fountain who are also enjoying the water, but they know that nobody is enjoying it as much as they are, that the horrible thirst and deprivation has increased their joyfulness and appreciation. That is what happens when all of the lights are on. When the lights weren't on, she could be by the fountain, drinking the water and feeling miserable about having been thirsty. As the lights go on, she is going, "Oh, my God, this tastes so good!" So, we want all the lights on. Make sense?

Tammy: Yes.

Jon: So, as we think about flower, that is symbolically representing our intention, what you and I are intending. We are intending you to be experiencing things. I want to show you a little something that is interesting about energy, intention, and what happens when we put it together. I think you will find it interesting. If you would put that arm kind of just like I have mine. Perfect. And then look at your hand. Look at a spot on the hand. Look at that spot. That's the exact right spot. Keep looking at it. Keep looking at it when I put my hand near yours. Notice I won't touch your hand, but just put it near yours. When I put it near yours, you start feeling something, like, right there. See, there it is, there it is, there it is. It's right there. Think about that energy you are feeling right there, as the energy in the intention between me to you, you to me, the intention that is meeting there. As you feel that energy there through your hand, through your fingers, don't do anything on purpose to move your hand or move your fingers. Instead, I am going to do that from here with that energy. You are going to notice that your hand begins to vibrate. Now, you are not going to move it on purpose, and you will notice that the vibrations that happen as your fingers, ever so slowly, separate, are movements that happen, that are different than the way that we could possibly consciously or purposely move a hand. It's going to start, that's it, with vibrations, but then you are going to find that there will be these kinds of click-clack, robot-like movements, strange movements, movements that are different than the way that most people would be moving their hand. As you notice your hand moving in that unusual way, you also notice that you are the observer. It's kind of a whole different relationship to be having with your hand because you can remember when you were the one directing what your hand did and now things are different. You are the one that is observing what your hand is doing instead of you directing it. I want to point out that all the movements that you are becoming aware of are movements that are happening.

Tammy: *(Laughter)*

Jon: Not because you are deciding to make them happen, but those movements are the outward and visible sign that inner mind is responding to what we are doing, to our intention, to what has been represented with "flower", that is underway right now. Each time we go through any kind of process like this, you become even more responsive to it. Imagine, next time, even faster and deeper and stronger. The time after that, even more. It just keeps increasing, stronger and stronger. And then back to here. All right. Good job. So, look again, if you will, at that design. If you'll remember, it was dark, and it was also jagged. Tell me what you notice as you look back at it now.

Tammy: Smoother.

Jon: Uh-huh. Let me explain what happened there because that is kind of interesting too, isn't it? You know that a thermometer is an instrument giving a reading on the environment. You know that when there is a different reading it's because there has been an environmental change. That picture, the design, like a thermometer, is an instrument. It's giving a reading on the internal environment within your mind. We didn't do anything to change it any more than we would change the thermometer. We might change the room temperature and then see a change in the thermometer. You have already successfully been altering the environment within your mind regarding this issue. Hence, different reading. We are already getting a response. We will get a far more profound response as we continue, but that response is already in gear. It's a happening thing.

TAMMY HAS NOT BEEN ABLE TO CHANGE THE WAY SHE FEELS AND THINKS. IT HAS FELT LIKE SHE COULDN'T GET HER MIND TO RESPOND TO WHAT SHE WANTS. NOW, SHE SEES THAT HER MIND IS DEFINITELY RESPONDING BECAUSE SHE WATCHED AND FELT HER HAND DOING THINGS SHE WAS NOT CAUSING. IF WE GET HER MIND RESPONDING, IT MEANS WE CAN GET A RESPONSE TO THOSE THINGS THAT WILL IMPROVE THE QUALITY OF HER LIFE.

Tammy: Ok.

Jon: Things are going on here. Make sense?

Tammy: Yes. Very much so.

Jon: When someone has experienced trauma, the mind is likely to continue to experience the event as happening or the meaning attached to the event as happening. It may read events that have some structural similarity, even remote similarity, as the same event when it is obvious, consciously, that they are different. When the mind is clear, that is no longer going on. All that has to happen for the impression left by the events to clear is to have the intention to be connecting to what is going on as we review info about what did go on. That intention is also that we are emotionally here. That also is clearing, not only the impression, but the meaning the mind attached to it. Then, the energy that is stuck there is freed and used in the transformation that is happening here. Make some sense?

This gal is going through all this clutter in a house and she finds a treasure. She is blowing off the dust and she is looking at this thing and she's saying, "Whoa! Is this a keeper or what?! This is so cool!" What's happening as she is finding the treasure is that the clutter is losing. It's kind of like it's becoming transparent as it shrinks. All of the gunk is just, on its own, disappearing and that's when the treasures arrange themselves. In other words, that picture finds the perfect place on the wall and hangs itself. The dining room table makes its way into the dining room by itself. There is a reunion, by the way, with his old friends, dining room chairs. The house becomes open, clear. You can find things. There is plenty of room to create. There is plenty of room to think and be. That is what we are up to as we are clearing things.

So, what to clear is not for you and me to decide. Instead, as we are looking toward "flower," your mind arranging toward what it represents, I ask your inner mind, your subconscious mind, because it's good at multi-tasking, to simultaneously scan back through your personal history in order to select whatever experience *(snap)* that left an impression, that would be the one for you and I to begin getting clear with. And then, a particular event comes to mind. Now, sometimes something might have happened three hundred times, but if it happened three hundred times, it must have happened once. We always want to get specific so that inner mind can deal with it because it doesn't deal so good with generalities or concepts. Specifics work for that. So, your mind will scan back, a particular experience that you had will come to mind. A particular experience that you had will come to mind that will be the first one for us to get cleared. Has it already come to mind?

HER MIND IS BEING CLEARED AND CLEANED, JUST LIKE THE HOUSE. AS THE CLUTTER DISAPPEARS, THERE ARE TREASURES THAT WILL BE FOUND. I ASK HER MIND TO PINPOINT AN EVENT THAT, AS WE LOOK AT IT, WILL FREE ENERGY TOWARD WHAT IT IS THAT WE INTEND TOGETHER. HER MIND SCANS THROUGH DATA AND PICKS AN EVENT THAT HAPPENED TO HER AS A CHILD. I DON'T ENGAGE HER CONSCIOUSLY IN DOING THIS AND I DON'T ASK HER TO BRING UP THE SOURCE OF THE PROBLEM. WHAT IS BEING BROUGHT UP IS THE SOURCE OF THE PROBLEM, BUT I AM NOT LOOKING TO FIND THE SOURCE OF THE PROBLEM, BUT INSTEAD, TO FUEL THE SOLUTION, THE TRANSFORMATION.

Tammy: Yeah.

Jon: And this thing happened about how long ago? Rough guess.

Tammy: Five years old.

Jon: Describe what happened but do it in less than seven seconds.

Tammy: Ok. My brother-in-law, I was left with him. It was a secret game. There was a gun.

Jon: Ok. Good job. And he was about how old?

Tammy: In his twenties.

I AM NOT EXPRESSING SYMPATHY OR TELLING HER WHAT HAPPENED WAS AWFUL. THAT WOULD IMPLY THAT IT IS AWFUL NOW THAT SOMETHING HAPPENED THEN.

Jon: I am going to tell you what happened that day and you will notice *(laughter)* that I am going to be wrong. So, you have a job to do as we do this. I am going to tell you what happened and, whenever you hear me make a mistake, you're going to do this. You're going to say, "No, that's wrong!" And then, you are going to correct it. Like, for instance, I am going to start by saying, "This is something that happened when you were twenty-seven-years old." You are going to go, "No, that's wrong. It happened when I was five-years-old." Now, occasionally, I will probably say something right. If that ever happens, you say, "Finally, you got it right" and then, again, tell me more about what happened and add more detail. So, here we go. This is something that happened when you were eleven years old.

THIS IS A WAY OF KEEPING HER EMOTIONALLY CONNECTED TO WHAT SHE AND I ARE DOING RATHER THAN RELIVING AND RE-EXPERIENCING THE TRAUMA. IT IS SILLY, SO I CAN MAKE HER LAUGH. IT INTERRUPTS THE TELLING OF THE STORY AND, IN SO DOING, TAKES AWAY THE POWER OF THE MEMORY. IT ALSO PUTS HER IN CHARGE BECAUSE SHE GETS TO CORRECT MY TELLING OF THE STORY.

Tammy: No, you got it wrong.

Jon: And then, it happened when?

Tammy: I was five.

Jon: Ok, it happened when I was five years old. Good. You were five years old, and you were out in a cornfield in the middle of Iowa.

Tammy: No, you're wrong. It happened in a home. In our home.

Jon: It happened up in the attic. There was dust in the air.

Tammy: No, you're wrong. It was in the living room.

Jon: You were in the living room and that's when this fat old lady walked in.

Tammy: No, you're wrong. It was my brother-in-law.

Jon: Ok, your brother-in-law walked in with three of his friends.

Tammy: No, you're wrong. He was by himself.

Jon: Good. He was by himself. He walked into the room. He immediately took his clothes off, fell to his knees and started crying.

Tammy: No, you're wrong. He was sitting in a chair.

Jon:	He was sitting in a chair. He took his clothes off and started crying.
Tammy:	No, you're wrong. He took his penis out of his pants.
Jon:	He took his penis out of his pants, looked down, saw that it was small, and started crying.
Tammy:	*(Laughter)* I'm sorry. No, you're wrong. He, *(laughter)* that was funny, sorry. He got his gun out after that.
Jon:	He thought his penis was his gun.

I GET TO MAKE THE STORY FUNNY AND THE LAUGHTER AND FUN DESTROY THE DISTORTION AND BRING HER INTO THE CONNECTION WITH ME.

Tammy:	No, you're wrong. I think he knew the difference between the two.
Jon:	He took the gun out and he said that it was time to play a game.
Tammy:	Yes.
Jon:	And he told you that he wanted you to rub the gun until it would shoot.
Tammy:	No, he told me he wanted me to rub his penis.
Jon:	When you started rubbing his penis, he started shooting the gun.
Tammy:	No, he never shot the gun.
Jon:	So, add more detail.
Tammy:	It's been so long…
Jon:	Make it up. It will work as well.
Tammy:	He had me sit in his lap. It just progressed.
Jon:	He asked you to sit in his lap and he took his penis and he stuck it into your butt and then he started crying.
Tammy:	No, he didn't stick it in my butt.
Jon:	He stuck his penis between your legs. It hurt like hell.
Tammy:	Yes.

Jon: He stuck his penis between your legs. It hurt like hell. It really scared you. He never touched who you actually are.

Tammy: Finally, you got it right.

Jon: Let me do that one again. He took his penis, he stuck it between your legs, it hurt like hell. He never touched who you really are.

Tammy: Finally, you got it right!

Jon: There we go. Kind of like an exasperated, "finally!" Got it? Say it.

Tammy: Finally! You got it right.

Jon: Yeah, good. Then he told you that you had to keep this secret, or he was going to take that gun and shoot his penis right off.

Tammy: No, you're wrong. He said he was going to shoot my family.

Jon: That's when you decided that it probably would be better not to tell.

Tammy: *(Laughing)* You're right! You finally got it right!

Jon: Ok, and you went to your room and began to play with your computer.

Tammy: No, you're wrong. I went to my room and actually hid in my closet.

Jon: Ok. Good job. We got all the way through that and, as we run through that, let's do this. We're going to chop it into ten chapters. I am going to say a chapter number, you watch it like a film. You know, kind of approximate what's in the chapter. So, ten, in the closet, it's finished. Nine, on the way to the closet. So, here we go. Do your best to keep up with me.

Tammy: Ok.

Jon: Ready, set, ten.

Tammy: Closet.

Jon: You don't even have to say, just think.

Tammy: Ok.

Jon: Watch that little film. And then there might be twelve, something you didn't mention later. Twenty, something that happened much later than that. So, ten. Twelve. Eight. Five. Two. Three. Seven. Eleven. Fifteen. One. Two. Four. Six. Nine. Twelve. Fifteen.

Keeping up with me? One, two, three, five, seven, nine, ten. Good. One, two, three, four, five, six, seven, eight, nine, ten. Good. And then, this whole thing is on little very transparent papers that are all triangles. There's one. There's three. There's two. And then you watch those transparent things like that. You look through the transparent things. There are flowers on the other side. You are looking at the flowers. You are looking through them at the flowers like if we were looking up at the ceiling and there were flowers on the other side. The ceiling is transparent. We can put these really transparent pieces of paper floating, floating, until you are just looking at the flowers, until the rest is just dust. Ok, and check out the design again. Remember dark, jagged. What does it look like as you look at it now?

Tammy: Gray, almost transparent.

Jon: Ah, so something just happened there, too. Excellent. Notice, now, what happens if you remember the thing that happened on that day. Yeah, good. And what was your sense as you just recalled it?

Tammy: Now it's different.

Jon: What is going on now as you remember what happened then? What is your experience now as you are remembering what happened then?

Tammy: I am almost happy.

THE CHAPTERS CHANGED THE ORDER OF WHAT HAPPENED AND FURTHER TOOK POWER FROM THE MEMORY BY MAKING IT VERY CLEAR TO ALL PARTS OF THE MIND THAT IT IS NOT HAPPENING AND THAT IT DOESN'T EXIST. IT BECOMES VISUAL AND IS ON SMALL PIECES OF PAPER THAT ARE TRANSPARENT. THIS IS NOT INTENDED TO CHANGE WHAT SHE KNOWS ABOUT WHAT HAPPENED TO HER AND IT WON'T. IT CHANGES THE WAY THIS INFORMATION IS CODED AND HOW IT WILL BE AFFECTING HER FEELINGS AND BEHAVIOR.

Jon: Good as one would be, drinking water after having been in the desert.

Tammy: Right, right. Yeah. I want to laugh hysterically almost.

Jon: Beautiful. So, what's going on now is your mind is applying this same discovery to many, many other events. Hence, we are not going to need to speak about every event any more than we would need to teach a kid to tie every pair of shoes that he's ever going to wear.

Tammy: Ok.

Jon: After about the second pair, he's going to say, "Hey, Lady, I think I got the concept here." Your mind gets the concept very quickly and begins going back and checking off and doing the same thing to all of them so that it has more to generalize from. Another event will come to mind. Mind will scan back through your personal history and another one pops up.

Tammy: Yes.

Jon: And you were about how old?

Tammy: Twenty-two.

Jon: Ok. And, when you were twenty-two, give me a headline.

Tammy: Ok. A police officer pulled me over for a dimmed taillight and proceeded to brutally molest me on the side of the road. *(Beginning to get very emotional)*

Jon: You and I are meeting. This is what's going on now. This is what's going on.

Tammy: Right.

Jon: It's like you call the dog. You just say, "Come." You don't have to say, "Come now." He could say, "As opposed to when?" because the dog knows what we are discovering which is that's all that is. This whole thing that we've been hearing about, that things that are in the past aren't actually in existence.

Tammy: Right.

Jon: Yeah. And isn't that good news? So, there is no past. There is no past. There is no past.

Tammy: Right.

Jon: You were twenty-two-years-old. You were driving home and saw the red light flashing behind you. You pulled the car over. This police officer walked over. He was very overweight. He was Chinese.

Tammy: No, you're wrong.

Jon: No? Go on.

Tammy: He pulled me over for a dimmed taillight and I jumped out of the car to check it out.

Jon: Ok, and he was Chinese.

Tammy: No, you're wrong. He wasn't Chinese.

Jon: He wasn't Chinese. So, this fat, black cop…

Tammy: *(Laughter)* He wasn't black.

Jon: So, there was this fat, Korean cop…

Tammy: No, you're wrong. He wasn't fat at all.

Jon: So, it was unusual to see a very short, female police officer.

Tammy: No, you're wrong. It was a male.

Jon: A male police officer, and you got out to check the taillight. He took off all his clothes and started to sing.

Tammy: No, you're wrong.

Jon: He didn't do that.

Tammy: No, he, off the side of the road, grabbed me and threw me on the ground.

Jon: He threw you on the ground, pulled your pants down and started singing.

Tammy: No, you're wrong. He ripped off all my clothes and handcuffed my hands to my feet.

Jon: After your hands were handcuffed to your feet, he stuck his penis into your butt and started screaming like a buffalo.

Tammy: *(Laughter)* No, you're wrong. He stuck his gun in my vagina.

Jon: He put his gun into your vagina and pulled the trigger.

Tammy: No, he threatened to pull the trigger.

Jon: And the thought of pulling the trigger got him so excited that he ejaculated, and it was like a fire hose.

Tammy: Yeah. You're right.

Jon: He apologized and asked you to please not to tell anyone.

Tammy: Yes, he did. You're right.

Jon: And you told him not to worry, you were just interested in going home.

Tammy: You're right. You got it!

Jon: Good. You got back into your car and he waited until you pulled away before he drove his car.

Tammy: Yes, you're right.

Jon: You were shaky, but you were also intent on getting the hell out of there. You did it. You turned the key, you heard it start, and you very carefully pulled out and drove. You looked in the mirror and he wasn't there.

Tammy: Yes, you're right.

Jon: And you got it that it's finished. See it on the paper triangles and now it is turning to dust. You look at that design and what do you notice now?

Tammy: I don't see anything.

Jon: Yeah, it's not there anymore. As you look at the flower…

Tammy: It looks really bright yellow.

Jon: Yeah. It's really vibrant yellow, now.

Tammy: Yes.

THE DESIGN THAT REPRESENTED THE PROBLEMATIC WAY HER MIND HAD BEEN PROCESSING DATA HAS DISAPPEARED AND THE FLOWER HAS BECOME MORE PROMINENT. AS TAMMY SEES THESE THINGS, THEY CONFIRM HOW MUCH SHE HAS BEEN ABLE TO GET DONE.

Jon: So, what's going to happen is that those two clearings, and you know what I'm talking about now with clearing, the same light is going to be applying to every single thing that ever disturbed you. Ok?

Tammy: Yes, very much so.

THE LEARNING, THE TRANSFORMATION THAT HAPPENED FOR THOSE TWO EVENTS CAN NOW BE AUTOMATICALLY APPLIED TO ALL OTHER EVENTS THAT HAD BEEN DISTURBING.

Jon: Here we go. You just put your arm like you had it before. Look right there. Here we go. You are going to notice your hand moving even much more than before. Every movement that is going on with your hand indicates another impression is being cleared. Things are getting cleared and moving and changing and shimmering inside so that all is light and bright and clear and good. From now on, you simply, naturally understand and follow through with those things that are best. Your mind entertains only those things that have benefit and possibility. You experience the world with an "I can do that. I can do that. I can do that. I can do that." What you are getting with every facet of your being is those guys messed with your stuff, but never touched you.

Tammy: *(Laughter)* Wow!

Jon: How does all of that leave you?

Tammy: It is very similar to looking up in the red wood, that awe.

Jon: You are becoming aware, more and more and more aware, of yourself. That's what you discovered by the red wood. That's what you are getting here. You are aware of you. Does it make sense?

Tammy: Yeah.

Jon: You did great.

Tammy: Thank you.

Jon: Anything you want to ask me about on any of what you and I have been doing today?

Tammy: No, I'm good. This has been wonderful.

Jon: Yeah, well, we went very quick because you are smart and responsive and cooperative and easy to just move ahead and go with. Didn't have to put the brakes on at all. Just went for it and it all happened, and you just did it perfectly.

Tammy: Thank you.

Jon: So, it was great fun to have a chance to meet you and work with you.

Tammy: Thank you.

Follow-Up Commentary

Six months after our meeting, Tammy reported that she continues to feel light and joyful.

Marc

Marc is a sales manager for a national corporation. He began working with a fitness trainer and the relationship continued for many years. In addition to their appointments for personal training, they would, from time to time, socialize and have drinks and visit in the trainer's apartment. After a long working relationship and friendship, he was raped by his trainer. He was reluctant to press charges but finally did so. He had great trepidation about what would happen in court and his physician suggested he meet with me.

Jon: Tell me what's going on.

Marc: I can only do so much. I have been a mess. There are so many simultaneous layers that I am just struggling to get through each day. I am pressing charges against the man who raped me.

Jon: Why? In order to what?

Marc: A resolution.

Jon: What do you mean?

Marc: The right thing.

Jon: Why is it the right thing?

Marc: Well, this is a conflict, but my brain knows it's the right thing.

Jon: Why is it the right thing?

Marc: Because it was a crime.

Jon: Yes, and so how is it valuable to go forward and get involved?

I WANT TO UNDERSTAND WHAT IS MOTIVATING MARC TO MOVE FORWARD WITH THIS. I WANT TO MAKE SURE I LEARN THIS FROM HIM RATHER THAN ASSUME IT IS WHAT I THINK IT MIGHT BE.

Marc: Because it shouldn't be allowed to happen. It suddenly hit me that I have a fifteen-year-old daughter and if it was her, not me, would I be walking around going, "Gee, I wonder what I should do about this?"

Jon: I've worked with many people who were assaulted in a way that was of sexual interest to the perpetrator and very few have moved forward to do what you're doing.

I AM STRENGTHENING MY CREDIBILITY BY LETTING HIM KNOW I AM EXPERIENCED WITH THIS. I AM ALSO LETTING HIM KNOW THAT REPORTING WHAT HAPPENED IS EXCEPTIONAL RATHER THAN EXPECTED SO HE RECEIVES CREDIT FOR IT. ALSO, I PURPOSELY DESCRIBE IT AS SOMETHING THAT THE PERPETRATOR HAD SEXUAL INTEREST IN.

Marc: It's such a weird thing. This is someone I've known for twelve years. He was my personal trainer. Is there something, something about me that it was ok to do it to me?

Jon: No. ***There is nothing about you that caused this to happen.*** Pressing charges is a powerful statement that this should not be allowed to happen.

I IMMEDIATELY AND AFFIRMATIVELY RESPOND TO THE THOUGHT THAT THIS HAS ANYTHING TO DO WITH SOMETHING ABOUT HIM. PEOPLE FREQUENTLY THINK THAT WHEN SOMETHING UNFORTUNATE HAPPENS THAT, SOMEHOW, THEY HAVE BROUGHT IT ON THEMSELVES AND I WANT HIM TO DISMISS THIS THOUGHT. I DO SO BY SHOWING NO HESITATION IN MY RESPONSE. I USE HIS WORDS "SOMETHING THAT SHOULDN'T BE ALLOWED TO HAPPEN." USING THE SAME WORDS BUILDS HIS EXPERIENCE OF BEING UNDERSTOOD AND CREATES THE EXPERIENCE OF CONNECTION.

Marc: No. No, it's not.

Jon: It's not ok with you for anyone to hurt you or to hurt anyone because they feel like it.

Marc: No.

Jon: I'm seeing you saying this is not okay and sending the message that **it's not ok to be violent and harm me or harm anybody.**

Marc: I went to a therapist after this happened to me. She told me that if I reported the rape it would be horrible for me and that it wouldn't do any good. She said it would be even harder because I was a man and I agree with that. I decided not to for a while but finally I went ahead and did it.

Jon: In spite of that, **you move forward.**

Marc: Yeah.

Jon: **You spoke up. You came forward. You do what there is for you to do** because it shouldn't be allowed to happen. You made a report to the police.

Marc: Yes.

Jon: And?

Marc: He was arrested.

Jon: If the detective just listened to you and didn't do anything, **you still did your job by coming forward.** Is your job to make the arrest?

Marc: No.

Jon: Was it your job to make the report?

Marc: Yes.

Jon: So, if you made the report and there was no arrest, then **you did what your job was.** Your job wasn't to make arrests or convictions. That's not your job. **You did your job. You did your job** and, after doing your job, they did some stuff and then they said, "Now there's other stuff for you to do." What there is for you to do is to describe what took place. Is there any other job?

Marc: No. I guess not.

Jon: Is it your job, therefore, to cause him to be convicted of that?

Marc: No.

Jon: Ok. Is it your job to imprison him?

Marc: No.

Jon: Your job ends, and the world does what it does.

Marc: I think that Sunday in the police station I got my first taste of what I've always heard about. It was like I was being interrogated. I said, "We had a few drinks together. Even though he was my trainer, sometimes we would have a few drinks and just talk. I liked him. I trusted him. There was no reason not to." The detective asked me if I had had sex with him previously. He asked me if I was attracted to him. I told him of course not. I got raped. That doesn't mean I am sexually attracted to men. I wonder if other people will have the same suspicions. I told the detective that he got up and locked the door and then the detective asked me, "He locked the door from the inside?" I said, "Yeah." But then he goes, "Well, then why didn't you just go unlock the door and leave?" He implied that it was my fault. He was suggesting that I let him do that to me. There was no way I could get away from him. He is much stronger than me and it seemed like this detective was acting like I could have stopped him. I couldn't have stopped him. There wasn't a chance in the world I could get near that door, but I had to prove to the detective that I couldn't get to the door.

Jon: He believed you since there was an arrest, but your job was not to be believed. His job is to determine when there's an allegation whether or not it has the validity for him to proceed. In order to do that, he does various things to check that. Sometimes those things are even designed to rattle the person making the accusation because an accusation could be made for a variety of reasons, right? And if it wasn't being made because the thing actually happened, it would be easier for the detective to ascertain that if the person was rattled. Right? Because if someone is trying to maintain a lie and you succeed in getting him off his game, it will be easier to decide these dots aren't connecting than if I'm just as calm as a cucumber. His job was to ascertain whether or not this thing was accurate enough to proceed, which he then did. But it was not your job to be believed. It was your job to state what it was. So, as you spoke to the detective, you told the story **and you were believed, but it wasn't your job to be believed.** It was only your job to tell the story.

Marc: Right.

Jon: So, if you told the story and he said, "You are full of shit," did you do your job?

Marc: Yes.

Jon: Yeah. So, if you did your job and he said, "Oh, you're ridiculous," did you do your job?

Marc: Yes.

Jon: Does that make some sense to you?

Marc: Yes.

Jon: Ok. So, get that, get that there's your job and then there are other people's jobs. You didn't have to, but you decided to do your job and the detective believed you. Had he not believed you, would you have done your job?

Marc: Yes.

Jon: And you can see if we talk about somebody else how super rapid you can answer that. So, Bill is eighteen years old, and these two guys who he knows took turns hurting him and raping him. He says, "It wouldn't be ok with me to act like that was ok so I'm going to go ahead and report it." And he does. And the detective says, "Bill, you've been arrested twice. You have been arrested for using heroin. You have needle marks on your arm and nobody in their right mind would believe anything you say." Would you say to him, "Well, Bill, you didn't do a good job"?

Marc: No.

Jon: Did he do his job?

Marc: Yes.

Jon: Ok. That's his job, then their job is to determine whether that is a legitimate allegation and they didn't do their job, but did he do his job.

Marc: Yes.

Jon: And now, other jobs are coming up and one job you may have is to describe what happened to you in court when you are asked.

Marc: Yeah.

Jon: Ok.

Marc: I've had an epiphany and I don't know if I should say it.

Jon: Well I'm interested in epiphanies.

Marc: Well, I know, it's a different thing but you said it was my job to report the rape whether I am believed or not.

Jon: Yes, you took it on as your job.

Marc: All of a sudden, it's exactly parallel to when I got divorced and my ex-wife had a really powerful attorney…

Jon: Yes.

Marc: …and she's a well-respected high school principle.

Jon: Yes.

Marc: People didn't believe me.

AS I INTEND FOR MARC'S MIND TO WORK IN HIS BEST INTEREST, AN EVENT THAT LEFT AN IMPRESSION CAME TO MIND. THE STRUCTURAL SIMILARITY BETWEEN THESE TWO EVENTS WAS CAUSING THE DATA MARC'S MIND HAD STORED ABOUT THE DIVORCE EXPERIENCE TO CAUSE MORE DISTURBANCES ABOUT REPORTING THE RAPE AND GOING TO COURT. BECAUSE IT CAME TO MIND, IT CAN THEREFORE BE ADDRESSED.

Jon: Right. Was it your job to be believed?

Marc: I thought so.

Jon: But was it? And the way to know is this. Was it Bill's job? Remember Bill? Was it Bill's job to be believed?

Marc: No.

Jon: Was it Bill's job to make an arrest?

Marc: No.

Jon:	So, there's a point where Bill's job ends, and the world begins. For Bill, I think it would be challenging enough to just do Bill. Don't you think?
Marc:	Yeah.
Jon:	Do you remember our meeting prior to the divorce?
Marc:	No, we never met prior to the divorce.
Jon:	Ok. That's right.
Marc:	I think I get it.

MARC UNDERSTANDS THAT HE IS NOW PREPARED AND THAT PREVIOUSLY HE WASN'T. HE REALIZES THAT NOW IS NOT THEN AND NOT THE SAME AS THEN. IN THIS WAY, THE DISTRESS HE EXPERIENCED DURING THE FIRST EVENT WILL NOT BE FUELING THIS EVENT.

Jon:	You got it?
Marc:	Yeah. I didn't know then what I am realizing now. I don't need to worry about being believed. I just have to state the truth.
Jon:	So, you felt like you were ineffectual during the divorce proceedings because people didn't believe you.
Marc:	Right.
Jon:	But **being believed was never your job anyway**. So, look back at when you were going through that divorce thing and thinking that your job was much bigger than it actually was. Be with me, look back at him, look back at the younger you as he is going through that divorce so that we know that **he's perfectly adequately doing his job. He is doing it fine**. Good. And as you know that, and I know that, and we know that together, close your eyes. Look at him and just hang with me knowing that I'm totally knowing it, you're knowing it and we're knowing it. We're looking back at him and he begins to get it. Yeah, there it is. He's beginning to get it. And the only difference is that he's getting it that he's completing his job in just the right way. That's it. Open your eyes. What was it like for him to notice that?
Marc:	I was so much calmer.
Jon:	Yeah.
Marc:	I felt more mature.

Jon: He's doing his job and he's satisfied doing his job. Oh, that's good. Yeah. So, next you go to court and the person who is paid to defend him is now going to do what she can do to cause you to lose credibility.

Marc: Yeah.

Jon: Ok, and is it your job to get her to be nice to you?

Marc: No. No.

Jon: Is it your job to get her to be moved by your story?

Marc: No.

Jon: No. So, she's going to do her job. So, there you are in the courtroom and she says something like this, "Well, sissy slut, isn't it actually the truth that all of this happened in your head because you were pissed off that he didn't have sex with you after you begged him to?"

MARC UNDERSTANDS THAT HE IS NOW PREPARED AND THAT PREVIOUSLY HE WASN'T. HE REALIZES THAT NOW IS NOT THEN AND NOT THE SAME AS THEN. IN THIS WAY, THE DISTRESS HE EXPERIENCED DURING THE FIRST EVENT WILL NOT BE FUELING THIS EVENT.

Marc: No, it's not true.

Jon: But, don't you have to get her to treat you respectfully?

Marc: It's not my job.

Jon: Ok. Your job is to just say what happened and if she says, "We happen to know that you were after him the whole time but because you couldn't seduce him, you cooked up this cockamamie scheme in your slutty sissy brain." Right? Then she gets really close to your face and she kinds of spits as she talks, she says, "Didn't you, sissy boy?"

Marc: No.

Jon: She shouldn't be saying that, should she? Don't you need to stop her?

Marc: No. I'm expecting it.

Jon: Yeah. So, let's expect her to do that. I'm expecting her to get her face really close so that you can actually feel the spittle because she has this salivary thing that shows up particularly when she says the word "sissy". She can't really say it without spitting and she likes to get really close when she says it. And you're saying, "no."

Marc:	No.

Jon:	So, now let's think about you doing your job, which is to say what comes to you to say about what happened without needing to convince anyone.

Marc:	Right, yeah.

Jon:	Good. Ok, so now, let's prepare even more for the trial. The trial is going on. The guy that raped you is looking at you, and he's hating you. Can you see that on his face? You need to get him happy with you, don't you?

Marc:	No.

Jon:	Is it ok with you that he's not happy being there?

Marc:	Yes.

Jon:	Well, don't you want him to be happy?

Marc:	No.

Jon:	Is it ok with you that he hates you?

Marc:	It's scary.

I WANT HIM TO NOT FEEL SCARED WHEN HE SEES HIS RAPIST LOOK ANGRY.

Jon:	Ok, now let's get perspective on this. Imagine that you are on trial and being accused of rape.

Marc:	That would be scary.

Jon:	It would be very scary, don't you think?

Marc:	I don't want to be him.

Jon:	Ok, you wouldn't want to be him. But he doesn't like being him at the moment either, so he will look hostile.

Marc:	Yes. Yes.

Jon:	So, you don't need to be making a lot of eye contact with him because he's really not the audience, is he?

Marc:	No.

Jon:	Who are you speaking to?
Marc:	The judge?
Jon:	No, you're just speaking to the attorney that's questioning you, the prosecutor or the defense attorney. You speak with that person. So, here's a defense attorney that says, "I'm sure this is not the first time you decided to accuse somebody of raping you because you didn't get your own way with him, isn't it?"
Marc:	No, it's not what happened.
Jon:	Good job. And that's it. So, whom were you speaking to? That attorney. That's the person talking to you. You're not speaking to the judge, you're not speaking to the jury, you're not speaking to the defendant, and you're not speaking to the court officers.
Marc:	Right.
Jon:	Do you have to convince the defense attorney that her client really was a bad guy?
Marc:	No.
Jon:	No. Good. So, would you have to get her to agree with you?
Marc:	No.
Jon:	All you have to do is answer questions. She asks you how many days before you made this accusation did you dream this up?
Marc:	No days, I didn't dream anything up.
Jon:	Good. Ok, there you go. And that's it. So, it's not necessary for you to convince her, just answer her questions. And her questions might very well be insulting.
Marc:	Yes.
Jon:	How will you know what to say?
Marc:	It's just the truth.
Jon:	There you go. That's it. So, now as you look toward doing this next job, how does it feel?
Marc:	Much easier.
Jon:	Yeah.

Marc: Easier and clearer and detached from the outcome. Yeah, just much clearer in thinking that it's not my job.

Jon: No, it's not your job. So, the best thing for you around this situation is to do this. The alternative which was to do nothing wouldn't have felt as good. **It feels better to do your job and have everybody think you're a malicious liar than not do your job.**

Marc: Yeah.

Jon: Yeah. Because being believed isn't up to you.

Marc: Yeah, it's a big relief. It's a huge relief. I feel so much better.

Jon: Yes.

Jon: Whatever happens, happens.

Marc: Yeah, my job is simple.

Jon: There you go.

Follow-Up Commentary

The trainer was convicted and sentenced. Marc told me that, although it was hard to do, it was much better to have done it. He told me, "If I had done nothing, it would still be haunting me. Now, it's behind me and I know I did the right thing."

Tom was twenty-nine-years-old when we met. His physician had participated in a training I provided for health professionals and suggested to Tom that he meet with me. I learned that, although he had completed medical school, he had yet to pass the board exam. He was working as a food server and had been for more than two years.

Jon: I know there was something you wanted to think about together.

Tom: I've had a bad experience haunt me. It's been about two and a half years ago. I was studying for the test and spent a lot of hours doing it. I took the test and missed the exam by approximately five or six points. I called a colleague who came and said that, "Maybe you need some help studying because things aren't sinking in as well as you want them to. I know somebody I want you to go to and they will help you out." He suggested that I make an appointment with a social worker that specialized in hypnotherapy. It was his sister. She explained to me that they were going to give me some hypnotic suggestions while I was in a trance and this would enhance my ability to be able to study. One of the complaints I had was that after studying for a few hours, I would fall asleep. Maybe, if I didn't fall asleep so easily, I would do better.

I was in an altered state and the lady asked a question and promptly got an answer. The question was, "What was I afraid of?" The answer I came up with was that I was afraid of death. I had no idea that I was afraid of death. Through medical school, I worked with cadavers; I worked in the emergency room and the operating room and certainly saw my share of death while I was in training, so I never felt that was an issue. But, nevertheless, the words came out of my mouth during the trance. She then said, "Why don't you go back to a period of time when death was an issue?" I don't know how it happened, but things started floating in my head when I got a picture, but I was seeing the picture through the eyes of somebody else, not what I thought of as me. A person dressed in a green, military uniform with a white lab coat and a stethoscope around his neck standing with two bodyguards, heavily armed, which didn't feel threatening to me at all.

THIS IS A DRAMATIC EXAMPLE OF PSYCHOTHERAPY CAUSING TRAUMA RATHER THAN RESOLVING TRAUMA. IT ISN'T UNUSUAL, HOWEVER, FOR ME TO SEE SOMEONE WHO HAS BEEN TRAUMATIZED BY A MENTAL HEALTH PROFESSIONAL WHO WAS TRYING TO HELP.

Jon: Were you seeing the person with the stethoscope or looking through his eyes?

Tom: I felt the stethoscope on my shoulders.

Jon: OK. You were looking through the eyes of somebody with green clothes and a stethoscope and there were two armed guards beside that person?

Tom: I believe that was me because, when I was in the trance, I felt the stethoscope; I felt the clothing on me. A peculiar odor started hitting me, which is very nauseating to me, very bothersome. It was very ugly to breathe this. *(His face becomes pale and he has an expression of disgust.)* Every time I even think about it, I get this horrible heaviness in my chest. I have it right now.

I QUICKLY AND FORCEFULLY INTERRUPT THIS.

Jon: I need your help. Get back here with me. Sometimes, when I walk through my neighborhood, I can see the television screens inside of other people houses. Have you ever noticed that?

Tom: Yeah, sure.

Jon: Let's imagine we are walking together, and we can see someone's television through the curtains of their home. On the screen, there is the guy with the stethoscope and the two guards. Look at the person's house again and then the television screen can be seen through the window. See what you are describing on the television through the person's window. What's going on?

Tom: *(He is still troubled, but his face is no longer pale and there is no longer the same look of disgust on his face.)* Why is it that the two guards are making me feel safe? Why am I just looking at what is happening? Why am I there? Why am I there? There are people throwing bodies into holes.

Jon: What is the guy on the television screen with the stethoscope doing?

I SEPARATE HIM FROM THE EVENT BY NOT SAYING "YOU", BUT SAYING, "THE GUY WITH THE STETHOSCOPE." I MATCH HIS VOICE VOLUME, BUT MY TONE IS MATTER OF FACT.

Tom: Just looking.

Jon: And then what happens?

Tom: The pain gets so great . . .

Jon: *(Loud and confused. I am trying to draw his attention back to me.)* Pain? Who is in pain?

Tom: Yes. The Medic.

Jon: What kind of pain?

Tom: The pain in his chest gets, so…

Jon: What's that coming from?

Tom: He's got pain in his chest. *(pause)* I don't know.

Jon: OK.

Tom: The odor is so nauseating that…

Jon: Is the guy with the stethoscope being held captive by the guards?

THIS ALL HAPPENED SO FAST FOR ME. TOM IS TELLING A STORY THAT IS VERY DIFFICULT FOR ME TO FOLLOW AND HE IS IN DISTRESS. I ASK HIM TO TELL IT FROM OUTSIDE OF IT AND THAT SEEMS TO HELP HIS DISTRESS SOMEWHAT, BUT NOT MY CONFUSION. FINALLY, I UNDERSTAND THAT HE IS TALKING ABOUT A SUPPOSED PAST-LIFE EXPERIENCE THAT CAME UP DURING HIS PREVIOUS HYPNOTIC SESSION. HE BELIEVES HE WAS A NAZI MEDIC SUPERVISING HORRIBLE STUFF AND BEING PROTECTED BY HEAVILY ARMED GUARDS.

Tom: He is being protected by these two guards.

Jon: He is protected by them. OK. And other people are throwing bodies into holes?

Tom: Ditches, yes.

Jon: OK. I'm following you. I'm with it so far, I think. Go ahead.

Tom: The pain gets so great and the odor gets worse, so I scream and I…

Jon: *(Said forcefully)* Get out of it. Look at the picture from outside of it. We are walking through a neighborhood looking through the window at someone's television screen.

Tom: *(Calmer)* The guy screams because he wants to get out of the picture. He doesn't want to stay in the picture.

Jon: Yeah. OK. And then?

Tom: Then I wake up.

Jon: OK. So, let me see if I got it. In order to **study better and study longer,** you went to a hypnotherapist. She was your friend's sister. She did some work with you and asked you some questions while you were in an altered state of consciousness. She asked what you were afraid of and you said death and were surprised at what you had said. She asked you to explore it further. Am I absolutely right so far?

Tom: Yes, sir.

Jon: OK. You found yourself looking through other eyes in a different sort of a situation. In this hypnotic kind of a dream, it seemed like that person had a stethoscope and a uniform. There was a pain, there was a stink, and there was a dreadful kind of a situation. Then, the pain increased and then **you get out of there.** Have I got it?

Tom: Yes, sir.

Jon: Then what?

Tom: I went back again.

Jon: You went back to see the hypnotherapist? *(Incredulous)*

Tom: Yes. And the next time was similar, and it was just as disturbing. I'm not happy with it.

Jon: Similar situation?

Tom: Yes, sir.

Jon: But not the same.

Tom: Yes. Slightly different. The bodies were not the same. The guards did not look the same. There was a similar appearance of everything.

Jon: What has this done to you?

Tom: It keeps coming back and sometimes, even if I am doing nothing at all, this will come up by itself. It always comes back if I think about studying or getting to sit in the test again. It gets me angry.

Jon: This has really been in your way.

Tom: Yes, sir. I tried joking about it and making it something funny that happened in my life, but it's not at all funny. I completed medical school and now I am waiting tables. I can't take the test again because I can't study. As we started talking today, the chest pain returned. I got anxious as we were going to start because I knew it was going to happen and I was afraid to have a flashback.

Jon: How are you doing now?

Tom: As soon as you asked me to look at the television through the window, the pain went away. I don't have the pain now.

Jon: Good, good.

Tom: I'm afraid to study. I've got to study, but I don't want to. I can't. I've got to pass the test for my license.

Jon: What have you been thinking this thing means?

Tom: I don't know. Am I afraid of death? I don't think so, but why would this thing come up?

Jon: What about having this come to mind was disturbing?

THERAPISTS FREQUENTLY TRY TO UNDERSTAND PEOPLE'S FEELINGS BY BEING EMPATHETIC. THEY TRY TO PUT THEMSELVES IN A SIMILAR SITUATION AND UNDERSTAND HOW OTHER PEOPLE ARE FEELING BY UNDERSTANDING HOW THEY WOULD FEEL. I THINK THIS IS A MISTAKE. IT ISN'T A GOOD IDEA FOR ME TO TRY TO UNDERSTAND TOM BY TRYING TO COMPARE HIM TO HOW I WOULD FEEL IN A SIMILAR SITUATION. INSTEAD, I BELIEVE IT IS MUCH BETTER TO LEARN ABOUT HIM FROM HIM.

Tom: That I would take part in killing people.

Jon: You took this thing to mean that you had taken part in killing people? *(Incredulous)*

Tom: Yes.

Jon: And that's what has been bothering you about it?

Tom: It's bothering me now.

Jon: You have been thinking that it meant that you had taken part in killing people? This thing meant that to you? **That is definitely not what it meant. You never took part in that stuff.** Something came to mind when you were hypnotized. That can come from anywhere. One possibility is that this thing was imagined from something you had viewed, seen or heard about and were horrified about. Sometimes people have nightmares. Don't you agree? Because someone has a dream, it doesn't mean the dream was true. This was a hypnotically induced bad dream. It has nothing to do with anything that actually happened. Am I making sense?

Tom: It's a possibility.

Jon: And the part of the dream, and that is definitely what it was, it was that, in the dream, you were part of it?

Tom: I didn't stop it.

Jon: Tom, you weren't involved in it. It was a manifestation of fear. For you, the fear was that you had hurt others or even that you had allowed it.

Tom: Yes.

Jon: Hey, the problem is you were thinking that this thing came to mind because of something you did. That isn't what it means. People don't have scary dreams because they did evil things in a past life. What it means is that you would hate to hurt people or even let people hurt people. So, the mind can bring something up because it's horrifying. That is why it is repulsive, that's why it's disturbing, that's why you have not wanted to deal with it. You find the thought of doing something bad for people to be horrifying. Don't you want to feel horrified by the thought of doing horrible things or even permitting anyone else to?

Tom: Yes, of course.

Jon: You find bad things repulsive. Have you got that?

Tom: Got it.

Jon: Tom, **you did not do any of those things.** That I can assure you of. **You did not do any of those things.** You find the idea of doing them or having done them repulsive.

Tom: Very repugnant.

Jon: Right. And that is exactly how you want it to be.

Tom: Yes. That's right.

Jon: You have it exactly the way you want it. Am I with you?

Tom: Yeah.

Jon: Then, what is the problem?

Tom: *(He pauses and seems confused)* I don't know.

Jon: Because it is solved.

Tom: It is? *(Sounds amazed)*

Jon: Imagine studying a medical book. It's about treating a gunshot wound.

Tom: Got it. Wow! It feels fine.

Jon: You are free of that. You never did anything. It was a nightmare. Nightmares happen when the conscious mind isn't present. Your conscious, logical mind was not present when your friend's sister hypnotized you. What happened is called "confabulation". It took place because of your concern about not having passed the test and because of the questions the hypnotherapist asked. Now, it is finished. Like any bad dream, it's over.

Tom: It's over. I can feel it. Thank you.

Follow-Up Commentary

Three months after our conversation, Tom told me he was free of anxiety and was busy studying for his licensure examination.

Paula was 38 years old when we had this conversation.

Jon: You attended a talk I gave recently and told me there was something you wanted to speak with me about.

Paula: Something that happened to me about fifteen years ago still has an influence on me. I think it's connected to a whole lot of other things in my life that are blocking me from where I want to go in my life and being what I want to be.

Jon: What was it that happened?

Paula: I was raped and beaten and run over. It has left me feeling badly about my body and myself.

PAULA SAYS, "I WAS RAPED AND BEATEN AND RUN OVER," AND, WHILE IT WOULD BE THE INCLINATION OF MOST PEOPLE AND MOST THERAPISTS WHO HEAR A STATEMENT LIKE THAT TO RESPOND WITH SYMPATHY, EMPATHY, OR COMPASSION, I DIDN'T DO THAT. IF I SHOW HER THAT I'M SYMPATHETIC WHILE SHE'S TALKING WITH ME, THEN I'M IMPLYING THAT SHE OUGHT TO BE SYMPATHIZED WITH RIGHT HERE AND NOW. IT WOULD IMPLY THAT, BECAUSE SOMETHING WAS AWFUL PREVIOUSLY, SHE OUGHT TO BE SYMPATHIZED WITH NOW. THAT THEN IMPLIES THAT SHE'S NOT CURRENTLY IN GOOD SHAPE, NOT EXPECTED TO BE IN GOOD SHAPE, ISN'T OKAY, AND SHOULDN'T BE OKAY. I THINK OF THAT MESSAGE AS "POISONOUS" BECAUSE OF THE EFFECT THAT WOULD HAVE ON HER SELF-CONCEPT AND ON THE WAY HER MIND READS INFORMATION.

Jon: On one level, you realize that **what happened to you was never about you.** Now, your mind can **take in what you know at an even deeper level** and integrate this understanding, so you **know what you know through every facet of your mind.**

BY SAYING, "WHAT HAPPENED TO YOU WAS NEVER ABOUT YOU...KNOW WHAT YOU KNOW THROUGH EVERY FACET OF YOUR MIND," I SEPARATE PAULA'S IDENTITY FROM THE EVENT. THERE ARE THREE STATEMENTS THAT CAN BE RESPONDED TO BY HER MIND. THE FIRST, "WHAT HAPPENED TO YOU WAS NEVER ABOUT YOU," AND THE SECOND, "TAKE IN WHAT YOU KNOW AT AN EVEN DEEPER LEVEL" AND THE THIRD "KNOW WHAT YOU KNOW THROUGH EVERY FACET OF YOUR MIND" ARE STATEMENTS THAT LIFT HER MOOD AND ORGANIZE THE WAY HER MIND SORTS AND READS INFORMATION. THEY MOVE HER TOWARD MY INTENTION FOR HER WHEN WE'RE DONE, WHICH IS TO FEEL GOOD ABOUT HAVING ALREADY SURVIVED THE WORST THINGS THAT HER LIFE WILL LIKELY EVER PRESENT, REALIZE THAT HAVING SURVIVED IS TO HER CREDIT, AND RECOGNIZE HER OWN STRENGTH, FLEXIBILITY, ENDURANCE AND POWER.

Paula: Yes, on this level, I'm real clear.

Jon: Good.

Paula: When I realized that I had physically survived, I was furious. I really did not, at that moment, want to be physically alive. For a very long time after that experience, I did a lot of things to try to off myself and to try and get the hell out of here because there was so much pain.

Jon: You wanted to **stop the pain and experience peace.** Makes sense to me.

WHEN I SAY, "YOU WANTED TO STOP THE PAIN AND EXPERIENCE PEACE...MAKES SENSE TO ME." I CONVEY TO HER THAT I EXPERIENCE HER AS SOMEONE WHO MAKES SENSE. THE WORDS, "STOPPING THE PAIN AND EXPERIENCING PEACE," DEMONSTRATE AN UNDERSTANDING OF WHAT SHE JUST SAID, WHILE RECOGNIZING THE POSITIVE INTENTION THAT WAS MOTIVATING THE SUICIDAL THOUGHT.

Paula: Right. It seemed to make sense.

Jon: Stopping pain and feeling peace. You <u>were</u> so hurt.

I ACKNOWLEDGE THAT THE EXPERIENCE WAS HORRIBLE WHEN I USE THE WORDS, "YOU WERE SO HURT," BUT THE WORDS ARE SAID IN THE PAST TENSE, WHICH PLACES THE HURT BEHIND HER.

Paula: Yes.

Jon: During that experience, you **fight to survive.**

Paula: During that experience, I made an effort to stay alive. I did a lot of things to try and maintain my life.

Jon: Yes. **You are all about survival. You are strong and tough.** When your survival is threatened, **you dig in**.

I SPEAK ABOUT STRUGGLING TO SURVIVE AS BEING WHO SHE REALLY IS USING THE DECLARATIVES, "YOU ARE ALL ABOUT SURVIVAL. YOU ARE STRONG AND TOUGH," AND, "WHEN YOUR SURVIVAL IS THREATENED, YOU DIG IN." I WANT HER TO IDENTIFY WITH FIGHTING TO SURVIVE RATHER THAN WANTING TO DIE.

Paula: Yeah, that's true. That's very true.

Jon: **You are a survivor.** That's what you do. That's who you are.

THE ISSUE OF HOW A PERSON VIEWS THEIR IDENTITY IS SIGNIFICANT. IT OFTEN STEMS FROM A FEELING, OR HOW THEY HAVE BEEN DOING THINGS OR SOMETHING ABOUT THEIR BODY. I TELL PAULA, "YOU ARE A SURVIVOR. THAT'S WHAT YOU'RE ABOUT. THAT'S WHAT YOU DO AND THAT'S WHO YOU ARE," BECAUSE I INTEND FOR HER TO EXPERIENCE HER IDENTITY AS ONE THAT IS DEDICATED TO SURVIVAL RATHER THAN THE FEELING OF WANTING TO DIE. I TELL HER THAT THE THOUGHTS SHE HAD AFTERWARD WEREN'T ACTUALLY HER, BUT HOW STRUGGLING TO SURVIVE IS WHO SHE IS.

Paula: Right.

Jon: This experience happened when you were about how old?

Paula: Fourteen.

Jon: What has it meant to you?

Paula: What it meant, because of the circumstances under which it happened to me at the time, was that I absolutely deserved every bit of it and that I was not worthy of anything better.

Jon: What gave you that idea?

Paula: Well, I was spending very little time living at home. I was going out on the street all the time. I was on my way to my 18-year-old boyfriend's house, which was, of course, a big issue, having an older boyfriend and being out on the street. I was walking down a dark street, acting as if I was perfectly safe, and I put myself in a very vulnerable position.

Jon: As you think back on it now, do you still have any thought that you deserved it?

Paula: I don't think intellectually that I deserved it, of course. No. Nobody deserves to have anything like that happen to them. There are crazy people running all over the planet and you could be in your home, snuggled up with a good book and have somebody break in and then rape you.

Jon: So, you know.

Paula: Yeah, I know those things.

Jon: Absolutely, you don't, and you never did, and you never will deserve anything bad to happen.

Paula: I think that there is a little part of me that is still not sure. I think that it keeps me from taking care of myself. It interferes with being happy. I don't sleep well. I am frequently depressed.

Jon: You realize it makes sense to **take care of yourself now**.

I DEBUNK ANY THOUGHT THAT SHE DESERVED WHAT HAPPENED TO HER, AND SHE SAYS THAT SHE BELIEVES THE EVENT HAS KEPT HER FROM TAKING CARE OF HERSELF. RATHER THAN RESPOND WITH, "IT STOPS YOU FROM TAKING CARE OF YOURSELF," I SAY, "YOU REALIZE IT MAKES SENSE TO TAKE CARE OF YOURSELF." THE WORDS, "TAKE CARE OF YOURSELF," ARE TAKEN AS A COMMAND BECAUSE, WHEN I SAY THOSE WORDS, THE VOLUME IS RAISED, AND EYE CONTACT IS MADE. THESE ARE SUBTLE CHANGES AND NOT RECOGNIZED BY THE CONSCIOUS MIND.

Paula: Right. Yes. I think that my relationship with people is sometimes tainted by my impression of extreme distrust. I'm so afraid that somebody is going to try to attack me or harm me. Sometimes, I think I wish that they would finish it. It's really weird.

As Paula describes how things have been, I see her as I intend her to be--strong, clear, secure and powerful. I think of this as "target". It is what goes on in my mind as I hear how she has been feeling and what she has been thinking. The target provides me with a clear direction as to what to say and do. Mental health professionals are usually taught that the client needs to be the one to determine the outcome. I believe I have more clarity and, therefore, it is my responsibility to determine what is best and facilitate it.

Jon:	I want to understand.
Paula:	I have had experiences in the past in therapy, trying to understand why I spend a lot of time reliving this experience.

Therapists frequently engage people in a process of trying to develop insight and understand themselves. I believe that introspection is symptomatic of emotional disturbance and, therefore, is not the cure. I may ask Paula what she thought something meant, but I will not encourage her to more deeply understand inner causes of emotional disturbance.

Jon:	When you said, "Wish they would..."
Paula:	Wish that somebody would go ahead and finish it, because I was...
Jon:	Kill you?
Paula:	Right. Kill me. Do it.
Jon:	"Wish somebody would finish it," is sort of a wishing thought about a way to get quiet from turmoil. It's just been at a wishing level. I guarantee that if somebody tried to kill you, you would object.
Paula:	Right.
Jon:	What it was really about was quiet from pain and turmoil.
Paula:	Right, and desperation.
Jon:	Yes, there was so much hurt, but, when it counts, **you fight and survive.**

The hurt is not minimized. It is acknowledged, but it is put in the past with this invisible tense change. If I had used the words "in the past" that would have made the tense change visible and she would have said or thought, "I still hurt". This way, I get it done and there is no dispute. I then end with the command "fight and survive". This is who she is, and this is what she does.

Paula:	Yes, I didn't really want it.
Jon:	No. Nor would you have been okay with it.
Paula:	Right.

Jon: You would **dig in and fight**.

Paula: Right.

I TEASE OUT THAT SHE HAS WISHED THAT THEY WOULD COME BACK AND KILL HER, SO I CAN DEAL WITH IT. I DEAL WITH IT BY DIMINISHING ITS POWER, BY CALLING IT A WISHING THOUGHT, AND BY EMPHASIZING THE POSITIVE INTENTION. I MOVE HER BACK TO BE A FIGHTER BY REFERENCING WHAT WOULD BE HER IMMEDIATE RESPONSE IF SOMEONE TRIED TO KILL HER NOW. THE DECLARATIVE, "YOU FIGHT AND SURVIVE," AND THE COMMANDS, "DIG IN AND FIGHT," AND, "TAKE GOOD CARE OF YOURSELF," CONTINUE TO REAFFIRM WHAT IT IS THAT'S INTENDED.

Jon: If you think of yourself at fourteen, how do you like her?

I SAY, "HOW DO YOU LIKE HER?" INSTEAD OF "HOW DO YOU LIKE YOURSELF?" BECAUSE I WANT TO SEPARATE HER IDENTITY FROM THAT 14-YEAR-OLD GIRL.

Paula: I don't.

Jon: What is it you don't like?

Paula: I don't like the fact that she did a lot of things that she thought were a lot of fun, but really were stupid. She didn't take good care of herself.

Jon: You realize what to do is **take good care of yourself**.

I AM ABLE TO DEMONSTRATE UNDERSTANDING FOR WHAT PAULA IS SAYING AND TELL HER TO TAKE CARE OF HERSELF AT THE SAME TIME.

Paula: Yes. I think that she had a lot of terrible experiences.

Jon: Tell me.

Paula: Well, she is doing dangerous drugs.

Jon: What kind of drugs?

Paula: Heroin.

Jon: Okay. What's that about?

Paula: It's about numb.

Jon: And?

Paula: It's about quiet.

Jon: Yes.

Paula: It's about being quiet.

Jon: It's about being quiet, so it's about peace and quiet.

USING HEROIN IS HORRIBLE FOR PEOPLE, BUT SO IS FEELING AWFUL ABOUT ONE'S SELF FOR HAVING DONE SO. I BEGIN TO SHIFT THAT BY RECOGNIZING PAULA WAS USING HEROIN TO EXPERIENCE PEACE AND QUIET.

Paula: It's kind of hard for me to think that I thought that that was my only resource.

Jon: Why?

Paula: Because what a "sucky" situation to be in!

Jon: Does having been in a sucky situation trouble you right now?

Paula: Well, I think that I deserve to be in a better situation.

Jon: No question. **You deserve much better**. But what about having been in a sucky situation bothers you now? It isn't bad to be in a better situation now than you were in then. It doesn't suck now, so now it doesn't suck.

I ASK HER, "DOES HAVING BEEN IN A SUCKY SITUATION TROUBLE YOU RIGHT NOW?" ADDRESSING IT IN THIS WAY AND BY USING THE PAST TENSE TO PLACE THE EVENT IN THE PAST CAUSES HER MIND TO UPDATE SO THAT SHE NO LONGER FEELS THAT SHE IS IN THAT SITUATION NOR DOES SHE FEEL BAD ABOUT HAVING FELT BAD ABOUT IT.
I HAVE TO REMAIN DETACHED AND OBJECTIVE. IF I SAID SOMETHING LIKE "YES, IT WAS SO DIFFICULT" I CAN GET DRAWN IN TO HER PERCEPTIONS. THEN, THE WRONG PERSON IS GETTING HYPNOTIZED. INSTEAD, I ASKED "WHY?", WHICH FACILITATES DETACHMENT AND OBJECTIVITY. I AM THEN CLEAR. FROM THAT PLACE OF CLARITY, I CAN SUGGEST THAT IT DOES NOT SUCK TO HAVE BEEN IN A BAD SITUATION. DRINKING WATER IN THE PRESENT DOESN'T SUCK EVEN IF ONE HAD BEEN THIRSTY IN THE DESERT. IN FACT, THE WATER IS EVEN BETTER.

I DON'T ACTUALLY AGREE WITH PAULA WHEN SHE SAYS THAT SHE DESERVES TO BE IN A BETTER SITUATION BECAUSE I DON'T THINK THE CONCEPT OF "DESERVING" IS EITHER ACCURATE OR USEFUL IN UNDERSTANDING HOW THINGS HAPPEN. IT SEEMS TO IMPLY THAT IT HAS OR THAT IT SHOULD HAVE AN EFFECT ON WHAT HAPPENS, BUT I DON'T SEE ANY INDICATION OF THAT. AT THIS POINT, HOWEVER, BRINGING PAULA TO THAT POINT OF VIEW WOULD BE A DISTRACTION, TAKING US AWAY FROM THE IMPORTANT WORK TO BE DONE FIRST.

Paula: Well, I guess nothing.

Jon: Good.

Paula: *(Uplifted)* I guess it just means that it happened.

Jon: Yes. Good. Something just shifted. Did you feel it?

Paula: Yes, I did.

Jon: I'd like you to close your eyes for a little while. Now you can open your eyes and see how things are different. When you were walking down the street, it meant...

I SAY, "SOMETHING JUST SHIFTED. DID YOU FEEL IT?" THEN, IMMEDIATELY AFTER, I SAY, "I'D LIKE YOU TO CLOSE YOUR EYES FOR A LITTLE WHILE." HAVING HER CLOSE HER EYES CREATES A PAUSE IN TIME, WHICH CAUSES WHAT HAS BEEN LEARNED TO BE PROCESSED ON A STILL DEEPER LEVEL.

Paula: Just that I was walking down the street.

I'M LOOKING TO ELIMINATE MEANINGS THAT HER MIND HAD ATTACHED TO WHAT SHE DID, LIKE SOMEHOW WALKING DOWN THE STREET CAUSED THE HORROR THAT TOOK PLACE. NOW, SHE GETS THAT WALKING DOWN THE STREET MEANT JUST THAT SHE WAS WALKING DOWN THE STREET. ITS MEANING HAS BEEN ELIMINATED. I BELIEVE THAT ALL MEANING IS DISTORTION, BUT THE MEANINGS THAT ATTACH TO DISTURBING EVENTS ARE EVEN MORE DISTORTED.

Jon: You were walking down the street. That was a sensible place to be walking.

Paula: Right.

Jon: If you were on a roof or a ledge or a tree, maybe not so much.

Paula: Right.

Jon: You were walking, and you got captured.

Paula: Yes. They pulled me down and forced me into a car.

Jon: They?

Paula: There were two men.

Jon: Okay.

Paula: And they threw me down and raped me.

Jon: Yes.

Paula: And then they ran me over.

Jon: Ran you over?

Paula: Yes, with their car. This was going on for a period of about five hours.

I NEED TO KEEP PRESENT AND STAY WITH MY INTENTION IN ORDER NOT TO PREVENT ANY REACTIVITY ON MY PART. THIS WAS QUITE CHALLENGING, AND HERE'S WHY. WHAT WE THINK OF AS NEGATIVE EMOTIONS ARE MORE POWERFUL THAN THOSE WE THINK OF AS POSITIVE. IMAGINE SIX PEOPLE ENTERING A ROOM. FIVE OF THEM ARE IN A PLEASANT MOOD AND ONE OF THEM IS FILLED WITH RAGE AND HATRED. IT'S MORE LIKELY THAT THE FIVE WILL FEEL WORSE THAN THE ONE WILL FEEL

CHEERFUL. IN ADDITION, THE PROCESS OF BEING COMPASSIONATE CAUSES ONE PERSON TO PUT HIMSELF IN ANOTHER'S SHOES. IF I TRY TO UNDERSTAND HER BY EXAMINING HOW I WOULD BE IN A SIMILAR SITUATION, THIS CAN PULL ME, THE FACILITATOR, INTO EXPERIENCING THE EMOTIONS OR THE PERSPECTIVE OF THE PARTICIPANT. I REFER TO THIS AS "THE WRONG PERSON GETTING HYPNOTIZED". I FOUND MYSELF REALLY LIKING PAULA AND THAT ALSO MAKES IT MORE LIKELY TO HAPPEN. I WAS CHALLENGED, BUT I CONTINUED TO RESET MY MIND TO BE INVOLVED IN THE WORK I WAS DOING. I HAVE HEARD PEOPLE USE PHRASES LIKE, "I FEEL YOU" OR "I FEEL YOUR PAIN." I DO MY BEST NOT TO.

Jon: You are doing great. Keep going.

Paula: And they tied me to a tree and pointed a gun at me, put it in my vagina, and put it down my throat.

Jon: You can remember having those hideous things done to you because they did happen.

Paula: Yes, it happened.

Jon: What do you think about that now?

Paula: It means that something horrible happened to me.

Jon: Which gives you what? Credibility. *(Said with certainty)* **You have major credibility**. Having had a gun put between your legs and down your throat at fourteen gives you lots of credibility.

Paula: Why is that?

Jon: **You really know.** You've been there, **you survived, and it's big time credibility**.

AS SHE TALKS ABOUT BEING RAPED, TORTURED, AND RUN OVER WITH A CAR, I DON'T HAVE A SYMPATHETIC RESPONSE. INSTEAD, I CONNECT WITH HER BY DRAWING HER ATTENTION TO WHAT SHE'S DOING RIGHT HERE WITH ME, WHICH CAUSES HER MIND TO ORIENT IN THE PRESENT EVEN THOUGH THERE'S DATA RECALL ABOUT THE PRIOR EVENT. I SAY, "YOU'RE DOING GREAT. KEEP GOING." AGAIN, I AM CHANGING HER SELF-CONCEPT AS I SPEAK TO HER SURVIVAL, POWER AND CREDIBILITY.

IN HEARING THESE HORRIFIC EVENTS, I NEEDED TO PULL MYSELF BACK FROM MY OWN EMOTIONAL REACTION. IT IS MY JOB TO MAKE EVERY PART OF HER REALIZE THAT SHE'S HERE, THAT SHE'S OKAY, AND THAT SHE'S ENGAGED IN A SHARED PROJECT THAT IS WORTHWHILE AND INTERESTING. IF I BECOME TROUBLED, THEN IT SUGGESTS THAT THERE IS SOMETHING THAT SHE OUGHT TO BE TROUBLED ABOUT HERE AND NOW. THAT'S NOT THE MESSAGE I WANT HER MIND TO RECEIVE. SINCE THE INFORMATION SHE CONVEYED WAS SO STARTLING TO ME, I HAD TO CONSCIOUSLY GRAB A HOLD OF WHAT SHE AND I WERE DOING IN THE MOMENT AND CONTINUE TO RESONATE EMOTIONALLY WITH THAT. BECAUSE I WANT THAT FROM HER, I HAVE TO MAKE SURE THAT I HAVE IT GOING FOR ME.

WHEN SHE ANSWERS MY QUESTION, "WHAT DO YOU THINK ABOUT THAT NOW?" WITH, "IT MEANS THAT SOMETHING HORRIBLE HAPPENED TO ME," THE EVENT IS BEING READ AS NO LONGER TAKING PLACE, AND THE MEANING IS BEING READ

BY HER MIND AS NOT TAKING PLACE. NOTHING IS TAKING PLACE, SO NOTHING NEEDS TO BE DONE. I SAY, "YOU HAVE MAJOR CREDIBILITY." THE FEELING OF SHAME DISAPPEARS, AND SHE IS FILLED WITH A SENSE OF POWER AND ACCOMPLISHMENT.

Paula: Yeah, it's when you know about that experience.

Jon: Yes, which makes you more powerful. Credibility relates to power, and certainly **you are powerful, and more powerful because of what happened.**

Paula: I haven't ever thought about that.

Jon: **You have major power and credibility.**

Paula: You are right. I do.

PAULA FEELS GREAT CONNECTION BECAUSE I AM REALLY INTERESTED IN HEARING HER. WHAT I SAY SHOWS UP AS ACCURATE AND IT IS INTERESTING BECAUSE IT IS DIFFERENT THAN THE WAY SHE WAS THINKING AND DIFFERENT THAN THE WAY THE PROFESSIONALS SHE HAD SPOKEN TO PREVIOUSLY WERE THINKING. BECAUSE OF THIS, I HAVE CREDIBILITY. WITH CONNECTION AND CREDIBILITY, SHE IS IN AGREEMENT WITH WHAT I SAY. I TELL HER SHE HAS MAJOR POWER AND CREDIBILITY AND SHE IMMEDIATELY AGREES.

Jon: Think about a group of people who are gathered to discuss some issue that in any way involves crime or abuse or trauma and somebody says, "I was violently assaulted." Who doesn't shut up and listen with electric interest? **You are highly credentialed in a way that very few people are.** As you think of it now and look at her with a gun shoved down her throat, what do you feel?

Paula: I feel that she has been in an experience that really hurt.

Jon: And now, with a gun shoved into the vagina.

Paula: She knows what that feels like. *(Her voice quivers with emotion.)*

Jon: There's still some pain. Tell me why?

I DON'T WANT TO UNDERSTAND HER THROUGH EMPATHY. THERAPISTS ARE TRAINED IN WAYS THAT ENCOURAGE EMPATHY, WHICH IS A PROCESS OF UNDERSTANDING WHAT SOMEONE ELSE IS FEELING BY CONSIDERING HOW YOU WOULD FEEL IN THE SAME OR A SIMILAR SITUATION. I THINK BEING EMPATHIC IS DISRESPECTFUL. TO BE RESPECTFUL, I LOOK TO UNDERSTAND WHAT SHE IS FEELING AND WHY, RATHER THAN WHAT I THINK I MIGHT BE FEELING. I SAY, "TELL ME WHY," SO I CAN UNDERSTAND FROM HER.

Paula: It really messed me up physically and, just this past summer, after years and years of feeling the physical repercussions, I needed to have a hysterectomy.

Jon: It <u>feels</u> so wrong.

RIGHT AND WRONG DON'T HAVE ANYTHING TO DO WITH WHAT CAUSES THINGS TO HAPPEN, BUT THIS IS PAULA'S EXPERIENCE OF THINGS. I ACKNOWLEDGE IT BUT USE THE WEDGE "FEELS" RATHER THAN CONFIRM THE MEANING BY USING THE WORD "IS".

Paula: Yes.

Jon: Being angry about it hurts.

Paula: It really hurts.

Jon: The only thing that can cause fear or anger is the perception of threat. Is there anything to be threatened about now about that gun that was in your vagina when you were fourteen?

Paula: Now? No. Not now.

Jon: Okay. If you are not threatened, then you will have to **be secure.** Sorry, but that's just the way that cookie crumbles. And if **you are secure**, then you are not angry. And if you are not angry, you are not attached to that.

Paula: Right.

THIS IS A CHALLENGING EVENT TO CLEAR BECAUSE OF BOTH THE MAGNITUDE OF THE EVENT AND THE CONTINUED REPERCUSSIONS REQUIRING A HYSTERECTOMY. EVEN SO, I SUGGEST THAT THE THING THAT'S BEEN HURTING HAS BEEN HER ANGER. THEN, IN A LIGHT, YET DECISIVE WAY, I LOOK TO ELIMINATE THAT ANGER.

WHAT HAS BEEN CAUSING THE PAIN IS THAT PAULA'S MIND HAS BEEN ATTEMPTING TO CAUSE HER TO DO SOMETHING TO STOP THE WRONGNESS. IT ISN'T TRYING TO CAUSE PAIN; IT IS TRYING TO CAUSE AN ACTION THAT DOESN'T NEED TO BE TAKEN. EMOTIONS ARE DESIGNED TO TURN ON, CAUSE THE ACTION, AND SNAP OFF. A PROLONGED EMOTIONAL REACTION IS DYSFUNCTIONAL AND PAINFUL. IT CAUSES PAIN AND AFFECTS BEHAVIOR NEGATIVELY.

CHRONIC ANGER NEGATIVELY IMPACTS HEALTH, RELATIONSHIPS, AND MOOD. IN OUR CULTURE, ANGER IS AN EMOTIONAL AND PHYSIOLOGICAL RESPONSE THAT IS DYSFUNCTIONAL. IN ANIMALS, IT STRENGTHENS PRIMARILY THE JAW SO THAT THE ANIMAL CAN BITE HARDER. THIS IS THE SAME FOR HUMANS AND FURTHER EXPLAINS WHY PEOPLE WITH CHRONIC ANGER DEVELOP PROBLEMS WITH THEIR TEETH AND JAW. ANGER IS VALUABLE FOR MORE PRIMITIVE LIFE FORMS FOR WHICH IT IS ADAPTIVE BUT HAS LITTLE OR NO VALUE FOR HUMANS. ANGER ALSO SLOWS DOWN THE PROCESS OF HEALING THROUGHOUT THE BODY. WHEN SOMEONE SAYS, "YOU MAKE ME SICK," IT'S LIKELY THAT THE ANGER IS, INDEED, NEGATIVELY AFFECTING THAT PERSON'S HEALTH.

I SAY, "WELL, IF YOU'RE NOT THREATENED, YOU'LL HAVE TO BE SECURE," AND THE ANGER'S NOW GONE. THERE IS SUCH A STRONG DEGREE OF CONNECTION AND CREDIBILITY AT THIS POINT THAT THOSE WORDS SAID IN THAT WAY MAKE THE ANGER DISAPPEAR EVEN THOUGH IT WAS PROLONGED AND HAD SIGNIFICANT REPERCUSSIONS. THE CONNECTION IS CAUSED BY HER FEELING OF CONNECTION TO ME AND HER EXPERIENCE THAT I AM CREDIBLE. WHEN I SAY, "IF YOU'RE NOT THREATENED, THEN YOU'LL HAVE TO BE SECURE...SORRY, BUT THAT'S THE WAY THE COOKIE CRUMBLES," I AM ABLE TO SAY SOMETHING LIGHT ABOUT SOMETHING SO PROFOUNDLY DISTURBING AND GET A RESPONSE OF LAUGHTER AND AGREEMENT BECAUSE OF

THAT CONNECTION. I CONTINUE TO ELIMINATE HER FEELINGS OF ANGER, NOT BY ENCOURAGING FORGIVENESS OR ACCEPTANCE, BUT BY MAKING IT CLEAR AT EVERY LEVEL THAT THE EVENT DOESN'T EXIST, THAT THE MEANING DOESN'T EXIST, AND WHEN BRAIN, AT THE DEEPEST LEVEL, GETS THAT IT DOESN'T EXIST, IT DOESN'T PRODUCE A FEELING. THE ONLY PURPOSE OF A FEELING IS TO CAUSE AN ACTION. NOTHING NEEDS TO BE DONE ABOUT WHAT HAPPENED WITH PAULA BECAUSE WHAT HAPPENED DOESN'T EXIST. NOTHING HAS TO BE DONE ABOUT THE MEANING THAT HER MIND ATTACHED TO WHAT HAPPENED BOTH BECAUSE THE MEANING DOESN'T EXIST AND ACTUALLY NEVER DID. FROM THE FULL REALIZATION THAT NOTHING NEEDS TO BE DONE, ALL THE ANGER IS GONE.

Jon: Because **you got away**.

Paula: Yes, I did.

Jon: **You did get away**. But since **you got the hell away**, get that **you did get away. You did get away.**

Paula: This is the first time that I have been happy I got away.

Jon: Well, because now you've absolutely got it. You got away. There is no threat because you got away.

Paula: I never felt like I really got away.

Jon: **You got away!** Yeah! You bet. **You got away!** You can remember it because **you got away**. And whenever you remember, it's clear that **you got away**.

IT USED TO BE THAT REMEMBERING THE EVENT COULD TRIGGER HER AND CAUSE A PAINFUL RELIVING AND THE EXPERIENCE OF FEAR, RESENTMENT, AND GUILT. I AM INSTEAD SAYING THAT IF SHE REMEMBERS IT, THEN SHE SURVIVED IT. IF YOU REMEMBER IT, THAT PROVES IT ISN'T TAKING PLACE. YOU DON'T REMEMBER THINGS AS THEY ARE HAPPENING.

Paula: Yes, it is amazing.

Jon: Let me in on that.

Paula: Well, just that whole trip. All of the therapists that I've seen have been encouraging my anger. I now realize that the anger was what was holding me back from feeling like I have a life. Encouraging me to be angry just made me feel worse and every therapist I saw did that.

Jon: They were doing what they learned, and I am sure they really wanted to help. But I believe something has shifted. Remember the gun in your vagina. That happened to you.

I TELL HER AGAIN THAT IT DID HAPPEN BECAUSE IT DID. I WANT HER OKAY KNOWING IT HAPPENED, NOT TRYING TO DISTRACT HERSELF. ACTIONS PEOPLE TAKE TO DISTRACT THEMSELVES FROM WHAT THEY HAVE EXPERIENCED CAN CAUSE ADDITIONAL PROBLEMS.

Paula:	Yes, it did.
Jon:	And?
Paula:	And it happened, but I don't have the fear with that anymore. I don't have the anger either.
Jon:	Is it unfortunate now that it did happen then?
Paula:	No.
Jon:	So, it's not unfortunate now.

I SAY, "YOU GOT AWAY. YOU DID GET AWAY. YOU GOT THE HELL AWAY. YOU DID GET AWAY." I REPEAT IT OVER, AND OVER, AND OVER TO GET IT DEEPLY INTO HER MIND. AS IT'S ABSORBED AND INTEGRATED, SHE ACKNOWLEDGES THAT THIS MOMENT WAS THE FIRST MOMENT SHE'S BEEN HAPPY THAT SHE GOT AWAY. PAULA REFLECTS ON HOW THERAPISTS HAVE ENCOURAGED ANGER AND HOW THE ANGER WAS HOLDING HER BACK. SHE EVEN MAKES THE GIGANTIC LEAP TO REALIZE THAT IT ISN'T UNFORTUNATE NOW WHAT HAPPENED THEN. THAT'S WHY THERE'S NO SYMPATHY, EMPATHY, OR COMPASSION NOW. ONE CAN DIFFERENTIATE BETWEEN THE WORDS "SYMPATHY," "EMPATHY" AND "COMPASSION", BUT I BELIEVE THAT ALL THREE WORDS HAVE ABOUT THE SAME EFFECT ON SOMEONE, WHICH IS THAT THEY CAUSE SOMEONE TO FEEL THAT THERE'S SOMETHING GOING ON RIGHT NOW THAT REQUIRES BEING SORRY FOR THEM. THIS EFFECT IS WHAT I WOULD CALL "POISONOUS," AND, ALTHOUGH THE WORDS HAVE SOMEWHAT DIFFERENT MEANINGS, THEY'RE ACTUALLY NOT SO DIFFERENT. WHAT I'M SUGGESTING IS QUITE DIFFERENT, WHICH IS WE THROW ALL OF THEM OUT.

I SAY, "YOU GOT AWAY. YOU GOT THE HELL AWAY," AND I REPEAT IT BECAUSE I BELIEVE THAT BELOW THE LEVEL OF HER CONSCIOUS AWARENESS, PAULA'S MIND CONTINUED TO READ THE EVENT AND THE MEANING IT HAD ATTACHED TO THE EVENT AS IF THEY WERE GOING ON AND NEEDED TO BE STOPPED. PAULA SAYS, "I NEVER FELT LIKE I REALLY GOT AWAY." WHEN I SAY, "WELL, THAT'S BECAUSE IT'S THE FIRST TIME THAT YOU'VE ABSOLUTELY GOT IT," IT'S THE FIRST TIME THAT THE PART OF HER MIND BELOW THE LEVEL OF CONSCIOUS AWARENESS IS REALIZING IT.

Paula:	No.
Jon:	So, now it's not unfortunate that somebody stuck a gun in your vagina.
Paula:	*(Paula begins laughing hard and speaks through her laughter.)* Sitting here talking about this, I'm laughing. I can't believe that! I'm not supposed to be laughing about this. This is supposed to be really serious.
Jon:	Yes, I know.
Paula:	*(She uses a funny British accent)* It's a serious event, you know.
Jon:	**You handled it wonderfully**. Look back and notice how well you did now that you are in a position to sit and critique.

Paula: That's true. I certainly cannot say there is something I should have done differently.

Jon: Would that be for us to say? I mean, for us to sit and watch that movie and say, "Well, I think she should have run a little faster, punched a little harder, begged a little better." Would that be nuts or what?

Paula: Yes, it would be.

Jon: Right.

Paula: I don't have the fear with that anymore.

Jon: It happened.

Paula: Yes. I've changed my production!

Jon: It can't be improved upon.

Paula: Right.

Jon: **You are proud of how well you did.**

Paula: I did everything correctly to survive.

Jon: Good. Think about one of the guys. If you were really enraged at somebody and you wanted to do something bad to that person and you could do magic like a magical witch, and you could change people into other people, would you consider making someone you were really mad at become that guy? Who would you be mad enough at anyone that you would make the person become him?

Paula: Nobody. Not even him.

Jon: No.

WITH FEAR AND ANGER BOTH GONE, I AFFIRM ONCE AGAIN, "YOU ARE FREE, ABSOLUTELY FREE. YOU SURVIVE." BECAUSE THERE IS A DEEP CONNECTION, HER MIND OPENS TO TAKE THINGS IN AT THE DEEPEST LEVEL. THESE STATEMENTS GO INTO HER THE WAY I THINK OF WATER BEING ABSORBED. TAKING CARE OF HERSELF IS NOW A PLEASURE.

Paula: I was just consumed with hateful feelings for these men. Now, I hope they are okay. *(She begins to cry.)*

Jon: And with that, **you are free, absolutely free. You absolutely got away.** You are crying in relief which is right on when you get away. **You survived,** and you are washed with tears of relief and joy.

Paula: Yes.

| Jon: | Your eyes want to close. *(A few moments of silence)* Now, they can open. What has opened up? |

Jon: Your eyes want to close. *(A few moments of silence)* Now, they can open. What has opened up?

Paula: What opens up is there are a whole lot of possibilities.

Jon: Yes.

Paula: Not being in pain. I'm free and I can do pretty much anything I want to.

Jon: Beautiful.

Paula: Yes, it is.

Jon: Tell me.

Paula: I think that the anger was connected to not taking care of myself.

Jon: Close your eyes. You **take care of yourself, take care of your body, nurture your body, protect your body**. **It's natural, it's automatic.** Take your time and, when you are ready, your eyes can open.

Paula: That felt really good.

Jon: Good, like?

Paula: I feel free.

Jon: You **take care of yourself** because **you made it, you survived, you are free**.

Paula: Yeah, it's like alive.

Jon: Alive.

Paula: Vibrant.

Jon: Yes, great. **It's such a joy to take care of yourself** because **it's such a pleasure.**

Paula: Yes, it is.

I SAY, "YOU SURVIVE," THEN TELL HER TO CLOSE HER EYES SO THAT, DURING THE PAUSE, WHAT'S BEING SAID CAN SINK DOWN DEEPER. AFTER THE PAUSE, SHE OPENS HER EYES AND THERE'S AN EXPERIENCE OF FEELING FREE. SO, IN THIS EXPERIENCE OF CONNECTION AND RECEPTIVENESS, I SAY TO HER, "TAKE CARE OF YOURSELF, TAKE CARE OF YOUR BODY, NURTURE YOUR BODY, PROTECT YOUR BODY," WHICH ARE COMMANDS TO HER INNER MIND.

WITH HER MIND CLEARED AND UPDATED, IT HAS BECOME NATURAL AND DESIRABLE FOR PAULA TO DO WHAT IS NURTURING AND PROTECTIVE TOWARD HER BODY. WITH THE ANGER NO LONGER SAPPING HER ENERGY, SHE IS NATURALLY AND

AUTOMATICALLY INTERESTED IN CARING FOR HER BODY. FOR PAULA, IN CLEARING THE IMPRESSION LEFT BY THE TRAUMATIC EXPERIENCE AND ELIMINATING ANGER TOWARD THE GUYS WHO TORTURED AND RAPED HER, IT WILL NOW BE NATURAL TO DO THINGS THAT ARE GOOD FOR HER BODY.

Jon: It's inviting to **take care of yourself**.

Paula: Yes, it is.

Jon: Take care of yourself how?

Paula: All kinds of ways.

Jon: Good.

Paula: Yes. I feel like I can move forward with those things with a lot more ease than I had before.

Jon: Yes.

Paula: I had this kind of head thing that said, "Yes, you'd better take care of yourself, otherwise you will not be alive and continue what you came here to do!" I didn't feel like it was especially pleasurable to do that.

Jon: Ah! Okay.

Paula: It was just part of a job. It was more work.

Jon: More like something you thought you were supposed to do.

Paula: Right. Exactly. This is what you are supposed to do. This is how you do it. Yes, it's a dirty job, but somebody has got to do it.

Jon: Now it's appealing.

Paula: And fun.

Jon: Lots of fun. Very inviting.

Paula: Yes.

Jon: Beautiful. Beautiful. What else should we look at together?

Paula: The only other piece that I felt like was relevant or related to all the stuff that we dealt with this evening was my basic distrust of people and situations, of course, especially pertaining to men in situations. That's the only piece that I'm not sure is really taken care of.

Jon: Okay. Think of a situation.

Paula: Okay. There are people at a party at any kind of social gathering.

Jon: What does that feel like?

Paula: I'm feeling suspicious.

Jon: Because?

Paula: Because I don't know them.

Jon: And?

Paula: Like somebody there might find out where I live and might follow me home or they might get angry with me for something that I said because I'm so opinionated and decide to do something to me or they might think I'm an asshole. I don't know.

Jon: What comes up as you approach them, or they approach you?

Paula: I should get to know about them before I trust them.

Jon: Why bother to trust them? Instead of bothering to trust them, just **interact with people, experience people, learn about people.**

TRUST IS OVER-RATED. PEOPLE THINK ABOUT EARNING TRUST AND TRUST BEING BETRAYED AND ESTABLISHING TRUST. THE PROBLEM WITH TRUST IS IT PUTS THE POWER OUTSIDE, AND, BECAUSE OF THIS, IT LEADS TO FEELINGS OF VICTIMIZATION. RATHER THAN PUTTING TRUST IN OTHER PEOPLE, DEVELOP YOUR OWN ABILITY TO ACCESS AND PREDICT BASED ON YOUR ASSESSMENT.

Paula: Yeah. I won't have to worry about anything because I'm not trusting them.

Jon: Right, just like you don't trust your best friend.

Paula: I trust her.

Jon: Do you think to yourself, "I'm going to go in the other room and trust her for a while?"

Paula: No, I don't do that. I just interact with her.

I AM LOOKING TO MAKE A POINT BUT LOOKING TO DO SO IN A WAY THAT IS LIGHT AND FUNNY. PAULA BELIEVED THAT SHE HAD A PROBLEM WITH TRUST AND THAT IT WOULD NEED TO BE FIXED IN ORDER FOR HER TO FEEL COMFORTABLE, PARTICULARLY WITH MEN. IT WOULD HAVE BEEN ALMOST IMPOSSIBLE TO ACCOMPLISH BECAUSE SHE ALSO FELT THAT BEING MORE TRUSTING WOULD THREATEN HER SAFETY. WHEN SOMEONE IS ON THE HORNS OF A DILEMMA, THEY ARE STUCK TRYING TO FIGURE OUT WHICH OF THE CHOICES WOULD BE BEST. PAULA WAS FEELING IT WOULD BE MORE COMFORTABLE IF SHE COULD TRUST, BUT SAFER NOT TO. SINCE SAFETY TRUMPED COMFORT, SHE WAS NOT TRUSTING, BUT WAS NOT HAPPY WITH

Life Changing Conversations with Rapid Resolution Therapy®

THE EFFECT IT WAS HAVING ON SOCIAL INTERACTIONS. I SUGGEST SOMETHING THAT HAD NOT BEEN CONSIDERED--SKIP TRUST ALL TOGETHER.

Jon: Right.

Paula: But I have a feeling of trust.

Jon: But you don't do any trusting. You interact with her.

Paula: That's true. I don't go around saying, "Oh, I'm going to call my friend so I can engage in some trust." She would think I was really weird if I did that. *(Laughter)*

Jon: Right. Let's say you are at this party and there are these people and you don't do any trusting of them.

Paula: Right. I just interact with them and learn about them.

Jon: How will that be?

Paula: I will be perfectly free to interact with them if I want to and, if I don't want to, I don't have to.

Jon: And it doesn't require any trust.

Paula: Right. It doesn't.

Jon: No need to trust, just relate.

Paula: Well, then, I'm fine. I don't feel compelled to trust them or be vulnerable in any way.

Jon: Give up trusting people.

Paula: Okay. I can do that.

Jon: Because it makes no sense to trust new people. You don't even bother to trust your friends.

Paula: *(Laughing)* Right.

Jon: If you don't engage in trust with your friends, why bother to try and trust people that you don't even know?

Paula: I like that.

Jon: Don't bother to trust anybody.

301

Paula: That makes a lot of sense. That's funny. That's a good one. I really like that. It's much easier.

PAULA TALKS ABOUT HOW WHAT'S HAPPENED HAS ELIMINATED HER ABILITY TO TRUST AND, IN A RATHER HUMOROUS WAY, I LOOK TO ELIMINATE THE IDEA THAT TRUST IS NECESSARY. I BELIEVE THAT PEOPLE HAVE THE IDEA THAT TRUST IS IMPORTANT AND THAT, ONCE VIOLATED, CAUSES ADDITIONAL EMOTIONAL ANGUISH, BUT NO OTHER LIFE FORM VIEWS THINGS IN THIS WAY.

TRUST IS OFTEN THOUGHT OF AS NECESSARY IN ORDER FOR RELATIONSHIPS TO BEGIN OR TO CONTINUE. RATHER THAN ENCOURAGING PAULA TO TRUST, I PREFER THAT SHE EXPERIENCE THE ABILITY TO SEE CLEARLY, PREDICT AND ADAPT. CLARITY AND OBJECTIVITY HEIGHTEN ONE'S ABILITY TO PREDICT. IF PAULA CAN APPROACH PEOPLE UNKNOWN TO HER WITH INTEREST IN WHAT CAN BE LEARNED THROUGH ENGAGEMENT, THEN EVERYTHING BECOMES SIMPLER. I SAY TO HER, "YOU DON'T EVEN TRUST YOUR FRIENDS." I'M UTILIZING HUMOR TO ENGAGE HER AND PROVIDE CLARITY.

Jon: Yes, much easier because trust is involved in a whole lot of expectations. Expectations weigh people down and you are lighter without them.

Paula: Yes. That's very true. And I can do that!

Jon: Sure.

Paula: I mean, I can really do this.

Jon: It's lighter for you. You won't have to say, "Excuse me, but I will be in with my expectations in a few minutes to talk to you?"

EVERYTHING IS LIGHTER NOW FOR PAULA. THE EVENT TOOK PLACE WHEN SHE WAS FOURTEEN YEARS OLD AND HAS AFFECTED THE WAY SHE MEETS AND RELATES TO PEOPLE. SHE IS SAFER AS SHE THINKS OF TAKING IN INFORMATION AND MAKING PREDICTIONS RATHER THAN TRUSTING. DISTORTION DISAPPEARS, AND THINGS BECOME CLEAR. WITH ADDITIONAL CLARITY, SHE SEES WHAT IS ACTUALLY THERE AND, BECAUSE THERE IS CLARITY AND LIGHT, SHE CAN ADAPT.

Paula: But it feels like there have been two classes of people. People I trust and have expectations of and people I don't trust and who can do anything. I might not like it, but I wouldn't be shocked or feel betrayed because I didn't trust them anyway.

Jon: Right.

Paula: So, if I threw them all into the same pot, then I don't have to worry about any of that.

Jon: Right.

Paula: I like that!

Jon: Good.

Paula: That makes good sense to me.

Jon: So, what else?

Paula: That was pretty much the whole ball of wax.

Jon: Good. Close your eyes. You get that there is nothing that you have to get. You understand that there is nothing you need to understand. It's all falling into place. **It's light...it's nice...light...enlightened...credibility...power...you take care of yourself... you take care of your body and you have so much fun.** Take your time. Only when you are ready...your eyes can open.

(A few minutes pass in silence as Paula sits with her eyes closed breathing quite slow.)

Paula: Thank you, this has been wonderful.

Jon: I have enjoyed it.

Follow-up Commentary

Six months after my conversation with Paula, she revealed to me that her life has become vastly improved. She is falling asleep easily and awakening refreshed in the morning. Her health and sense of well-being have improved. She is making good friends, having more fun, and no longer feels depressed. She seldom thinks about the trauma and is more peaceful with day-to-day living. If the memory occurs to her, she simply remembers and feels good about how well she handled a difficult event in her life.

Afterword

The most dangerous thing in the world is communication. Without communication, there could never have been Hitler, the Ku Klux Klan, Jonestown, the Witch Trials or anything else we think of as horrific. The only thing more dangerous than communication is the attempt to censor or limit it.

Communication is like fire. It can do tremendous harm, yet it can cause things that are amazing and wonderful. Precise and intentional communication can free people from emotional turmoil, negative thoughts, destructive behaviors and even chronic pain.

Intend what is best for the individual you are speaking with and what is best for the world.

About the Author

Dr. Jon Connelly is the founder of Rapid Resolution Therapy (RRT), a revolutionary psychotherapeutic approach to resolving emotional and behavioral difficulties. Thousands of mental health professionals have attended RRT training and his students state that it has enabled them to become much more powerful and effective healers. Dr. Connelly also founded the Institute for Survivors of Sexual Violence, a non-profit (501-C3) organization that provides state of the art clinical treatment to individuals who have been traumatized regardless of their ability to pay. His early career experiences as a child protective service worker and clinical supervisor in a program that supported teens who had experienced emotional trauma, childhood abuse or sexual violence helped to shape the birth of RRT. As a result of these experiences, he became committed to finding a way to relieve suffering. Dr. Connelly has taught college classes in human sexuality and group dynamics prior to providing post-graduate training programs for health and mental health professionals. He continues to provide individual treatment and training. Dr. Connelly is licensed as a clinical social worker and holds a Doctorate in Clinical Pastoral Counseling.

Made in the USA
Monee, IL
08 February 2020